Pandæmonium
1660–1886

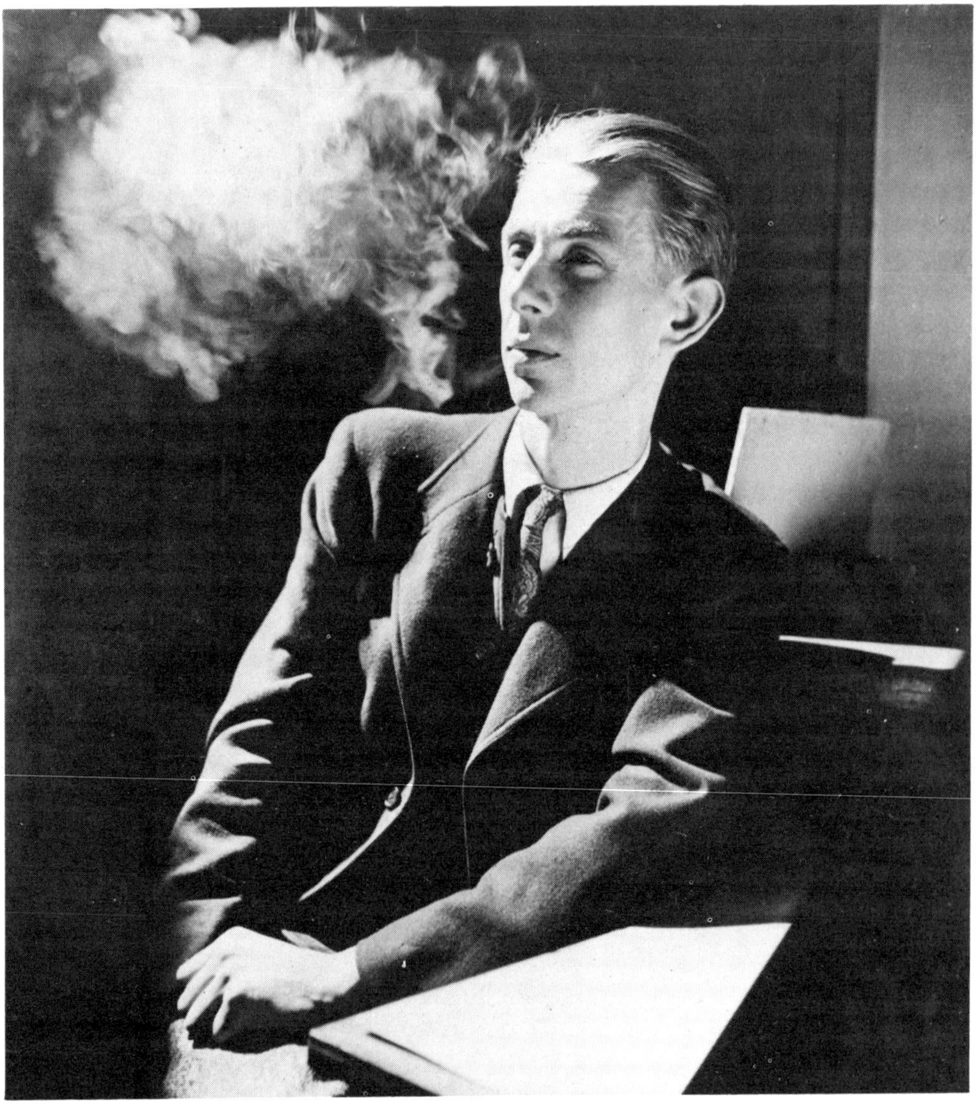

HUMPHREY JENNINGS

PANDÆMONIUM
1660–1886

The Coming of the Machine
as seen by contemporary observers

Edited by Mary-Lou Jennings
and Charles Madge

ANDRE DEUTSCH

First published 1985 by
André Deutsch Limited
105 Great Russell Street London WC1

Copyright © 1985 by Mary-Lou Jennings

All rights reserved

ISBN 0 233 97808 9

Typeset by Inforum Ltd, Portsmouth
Printed in Great Britain by the
Bath Press, Bath, Avon

Contents

Humphrey Jennings and This Book   vii
MARY-LOU JENNINGS

Editorial Tasks and Methods   xv
CHARLES MADGE

The Images: a Chronological List   xxiii

List of Illustrations   xxxiii

Introduction   xxxv
HUMPHREY JENNINGS

PART ONE
1660–1729: Observations and Reports   1

PART TWO
1730–1790: Exploitation   45

PART THREE
1791–1850: Revolution   93

PART FOUR
1851–1886: Confusion   251

Theme Sequence   358

Index   369

Humphrey Jennings
and This Book

My father, Frank Humphrey Sinkler Jennings, was born in 1907 in Walberswick, Suffolk. He was the elder son of Frank Jennings, an architect, and Mildred Hall, an artist. His father was the fourteenth child of a successful racehorse trainer; his mother the only child of a London solicitor. My grandfather restored and designed houses, using materials from demolished sixteenth century buildings, and travelled around East Anglia collecting beams, bricks and stained glass. He was a gentle, unworldly man, deaf because of service in the First World War. My grandparents subscribed to the tenets of guild socialism, which took its ideals from John Ruskin and William Morris, believing that the devaluation of the workman's labour in a capitalist society could only be arrested by the creation of small, self-governing groups of craftsmen. My grandparents founded such a workshop, the Walberswick Peasant Pottery Company, which bought, made and sold furniture and pottery. My grandmother was the stronger character; of her my father said, 'My mother believes she carries the keys of the universe in her pocket'. They read the radical weekly magazine, *The New Age*, founded by A.R. Orage as a bulletin for socialist ideas on culture. Like Orage himself, my grandmother became involved with the mystic world of Gurdjieff and 'the Work', and by the end of the 1930s she had left my grandfather and lived in a community near London. Throughout their married lives my grandparents had little money, and as far as I know my father never inherited any during his lifetime.

As a result of a recommendation by Orage, my father was sent at the age of eight to the Perse School, Cambridge. The headmaster then was W.H.D. Rouse, a liberal eccentric, who made the Perse very different from the other minor public schools of the period. What he described as his 'wild, lonely childhood' gave my father a considerable knowledge of English literature which was enlarged by the teaching of English at school by Caldwell Cook, who encouraged boys to write and act plays and to stage dramatic disputations. Acting, set building and design appealed strongly to my father and he continued to work on Perse productions after he left. The Perse also gave him – again through unconventional teaching methods – an ease and fluency in French, Latin and Greek. Later he told my mother that in his early school days he was lonely and bullied, but he was in fact very successful though this success may well have made him difficult for others to tolerate. Excelling at academic subjects, he also led in acting and in sport. He refused to join in the other conventional organised groups of a public school, and was dismissed for misconduct from both the Officers' Training Corps and the Scouts.

From the Perse he gained a scholarship to Pembroke College, Cambridge to read English. At that time the English school was particularly exciting, before what William Empson has called 'the great wave of self-righteous dismalness broke into "Eng-Lit" '. He attended lectures by I.A. Richards and Mansfield Forbes, of whose work Richards wrote: 'He gave original character to the English Tripos – an imagination from which ours caught fire – a sureness of taste and rightness of judgment.' Empson wrote of my father at that time: 'He was, though quite unaffectedly a leader, not at all a bully. He was not interested in "mastering" people or "possessing" them, let alone frightening them or bribing them – in fact he was rather unconscious of other people, except as an audience – he did have a good deal of consciousness of whether he was swinging round his audience to vote to his side.' Of my father's later academic work, Richards wrote that 'his powers of assimilation, of perceiving possible and hitherto unnoticed connections and synthesising his perceptions with systems are most impressive... his work may be of real importance in illuminating the tradition of English Literature.' Between 1926 and 1929, while he was at Pembroke, he designed and acted in seven productions at the Amateur Dramatic Club and the Festival Theatre, among them Thomas Heywood's *Fair Maid of Perth* and the first production in Britain of Stravinsky's *A Soldier's Tale*, with Lydia Lopokova. During his finals in May 1929 he designed the first production of Honegger's *King David* as a theatrical pageant, supervising the scenery and forty costumes. He went on to gain first class honours in both parts of the tripos examinations with a mark of distinction.

In late 1929 my parents married in the face of strong family opposition. It is not hard to see why: my father had an income of £1 a week from a scholarship for postgraduate work, supplemented occasionally by money for designing and painting scenery at the Festival Theatre. My mother, Cicely Cooper, who was tall and elegant, beautifully dressed in clothes from Paris and Brussels, came to Cambridge with a white Pekinese dog and no income of her own. They lived in a flat above a gallery of modern art which they attempted to run with the painter Julian Trevelyan. My mother hated Cambridge. It was not just that they were poor: it was her feeling of isolation and exclusion from my father's circle. When Jacob Bronowski, Empson and my father had what Empson has described as 'heady, bouncy' talk, my mother, extremely shy, felt unable to join in. They appreciated her elegance and taste but she could not share their lives.

My father began research for a doctoral thesis on Thomas Gray, supervised by Richards with whom he kept in touch until the end of his life. He edited Shakespeare's 1593 Quarto of *Venus and Adonis*, and together with

Bronowski and others founded and wrote for the magazine, *Experiment*. His knowledge of the state of modern art in France in the late 1920s and early 1930s put him ahead of others in the use of colour and materials and he designed sets and costumes for productions of Locke and Gibbons' *Cupid and Death*, Purcell's *Dido and Aeneas* and *King Arthur*, and *The Bacchae* of Euripides. From this one might have thought he would go on to gain a fellowship, remaining for the whole of his life in Cambridge, or that he would work in the theatre. But to his wife he wrote in 1929: 'You know I hate "Art", but I want to draw and that is the business of a lifetime, not of leisure hours.' This, in part, may have been why he gave up his work on Gray. He taught in a boys' school for a term in 1931 and then went to Paris for two months to paint, supported by my mother who worked as a fashion model. In 1932 a small legacy enabled them to live in the south of France for a few months, and in 1933 they were back in Cambridge, where my father painted scenery at the Festival Theatre and where I was born. However, any progress at the theatre was blocked by a serious disagreement with the director, Terence Gray, who wrote to him: 'Surely your experience of the theatre has shown you that, without unity of conception, a play can only succeed by accident. Giving artists an opportunity does not mean offering them the stage as a canvas independently of the play and its method of performance. A scenic artist needs a capacity for co-operation.' The difficulty was one for which my father was open to criticism later in life. A failure to submit coherent designs, clear synopses and final film scripts, and a working method written on the backs of envelopes caused panic and resulted too often, and perhaps not surprisingly, in producers being unable or unwilling to back his ideas. At this point too, in a serious emotional and financial crisis, my mother with a small baby had had enough of a cold basement flat and lack of money and Cambridge, and returned to her parents. At this my father seriously attempted to get his material on Gray published and to return to academic work. He obtained testimonials from Richards and from his former tutor and in early 1934 sent a long piece, 'A Passage on the Progress of Poesy' to T.S. Eliot at *The Criterion*. Eliot welcomed its content and asked him to shorten it for publication. My father seems never to have replied, probably because by the end of the year he had left Cambridge to work for the GPO Film Unit, and we had settled in London where my sister was born.

   Stuart Legg, a contemporary at Cambridge, had introduced my father to John Grierson, the founder of the Unit. Although Grierson gave my father a job editing, designing and directing documentary film, they did not get on well. Their views of the role of public service cinema could never be reconciled. Between 1934 and 1939 my father was involved in twelve films, some lightweight (*Post Haste* and *Pett and Pott*), some visually experimental (*The Birth of a Robot*), and a number which demonstrated his interest in the machine. While making films he was still painting and by the mid-1930s had become involved in surrealism. He had by then met Roland Penrose the painter and art collector, and Edouard Mesens, a Belgian painter and gallery owner. Penrose's close friendship with Picasso and André Breton was instrumental in bringing surrealist ideas to this country and in the scheme for an International Surrealist Exhibition in 1936. My father translated the poetry of the surrealist, Paul Eluard, and Eluard and his wife Nusch remained my parents' close friends. The International Surrealist Exhibition was a *jeu d'esprit* but from it came Edouard Mesens' London Gallery in Cork Street and the magazine, *London Bulletin*, on which both my parents worked at one time or another. At this moment my father saw himself as having 'survived the Theatre and English Literature at Cambridge and . . . connected with colour film direction and racehorses'. But 'to be already a "painter", a "writer" an "artist", a "surrealist" what a handicap'.

In 1936, the public debate about the abdication of Edward VIII saw politicians and the press asserting that they knew what the public really felt about the conduct and ultimate fate of the King and Mrs Simpson. My father, together with Stuart Legg and David Gascoyne, felt strongly that more should be done to attempt to discover the national consciousness through 'an anthropology of our own people'. In a letter to *The New Statesman* signed by the anthropologist Tom Harrisson, Charles Madge, then working on the *Daily Mirror*, and my father, the aims of Mass Observation were set out – an invitation to self-selected 'Mass Observers' from all over the country who would be ready to write 'reports' on their day-to-day lives. My father's involvement in Mass Observation was, in fact, short-lived. He worked on one large project with Charles Madge, publishing observers' 'reports' on Coronation Day, May 12th 1937, but then moved back into film. The scientific analysis of the 'reports' did not interest him; what was important to his work was the content. He himself had written poetry in report form before 1936, and in 1937 he wrote monthly reports on his own day on the 12th of each month. In later life he would occasionally write reports of a particular day: the weather; how he felt mentally and physically; the content of the day's newspapers and his work.

At this point it is possible to discern a change in my father's work. England was a more serious place at the end of the decade: unemployment and the real threat of war affected everyone physically and intellectually. My mother's younger brother had been killed fighting for the Spanish Republic at Jarama. Until the late 'thirties it seemed as though my father had dealt only in ideas. Now other peoples' daily concerns became important. In 1938 he did a series of talks on the radio on poetry and national life. Poetry he said, enabled man to deal with himself: to protect and arm himself. He spoke of Apollinaire who said that the poet must stand with his back to the future because he was unable to see it: it was in the past that he would discover who he was and how he had come to be. In this sense my father began to work on material that was later built into *Pandæmonium*. In July 1938 he edited an issue of the *London Bulletin* devoted to the machine. A 'collection of texts on the Impact of the Machine' was included: these were the germ of *Pandæmonium*. In 1939 he went north to make a film, *Spare Time* which drew directly on his Mass Observation work. This visit he later described to Allen Hutt as the most important turning point in his life. He had never been to the industrial north before and wrote to my mother, 'Cotton seems to produce a desolation greater – more extended – than any other industry. . . . The desolation – the peculiar kind of human misery which it expresses comes I think from the fact that "Cotton" simply means *work*: At Manchester there was a sort of thin wet sunlight which makes it look pathetic. It has a grim sort of fantasy. And a certain dignity of its own from being connected with certain events in history.'

With the outbreak of war, my father's work with what later became the Crown Film Unit had intensified; between 1939 and 1950 he worked on twenty films. My mother, my sister and I went to America in 1940 and he had no permanent base: his books and our furniture went into store, and he worked all over the country on location: not the ideal conditions for working on an extended literary project. It is for the films made between 1940 and 1944 that he is best known. In 1941 he made *Listen to Britain*, a film without commentary which is close in some ways to the construction of *Pandæmonium*: each a series of images carefully placed to illuminate not just themselves in isolation but each other. In 1943 he wrote and directed *Fires were Started* which used amateurs as actors. His relations with other people had changed for the better, as he himself admitted. The men and women in the film were asked to stage real fires in a phoney blitz and it was dangerous. The writer, William Sansom, who served as a fireman during the war and acted in the film wrote 'Why did we do these things? In a way, they looked and felt more dangerous than they were, and we were in uniform and duty bound. Yet I think also our immediate acceptance came because it was Jennings who asked for it, and we had by then developed a kind of hero worship for him. Humphrey had a personal passion, an obsessive drive and the knowledge that he was a thoroughly intelligent tough æsthete carried him way above the ordinary run.' Making a film in Wales about the destruction of Lidice in 1943 my father wrote 'I feel we have really begun to get close to the men – not just as individuals – but also as a class – with an understanding between us: so they don't feel we are just photographing them as curios or wild animals or "just for propaganda",' adding that he had got out the material assembled years back on the Industrial Revolution to give a series of talks to miners in the Swansea Valley on poetry and the Industrial Revolution which is 'really a golden opportunity – so doing some work on that, I have got as far once again as thinking of it as a book and looking for a publisher and so on. Masses of new material – but again no time, or very little.' He made contact with Herbert Read at Routledge, who gave him a contract for a book to be delivered by June. But film location work, including filming the invasion of Sicily, made that impossible.

In early 1944 he moved to Allen Hutt's house in Camden Town, where he lived until his death in 1950. Here he had not only his books and a settled life but also Allen Hutt's encouragement. My father's politics have been crudely assigned to being of the left. But it was not as simple as that. He described them in 1944 as 'those of William Cobbett'. Like Orwell in *The Lion and the Unicorn* he was intensely patriotic, believing that patriotism was not just the possession of the right. His view of Britain at the end of the war is expressed in the film *Diary for Timothy* which reflects on how life would be in post-war years. 'England has, you will find, changed a great deal', he wrote to my mother, 'not so much any one person is different but the young coming up are pretty determined – and people in general have had a good think . . . are very definite as to what went wrong five years ago.'

After the war, my father left the Crown Film Unit to work with Ian Dalrymple, the producer with whom he had the greatest rapport during the war. Together they looked at a number of possibilities: a film of H.E. Bates' *The Purple Plain*, for which he went to Burma for three months in 1947; a film about the century of industrialism between 1846 and 1946; a film on the London Symphony Orchestra at work. None of these came to anything. He made three films between 1947 and 1950 which are generally regarded as a critical disappointment. In 1950 he went to Greece to make a film on health for the European Economic Commission. He died on Poros in an accident in September. He was forty-three years old.

Pandæmonium was never delivered to Routledge. When my father died he said that it was practically finished, as Charles Madge describes. It was not a case of failing to deliver a book because he was incapable of finishing it. He had to earn his living in films and the nature of this work made it impossible for him to give the book the six months' sustained work it required. After his death Charles Madge worked on the manuscript and prepared a series of extracts to show to publishers to give them an idea of the whole. Charles had to go abroad for the United Nations, and Stuart Legg began to investigate the possibility of publication. He wrote to the Cambridge University Press and to Allen Lane at Penguin Books, but with little success. In 1954, Jacob Bronowski prepared a report on Charles's prospectus. Bronowski suggested that a book of the size that is now being published might be possible. But elsewhere, and later in the 1950s, Bronowski wrote that the manuscript needed more work than anyone except my father would have put into it, and 'alas he would not have put the work in either . . . he was too subtle and too nimble-minded to get down on the page all he wanted to say.' Hutchinson Educational Books then wanted to look at the book because it sounded 'a perfect book for the brighter sixth former'. Later they wrote that Raymond Williams would be interested in editing it, but in 1961 he withdrew because of pressure of other work. Granada TV took a fleeting interest in the book as the basis of a TV series. In 1967 the University of California Press learned of the book from Bronowski, but eventually they too withdrew because of the need for extensive editorial work. Nobody had the time to give to it. My mother, who had done much to get it known, died in 1975. In 1980 a new prospectus was prepared and was rejected by Gollancz, Secker and Warburg and the Scolar Press.

In 1982 Riverside Studios staged a retrospective exhibition of Jennings's paintings and films and it was then that, as a result of a talk with Hilary Rubinstein, I approached Charles Madge and asked him if he would complete his original work on the manuscript by helping me to prepare a final version. He went through the whole of the original material yet once more, and together we decided on the final selection. A generous grant was made by the Elephant Trust to enable me to work on checking texts and tracing sources, and to have the manuscript typed. I also undertook the picture research. I will leave to Charles Madge the description of editorial method, adding only that without his commitment over so many years this book would never have been published.

My father's method of working on *Pandæmonium* has been compared with Isaiah Berlin's artist who hopped from subject to subject: the fox who had no continuity of thought and aesthetic approach, no evolution. I believe that although on the surface he gave the impression of being foxlike, my father was inwardly more like Berlin's hedgehog: he might seem to be hopping about, but in fact he was in pursuit of one end: the purpose of the poet.

Mary-Lou Jennings

ACKNOWLEDGMENTS. We are grateful to the Elephant Trust for a grant to help with editorial and typing work on the manuscript; to the staff of the London Library; to the Library at Senate House, University of London; to the Dr Williams's Library; to the British Museum; and to the Science Museum for permission to use 'Coalbrook Dale at Night' by P.J. de Loutherburg. We also thank Alison Slienger, Judy Collingwood and Fiona MacDonald for creating an immaculate typescript from an impossibly difficult text, and lastly Diana Athill for invaluable encouragement and support.

Editorial Tasks and Methods

The original material of *Pandæmonium* consists of twelve books, which from the colour of their binding I shall refer to as the Red Books. In these are bound up well over a thousand photocopied pages, some handwritten, some typewritten, comprising *texts* selected by Humphrey Jennings for possible inclusion in the completed work; *notes*, or indications for notes, which he intended to accompany them; and numerous annotations which were working notes addressed to himself.

Jennings was involved in this work from about 1937 until his death in 1950, a period of at least thirteen years. During this time many texts were dropped and many added, as the work grew both in length and, one might say, in depth. If he himself had prepared it for publisher and printer, he would no doubt have filled certain gaps, and tied up loose ends here and there, but he would also almost certainly have reduced its total length, not by cutting or abridging texts, but by leaving many of them out altogether. This is the work which I have tried to do in his place – in fact I have done it twice, the first time shortly after his death, and now for a second time thirty-two years later.

A few days before he died, he had a conversation with a friend, Miss Dillon Barry, about which she wrote me a letter which gives a valuable indication of his intentions for *Pandæmonium* at this time:

> 'He felt that it needed a good six months full time work to complete it, and explained to me in some detail the important points he was bearing in mind. He wished to have the book published in a popular edition, such as the Penguin series, possibly in several volumes. He said that he had put aside one offer from a publisher who wished to have an abridged version made. He said that the 17th century required the greater part of the further research required, the rest was more or less complete . . .
>
> 'He stressed that on no account would he cut down the extracts as opposed to eliminating them. Apparently when he first started on this work he had tried to condense the extracts and shorten them in some cases. He then found that in doing this, seemingly irrelevant facts were cut out, and then in the light of his later work he found that these seemingly irrelevant facts formed a vital part of the extract. In other

words he made it a principle, and he was very definite about this, that one can take *out* an extract from a main work, but that in cutting it *down* one interferes with the basic structure of the thought expressed, and this one should not do. . . .

'Finally I asked him about the purpose of the book. He said it was to illustrate the coming of the Machine, using the words of contemporary observers. I asked him if he was entirely objective in his choice of extracts. Whether in fact, he chose these in praise or blame of the Machine alike, or whether he almost in spite of himself chose those that suited a theme he was bearing in mind. He hesitated over this, and then said that his purpose and choice were entirely objective, but that he found a theme emerging from the collection almost spontaneously, – that the coming of the Machine was destroying something in our life. . . .'

Humphrey's wife Cicely gave me the *Pandæmonium* material soon after his death, and soon after I had gone to Birmingham University. I had not therefore a great deal of time to spare but I worked at the material whenever I could, sorting it out into chronological order, numbering each page or item, selecting from the texts those which I felt that Humphrey might have selected in his final recension, numbering these also, deciphering and filling out the notes which Humphrey had intended to accompany them, adding a few notes of my own on some of the 17th century material. This was the form in which I handed the material back to Cicely Jennings, and this is the form in which it was recently passed back to me again by her daughter Mary-Lou Jennings, photocopied and bound up in the twelve Red Books. Also bound up in the Red Books, but not, I think, made available to me in 1950, are about a hundred unnumbered items, distinguished by a small green disc.

In preparing the present edition, in consultation with Mary-Lou Jennings, I have in most cased adopted the same selection of items as in 1950 and used the same version of the notes. But I have re-read every item, including the green disc items, deciphered and added some further notes, and have left out some texts included in the former selection while adding others not previously selected. The material in the Red Books could provide the basis for a different selection of texts, longer or shorter, and a different version of the notes, if at any time in the future a new edition was thought desirable.

Among the notes for an introduction to *Pandæmonium* is the pencilled sentence: 'The poets are the guardians of the Animistic system, the scientists of the Materialist system.'

In the conflict between these two basic systems, it is the materialist system which has prevailed, and Humphrey, for all his essentially poetic vision, accepted that this must be so. But he could see and feel the immense loss which it had brought upon his own and succeeding generations. Perhaps he was not able to surmount this contradiction, but in the latter part of his notes for an introduction, where he sets forth a post-Marxist position in which the means of production are parallelled by equally important means of vision, he is thereby able to escape, if only poetically, the constriction inherent in Marxism.

Humphrey Jennings was well aware that his choice of texts was contradictory and inconsistent, but he believed that it was imaginatively valid. In another pencilled sentence he wrote: 'The presence of *Imagination* is apprehended by the *Imagination*: therefore the reasons for choice are not reasonable.' There is no call, then, to try to rationalize his method of selection. The apprehension of the imagination by the imagination is, as he says, a matter far more difficult and delicate to handle 'than the facts and events and ideas of which history is usually constructed'. Nor is there any way of demonstrating whether this 'apprehension' is or is not correct. Imagination itself might be a purely imaginary concept – as a word it is all too often trivialized and diminished in contemporary parlance. The most I can myself say of *Pandæmonium* is that for me reading it has had the effect of enlarging and potentiating my own imagination – or so I imagine.

Yet another pair of pencilled sentences, perhaps addressed to a possible publisher, reads as follows: 'A certain number of the proposed type of extracts are appended. But clearly a great deal of the effect of the book must lie in the order and arrangement of them.'

Something needs to be said about this order and arrangement. The order so far as possible is strictly chronological. The exact date is given – day, month and year – if it can be reliably assigned. This is not always possible – for example the date of the extract with which the book begins, from the first book of *Paradise Lost*, is given as 'c. 1660', the date at which it may be supposed to have been written. In the many extracts from letters or from journals, there is generally a precise date. In the case of a book, we may have to make do with the date when it was published, but the date at which it was written or to which it refers is preferred. The chronological sequence throws up both similarities and differences between the subject-matter of passages written at around the same time. The juxtaposition of one passage and another may either reinforce a common theme or point up a contrast. Besides the effect of juxtaposition, there is the effect of the theme which recurs at intervals, sometimes widely spaced, over the two hundred and twenty-six years which the book covers.

There is also, for the work as a whole with its three hundred and seventy-two texts, an overall historical pattern (a pencilled note suggests one possible pattern: '17th Cent. The Idea. 18th Cent. The Means. 19th Cent. The Man.'); and, in the Red Books, there are notes suggesting various ways of subdividing the period. As the period progresses, the number of extracts per year or per decade steadily increases – not I think by design, but because there is more material to choose from. For the period of one hundred and forty years from 1660 to 1800 there are one hundred and nine texts, an average of less than one a year; for the remaining period of eighty-five years up to 1886, there are two hundred and sixty-three texts, an average of about three a year.

In his notes for an introduction, Humphrey calls his extracts 'images', a term which, in the way he uses it, can cover a wide range of meanings. He chose the extracts because, for him, they had an imaginative impact. An image, in his sense, may be a poem, or part of one, or an account of a railway journey or an anecdote about a scientist. In some cases the extract seems more prosaic than imaginative: for example the second one, the memorandum recording Mr Wren's lecture on November 28, 1660, and how it led to the founding of the Royal Society. What gives this its force as an 'image' is its place in Humphrey's 'unrolling film'. The meeting at Gresham College is the quiet beginning of the great developments in natural science and scientific technology which led on to the Industrial Revolution. Humphrey undoubtedly had an eye for such passages, a painter's eye, and a film-maker's, for whom the visual complement of the written word was never far away. If at first one does not see the image through his eyes, on a further reading and after the impact of other images, a stronger sense of it may follow.

The titles which Humphrey gave to his extracts, and in which I have scrupulously followed him, are signals to us that the extracts have passed through his own imagination and have been apprehended as imaginative entities.

There are long extracts and short extracts, there are some which convey a single powerful image and others in which a variety of images appear to be compounded. On the same page of his notes as the previously quoted statement – that the effect of the book *must* largely lie in the order and arrangement of the extracts – Humphrey has the following passage, headed TO THE READER:

'There are at least three different ways in which you may tackle this book. First, you may read it straight through from the beginning as a continuous narrative or *film* on the Industrial Revolution. Second, you may open it where you will, choose one or a group of passages and study in them details of events, persons and thoughts as one studies the material and architecture of a poem. Third way, you begin with the Index – look up a subject or an idea, and follow references skipping over gaps of years to pursue its development.'

There are no traces of such an index having been compiled that I can find, so I have attempted to construct one in addition to the more orthodox index. I cannot of course be sure of having carried this out as Humphrey would have done. Possibly he would have found it difficult to do in practice – I certainly did. My attempt is therefore not definitive and has no particular authority. The problem is a double one – that of finding workable headings and that of deciding which of the texts come under that heading. Of course a good many texts will fall under more than one heading, and a few will not seem to fall convincingly under any. The justification for this exercise however is that, in my own practical experience, assembling texts in this way and following the subject or idea behind them through its different appearances and manifestations, does in many cases give extra depth and dimension to the idea.

The resulting list is not an index in the usual sense: for one thing, it is not in alphabetical order. I have called it THEME SEQUENCES for want of a better name. It was not easy to decide on names for the different themes which would do them justice. In some cases, there was no problem, as in the series of thirty texts which evoke in various forms the image of London: this sequence, which I have put last because in some ways it is the most comprehensive, I have headed simply LONDON. Another sequence with an obvious heading was DÆMONS AT WORK, the title which Humphrey had given to text No. 54, an extract from Thomas Gray's *Journal of a Tour in the Lakes*, 1769, immediately recalling the text with which the book opens, 'The Building of Pandæmonium', and leading on to twenty-two other texts which include a similar image.

My first group of headings: THE MAN OF SCIENCE, POETRY AND SCIENCE, THEOLOGY AND SCIENCE, is all right so far as it goes, but is more descriptive than evocative. However in following these through the reader will witness the development of the scientific vision – imaginatively, that is, and not in the form of a history of science – and will see the scientist as he saw himself and as he was seen by others, both those who admired him and those, like Swift and Blake, who made fun of him or opposed their vision to his. The 'Man of Science' heading, with thirty-five texts, and the 'Industrial Man' heading, with forty-six, are the two longest sequences, and for that reason the heading seems perhaps to be too comprehensive, and to need breaking down under sub-headings. This may be so, but there is something to be said for reading through each sequence as a whole, to watch the theme develop as decades and centuries pass, and to note constrasting attitudes towards it.

The remaining themes proceed from these two, and the order in which I have placed them has no particular validity. The sequences on DÆMONS AT WORK and MINERS obviously follow on from INDUSTRIAL MAN, and so in a sense does the next – I am afraid unpoetic – heading, POPULATION AND SUBSISTENCE. The twenty-eight texts under this heading illustrate both the apparently cold and calculating attitude to these problems of demographers and economists, and the hostile reaction they evoked. The mass of the people appear in a different guise under THE POWER TO COME, its thirty-one texts ranging from John Wesley's mission to the miners to the Peterloo massacre and beyond, down to William Morris's 'March of the Workers'.

The next heading, MAN – ANIMAL – MACHINE, includes images in which animals are viewed as machines, and machines are viewed as animals, and goes somewhat beyond this to cover images of Man and Robot, and Man as Animal. Linked with it is the heading THE WEATHER IN THE SOUL, interpreted as having a life of its own, perhaps as an outward projection of human emotions.

Some of the remaining headings are rather more difficult to justify or explain. The heading MUSIC AND ARCHITECTURE brings together two kinds of expressive structure that are only tenuously linked. In the first extract, from *Paradise Lost*, Pandæmonium rises like music through the pipes of an organ, and subsequent references to either music or architecture sometimes appear to hark back to this, whether accidentally or because of some inherent imaginative affinity.

The twenty-nine texts listed under the heading EARTH AND CREATION can loosely be linked to ideas about how the earth was created, and what is the nature of creation by man as well as by god. The earth is the province of agriculture, and is pre-industrial and animistic. Pollution of the earth is desecration. The return to the earth, or the wish to do so, is a reassertion of animism, though the earth itself is material in the sense of being earthy, 'down to earth'.

The next heading, LIGHT, needs no particular explanation, though there is something mysterious about it. THE RAILWAY and MEN AND MOLECULES are images which become important in the nineteenth century, and the latter has inner complexities which are explained in the long note to text No. 362, 'The Crown and the Runner'. These two lead naturally on to LONDON, the last of the series.

That Humphrey intended to provide illustrations for *Pandæmonium* is evidenced by a single closely written page of notes. To follow out these indications was even more difficult than making an 'Index' on the lines he suggested. It demanded the same kind of imagination as the selection of the texts, with an added visual element. For Humphrey Jennings, painter and film-maker, this would have presented no problem. My first inclination was to leave out the illustrations altogether, for fear of compromising the book as a whole by inept selection of visual images. But we came round to them in the end. There were two criteria for selection that I felt would be consistent with Humphrey's practice in selecting texts. Whenever possible the illustration should form an integral part of the text, as in text No. 9, which when first published included a Figure of the Water-Insect or Gnat (from Robert Hooke's *Micrographia*, 1644). Failing that, the illustration should be contemporary with the text, and should therefore convey a parallel way of looking at things. Some of the suggestions in Humphrey's page of notes have pointed to the right source, for example the illustrations to Mayhew and Binny's *The Criminal Prisons of London*, 1862, and, as indicated in text No. 190, John Martin's depiction of 'The Country of the Iguanodon'. Given that a certain opportunism has been needed in practice, I think that on balance the illustrations feed in a visual element which helps to make the 'images' appear more clearly.

In editing this extraordinary work, it was from the beginning my aim to intervene as little as possible: an attitude shared by Mary-Lou Jennings. The work must speak for itself, not only through the words of those who, from 1660 to 1886, wrote the texts, but also through Humphrey Jennings's own creative acts of selection and comment. He died thirty-five years ago, and since then there has been an immense volume of writing, critical, historical, biographical, relevant to the themes of *Pandæmonium*. Whole schools of criticism have risen and fallen since he wrote. New primary material has been published, new sources discovered. Marxism, literary and political, has been through various transformations. Science has taken great new strides forward, the political world of the nations has evolved new boundaries. As the years go by, the formidable gap will widen, perhaps at an accelerating pace. Although *Pandæmonium* is concerned with the period from 1660 to 1886, that period is re-created through the imagination of Humphrey Jennings looking at it over the years 1937 to 1950. Readers of later generations must bear that in mind. Yet the passage of time has not invalidated Humphrey Jennings's historical imagination. In some ways it has validated it, and it is my belief that it will continue to do so.

Charles Madge

THE IMAGES
A Chronological List

PART ONE
1660–1729: Observations and Reports

1.	c.1660	THE BUILDING OF PANDÆMONIUM: John Milton
2.	1660	MEMORANDUM: Journal of the Royal Society
3.	c.1660	GOD WOULD BE MUCH HONORED: William Petty
4.	c.1660	THE BOYHOOD OF GENIUS: Dr. Stukeley
5.	c.1660	THE MOST STUPENDIOUS WORK IN THE WHOLE WORLD: The Marquis of Worcester
6.	1661	THAT HELLISH AND DISMAL CLOUD: John Evelyn
7.	1662	TO COMMAND THE RAIN: Samuel Pepys
8.	c.1662	THE FACES OF THE SKY: Robert Hooke
9.	1663	THE WATER-INSECT OR GNAT: Robert Hooke
10.	1663	A HEATHEN PLACE: Samuel Pepys
11.	1666	THE NATURE OF SOUNDS: Samuel Pepys
12.	1667	OBSERVATIONS: Thomas Sprat
13.	1669	THE NEW THEATER: John Evelyn
14.	1669–70	A MECHANICAL MUSCLE: Minutes of the Royal Society
15.	1675–76	SOUND: Robert Hooke
16.	1675–76	THE ANALOGY OF NATURE: Isaac Newton
17.	1680–81	THE FACE OF THE EARTH: Isaac Newton
18.	1681	THE GREAT GOGLE-EYED BEETLE: Nehemiah Grew
19.	1682	RESEMBLANCE: Nehemiah Grew
20.	1684	ARTIFICIAL SPRING: Hans Sloane
21.	1685	HOMOGENEOUS PARTICLES: John Ray
22.	1685	THE EDUCTION OF LIGHT: John Evelyn
23.	1686	LONDON: Robert Southwell
24.	c.1687	OF DOUBLING THE PEOPLE IN 25 YEARS: William Petty
25.	1690–91	THE SOUL OF BRUTES: John Ray
26.	1696	COLLEDGE OF INDUSTRY: John Bellars
27.	1699	THE MINE-MAN: Samuel Sturmy
28.	c.1704	COMPRESSING ENGINES: W. Derham
29.	c.1706	HÆMASTATICS: Stephen Hales
30.	c.1713	MARTINUS SCRIBLERUS: Jonathan Swift

31.	1715–16	A CORONA, OR IMAGE: Edmund Halley
32.	1724	THE SOLEMNITY OF THE SIGHT: William Stukeley
33.	1725	THE WONDERS OF THE PEAK: Daniel Defoe
34.	1725	EFFECTS OF LIGHTNING IN NORTHAMPTONSHIRE: J. Wasse
35.	1725	THE YORK BUILDINGS DRAGONS: *Read's Weekly Journal*
36.	1729	THE CHILDREN OF IRELAND: Jonathan Swift

PART TWO
1730–1790: Exploitation

37.	1730	EXPERIMENT: Stephen Gray
38.	c.1730	THE DERBY SILK-MILL: William Hutton
39.	1733	THE HOE-PLOW: Jethro Tull
40.	1738	THE FIRST SPRINGS: Voltaire
41.	1739	THE COLLIERS OF KINGSWOOD: John Wesley
42.	1742	EASTER: John Wesley
43.	1750	A LOVE OF SYSTEM: Thomas Gray
44.	1753	ELECTRICAL FIRE: John Wesley
45.	1757	PURE WARM AIR: Stephen Hales
46.	c.1758	TO THE DUKE OF BEDFORD, PRESIDENT OF THE FOUNDLING HOSPITAL: Lewis Paul and Dr Johnson
47.	1759	WESLEY IN CUMBERLAND: John Wesley
48.	c.1760	PROVIDENCE: John Ramsay of Ochtertye
49.	c.1761	WRITTEN IN BEDLAM: Christopher Smart
50.	1761–62	THE MATERIALIST CONCEPTION OF MUSIC: John Robison on James Watt
51.	c.1765	A PERFECT STEAM-ENGINE: John Robison on James Watt
52.	c.1767	THE FORMING OF A TEA-POT: Josiah Wedgwood
53.	1768	THE WOODEN HORSE: Richard Lovell Edgeworth
54.	1769	DÆMONS AT WORK: Thomas Gray
55.	1770	ON THE WYE: Thomas Whateley
56.	1770	THE ENCLOSURES: Oliver Goldsmith
57.	1770	AN IMMENSE WILDERNESS: Tobias Smollett
58.	1770	ALLOA: Tobias Smollett
59.	c.1770	INSPIRATION: John Aikin
60.	c.1770	SLEEP: Erasmus Darwin
61.	1772	THE ISLE OF RUM: Thomas Pennant
62.	1773	THE SONG OF BIRDS: Daines Barrington
63.	1773	TRADE: James Boswell
64.	1776	AN IRON CHIEFTAIN: James Boswell
65.	1776	GENIUS: John Wesley
66.	1777	MEMORANDUM: Matthew Boulton

67.	1778	SELBORNE ECHO: Gilbert White
68.	1779	THE INVENTION OF ARTS: Lord Monboddo
69.	1779	LETTER TO MATTHEW BOULTON: James Watt
70.	1779	THE MOB: Josiah Wedgwood
71.	1782	BLIND JOHN METCALF: Mr Bew
72.	1783	THE COMPOSITION OF WATER: James Watt
73.	1783	COALBROOK DALE: Arthur Young
74.	1784	THE EVIL ONE: William Buckle
75.	1784	THE FIRST AERIAL VOYAGE: Vincent Lunardi
76.	1784	ELIZABETH BRETT, SPINSTER: a deposition
77.	1784	FARM SERVANTS: William Marshall
78.	1784	THE PANTHEON: William Hutton
79.	c.1785	YOUNG GEORGE CROMPTON: Samuel Crompton
80.	1785	OLD GEORGE BARWELL: William Marshall
81.	c.1785	RICHARD REYNOLDS: Mary Anne SchimmelPenninck
82.	c.1785	BANKS: Erasmus Darwin
83.	c.1787	THE LUNATICS: Mary Anne SchimmelPenninck
84.	1788	YEAR 1788: John Galt
85.	1788	IN THE CAVERN: Erasmus Darwin
86.	1789	THE FRENCH REVOLUTION: Mary Anne SchimmelPenninck
87.	1789	THE CHILDHOOD OF MARY ANNE SCHIMMELPENNINCK

PART THREE
1791–1850: Revolution

88.	1791	FOR CHURCH AND KING: Joseph Priestley
89.	1791	GLEANING: Anonymous
90.	1792	EPITAPH IN WHITKIRK PARISH CHURCH: From Samuel Smiles
91.	1791–92	PANOPTICON: Jeremy Bentham
92.	1793	YEAR 1793: John Galt
93.	c.1793	TOM PAINE: Samuel Bamford
94.	c.1793	LONDON: William Blake
95.	1793	MY PLAN: Tom Poole
96.	1793	THE RIOT: Hannah More
97.	1794	PANTISOCRACY: Tom Poole
98.	1795	THE SONG OF THE KINGS OF ASIA: William Blake
99.	1795	FOOD OF THE POOR OF INGLETON: Capel Lofft
100.	1796	MR DALE'S COTTON-WORKS AT NEW LANARK: Charles Manners, Duke of Rutland
101.	1796	FACTS OF MIND: Samuel Coleridge
102.	1797	THE REVERIE OF POOR SUSAN: William Wordsworth

103.	1797	PETITION AGAINST ENCLOSURE: House of Commons Journal
104.	1798	INFANT MAN: Jeremy Bentham
105.	1798	AFTER TEA: Elizabeth Fry
106.	1799	COLERIDGE IN LONDON: Samuel Coleridge
107.	1800	THE POET AND THE MAN OF SCIENCE: William Wordsworth
108.	1800	BLAKE AT FELPHAM: William Blake
109.	1800	COLERIDGE AT KESWICK: Samuel Coleridge
110.	1801	THE DOMESTIC AFFECTIONS: William Wordsworth
111.	1801	LONDON: Charles Lamb
112.	1801	NEWTON: William Blake
113.	1801	NEWTON: Samuel Coleridge
114.	1801	SOMERSET: Tom Poole
115.	1801	THE CHILDREN: Joseph Farington
116.	1801	CHEMISTRY: Samuel Coleridge
117.	1802	THE CURSED BARBAULD CREW: Charles Lamb
118.	1803	SIMPLE NAKED SCOTLAND: Dorothy Wordsworth
119.	1804	THE ENGINE: Richard Trevithick
120.	1804	PORTSMOUTH: Samuel Coleridge
121.	1804	CANDLE-POWER OF VENUS: George Cayley
122.	1805	OMNIPRESENCE: Samuel Coleridge
123.	1805	NIGHT IMAGES: Samuel Coleridge
124.	1806	THE SMOKE OF LONDON: Benjamin Robert Haydon
125.	1806	THE EXTREME DELIGHT: John Davy
126.	1806	RATIONAL TOYS: Thomas Beddoes and others
127.	c.1808	THE ISLAND OF BRITAIN: Samuel Coleridge
128.	1804–08	JERUSALEM: William Blake
129.	1808	ENCAGED: Samuel Coleridge
130.	1808	THE ENGINE IS THE FAVORITE: *The Times*
131.	1808	MY FIRST SIGHT OF THE ELGIN MARBLES: Benjamin Robert Haydon
132.	c.1810	WHEN THE SUN RISES: William Blake
133.	1810	COTTLE'S FREE VERSION OF THE PSALMS: Samuel Coleridge
134.	1811	MACHINE FOR COPYING SCULPTURE: James Watt
135.	1811	SEARCH FOR BEAUTIFUL FORMS: Dr Patrick Wilson
136.	1812	SPIDER-WORK: Lord Byron
137.	1812	THE FELLING COLLIERY DISASTER: The Rev. John Hodgson
138.	1813	DAVY IN PARIS: J.A. Paris
139.	1813	A REFORM: Benjamin Robert Haydon
140.	1814	ALMOST ORGANIC: *The Times*
141.	c.1814	DEMONSTRATION: William Blake

142.	c.1815	THE ROAD TO PUTNEY: Richard Phillips
143.	c.1815	MECHANIC POWERS: Richard Phillips
144.	1815	PERSONIFICATION OF FICTIONS: Jeremy Bentham
145.	1816	TEREDO NAVALIS: Richard Beamish
146.	1816	THE GREATNESS OF GREAT BRITAIN: Benjamin Newton
147.	1816	FRANKENSTEIN: Mary Wollstonecraft Shelley
148.	1816	THE PRODUCE OF THE MIND: William Cobbett
149.	1816	LETTER FROM VENICE: Lord Byron
150.	before 1817	'THE MACHINE-WRECKERS OF ARMATA: Thomas, Lord Erskine
151.	1817	SUNDAY IN THE BREW-HOUSE: Thomas Fowell Buxton
152.	1817	THE IMMORTAL DINNER: Benjamin Robert Haydon
153.	1818	KEATS IN THE LAKES: John Keats
154.	1819	PETERLOO: Samuel Bamford
155.	1819	UTOPIA: Robert Southey
156.	1819	THE BIRTH OF THE CYLINDER: Henry Reveley and P.B. Shelley
157.	1820	PROFESSIONAL FANCIES: Michael Faraday
158.	1821	THE WIND OF HEAVEN: Samuel Bamford
159.	1822	THE DEATH-BED OF HERSCHEL: Caroline Herschel
160.	1823	WILLIAM BLAKE: Alexander Gilchrist
161.	1823	EXTRACT FROM A PLAY: Alfred Tennyson
162.	1824	SAINT PAUL'S: Thomas Carlyle
163.	1824	USE OF THE CAMERA OBSCURA: *Glasgow Mechanics' Magazine*
164.	1824	THE BLACK COUNTRY: Thomas Carlyle
165.	1824	CARLYLE IN LONDON: Thomas Carlyle
166.	1826	HARRY AND LUCY: John Ruskin
167.	1827	RAYS OF DARKNESS: Michael Faraday
168.	1827	THE BEAUTIFUL ROAD TO HADES: Fanny Kemble
169.	1827	THE LORD'S PRAYER: William Blake
170.	1829	LONDON LIFE: Felix Mendelssohn
171.	1830	THIS SHEFFIELD: William Cobbett
172.	1830	THE BLACK COUNTRY: James Nasmyth
173.	1830	MR STEPHENSON: Fanny Kemble
174.	1830	OPENING OF THE RAILWAY: *Mechanics Magazine*
175.	1830	A REPRESENTATIVE MAN: Fanny Kemble
176.	1830	A GLOSS: Alfred Tennyson
177.	c.1830	COPY OF UNION CLUB OATHS: *The Cambrian*
178.	1831	MR TOOGOOD: Thomas Love Peacock
179.	1831	CRISPATIONS: Michael Faraday
180.	1831	GALVANISM: Samuel Coleridge
181.	1831–32	THE SALVATION OF THE TRIATARSOSTINUS: Thomas Hawkins

182.	1832	OASTLER ON THE TEN HOURS' BILL: Richard Oastler
183.	1832	CHOLERA COMES TO MANCHESTER: James Kay-Shuttleworth
184.	1832	MAN AND MACHINE: James Kay-Shuttleworth
185.	1833	WHEN THE SAVAGE SETTLES DOWN: Robert Owen and Robert Dale Owen
186.	1833	THE ASPECT AND CHARACTER: Thomas Chalmers
187.	1833	THE STEAM-CARRIAGES: Henry Crabb Robinson
188.	1833	VILLE UNIVERSELLE: William Beckford
189.	1834	THIS NEW DESCRIPTION OF PROPERTY: George Head
190.	1834	THE COUNTRY OF THE IGUANODON: Gideon Mantell
191.	1834	THE PHILOSOPHER'S OPINION OF THE WHITBY SNAKES: William Martin
192.	1835	LETTER TO FRANCIS PLACE: Henry Drummond
193.	c.1835	THE IRON MAN: Andrew Ure
194.	c.1835	THE PHILOSOPHY OF MANUFACTURES: Andrew Ure
195.	1835	CARLYLE IN LONDON: Thomas Carlyle
196.	1835	THE POWERS OF THE MACHINE: George Ticknor
197.	1835	PHOTOGENIC DRAWING: Henry Fox Talbot
198.	1835	QUALITY AND QUANTITY: George Head
199.	1835	THE ICHTHYOSAURUS: Thomas Hawkins
200.	1836	THOSE BEAUTIFUL FACES: Najaf Koolee Meerza
201.	1836	THE REAL SIGHTS: Najaf Koolee Meerza
202.	1836	BLACK SWANS: William Howitt
203.	1837	OUR ORIGIN: Charles Darwin
204.	c.1837	COAL-PIPES: Charles Lyell
205.	1837	IMAGINATION: Benjamin Robert Haydon
206.	1838	BRIGHTON: Gideon Mantell
207.	1838	SEDGWICK AT NEWCASTLE: John Herschel
208.	1838	INDIANS AT THE POLYTECHNIC: Jehangeer Nowrojee and Hirjeebhoy Merwanjee
209.	1838	PAUPER CHILDREN FARMED OUT: James Kay-Shuttleworth
210.	c.1839	TWO HEARTS: Charles Dickens
211.	1839	FROM AN OLD JOURNAL: Elizabeth King
212.	1839	KERSALL MOOR: General Sir Charles Napier
213.	1839	THE DEVIL: Lord Shaftesbury
214.	1839	FAUST'S FLIGHT: Thomas Carlyle
215.	1840	MIND AND MATTER: Henry Crabb Robinson
216.	1840	THE MONSTER: Thomas Carlyle
217.	1841	CARLYLE AT LEEDS: Thomas Carlyle
218.	1841	A TOO MUCH DIVIDED HEART: Edward Pease
219.	c.1842	A YORKSHIRE CHILDHOOD: George Oldfield
220.	1842	SHAFTESBURY'S MINES BILL: Lord Shaftesbury

221.	1842	CIVILITY TO VULCAN: James Nasmyth
222.	1842	POEMS: Ralph Waldo Emerson
223.	1843	THE CONDITION OF ENGLAND: Thomas Carlyle
224.	1843	THE COMPANY'S ENTERPRISE AND TASTE: Augustus Welby Pugin
225.	1843	A CONVERSATION: Alexander Somerville
226.	1843	IN BEDLAM: Thomas Carlyle
227.	1843	PROSE: Ebenezer Elliott
228.	1843	CHRISTMAS DAY: Lord Shaftesbury
229.	1843	SCROOGE AND THE SECOND SPIRIT: Charles Dickens
230.	1844	CLASSIC SOIL: Friedrich Engels
231.	1844	THE MORAL MACHINERY: *The Penny Magazine*
232.	1844	THE DUE REWARD: Arthur Hugh Clough
233.	1844	HALF-TIMERS: Minutes of the Committee of the Privy Council
234.	1844	CHICKABOBBOO: George Catlin
235.	1844	THE PHILISTINE: Lord Shaftesbury
236.	1845	WORDSWORTH: Barron Field
237.	1845	AT FURNESS ABBEY: William Wordsworth
238.	1845	WORDSWORTH: Isabella Fenwick
239.	1845	LETTER TO THOMAS COOPER: Thomas Carlyle
240.	1845	MANCHESTER: Hugh Miller
241.	1846	BIRMINGHAM: Hugh Miller
242.	1846	DOMBEY IN THE TRAIN: Charles Dickens
243.	1847	BEYOND ANY DREAMS: Alexander Somerville
244.	1847	A GREATER EPIC: Edward Fitzgerald
245.	1847	OUR PHILOSOPHY: Michael Faraday
246.	1847	ROCHDALE: Thomas Carlyle
247.	1847	THE METROPOLITAN POOR: Charles Cochrane
248.	1848	GOD'S HANDWRITING: Charles Kingsley
249.	1848	THINKING BY DREAMING: James Clerk-Maxwell
250.	1848	A QUIET TALK: Miss Rundle Charles
251.	1848	LINE IRON: Charles Kingsley
252.	1848	THE EUSTON STATION: Francis Head
253.	1849	ROOMS NOT CHURCHES: Augustus Welby Pugin
254.	1849	THE SHADOW: Charles Dickens
255.	1849	A POET'S OLD AGE: Elizabeth Gaskell
256.	1849	THE IMPRISONMENT OF ERNEST JONES: Anonymous
257.	1849	A CITY OF DIS: Herman Melville
258.	c.1850	OLD GILHAM: Henry Mayhew
259.	1850	THE COUNTRY: Frederick Law Olmsted
260.	1850	A STREAM OF GOLDEN CLOUD: Michael Faraday
261.	1850	THE SCENERY OF HEAVEN: Michael Faraday

PART FOUR
1851–1886: Confusion

262.	1851	THE GREAT EGGS AND BACON: Henry Mayhew
263.	1851	MAYHEW ON HIS WORK: Henry Mayhew
264.	1851	THE TEMPEST PROGNOSTICATOR: George Merryweather
265.	1851	I CAN'T GET OUT: Thomas Carlyle
266.	1851	THE OPENING: Lord Macaulay
267.	1851	THE SHILLING PEOPLE: Henry Mayhew and George Cruikshank
268.	1851	ALL PEOPLE THAT ON EARTH DO DWELL: Hector Berlioz
269.	1851	ONLY MAGIC: Charlotte Brontë
270.	1851	THE LIVING AND THE MARBLE: Gideon Mantell
271.	1851	FOG: Charles Dickens
272.	1852	LANE'S NET: Hugh Miller
273.	1852	A BALLOON VIEW OF LONDON: Henry Mayhew and John Binny
274.	1852	HERZEN IN LONDON: Alexander Herzen
275.	1853	REFLEX MUSINGS: REFLECTION FROM VARIOUS SURFACES: James Clerk-Maxwell
276.	1853	THE CONCEALED YEARNING: Mary Howitt
277.	1853	THE MIND OF MAN: Michael Faraday
278.	1853	LIVERPOOL: Nathaniel Hawthorne
279.	1853	A TERRIFIC BANQUET IN AN IGUANODON: E. MacDermot
280.	1854	COKETOWN: Charles Dickens
281.	1855	BOTTLED COMPASSES: Caroline Fox
282.	1855	PHILANTHROPY: Lord Shaftesbury
283.	1856	THE SILENT SYSTEM: Henry Mayhew and John Binny
284.	1856	TERRESTRIAL ALL IN CHAOS: James Clerk-Maxwell
285.	1857	THE RAILWAY TO HEAVEN: Walter White
286.	1857	THE ROAD TO HAWORTH: Elizabeth Gaskell
287.	c.1857	SALTAIRE: Walter White
288.	1857	SATURN: James Clerk-Maxwell
289.	1857	THE GREAT MYSTERY: James Clerk-Maxwell
290.	1857	THE MATERIAL WORLD: Nathaniel Hawthorne
291.	1858	LAW AND LIBERTY: James Clerk-Maxwell
292.	1859	CHANCE: Charles Darwin
293.	c.1859	VISIBLE SYMBOL: Gilbert French on Samuel Crompton
294.	1859	LETTER FROM EDWARD LEAR
295.	1859	DARWIN ON PIGEONS: Charles Darwin
296.	1860	DARWIN ON THEOLOGY: Charles Darwin
297.	c.1861	THE SPREAD OF EDUCATION: Bracebridge Hemyng

298.	1862	ODE SUNG AT THE OPENING OF THE INTERNATIONAL EXHIBITION: Alfred Tennyson
299.	1862	THE LOWER PTHAH: John Ruskin
300.	1862	THE QUESTION OF QUESTIONS: Thomas Huxley
301.	1862	BODY AND SOUL: James Clerk-Maxwell
302.	1862	TRAVELS IN THE AIR: James Glaisher
303.	1862	THE UNEMPLOYED: Edwin Waugh
304.	1862	A VERY UNUSUAL THING: Edward Lear
305.	1863	GOOD AND EVIL: Samuel Smiles
306.	1863	SCREAMY GANDERS: Edward Lear
307.	1863	THE GREAT GULF: Thomas Huxley
308.	1863	TO HIS NIECE IN HIS OLD AGE: Michael Faraday
309.	1863	OVER LONDON: James Glaisher
310.	1864	HERSCHEL AND NASMYTH: James Nasmyth
311.	c.1864	ETERNAL JUSTICE: Henry Bessemer
312.	1865	THE LITTLE GARRET AT HEATHFIELD: Samuel Smiles
313.	1865	THE TENTH MUSE: John Ruskin
314.	1865	THE HUMAN ELEMENT: Lewis Carroll
315.	1865	THE ENGLISH MIDDLE-CLASS: Matthew Arnold
316.	1865	THE 'FACTORY KING': Annals of Yorkshire
317.	1865	THE SUICIDE OF BETTY HIGDEN: Charles Dickens
318.	1866	THE POOLS OF CARSHALTON: John Ruskin
319.	1866	ENGLAND: Edward Lear
320.	1867	THE SWINDON RAILWAY WORKS: Richard Jefferies
321.	1867	IN A RAILWAY CARRIAGE: Edward Lear
322.	c.1867	THE VOWEL FLAME: John Tyndall
323.	1867	THE DAMAGE: W. Rothwell
324.	1867	THE FIRE OF LABOUR: Karl Marx
325.	1867	THE QUEEN OF RED CLAY: Elihu Burritt
326.	c.1868	NORTHERN FARMER – NEW STYLE: Alfred Tennyson
327.	1869	THE FIRST TASK: John Ruskin
328.	1869	THE GREATNESS OF ENGLAND: Matthew Arnold
329.	1870	ROUGH-SPUN NATURE: Edward Fitzgerald
330.	1870	LANCASHIRE: Thomas Cooper
331.	1870	FREEDOM: Thomas Huxley
332.	1870	MORECAMBE BAY: Adam Sedgwick
333.	1871	A VAST NUMBER: R.M. Ballantyne
334.	1871	EVAPORATION: Gerard Manley Hopkins
335.	1871	CLOUDS: John Tyndall
336.	1871	THE SUN-FORCE: Charles Kingsley
337.	1871	THE GODS: John Ruskin
338.	1871	ANIMISM: Edward Burnett Tylor
339.	1871	THE PLAGUE-WIND: John Ruskin
340.	1871	A LIVING OPTICAL INSTRUMENT: Charles Darwin

341.	1872	AN AFFECTIONATE MACHINE-TICKLING APHID: Samuel Butler
342.	1872	EXTRAORDINARY THINGS: Francis Galton
343.	1873	MANUFACTURED ARTICLES: James Clerk-Maxwell
344.	1873–74	THE DISTURBER: Thomas Hardy
345.	1873	A MEMORABLE FOG: John Tyndall
346.	1874	THE LUNAR LANDSCAPE: James Nasmyth and James Carpenter
347.	1875	THE POWER TO COME: George Meredith
348.	c.1875	DELUSIONS OF CRIMINAL PRISONERS: Arthur Griffiths
349.	1877	THE TWO CLAVIGERAE: John Ruskin
350.	1878	AREOI: Charles Darwin
351.	1878	A PARADOXICAL ODE: James Clerk-Maxwell
352.	1879	THE ELECTRIC LIGHT: Samuel Butler
353.	1879	THE EDISON TELEPHONE: John Tyndall
354.	1879	NOTHING LIKE THE EARTH: Richard Jefferies
355.	1879	MANCHESTER DEVIL'S DARKNESS: John Ruskin
356.	1879	THE ROMANCE HAS DEPARTED: Richard Jefferies
357.	c.1880	THE PRINCIPLE OR FOUNDATION: Gerard Manley Hopkins
358.	1880–81	THE VIEW DOWN FLEET STREET: Samuel Butler
359.	1881	SCIENCE AND POETRY: Charles Darwin
360.	c.1881	IN A MANUFACTURING TOWN: Edward Carpenter
361.	1882	THE FIRST WHISPER: Annie Besant
362.	1882	THE CROWD AND THE RUNNER: John Tyndall
363.	1882	THE NUMBER OF PASSENGERS: James Nasmyth
364.	1882	MENTAL CHOKING: Herbert Spencer
365.	1883	PHANTASMAGORIA: Francis Galton
366.	1883	HOLLAND HOUSE: Lord Shaftesbury
367.	1884	THE STORM-CLOUD OF THE NINETEENTH CENTURY: John Ruskin
368.	1885	THE MARCH OF THE WORKERS: William Morris
369.	c.1885	BLOOD TEST: Arthur Conan Doyle
370.	1885	AFTER LONDON: Richard Jefferies
371.	1886	APOCALYPTIC VISIONS: Thomas Huxley
372.	1886	THE DAY OF THE EARTH: William Morris

ILLUSTRATIONS

Humphrey Jennings, Lee Miller, 1944. Frontispiece.
The Water-Insect or Gnat. From *Micrographia*, Robert Hooke, 1663. Page 11.
The Great Gogle-Eyed Beetle. From *Musaeum Regalis Societatis*, Nehemiah Grew, 1682. Page 18.
The Anatomy of Trunks. From *The Anatomy of Plants*, Nehemiah Grew, 1682. Page 19.
The East Prospect of Derby. From *History of Derby*, William Hutton, 1791. Page 48.
The Hoe-Plough. From *Horse-Hoeing Husbandry*, Jethro Tull, Dublin, 1733. Page 49.
The English Balloon and Appendages. From *An Account of the First Aërial Voyage*, Vincent Lunardi, 1748. Page 81.
Banks. From *Zoonomia*, Erasmus Darwin, 1785. Page 86.
Tailpiece from *Horse-Hoeing Husbandry*, Jethro Tull, Dublin, 1733. Page 111.
Trapper in the Lancashire and Cheshire Coal-Pits. From *Cyclopaedia of Useful Arts*, Charles Tomlinson, 1854. Page 121.
The Great World of London. From *The Criminal Prisons of London*, Henry Mayhew and John Binney, 1862. Page 124.
Admission card to Trevithick's Railway. From *Richard Trevithick*, H.W. Dickinson and A. Titley, 1934. Page 128.
The Country of the Iguanodon by John Martin. From *The Book of the Great Sea Dragons*, Thomas Hawkins, 1834. Page 189.
Ichthyosaurus Chiroparamekostinus. From *Memoirs of the Ichthyosauri*, Thomas Hawkins, 1834. Page 199.
Entrance Gateway for a New Cemetary. From *Apology to the Christian Church*, A.W. Pugin, 1843. Page 218.
Premium, Par, Discount. From *Table Book*, George Cruickshank, 1845. Page 234.
The Poor Man's Guardian, Saturday, November 6, 1847. Page 239.
The Railway Juggernaut of 1845. From *Punch*, 1845. Page 242.
The Crippled Street Bird-Seller. From *London Labour and the London Poor*, Henry Mayhew, 1851. Page 247.
The Tempest Prognosticator, George Merryweather, 1851. Page 255.
The First Shilling Day – Going In. From *1851, The Adventures of Mr and Mrs Sandboys at the Great Exhibition*, Henry Mayhew and George Cruickshank, 1851. Page 259.
Calico Pattern and Smithia Pangellyi. From *The Testimony of the Rocks*, Hugh Miller, 1857. Page 264.

The Workshop under the Silent System at Millbank Prison. From *The Criminal Prisons of London*, Henry Mayhew and John Binny, 1862. Page 275.

Octagonal Chimney Shaft at Bolton. From *Cyclopaedia of Useful Arts*, Charles Tomlinson, 1854. Page 284.

The Suburbs of London in the Distance. From *Travels in Air*, James Glaisher, 1871. Page 300.

Watt's Garret at Heathfield. From *Lives of Boulton and Watt*, Samuel Smiles, 1865. Page 304.

In A Railway Carriage. From *More Nonsense*, Edward Lear, 1867. Page 313.

The Vowel Flame. From *Sound*, John Tyndall, 1867. Page 314.

Ludgate Hill. From *London*, W. Blanchard Jerrold and Gustave Dore, 1872. Page 242.

Tailpiece. From *A Life of Sir Titus Salt, Bart.*, A. Holroyd, 1871. Page 356.

INTRODUCTION

In this book I present the imaginative history of the Industrial Revolution. Neither the political history, nor the mechanical history, nor the social history nor the economic history, but the imaginative history.

I say 'present', not describe or analyse, because the Imagination is a function of man whose traces are more delicate to handle than the facts and events and ideas of which history is usually constructed. This function I believe is found active in the areas of the arts, of poetry and of religion – but is not necessarily confined to them or present in all their manifestations. I prefer not to try to define its limits at the moment but to leave the reader to agree or not with the evidence which I shall place before him. I present it by means of what I call Images.

These are quotations from writings of the period in question, passages describing certain moments, events, clashes, ideas occurring between 1660 and 1886 which either in the writing or in the nature of the matter itself or both have revolutionary and symbolic and illuminatory quality. I mean that they contain in little a whole world – they are the knots in a great net of tangled time and space – the moments at which the situation of humanity is clear – even if only for the flash time of the photographer or the lightning. And just as the usual history does not consist of isolated events, occurrences – so this 'imaginative history' does not consist of isolated images, but each is in a particular place in an unrolling film.

And these images – what do they deal with? I do not claim that they represent truth – they are too varied, even contradictory, for that. But they represent human experience. They are the record of mental events. Events of the heart. They are facts (the historian's kind of facts) which have been passed through the feelings and the mind of an individual and have forced him to write. And what he wrote is a picture – a coloured picture of them. His personality has coloured them and selected and altered and pruned and enlarged and minimised and exaggerated. Admitted. But he himself is part, was part of the period, even part of the event itself – he was an actor, a spectator in it. So his distortions are not so much distortions as one might suppose. Moreover they altered him. The event had its effect on him. Undistorted him, opened his eyes.

What have these extracts in common? They have no political or economic or social homogeneity. They are all *moments* in the history of the

Industrial Revolution, at which clashes and conflicts suddenly show themselves with extra clearness, and which through that clearness can stand as symbols for the whole inexpressible uncapturable process. They are what later poets have called 'Illuminations', 'Moments of Vision' – some obviously clearer than others – some intentional, others unintentional – but all in some degree with this window-opening quality – it is this which differentiates these pieces of writing from purely economic or political, or social analyses. Theirs is a different method of tackling, of presenting the same material, the same conflicts, the method of poetry.

These extracts are to be considered as documents which illuminate – in one way or another – the conflicts of the Industrial Revolution in Britain.

In what ways? What conflicts?

1. Class conflicts – in their simplest form Luddite riots, Peterloo
2. The conflict of animism and materialism
3. The conflict of the expropriated individual with his environment
4. Conflicts of ideas
5. Conflicts of systems – religious systems
    political systems
    moral systems

But do not expect to find each of the extracts dealing with one of these conflicts only. That is precisely what they do not do. They are *not* texts to illustrate histories of economics etc. In treating separately the Trades Union, the political-historical, the social, the economic sides of the Industrial Revolution, the writers have themselves simply perpetuated the law of division of labour. But this should not blind us to the fact that Life – of which their analyses are analyses – is a synthesis and that the interactions between its parts are infinitely more complex than any analytical machine can follow. This is not in any way to invalidate the analytical method – or to suggest that the poet, for example, is more capable of presenting the whole – of course he is not. But what he can present is the sense of complexity – the type of pattern and so the type of inter-actions of which it consists. The analytical historian's business is to disentangle shred by shred like plucking the strand out of a rope. The result is the length of the rope but only one strand's thickness, and although the strand may still be twisted from its position among the other strands it is presented nevertheless alone. The poet might be compared to a man who cuts a short section of the whole rope. The only thing is he must cut it where it will not fall to pieces.

The history of poetry is itself a history of mechanisation and specialisation. At the time of Homer, Hesiod, Moses, Lao-Tze, poet-sages dealt with *all* problems of life – religious, scientific, social and personal. In the course of history, the actual mental process of poetic production has hardly altered, but the division of labour has produced specialisation here as everywhere. Since that time we have seen the appearance of specialist writers on every subject, who have in the main avoided poetry as far as possible – since their reason for specialisation was in reaction against the universal poetic writer. In the last two hundred years the division of labour and specialisation have gone so far that the poet can only write about the subject of poetry itself (Gray, 'The Progress of Poesy') or definitely poetic subjects (Keats – supreme example) or his own thoughts.

It would take a large work on its own to show, in the great period of English poets 1570–1750, the desperate struggle that poets had to keep poetry head into the wind: to keep it facing life. But by 1750 the struggle – like that of the peasants – was over. *In other words poetry has been expropriated.*

Poetry was created in primitive and feudal societies – patriarchal societies – and in these societies the subjects with which the poet dealt were not *then* poetical subjects; they were vital everyday facts and necessities – *religion* – the cosmos and the fate of the human soul . . . *kingship* – the character of the man in power and the fate of the people under him. As agriculture was the principal means of subsistence of these societies, the language and metaphors of poetry (what is called 'flowery' language) are full of agricultural memories.

But in a process (conflict) which culminated between 1660 and 1880 the peasants were destroyed and the land capitalised – the power of money – capital – substituted for the power of the Crown and the religion. The poet – as an individual – reacted to this major crisis of his career in many differing ways but it must be admitted not very successfully. We cannot say that any poet understood this process – much less applied it to his own view of the world or in any way modified his writings through it.

But the written language itself – the poets' raw material – did not stand about unused – unwritten. I mean that the conflict between animism and materialism – between poetry and science – the conflicts between agriculture and industrialisation – the fundamental class conflicts – did not go unrecorded. *Poetry survived* – although it would be untrue to say that a synthesis was evolved from any of the above conflicts. In what ways may we say it survived?

In the work of certain well-known poets – Milton, Blake, Shelley; plus novelists – Disraeli, Dickens: who from time to time but only rarely, found a point in their work where it *met*, so to speak, the current economic and political and social revolutions on equal ground and where they were capable of recording the conflict: adaptation of the classic line of poetry to industrial revolution.

In the work of scientists and philosophers (natural philosophers as they were called) where very occasionally they are looking beyond the immediate scientific issues and recording the conflict of their own new systems with others such as religion – Newton, Berkeley, Darwin.

In the work of social critics as we may call them – Cobbett, Swift, Carlyle, Ruskin, Arnold – who made it their business of life to comment on the conflicts they saw in front of them and whose commentaries are often passionate, and lively. Also social documents as by Defoe, Head, Hawthorne.

In the autobiographies, memoirs, letters, diaries and so on of scientists, artists and especially in the 19th century of working men and social workers – Samuel Bamford, Hugh Miller, Charles Kingsley, Caroline Fox – which not only record some of the conflicts but also show the growing consciousness of those conflicts among the people most nearly involved in them: principally the newly-formed working class.

In other documents in which the authors were in the main unconscious of the effect and value of what they were recording – memoirs of capitalists (Nasmyth, Bessemer) – newspaper accounts – would-be comic writers.

THE MEANS OF VISION AND THE MEANS OF PRODUCTION

The Means of Vision – matter (sense impressions) transformed and reborn by Imagination: *turned into an image.*

The Means of Production – matter is transformed and reborn by *Labour.*

At a certain period in human development the means of vision and the means of production were intimately connected – or were felt to be by the people concerned – I refer to the Magical systems under which it was not possible to plow the ground without a prayer – to eat without a blessing, to hunt an animal without a magic formula. To build without a sense of glory.

In the two hundred years 1660–1860 the means of production were violently and fundamentally altered – altered by the accumulation of capital, the freedom of trade, the invention of machines, the philosophy of materialism, the discoveries of science.

In what sense have the Means of Vision kept pace with these alterations? I am referring not to the Arts as a commodity for Bond Street, or as a piece of snobbery in Mayfair, or as a means of propaganda in Bloomsbury, or as a method of escapism in Hampstead . . . but to the Means of Vision by which 'the emotional side of our nature' (Darwin's phrase) is kept alive and satisfied and fed – our nature as Human Beings in the anthracite drifts of South Wales, in the cotton belt of Lancashire, in the forges of Motherwell – how the emotional side of their nature has been used, altered, tempered, appealed to in these two hundred years.

Man as we see him today lives by production and by vision. It is doubtful if he can live by one alone. He has occasionally however tried. Dr Ure speaks of a factory as ideally 'a vast automaton, composed of various mechanical and intellectual organs, acting in an uninterrupted concern for the production of a common object, all of them being subordinated to a self-regulated moving force'.*

---

* Quoted by Marx in *Capital* where he calls Ure 'the Pindar of the automatic factory'.

At the other extreme we have the Tibetan living naked in the caves of the Himalayas, eating only nettles and devoting himself to contemplation, and turning green in consequence. But in fact the factory man is living on the vision of others and the Buddhist Yogi on the production of others. In some societies (civilisations) the two have been mixed, in others clearly distinguishable. The relationship of production to vision and vision to production has been mankind's greatest problem.

Unless we are prepared to claim special attributes for the poet – the attribute of vision – and unless we are prepared to admit the work of the artist (that is to say the function of 'imagination') as an essential part of the modern world there is no real reason for our continuing to bother with any of the arts any more, or with any imaginary activity. No reasons except money, snobbery, propaganda or escapism. In this book however it is assumed that the poet's vision does exist, that the imagination is a part of life, that the exercise of the imagination is an indispensable function of man like work, eating, sleeping, loving. I do not propose to ask the obvious next question 'What then is the place of imagination in the world of today?' I prefer to inquire what may have *been* the place of imagination in the making of the modern world.

This introduction was written up by Charles Madge from extensive notes left by Humphrey Jennings.

PART ONE

1660–1729
Observations and Reports

1   THE BUILDING OF PANDÆMONIUM   c.1660

There stood a Hill not far whose griesly top
Belch'd fire and rowling smoak; the rest entire
Shon with a glossie scurff, undoubted sign
That in his womb was hid metallic Ore,
The work of Sulphur. Thither wing'd with speed
A numerous Brigad hasten'd. As when bands
Of Pioners with Spade and Pickaxe arm'd
Forerun the Royal Camp, to trench a Field,
Or cast a Rampart. *Mammon* led them on,
Mammon, the least erected Spirit that fell
From heav'n, for ev'n in heav'n his looks and thoughts
Were always downward bent, admiring more
The riches of Heav'ns pavement, trod'n Gold,
Then aught divine or holy else enjoy'd
In vision beatific: by him first
Men also, and by his suggestion taught,
Ransack'd the Center, and with impious hands
Rifl'd the bowels of thir mother Earth
For Treasures better hid. Soon had his crew
Op'nd into the Hill a spacious wound
And dig'd out ribs of Gold. Let none admire
That riches grow in Hell; that soyle may best
Deserve the pretious bane. And here let those
Who boast in mortal things, and wondring tell
Of *Babel*, and the works of *Memphian* Kings,
Learn how thir greatest Monuments of Fame,
And Strength and Art are easily outdone
By Spirits reprobate, and in an hour,
What in an age they with incessant toyle
And hands innumerable scarce perform.
Nigh on the Plain in many cells prepar'd,
That underneath had veins of liquid fire
Sluc'd from the Lake, a second multitude
With wondrous Art founded the massie Ore,
Severing each kinde, and scum'd the Bullion dross:
A third as soon had form'd within the ground
A various mould, and from the boyling cells
By strange conveyance fill'd each hollow nook,
As in an Organ from one blast of wind
To many a row of Pipes the sound-board breaths.
Anon out of the earth a Fabrick huge
Rose like an Exhalation, with the sound

Of Dulcet Symphonies and voices sweet,
Built like a Temple, where *Pilasters* round
Were set, and Doric pillars overlaid
With Golden Architrave; nor did there want
Cornice or Freeze, with bossy Sculptures grav'n,
The roof was fretted Gold. Not *Babilon*,
Nor great *Alcairo* such magnificence
Equal'd in all thir glories, to inshrine
Belus or *Serapis* thir Gods, or seat
Thir Kings, when *Ægypt* with *Assyria* strove
In wealth and luxurie. Th' ascending pile
Stood fixt her stately highth, and strait the dores
Op'ning thir brazen foulds discover wide
Within, her ample spaces, o're the smooth
And level pavement; from the arched roof
Pendant by suttle Magic many a row
Of Starry Lamps and blazing Cressets fed
With *Naphtha* and *Asphaltus* yeilded light
As from a sky. The hasty multitude
Admiring enter'd, and the work some praise
And some the Architect: his hand was known
In Heav'n by many a Towred structure high,
Where Scepter'd Angels held thir residence,
And sat as Princes, whom the supreme King
Exalted to such power, and gave to rule,
Each in his Hierarchie, the Orders bright.

From Paradise Lost *Book I by John Milton, published 1667, written c.1660.*

The first image, and in some sense the origin of all that follow, is the passage towards the end of Book 1 of Milton's Paradise Lost *describing the fallen angels setting to work to mine, smelt, forge and mould the metals in the soil of hell.*

In the lines that follow, Lucifer is equated with Vulcan or Mulciber, also thrown down from heaven and in ancient Greece and Rome the god of the forge:

nor aught avail'd him now
To have built in Heav'n high Towrs; nor did he scape
By all his Engins, but was headlong sent
With his industrious crew to build in hell.
Meanwhile the winged Haralds by command
Of Sovran power, with awful Ceremony
And Trumpets sound throughout the Host proclaim

> A solemn Councel forthwith to be held
> At *Pandæmonium*, the high Capital
> Of Satan and his Peers. . . .

In this book, the building of Pandæmonium is equated with the industrial revolution and the coming of the machine. One of the early 'notes for an introduction' reads: 'Pandæmonium is the Palace of All the Devils. Its building began c.1660. It will never be finished – it has to be transformed into Jerusalem. The building of Pandæmonium is the real history of Britain for the last three hundred years. That history has never been written. The present writer has spent many years collecting materials for it. From this mass of material the present book is a selection. A foretaste of the full story.'

2   MEMORANDUM   1660

Memorandum that, November 28, 1660, these persons following, according to the usual custom of most of them, mett together at Gresham College, to hear Mr Wren's lecture, viz., the Lord Brouncker, Mr Boyle, Mr Bruce, Sir Robert Moray, Sir Paule Neile, Dr Wilkins, Dr Goddard, Dr Petty, Mr Ball, Mr Rooke, Mr Wren, Mr Hill. And after the lecture was ended they did, according to the usual manner, withdrawe for mutualle converse. Where, amongst other matters that were discoursed of, something was offered about a designe of founding a Colledge for the promoting of Physico-Mathematicall Experimentall Learning; and because they had these frequent occasions of meeting with one another, it was proposed that some course might be thought of to improve their meeting to a more regular way of debating things, and, according to the manner in other countries, where there were voluntary associations of men in academies for the advancement of various parts of learning, soe they might do something answerable here for the promoting of experimentall philosophy.

In order to which it was agreed that this Company would hold their weekly meetings on Wednesday, at 3 o'clock, of the term time, at Mr Rooke's chamber at Gresham Colledge; in the vacation at Mr Ball's chamber in the Temple.

This 'memorandum' is quoted in an extract from the Journal *of the Royal Society in* The Royal Society, 1660–1940 *by Sir Henry Lyons, 1944. A similar text is printed in* The History of the Royal Society *by Thomas Birch, 1756.*

3   GOD WOULD BE MUCH HONORED   c.1660

God would be much honored

1 By finding out the use of the fixed stars.
2 Of the matter wherewith the Globe of the Earth is fill'd.

3 The use of most animalls, vegetables, & mineralls.
4 The origins of man & animalls.
5 Of animals eating one another.
6 Of the paines & evills which animalls suffer.
7 Of generation by the way of male & female.
8 Of the different ages & gestation of animals.
9 Of germination in animalls, vegeatables &c.

From the MSS of Sir William Petty in The Petty Papers, *edited by the Marquis of Lansdowne, 1927.*

4   THE BOYHOOD OF GENIUS   c.1660

Every one that knew Sir Isaac, or have heard of him, recount the pregnancy of his parts when a boy, his strange inventions, and extraordinary inclination for mechanics. That instead of playing among the other boys, when from school, he always busied himself in making knick-knacks and models of wood in many kinds. For which purpose he had got little saws, hatchets, hammers, and all sorts of tools, which he would use with great dexterity. In particular they speak of his making a wooden clock. About this time, a new windmill was set up near Grantham, in the way to Gunnerby, which is now demolished, this country chiefly using water mills. Our lad's imitating spirit was soon excited and by frequently prying into the fabric of it, as they were making it, he became master enough to make a very perfect model thereof, and it was said to be as clean and curious a piece of workmanship, as the original. This sometimes he would set upon the house-top, where he lodged, and clothing it with sail-cloth, the wind would readily turn it; but what was most extraordinary in its composition was, that he put a mouse into it, which he called the miller, and that the mouse made the mill turn round when he pleased; and he would joke too upon the miller eating the corn that was put in. Some say that he tied a string to the mouse's tail, which was put into a wheel, like that of turn-spit dogs, so that pulling the string, made the mouse go forward by way of resistance, and this turned the mill. Others suppose there was some corn placed above the wheel, this the mouse endeavouring to get to, made it turn.

From a letter from Dr Stukeley to Dr Mead, printed in Collections for the History of the Town and Soke of Grantham *by Edmund Turnor, 1806.*

Note on 2, 3 and 4. *The first stage (1660–1730) is a phase of pure science, direct experiments and clear philosophical and materialist thinking. The invention as yet was only on paper. The people – the impact on life – and consequent exploitation had not yet arrived.*

Suggestion: when these ideas, scientific and mechanical, began to be exploited by capital and to involve many human beings, was not this the period of the repression of the clear imaginative vision in ordinary folk? And hence for its being possible for them to be emotionally exploited, e.g. by Wesley?

5 THE MOST STUPENDIOUS WORK IN THE WHOLE WORLD   c.1660

98. An Engine so contrived, that working the *Primum mobile* forward or backward, upward or downward, circularly or corner-wise, to and fro, streight, upright or downright, yet the pretended Operation continueth, and advanceth none of the motions above-mentioned, hindering, much less stopping the other; but unanimously, and with harmony agreeing they all augment and contribute strength unto the intended work and operation: And therefore I call this *A Semi-omnipotent Engine*, and do intend that a Model thereof be buried with me.

99. How to make one pound weight to raise an hundred as high as one pound falleth, and yet the hundred pound descending doth what nothing less than one hundred pound can effect.

100. Upon so potent a help as these two last-mentioned Inventions a Waterwork is by many years experience and labour so advantageously by me contrived, that a Child's force bringeth up an hundred foot high an incredible quantity of water, even two foot Diameter, so naturally, that the work will not be heard even into the next Room; and with so great ease and Geometrical Symmetry, that though it work day and night from one end of the year to the other, it will not require forty shillings reparation to the whole Engine, nor hinder ones day-work. And I may boldly call it *The most stupendious Work in the whole world*: not onely with little charge to drein all sorts of Mines, and furnish Cities with water, though never so high seated, as well to keep them sweet, running through several streets, and so performing the work of Scavengers, as well as furnishing the Inhabitants with sufficient water for their private occasions; but likewise supplying Rivers with sufficient to maintaine and make them portable from Towne to Towne, and for the bettering of Lands all the way it runs; with many more advantageous, and yet greater effects of Profit, Admiration, and Consequence. So that deservedly I deem this Invention to crown my Labours, to reward my Expences, and make my Thoughts acquiesce in way of further Inventions: this making up the whole Century, and preventing any further trouble to the Reader for the present, meaning to leave to Posterity a Book, wherein under each of these Heads the means to put in execution and visible trial of all things belonging to them, shall be printed by Brass-plates.

From A Century of Inventions *by the Marquis of Worcester, 1663.*

For first, the City of *London* is built upon a sweet and most agreeable Eminency of Ground, at the North-side of a goodly and well-conditioned River, towards which it hath an Aspect by a gentle and easie declivity, apt to be improved to all that may render her Palaces, Buildings, and Avenues usefull, gracefull, and most magnificent: The *Fumes* which exhale from the Waters and lower Grounds lying Southward, by which means they are perpetually attracted, carried off or dissipated by the Sun, as soon as they are born, and ascend.

Adde to this, that the Soil is universally Gravell, not onely where the City itself is placed, but for severall Miles about the Countreys which environ it: That it is plentifully and richly irrigated, and visited with Waters which Christalize her Fountains in every Street, and may be conducted to them in such farther plenty, as *Rome* herself might not more abound in this liquid ornament, for the pleasure and divertisement, as well as for the use and refreshment of her Inhabitants. I forbear to enlarge upon the rest of the conveniences which this August and Opulent City enjoies both by Sea and Land, to accumulate her *Encomiums*, and render her the most considerable that the *Earth* has standing upon her ample bosome; because, it belongs to the *Orator* and the *Poet*, and is none of my Institution: But I will infer, that if this goodly City justly challenges what is her due, and merits all that can be said to reinforce his Praises, and give her *Title*; she is to be relieved from that which renders her less healthy, really offends her, and which darkens and eclipses all her other Attributes. And what is all this, but that Hellish and dismall Cloud of SEA-COALE? which is not onely perpetual imminent over her head; For as the Poet[*],

Conditur in tenebris altum caligine cœlum;

but so universally mixed with the otherwise wholesome and excellent *Aer*, that her *Inhabitants* breathe nothing but an impure and thick Mist, accompanied by a fuliginous and filthy vapour, which renders them obnoxious to a thousand inconveniences, corrupting the *Lungs*, and disordering the entire habit of their Bodies; so that *Catharrs, Phthisicks, Coughs* and *Consumptions*, rage more in this one City, than the whole Earth besides.

I shall not hear much descant upon the Nature of *Smoakes*, and other Exhalations from things burnt, which have obtained their several *Epithetes*, according to the quality of the Matter consumed, because they are generally accounted noxious and unwholesome; and I would not have it thought, that I do here *Fumos vendere*, as the word is, or blot paper with insignificant remarks: It was yet haply no inept derivation of that *Critick*, who took our

---

[*] Æneid xi

English, or rather, *Saxon* appellative, from the Greek word σμυχω *corrumpo* and *exuro*, as most agreeable to its destructive effects, especially of what we doe here so much declaim against, since this is certain, that of all the common and familiar materials which emit it, the immoderate use of, and indulgence to *Sea-coale* alone in the City of *London*, exposes it to one of the fowlest Inconveniences and reproaches, than possibly beffall so noble, and otherwise incomparable City: And that, not from the *Culinary* fires, which for being weak, and less often fed below, is with such ease dispelled and scattered above, as it is hardly at all discernible, but from some few particular Tunnels and Issues, belonging only to *Brewers, Diers, Lime-burners, Salt,* and *Sope-Boylers*, and some other private Trades, *One* of whose *Spiracles* alone, does manifestly infect the *Aer*, more than all the Chimnies of *London* put together besides. And that this is not the least *Hyperbolic*, let the best of Judges decide it, which I take to be our senses: Whilst these are belching it forth their sooty jaws, the City of *London* resembles the face rather of *Mount Ætna*, the *Court of Vulcan, Stromboli*, or the Suburbs of *Hell*, than an Assembly of Rational Creatures, and the imperial seat of our incomparable *Monarch*. For when in all other places the *Aer* is most Serene and Pure, it is here Ecclipsed with such a Cloud of Sulphure, as the Sun itself, which gives day to all the World besides, is hardly able to penetrate and impart it here; and the weary *Traveller*, at many Miles distance, sooner smells, than sees the City to which he repairs. This is that pernicious Smoake which sullyes all her Glory, superinducing a sooty Crust or Fur upon all that it lights, spoyling the moveables, tarnishing the Plate, Gildings and Furniture, and corroding the very Iron-bars and hardest Stones with those piercing and acrimonious Spirits which accompany its Sulphure; and executing more in one year, than exposed to the pure *Aer* of the Country it could effect in some hundreds.

From Fumifugium *by John Evelyn, 1661.*

7	**TO COMMAND THE RAIN**	July 19, 1662

In the afternoon I went upon the river to look after some tarr I am sending down and some coles, and so home again; it raining hard upon the water, I put ashore and sheltered myself, while the King came by in his barge, going down towards the Downs to meet the Queen; the Duke being gone yesterday. But methought it lessened my esteem of a king, that he should not be able to command the rain.

From the Diary *of Samuel Pepys edited by H.B. Wheatley, 1904.*

8 THE FACES OF THE SKY c.1662

But for the Faces of the Sky, they are so many, that many of them want proper Names; and therefore it will be convenient to agree upon some determinate ones, by which the most usual may be in brief expressed. As let *Cleer* signify a very cleer Sky without any Clouds or Exhalations: *Checker'd* a cleer Sky, with many great white round Clouds, such as are very usual in Summer. *Hazy*, a Sky that looks whitish, by Reason of the Thickness of the higher parts of the Air, by some Exhalation not formed into Clouds. *Thick*, a Sky more whitened by a greater Company of Vapours: these do usually make the *Luminaries* look bearded or hairy, and are oftentimes the Cause of the appearance of Rings and Haloes about the *Sun* as well as the *Moon*. *Overcast*, when the Vapours so whiten and thicken the Air, that the Sun cannot break through; and of this there are very many degrees, which may be express'd by a *little, much, more, very much overcast*, &c. Let *Hairy* signify a Sky that hath many small, thin, and high Exhalations, which resemble locks of hair, or flakes of Hemp or Flax: whose Varieties may be express'd by *straight or curv'd*, &c. according to the resemblance they bear. Let *Water'd* signify a Sky that has many high thin and small Clouds, looking almost like water'd Tabby, called in some places a Mackeril Sky. Let a Sky be called *Wav'd*, when those Clouds appear much bigger and lower, but much after the same manner. *Cloudy*, when the Sky has many thick dark Clouds. *Lowring*, when the Sky is not very much overcast, but hath also underneath many thick dark Clouds which threaten rain. The signification of *gloomy, foggy, misty, sleeting, driving, rainy, snowy*, reaches or racks variable, &c. are well known, they being very commonly used. There may be also several faces of the Sky compounded of two or more of these, which may be intelligibly enough express'd by two or more of these Names.

From A Method for Making a History of the Weather *by Robert Hooke, printed in* The History of the Royal Society *by Thomas Sprat, 1667.*

Hooke is secularizing the sky, or heaven, long thought of as a divinity or home of divinities, its aspects exerting magical influence on the lives of man. He is making out of it the subject matter for the new science of meteorology. But in doing so he continues to use animistic language. The sky has 'faces' that are sometimes 'bearded or hairy'.

9 THE WATER-INSECT OR GNAT September 1663

'Tis a creature, wholly differing in shape from any I ever observ'd; nor is its motion less strange. It has a very large head, in proportion to its body, all covered with a shell, like other *testaceous* animals, but it differs in this, that it has, up and down several parts of it, several tufts of hairs, or bristles, plac'd in the order express'd in the Figure; it has two horns, which seem'd almost like the horns of an Oxe, inverted, and, as neer as I could guess, were hollow, with tufts of bristles, likewise at the top; these horns they could move easily this or that way, and might, perchance, be their nostrils. It has a pretty large mouth, which seem'd contriv'd much like those of Crabs and Lobsters, by which, I have often observ'd them to feed on water, or some imperceptible nutritive substance in it.

I could perceive, through the transparent shell, while the Animal surviv'd, several motions in the head, thorax, and belly, very distinctly, of differing kinds which I may, perhaps, elsewhere endeavour more accurately to examine, and to shew of how great benefit the use of a *Microscope* may be for the discovery of Nature's course in the operations perform'd in animal bodies, by which we have the opportunity of observing her through these delicate and pellucid teguments of the bodies of insects acting according to her usual course and way, undisturbed, whereas, when we endeavour to pry into her secrets by breaking open the doors upon her, and dissecting and mangling creatures whil'st there is life yet within them, we find her indeed at work, but put into such disorder by the violence offer'd, as it may easily be imagin'd, how differing a thing we should find, if we could, as we can with a *Microscope*, in these smaller creatures, quietly peep in at the windows, without frighting her out of her usual byas.

From Micrographia *by Robert Hooke, published 1664 but probably written September 1663.*

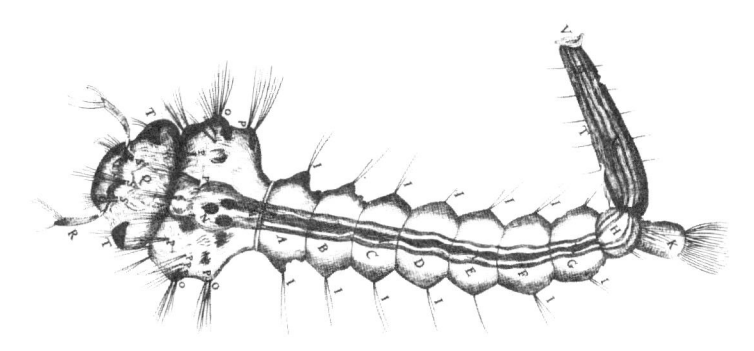

THE WATER-INSECT OR GNAT

Here too Hooke is seeing things in a new way that is still partly the old way. His microscope enables him to see a water-insect as though it were 'an Oxe'. What had been a negligible gnat is now a monster. But what he sees when he 'peeps in at the windows' of this creature suggests to him that it is a mechanical rather than a magical contrivance. The idea that living creatures are machines is in these years gaining ground. God is admired as an inventor or engineer and the scientists are in the god-like position of being able to create machines which are like living creatures. The analogy which begins with insects, whose movements are compulsive, is not at first openly continued up to man, the animal with a soul. But the distinction is dropped in practice, or blurred, when human labour begins to be organised on a ruthlessly rational basis.

10 A HEATHEN PLACE September 1663

17th. Up, and my father being gone to bed ill last night and continuing so this morning, I was forced to come to a new consideration, whether it was fit for me to let my uncle and his son go to Wisbeach about my uncle Day's estate alone or no, and concluded it unfit; and so resolved to go with them myself, leaving my wife there, I begun a journey with them, and with much ado, through the fens, along dikes, where sometimes we were ready to have our horses sink to the belly, we got by night, with a great deal of stir and hard riding, to Parson's Drove, a heathen place, where I found my uncle and aunt Perkins, and their daughters, poor wretches! in a sad, poor thatched cottage, like a poor barn, or stable, peeling of hemp, in which I did give myself good content to see their manner of preparing of hemp; and in a poor condition of habit took them to our miserable inn, and there, after long stay, and hearing of Frank, their son, the miller, play upon his treble, as he calls it, with which he earns part of his living, and singing of a country bawdy song, we sat down to supper; the whole crew, and Frank's wife and child, a sad company, of which I was ashamed, supped with us.

From the Diary of Samuel Pepys, *edited by H.B. Wheatley, 1904.*

While Hooke was writing his observations on insects, Pepys was travelling through the fens, which at that time and up to two hundred years later, were haunted by mosquitoes and malaria. Here he finds the depressed conditions which are still to be found among peoples who live in undrained swampland.

11 THE NATURE OF SOUNDS August 1666

Up, and with Reeves walk as far as the Temple, doing some business in my way at my bookseller's and elsewhere, and there parted, and I took coach, having first discoursed with Mr. Hooke a little, whom we met in the streete, about the nature of sounds, and he did make me understand the nature of musicall sounds made by strings, mighty prettily; and told me that having come to a certain number of vibrations proper to make any tone, he is able to tell how many strokes a fly makes with her wings (those flies that hum in their flying) by the note that it answers to in musique during their flying.

That, I suppose, is a little too much refined; but his discourse in general of sound was mighty fine.

From the Diary *of Samuel Pepys, edited by H.B. Wheatley, 1904.*

12   OBSERVATIONS   1667

Observations of the fix'd Stars for the perfecting of *Astronomy*, by the help of *Telescopes:* of the *Comets* in 1665, and 1666, which were made both in *London*, and elsewhere; and particularly of the first *Comet*, for above a month after, it disappear'd to the naked eye, and became Stationary, and Retrograde.

Observations about *Saturn*, of the proportion, and position of its *Ring*, of the motion and Orbit of its *Lunale*, of the shadow of the *Ring* on the *Body*, and of the *Body* on the *Ring*; and of its *Phases, &c.* of *Jupiters Belts*, and of its spots, and verticity about its *Axis*, of its eclipsing its *Satellites*, and being eclips'd by them; of the Orbs, Inclinations, Motions, &c. of the *Satellites*, together with *Tables*, and *Ephemerides* of their motions.

Observations of the Spots, about the Body of *Mars*, and of its whirling motion about its Center: of several Eclipses of the *Sun*, and *Moon*, and some of them as were not taken notice of, by *Astronomers*, or Tables commonly us'd: of the spots in the *Moon*, and of the several appearances in the Phases of it: of the *Moon* at the same time, by *Correspondents* in several parts of the World, towards the finding her Parallax, and distance.

Observations of the Eliptical and waved Figures of the *Planetary Bodies*, near the *Horizon* from the refraction of the Hemisphere: of the effects of *Lightning:* of the various pressure of the Atmosphere, by a *Wheel-barometer* for several years, and of its usefulness for predicting the changes of Weather.

Observations on frozen Beer: on the Figures of *Snow*, frozen Water, *Urine* congeal'd: on the suspension of *Mercury* at a great height: On *Mines* and *Minerals*: on the Concretions of *Wood, Plants, Shells*, and several *Animal* Substances: on the effects of Earthquakes, Fiery Eruptions, and Inundations: on Lakes, Mountains, Damps, subterraneous Fires: on Tides, Currents, and the Depth of the Sea.

Observations of the liming of *Ground*, for improvement of the Bodies of Sheep, but spoiling their Wool: of several ways for preventing smutty *Corn*: of the importance of changing Seed-Corn: of the alteration of the Horns of *Sheep*, and other *Cattel*, by the change of Pasture: of the Pores and Valves in *Wood*: the Anatomy of *Trees*: of the sensitive, and humble *Plant*.

Observations on the *Bills* of *Mortality*: on the leaves of *Sage:* on small living

Flies in the Powder of *Cantharides:* of insects bred in *Dew*: of *Virginian* Silk-Bottoms: of the Parts, and Anatomy of *Fishes*: of *Bernacles*: of the calcin'd Powder of *Toads*: of an Outlandish *Deer*-skin, and hair: of the parts of *Vipers*: of Stones taken out of the Heart of a *Man*: of young *Vipers*, that they do not eat holes through their old ones Bellies as is commonly affirm'd.

From The History of the Royal Society *by Thomas Sprat, 1667.*

13   THE NEW THEATER   July 9, 1669

In the morning was celebrated the Encenia of the New Theater, so magnificently built by the munificence of Dr. Gilbert Sheldon, Abp. of Canterbury, in which was spent £25,000, as Sir Christopher Wren, the architect, (as I remember) told me; and yet it was never seene by the benefactor, my Lord Abp. having told me that he never did nor ever would see it. It is in truth a *fabrick* comparable to any of this kind of former ages, and doubtless exceeding any of the present, as this University does for Colledges, Librairies, Scholes, Students, and order, all the Universities in the world. To the Theater is added the famous Sheldonian Printing-house. This being at the Act and the first time of opening the Theater (Acts being formerly kept in St. Mary's Church, which might be thought indecent, that being a place set apart for the immediate worship of God, and was the inducement for building this noble pile) it was now resolved to keep the present Act in it, and celebrate, and therefore drew a world of strangers and other companie to the Universitie from all parts of the nation.

The Vice Chancellor, Heads of Houses and Doctors, being seated in magisterial seates, the Vice Chancellor's chaire and deske, Proctors, &c. cover'd with Brocatall (a kind of brocade) and cloth of gold; the Universitie Register read the founder's grant and gift of it to the Universitie for their scolastic exercises upon these solemn occasions. Then follow'd Dr. South, the Universitie's Orator, in an eloquent speech, which was very long, and not without some malicious and indecent reflections on the Royal Society, as underminers of the Universitie, which was very foolish and untrue, as well as unreasonable. But to let that pass from an ill natured man, the rest was in praise of the Archbishop and the ingenious architect. This ended, after loud musiq from the corridor above, where an organ was plac'd, there follow'd divers panegyric speeches both in prose and verse, interchangeably pronounc'd by the young students plac'd in the rostrums, in Pindarics, Eclogues, Heroics, &c. mingled with excellent musiq, vocal and instrumental, to entertain the ladies and the rest of the company. A speech was then made in praise of Academical learning. This lasted from 11 in the morning till 7 at night, which was concluded with ringing of bells and universal joy and feasting.

From the Diary *of John Evelyn.*

Note the attack on the Royal Society; and the parallel between the new secular building and the 'Fabrick' that 'rose like an exhalation' in the opening passage from Milton, which also compares the way Pandæmonium was built to the passage of air into the pipes of an organ. All organs had been removed from churches by an ordinance dated 1644, and it was a long time after the Restoration before they could all be replaced.

The architecture of the Sheldonian, designed by Sir Christopher Wren, was based on a study of the classical theatre. Like St Pauls, and later in the Panopticon and the Crystal Palace, it was an architectural symbol. Some of the classical rationalism which it expressed would later be borrowed for the purposes of science and industry. The word theatre reappears in the surgeon's operating theatre. The machinery of the theatrical masque reappears in the factory. The division of labour in the musical orchestra has its industrial parallel.

14   A MECHANICAL MUSCLE   1669–70

Feb.3. Mr Hooke produced a contrivance of his to try, whether a mechanical muscle could be made by art, performing without labour the same office, which a natural muscle doth in animals. It was so contrived, as that by the application of heat to a body filled with air for dilatation, and by the application of cold to the same body for contraction, there might follow a muscular motion. It was objected, that it did not appear, how this agent, that was to produce heat and cold, could be applied for use, so as to cause this motion immediately, and with that speed, as it is done in animals. However Mr Hooke was ordered to consider more fully of it, and to acquaint the Society with the result of his further considerations.

He suggested, that if it could be done leisurely this way, the motion might be rendered quick by springs.

From the Minutes of the Royal Society, reprinted in The History of the Royal Society *by Thomas Birch, 1756.*

15   SOUND   1675–76

Saturday, January 15th – At home with Scarborough till 12. To Garaways. With Cox and Neale. Advised to work chain pump at bottom. With Sir R. Redding to Davys. Cald on Hammond at Mayors. Both abroad. Met Mrs Mayor. DH. Tryed glasses on turret. Haak chesse. Mary out. To Sir Chr. Wrens, Dr Holder and I discoursed of musick, he read my notes and saw my designs, then he read his which was more imperfect. I told him but *sub sigillo* my notion of sound, that it was nothing but strokes within a Determinate degree of velocity. I told them how I would make all tunes by strokes of a hammer. Shewd them a knife, a camlet coat, a silk lining. Told them there was no vibration in a puls of sound, that twas a pulse propagated forward, that the sound in all bodys was the striking of the parts one against the other and not the vibration of the whole. Told them my experiment of the vibrations of a magicall string without sound by symphony that touching of it which made the internall parts vibrate – caused the sound, that the vibrations of a string were not Isocrone but that the vibration of the particals was. Discoursd about the breaking of the air in pipes, of the musick of scraping trenchers, how the bow makes the fidle string sound, how scraping of metal, the scraping the teeth of a comb, the turning of a watch wheel &c., made sound. Compard sound and light and shewd how light produced colours in the same way by confounding the pulses. Eat cake and cheese, bread, ale and claret. Walkd hard to Garaways. Met Hammond drunk. he denyd to meddle with theater. Another with him. Cacao Nutts.

From The Diary of Robert Hooke: *first published, edited by H.W. Robinson and W. Adams, from the original MS, 1935.*

On March 10, 1671/2, Robert Hooke began to keep a diary or as he expressed it 'Memoranda'. For the first nine months or so the pages were divided into two columns. In the left-hand column he noted down weather observations. In the right-hand the personal jottings of which diaries usually consist. Later the weather observations fade out and the whole page is taken up with personal memoranda. Before this Hooke had already made a proposal for keeping a History of the Weather (see 8).

This diary of Hooke's was of course only a small one, overshadowed by the diaries of Pepys and Evelyn. Other diarists of the period include Sir William Dugdale the antiquarian, Bulstrode Whitelocke, lawyer and parliamentarian, and George Fox the Quaker. Historians have related the keeping of personal diaries to the development of capitalism and protestantism, while the idea that they record personal revelations links them with the inner voices heard by mediaeval mystics, such at St Hildegard.

The diaries of Hooke, Pepys and Evelyn are the diaries of realism, connected with the novel, and later with poetry, as in the case of Smart, Blake, Coleridge, Wordsworth and Hopkins. The weather is important throughout (the weather in the Englishman's soul), weather equalling the soul outside *the body: 'My tables, meet it is I set it down.'*

There is a further connection between diaries and the idea of a 'Universal Character', as proposed by John Wilkins, whose 'Essays towards a Real Character' was closely studied and highly praised by Pepys, who himself wrote in a shorthand cypher, as originally devised by Thomas Shelton. There are links with the symbols used by alchemists and in medical prescriptions, with mathematical researches and early calculating machines, all expressing a trend towards the 'mechanisation of thoughts'. The use of abbreviations is partly for the sake of compression, as in Hooke's diary, partly to hide or disguise reference to sexual activities, as in much of Pepys'.

The Diary diverged into a journal of scientific observations (as in the

Philosophical Transactions *of the Royal Society*), *as an alternative method of record and communication to letters, or (at a further remove) to poems. The diary is written late at night, as a record of the past day, and of the diarist's life up to that point in time. The diary remains the domain of mixed observations, recording the personal idiosyncrasies of the up and coming middle class. Hence the preponderance of Quakers' and dissenters' diaries.*

The idea of the diary as a form of expression is present in the design of this book, since it consists of 'images' – pages from a mass-diary.

16 THE ANALOGY OF NATURE January 25, 1675–76

I suppose that as bodies of various sizes, densities, or tensions, do by percussion or other action, excite sounds of various tones, and consequently vibrations in the air of various bignesses; so, when the rays of light, by impinging on the stiff refracting superficies, excite vibrations in the æther, those rays, whatever they are, as they happen to differ in magnitude, strength or vigour, excite vibrations of various bignesses; the biggest, strongest, or most potent rays, the largest vibrations, and others shorter, according to their bigness, strength, or power; and therefore the ends of the capillamenta of the optic nerve, which front or face the retina, being such refracting superficies, when the rays infringe on them, they must there excite these vibrations; which vibrations (like those of sound in a trumpet) will run along the aqueous pores or crystalline pith of the capillamenta, through the optic nerves into the sensorium; (which light itself cannot do) and there, I suppose, affect the sense with various colours, according to their bigness and mixture: the biggest with the strongest colours, reds and yellows; the least with the weakest, blues and violets; the middle with green, and a confusion of all, with white; much after the manner that in the sense of hearing nature makes use of aërial vibrations of several bignesses, to generate sounds of divers tones; for the analogy of nature is to be observed! And further, as the harmony and discord of sounds proceed from the proportions of the aërial vibrations, so may the harmony of some colours, as of a golden and blue, and the discord of others, as of red and blue, proceed from the proportions of the ætherial. And possibly colour may be distinguished into its principal degrees: red, orange, yellow, green, blue, indigo, and deep violet, – on the same ground that sound within an eighth is graduated into tones.

From a letter of Sir Isaac Newton to Mr Oldenburgh, printed in Memoirs of Sir Isaac Newton *by Sir David Brewster, 1855.*

17 THE FACE OF THE EARTH January 1680–81

But you will ask how could an uniform chaos coagulate at first irregularly into heterogeneous veins or masses to cause hills. Tell me then how an uniform solution of saltpetre coagulates irregularly into long bars; or to give you another instance, if tinn (such as the pewterers bring from ye mines in Cornwel to make pewter of) be melted and then let stand to cool till it begin to congeal, and when it begins to congeale at ye edges, if it be inclined on one side for ye more fluid part of ye tin to run from those parts wch coagulate first, you will see a good part of ye tin congealed in lumps which after the fluider part of ye tin which congeals not so soon is run from between them, appear like so many hills, with as much irregularity as any hills on ye earth do. Tell me ye cause of this, and ye answer will perhaps serve for the chaos.

From a letter by Sir Isaac Newton to Dr Burnet, quoted in Memoirs of Sir Isaac Newton *by Sir David Brewster, 1855.*

18   THE GREAT GOGLE-EYED BEETLE   1681

Carabus Indiae Orientalis maximus. I find it no where described or pictur'd. Two inches and ½ long, and an inch broad. His Head of a middle size. His Face perpendicular, about ⅓ of an inch long, in the middle of a golden green. His Teeth like polish'd *Steel*, of great thickness and strength. His Eyes of a fine colour betwixt a light *Chesnut*, and that of red *Coral*; of an Oval figure; and ratably, very great, *sc.* ¼ of an inch long. Which also, so far as I have observ'd, is the principal Character of all the *Carabus*-kind, so far, as distinct from the *Capricorne*: whence I take leave for the *English* Name. His Horns rooted between the Eyes and the Snout; but they are here broken off. His Shoulder or Back-Piece almost square; yet edged with a Convex Margin on each side; above ¾ of an inch broad, and ½ an inch by the length of the *Insect*; burnish'd with two large spots of the colour of polish'd *Bellmettle*; betwixt which, and on the edges or margins of a shining-green.

The *Wing-shells* almost two inches long, with small furrows running by the length, and united with short transverse lines, all together, like Network. Not Oval, but rather expressing the figure of a *Speer-Mint-Leaf*. At the end of each, two very small points or prickles. In the middle, of a glorious golden red like that of burnish'd *Copper*; On the edges of a shining blewish green. The Belly of the same colour with the middle of the *Wing-shells*; saving, that the fore part of every Ring (where there are three) and the Tail-piece, is also variegated with a curious sort of small white Streaks, which, at the first, look like fine Hair.

The great Joynts of the Legs (as is also best observable in other larger *Insects*) are joyn'd together, not only

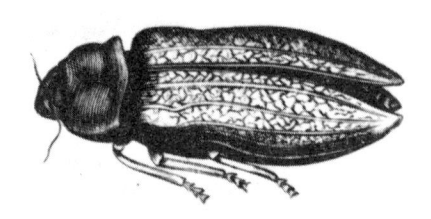

THE GREAT GOGLE-EYED BEETLE

by Ligaments, as are the Bones in other Animals; but also the globular knob of one, is entirely inclosed, and so winds, within the globular Concave of another. The imitation whereof, may be seen in the *Joynted Images*, which some *Stone-Cutters* make use of, for their direction as to *Postures*.

From Musæum Regalis Societatis *by Nehemiah Grew, 1681.*

19 RESEMBLANCE 1682

The most infeigned and proper resemblance we can at present make of the whole *Body* of a Plant, is, To a piece of *fine* Bone lace, when the Women are working it upon the *Cushion*; For the *Pith*, *Insertions* and *Parenchyma* of the *Barque*, are all extream *Fine* and Perfect *Lace-work*: the *Fibres* of the *Pith* running *Horizontally*, as do the *threds* in a Piece of *Lace*; and bounding the several *Bladders* of the *Pith* and *Barque*, as the *Threds* do the several *Holes* of the *Lace*; and making up the *Insertions* without *Bladders*, or with very small ones, as the same *Threds* likewise do the *close* Parts of the *Lace*, which they call the Cloth-Work. And lastly, both the *Lignous* and Aer-Vessels, stand all *Perpendicular*, and so cross to the *Horizontal Fibres* of all the said *Parenchymatous Parts*; even as in a Piece of Lace upon the *Cushion*, the *Pins* do to the *Threds*. The *Pins* being also conceived to be *Tubular*, and prolonged to any length; and the same *Lace-Work* to be wrought many Thousands of times over and over again, to any thickness or hight, according to the hight of any Plant. And this is the true *Texture* of a *Plant*; and the *general composure*, not only of a *Branch* but of all other parts from the Seed to the Seed.

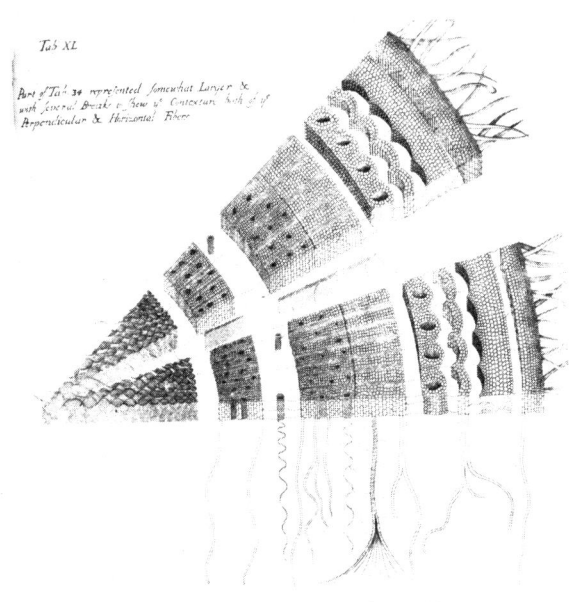

THE ANATOMY OF TRUNKS

From 'The Anatomy of Trunks', in The Anatomy of Plants *by Nehemiah Grew, 1682.*

Notes on 16, 17, 18, 19. *These four passages exemplify new problems of description and comparison. Newton, Grew, Hooke, etc. use descriptions of manufacture to describe natural objects or phenomena and homely images to illustrate their hypotheses. This had begun with William Harvey's note-book on the circulation of the blood (reproduced facsimile in C. Singer,* Discovery of the Circulation of the Blood) *and goes on at least as late as Thomas Young (1773–1829) on the hydraulic system in human muscles etc. Later we may note the influence of such analogies on nineteenth century descriptions of people, for example by Galton and Nasmyth. In the nineteenth-century there was the opposite use of natural objects etc. to describe machines and industrial phenomena. Compare Samuel Butler,* Darwin among the Machines *(1863).*

20   **ARTIFICIAL SPRING**   November 11, 1684

Mr *Watts* having a new Contrivance, (at least in this Countrey) *viz.* he makes under the Floor of his Green-house a great Fire-place with Grate, Ash-hole, &cc and conveys the Warmth through the whole House, by Tunnels; so that he hopes, by the Help of Weather-Glasses within, to bring or keep the Air at what Degree of Warmth he pleases, letting in upon Occasion this outward Air by the Windows. He thinks to make, by this Means, an artificial Spring, Summer, Winter, &c.

From a letter of Sir Hans Sloane to John Ray, printed in Philosophical Letters of Ray, *edited by W. Derham, 1718.*

21   **HOMOGENEOUS PARTICLES**   May 12, 1685

. . . From the figures of homogeneous particles, or such as are of the same shape, no considerable varieties can proceed; for, from suppose a bag of shot, perfectly spherical and solid, should I shake or move them to the world's end, I should get a body of no other texture than I had at first . . . .

From a letter of John Ray to Dr Tancred Robinson, printed in Philosophical Letters of Ray, *edited by W. Derham, 1718.*

This is clearly a reference to Hooke, Micrographia, *which in turn is the first clear statement in English of the atomic theory. Compare the argument of 'golden letters' from Cicero,* de Natura Deorum *quoted in* The Wisdom of God *by John Ray. And compare William Blake, 'The atoms of Democritus and Newton's particles of light'.*

| 22 | THE EDUCTION OF LIGHT | December 13, 1685 |

Dining at Mr Pepys's, Dr Slayer shewed us an experiment of a wonderful nature, pouring first a very cold liquor into a glass, and super-fusing on it another, to appearance cold and clear liquor also; it first produced a white cloud, then boiling, divers corruscations and actual flames of fire mingled with the liquor, which being a little shaken together, fixed divers sunns and starrs of real fire, perfectly globular, on the sides of the glasse, and which there stuck like so many constellations, burning most vehemently, and resembling starrs and heavenly bodies, and that for a long space. It seemed to exhibit a theorie of the eduction of light out of chaos, and the fixing or gathering of the universal light into luminous bodys. This matter or phosphorus was made out of human blood and urine, elucidating the vital flame or heate in animal bodys. A very noble experiment.

From the Diary *of John Evelyn.*

| 23 | LONDON | October 4, 1686 |

Now as to the Grandour of London, Would not England be easier and perhaps stronger if these vitalls were more equally dispersed? Is there not a Tumour in that place, and too much matter for mutiny and Terrour to the Government if it should Burst? Is there not too much of our Capital in one stake, liable to the Ravage of Plague and fire? Does not the Assembly too much increase Mortality and lessen Births, and the Church-yards become Infectious? Will not the Resort of the Wealthy and emulation to Luxury, melt down the order of Superiors among and bring all towards Levelling and Republican?

From a letter of Robert Southwell to Sir William Petty, published in the Petty–Southwell Correspondence, *edited by the Marquis of Lansdowne, 1928.*

| 24 | OF DOUBLING THE PEOPLE IN 25 YEARS | c.1687 |

1. Itt hath been showen that if all, or near all, the teeming women aged between 18 and 44 yeares old, were married & did bear a Child in every 2 yeares & a halfe, that the work here propounded will be efectually done.

2. Now though there be in efect 112 males for 651 females, yett it is found by observation that but between 30 & 40 of the teeming women are att present married, by reason the prolifick people are afraid they shall not be able to maintaine the Children they shall begett. Now if there be 72 millions of Statute acres in Great Brittan & Ireland & the adjacent Islands above named, Then when the propounded number of 9300^m are doubled, there

will be neare 4 acres of Land to every head, which with moderate Labour will afoord necessarys unto them. And Consequently if there be a suficiency wherewith to maintaine the Double, It is meere mismanagement if there be not a sufficiency to maintaine lesser numbers.

3. Wherefore – leaving itt to God to punish the sin of women who become with Child against his Comandments, and leaving it to the world to punish such women with Contempt & Dirision, & leaving it to the women themselves to suffer for their folly in not oblidging the men they deale with to provide for their Children, – Lett the Government in humanity make provision for every woman with Child for 30 days, the woman leaving her Child to be a servant to the Government for 25 yeares, suppressing the names of their parents.

4. The Charge of maintaining a woman 30 dayes in Child bed may well be defrayed for under 30 shillings; but if the value of mankind be in this age & country 70£ per head, a new born Child, bread up to fair hard work for 25 yeares, will be very well worth 3 times 30 shillings, as may be seen in the price of Negros Children in the American plantations.

From MSS by Sir William Petty printed as The Petty Papers, *edited by the Marquis of Lansdowne, 1927.*

25 THE SOUL OF BRUTES 1690–91

That the Soul of Brutes is material, and the whole Animal, Soul and Body, but a meer Machine, is the Opinion publickly own'd and declar'd of *Des Cartes, Gassendus*, Dr *Willis* and others; the same is also necessarily consequent upon the Doctrine of the Peripateticks, *viz.* That the sensitive Soul is educed out of the Power of the Matter, for nothing can be educed out of the Matter, but what was there before, which must be either Matter or some Modification of it. And therefore they cannot grant it to be a spiritual Substance, unless they will assert it to be educed out of nothing. This Opinion, I say, I can hardly digest. I should rather think Animals to be endu'd with a lower Degree of Reason, than that they are meer Machines. I could instance in many Actions of *Brutes* that are hardly to be accounted for without Reason and Argumentation; as that commonly noted of Dogs, that running before their Masters they will stop at a divarication of the way, 'till they see which Hand their Masters will take; and that when they have gotten a Prey, which they fear their Masters will take from them, they will run away and hide it, and afterwards return to it. What account can be given why a Dog, being to leap upon a Table, which he sees to be too high for him to reach at once, if a Stool or Chair happens to stand near it, doth first mount up that, and from thence the Table? If he were a Machine or Piece of Clockwork, and this motion caus'd by the striking of a Spring, there is no reason imaginable why the Spring being set on work, should not carry the

Machine in a right line toward the Object that put it in motion, as well when the Table is high as when it is low: whereas I have often observ'd the first leap the Creature hath taken up the Stool, not to be directly toward the Table, but in a line oblique and much declining from the Object that mov'd it, or that part of the Table on which it stood.

From The Wisdom of God *by John Ray, written 1690, published 1691.*

Compare Wesley in 41 on 'the beasts that perish', i.e. the workers. In 1690, Locke published his Essay concerning Human Understanding *in which there is the image of the mind at birth as a blank sheet to be written on by experience. The child as virgin soil to be exploited. Compare Wordsworth:*

> Not in entire forgetfulness,
> And not in utter nakedness,
> But trailing clouds of glory do we come. . . .

26 COLLEDGE OF INDUSTRY 1696

Why the name Colledge, and not a community, or work-house?

A work-house bespeaks too much of servitude, for people of estates to send their children for education; and too much of Bridewel, for honest tradesmen to like it, and the name community implies a greater unity in spirit, than colledge doth; and therefore not so proper to be used to such a mixt multitude of men and boys; the word colledge more relates to an outward fellowship than an inward communion, and therefore better suits the subject.

From Proposals for Raising a Colledge of Industry *by John Bellars.*

Compare Locke's report in 1697 for the newly instituted Board of Trade on the problem of poverty and poor relief, in which he recommended that all children over three should be taught to earn their living at working schools for spinning and knitting.

27 THE MINE-MAN 1699

Upon the 2d of *July*, 1699, I descended by Ropes affix'd at the top of an old *Lead-Ore Pit*, 4 Fathoms almost perpendicular; and from thence 3 Fathoms more obliquely, between two great Rocks, where I found the Mouth of this spacious Place; from which a *Mine-Man* and my self lower'd ourselves by ropes 25 Fathoms perpendicular, into a very large Place, which resembled to us the form of a Horse-shoe; for we stuck lighted Candles all the way we went to discover what we could find remarkable. At length we came to a River or great Water, which I found to be 20 Fathoms broad, and 8 Fathoms deep. The *Mine-Man* would have persuaded me, that this River ebbed and flowed; for that some 10 Fathoms above the Place we now were in we found the Water had sometimes been: But I proved the contrary, by staying there from 3 Hours *Flood* to 2 Hours *Ebb*, in which time we found no alteration of this River. Besides, its Waters are Fresh, Sweet, and Cool; and the Surface of this Water, as it is now at 8 Fathom deep, lies lower than the bottom of any part of the *Severn Sea* near us, so that it can have no Community with it. As we were walking by this River, 32 Fathoms under the Ground, we discovered a great Hollowness in a Rock some 3 Foot above us; so that I got a Ladder down to us, and the *Mine-Man* went up the Ladder to that Place, and walk'd into it about 70 Paces, till he just lost sight of me, and from thence chearfully called unto me, and told me he had found what he look'd for, a *Rich Mine*. But his Joy was presently turned into Amazement, and he returned affrighted by the sight of an *Evil Spirit*, which we cannot persuade him but he saw, and for that Reason will go thither no more.

From a paper by Captain Samuel Sturmy in Philosophical Transactions of the Royal Society, *No.343, published 1700–1701.*

With this story compare the section 'Romances of the Miners' in Popular Romances of the West of England *by Robert Hunt, F.R.S., 1881, showing that at the end of the period 1660–1881 the superstitions of underground workers were still alive.*

28 COMPRESSING ENGINES c.1704

As the Air is of absolute Necessity to Animal Life, so it is necessary that it should be of a due Temperament or Consistence; not foul, by reason that suffocateth; nor too rare and thin, because that sufficeth not: with Examples of each which, I shall a little Entertain the Reader. In one of Mr. Hawksbee's Compressing Engines, I closely shut up a Sparrow, without forcing any Air in; and in less than an Hour the Bird began to pant, and be concerned; and in less than an Hour and a half to be sick, vomit, and more out of Breath; and in two Hours time was nearly expiring.

Another I put in and compressed the Air, but the Engine leaking, I frequently renewed the Compressure; by which Means, (although the Bird panted a little after the first Hour) yet after such frequent compressures, and Immission of fresh Air, it was very little concerned, and taken out seemingly unhurt after three Hours.

After this I made two other Experiments in compressed Air, with the Weight of two Atmospheres injected, the Engine holding tight and well; the one with the Great Titmouse, the other with a Sparrow. For nearly an Hour they seemed but little concerned; but after that grew fainter, and in two Hours time sick, and in three Hours time died. Another thing I took Notice of, was, that when the Birds were sick, and very restless, I fancied they were somewhat relieved for a short Space, with the Motion of the Air, caused by their fluttering and shaking their Wings, (a Thing worth trying in the Diving-Bell.) I shall leave the ingenious Reader to judge what the Cause was of both the Birds living longer in compressed, than uncompressed Air; whether a less quantity of Air was not sooner fouled and render'd unfit for Respiration, than a greater.

From a note in Physico-Theology or, a Demonstration of the Being and Attributes of God *by W. Derham.*

29   HÆMASTATICS   c.1706

1. In *December* I caused a mare to be tied down alive on her back; she was fourteen hands high, and about fourteen years of age, had a *Fistula* on her Withers, was neither very lean, nor yet lusty: Having laid open the left crural Artery about three inches from her belly, I inserted into it a brass Pipe, whose bore was one sixth of an inch in diameter; and to that, by means of another brass Pipe which was fitly adapted to it, I fixed a glass Tube, of nearly the same diameter, which was nine feet in Length: Then untying the Ligature on the Artery, the blood rose in the Tube eight feet three inches perpendicular above the level of the left Ventricle of the heart: But it did not attain to its full height at once; it rushed up about half way in an instant, and afterwards gradually at each Pulse twelve, eight, six, four, two, and sometimes one inch: When it was at its full height, it would rise and fall at and after each Pulse two, three, or four inches; and sometimes it would fall twelve or fourteen inches, and have there for the same Vibrations up and down at and after each Pulse, as it had, when it was at its full height; to which it would rise again, after forty or fifty Pulses.

2. The Pulse of a horse that is well, and not terrified, nor in any pain, is about thirty six Beats in a minute, which is nearly half as fast as the Pulse of a man in health: This mare's Pulse beat about fifty-five times in a minute, and sometimes sixty or a hundred, she being in pain.

3. Then I took away the glass Tube, and let the blood from the Artery mount up in the open air, when the greatest height of its Jet was not above two Feet.

4. I measured the blood as it run out of the Artery, and after each quart of blood was run out, I refixed the glass Tube to the Artery, to see how much the force of the blood was abated; this I repeated to the eighth quart, and then its force being much abated, I applied the glass Tube after each pint had flowed out: The result of each trial was as is set down in the following Table, in which are noted the greatest heights it reached after every

Evacuation. It was usually about a minute before it rose to these heights, and did not rise gradually, but would stand during several Pulses much lower, than what it would at length reach to; so that I often thought it had done rising, when on a sudden it would rise for some time four, eight, twelve or sixteen inches higher, where it would stay for some time, and then on a sudden fall four, eight, twelve or sixteen inches.

From 'An Account of some Hydraulic and Hydrostatical experiments made on the Blood and Blood-Vessels of Animals' in Statical Essays, *Vol.II: Haemastatics by Stephen Hales, c.1706.*

30   MARTINUS SCRIBLERUS   c.1713

And here, O Reader, we entreat thee utterly to forget all thou hast hitherto read, and to cast thy eyes only forward, to that boundless Field the next shall open unto thee; the fruits of which (if thine, or our sins do not prevent) are to spread and multiply over this our work, and over all the face of the Earth.

In the mean time, we know what thou owest, and what thou yet may'st owe, to this excellent Person, this Prodigy of our Age; who may well be called The Philosopher of Ultimate Causes, since by a Sagacity peculiar to himself, he hath discover'd Effects in their very Cause; and without the trivial helps of Experiments, or Observations, hath been the Inventor of most of the modern Systems and Hypotheses.

He hath enrich'd Mathematicks with many precise and Geometrical Quadratures of the Circle. He first discover'd the Cause of Gravity, and the intestine Motion of Fluids.

To him we owe all the observations on the Parallax of the Pole-Star, and all the new Theories of the *Deluge*.

He it was, that first taught the right use sometimes of the Fuga Vacui, and sometimes the Materia Subtilis, in resolving the grand Phœnomena of Nature.

He it was that first found out the Palpability of Colours; and by the delicacy of his Touch could distinguish the different Vibrations of the heterogeneous Rays of Light.

His were the Projects of Perpetuum Mobiles, Flying Engines, and Pacing Saddles; the Method of discovering the longitude, by Bomb-Vessels, and of increasing the Trade-Wind by vast plantations of Reeds and Sedges.

I shall mention only a few of his philosophical and Mathematical Works.

1. A compleat Digest of the Laws of Nature, with a Review of those that are obsolete or repealed, and of those that are ready to be renew'd and put in force.

2. A Mechanical Explication of the Formation of the Universe according to the Epicurean Hypothesis.

3. An Investigation of the Quantity of real Matter in the Universe, with the proportion of the specific Gravity of solid Matter to that of fluid.

4. Microscopical Observations of the Figure and Bulk of the constituent Parts of all Fluids. A Calculation of the proportion in which the Fluids of the earth decrease, and of the period in which they will be totally exhausted.

5. A Computation of the Duration of the Sun, and how long it will last before it be burn'd out.

6. A method to apply the Force arising from the immense Velocity of Light to mechanical purposes.

7. An answer to the question of a curious Gentleman; How long a New Star was lighted up before its appearance to the Inhabitants of our earth? To which is subjoin'd a Calculation, how much the Inhabitants of the Moon eat for Supper, considering that they pass a night equal to fifteen of our natural days.

8. A Demonstration of the natural Dominion of the Inhabitants of the Earth over those of the Moon, if ever an intercourse should be open'd between them. With a Proposal of a Partition-Treaty, among the earthly Potentates, in case of such discovery.

9. Tide-Tables, for a Comet, that is to approximate towards the Earth.

10. The Number of the Inhabitants of London determin'd by the Reports of the Gold-finders, and the tonnage of their Carriages; with allowance for the extraordinary quantity of the Ingesta and Egesta of the people of England, and a deduction of what is left under dead walls and dry ditches.

From The Memoirs of Martinus Scriblerus, *probably by Jonathan Swift, written c.1713–14, first published in the* Prose Works *of Pope, 1741.*

31   A CORONA, OR IMAGE   March 6, 1715–16

On Tuesday the sixth of *March, st. vet.* in the current Year 1716, (the Afternoon having been very serene and calm, and somewhat warmer than ordinary) about the Time it began to grow dark, (much about seven of the Clock) not only in *London*, but in all Parts of *England*, where the Beginning of this wonderful Sight was seen; out of what seem'd a dusky Cloud, in the N.E. Parts of the Heavens, and scarce ten Degrees high, the Edges whereof were tinged with a reddish Yellow, like as if the Moon had been hid behind it, there arose very long luminous Rays or Streaks perpendicular to the Horizon, some of which seem'd nearly to ascend to the Zenith. Presently after, that reddish Cloud was swiftly propagated along the Northern Horizon into the N.W. and still farther Westerly; and immediately sent forth its Rays from all Parts, now here, now there, they observing no Rule or Order in their rising. Many of these Rays seeming to concur near the *Zenith*, formed there a *Corona*, or Image which drew the Attention of all Spectators. Some liken'd it to that Representation of *Glory* wherewith our Painters in Churches surround the Holy *Name of God*. Others to those radiating *Stars*, wherewith the Breasts of the *Knights* of the Order of the *Garter* are adorn'd. Many compar'd it to the *Concave* of the great *Cupola* of St. Paul's Church, distinguish'd with Streaks alternately light and obscure, and having in the middle a Space less bright than the rest, resembling the Lantern. Whilst others, to express as well the Motion as Figure thereof, would have it to be like the Flame in an Oven, reverberated and rouling against the arched Roof thereof: Some thought it liker to that tremulous Light which is cast against a Ceiling by the Beams of the Sun, reflected from the Surface of Water in a Bason that's a little shaken; whose reciprocal Motion it very much imitated. But all agree, that this *Spectrum* lasted only a few Minutes, and exhibited itself variously tinged with Colours, Yellow, Red, and a dusky Green: Nor did it keep in the same Place; for when first it began, it appear'd a little to the Northwards of the *Zenith*, but by Degrees declining towards the South, the long *Striae* of Light, which arose from all Parts of the Northern Semicircle of the Horizon, seem'd to meet together, not much above the Head of *Castor*, or the Northern Twin, and there soon disappear'd.

From 'An Account of Lights seen in the Air, March 6, 1715–16' by Dr Edmund Halley, in Philosophical Transactions of the Royal Society, *XXVI, No.347.*

This passage and others of this period illustrate new modes of observation. Defoe in The Storm *(1704) suggested there should be a collection of 'such authentick Accounts of the Mischiefs, Damages and Disasters . . .' from people in the country. Woodward wrote: 'I drew up a List of* Quaerites *upon this Subject, which I dispatch'd into all parts of the world . . .' (1696).*

This was the time of the emergence of reporting both in the newspaper sense and for the special purposes of scientists. Merchants were interested in news of prices: John Houghton's Bulletin of Stock Prices *was issued in 1694. Philosophers were interested in factual accounts, observations, descriptions of experiments, annals and diaries. The majority of images however were not written for publication or were slipped in unawares.*

The total eclipse of 1715 was recorded by Halley in the Philosophical Transactions. *He caused 'a small map of England describing the Track and Bounds of the Shade to be dispersed all over the Kingdom, with a request to the Curious to observe what they could about it'.*

THE SOLEMNITY OF THE SIGHT May 10, 1724
To Dr. Edmund Halley.

According to my promise, I send you what I observed of the solar eclipse, though I fear it will not be of any great use to you. I was not prepared with any instruments for measuring time, or the like, and proposed to myself only to watch all the appearances that Nature would present to the naked eye on so remarkable an occasion, and which generally are overlooked, or but grosly regarded. I chose for my station a place called Haradon hill, two miles eastward from Amsbury, and full east from the opening of Stonehenge avenue, to which it is as the point of view. Before me lay the vast plain where that celebrated work stands, and I knew that the eclipse would appear directly over it: beside, I had the advantage of a very extensive prospect every way, this being the highest hill hereabouts, and nearest the middle of the shadow. Full west of me, and beyond Stonehenge, is a pretty copped hill, like the top of a cone lifting itself above the horizon: this is Clay hill, near Warminster, twenty miles distant, and near the central line of darkness, which must come from thence; so that I could have notice enough before-hand of its approach. Abraham Sturgis and Stephen Ewens, both of this place and sensible men, were with me. Though it was very cloudy, yet now and then we had gleams of sun-shine, rather more than I could perceive at any other place around us. These two persons looking through smoked glasses, while I was taking some bearings of the country with a circumferentor, both confidently affirmed the eclipse was begun; when by my watch I found it just half an hour after five: and accordingly from thence the progress of it was visible, and very often to the naked eye; the thin clouds doing the office of glasses. From the time of the sun's body being half covered, there was a very conspicuous circular *iris* round the sun, with perfect colours. On all sides we beheld the shepherds hurrying their flocks into fold, the darkness coming on; for they expected nothing less than a total eclipse, for an hour and a quarter.

When the sun looked very sharp, like a new moon, the sky was pretty clear in that spot: but soon after a thicker cloud covered it; at which time the *iris* vanished, the copped hill before mentioned grew very dark, together with the horizon on both sides, that is, to the north and south, and looked blue; just as it appears in the east at the declension of day: we had scarce time to tell then, when Salisbury steeple, six mile off southward, became very black; the copped hill quite lost, and a most gloomy night with full career came upon us. At this instant we lost sight of the sun, whose place among the clouds was hitherto sufficiently distinguishable, but now not the least trace of it to be found, no more than if really absent: then I saw by my watch, though with difficulty, and only by help of some light from the northern quarter, that it was six hours thirty-five minutes: just before this the whole compass of the heavens and earth looked of a lurid complexion, properly speaking, for it was black and blue; only on the earth upon the horizon the blue prevailed. There was likewise in the heavens among the clouds much green interspersed; so that the whole appearance was really very dreadful, and as symptoms of sickening nature.

Now I perceived us involved in total darkness, and palpable, as I may aptly call it: though it came quick, yet I was so intent that I could perceive its steps, and feel it as it were drop upon us, and fall on the right shoulder (we looking westward) like a great dark mantle, or coverlet of a bed, thrown over us, or like the drawing of a curtain on that side: and the horses we held in our hands were very sensible of it, and crouded close to us, startling with great surprise. As much as I could see of the men's faces that stood by me, had a horrible aspect. At this instant I looked around me, not without exclamations of admiration, and could discern colours in the heavens; but the earth had lost its blue, and was wholly black. For some time, among the clouds, there were visible streaks of rays, tending to the place of the sun as their centre; but immediately after, the whole appearance of the earth and sky was intirely black. Of all things I ever saw in my life, or can by imagination fancy, it was a sight the most tremendous.

Towards the north-west, whence the eclipse came, I could not in the least find any distinction in the horizon between heaven and earth, for a good breadth, of about sixty degrees or more; nor the town of Amsbury underneath us, nor scarce the ground we trod on. I turned myself round several times during this total darkness, and remarked at a good distance from the west on both sides, that is, to the north and south, the horizon very perfect; the earth being black, the lower part of the heavens light: for the darkness above hung over us like a canopy, almost reaching the horizon in those parts, or as if made with skirts of a lighter colour; so that the upper edges of all the hills were as a black line, and I knew them very distinctly by their shape or profile: and northward I saw perfectly, that the interval of light and darkness in the horizon was between Martinsal hill and St. Ann's hill; but southward it was more indefinite. I do not mean that the verge of the shadow passed between those hills, which were but twelve miles distant from us: but so far I could distinguish the horizon; beyond it, not at all. The reason of it is this: the elevation of ground I was upon gave me an opportunity of seeing the light of the heavens beyond the shadow: nevertheless this verge of light looked of a dead, yellowish and greenish colour: it was broader to the north than south, but the southern was of a tawny colour. At this time, behind us or eastward toward London, it was dark too, where otherwise I could see the hills beyond Andover; for the foremost end of the shadow was past thither: so that the whole horizon was now divided into four parts of unequal bulk and degrees of light and dark; the part to the north-west, broadest and blackest; to the south-west, lightest and longest. All the change I could perceive during the totality, was that the horizon by degrees drew into two parts, light and dark; the northern hemisphere growing still longer, lighter, and broader, and the two opposite dark parts uniting into one, and swallowing up the southern enlightened part.

As at the beginning the shade came feelingly upon our right shoulders, so now the light from the north, where it opened as it were: though I could discern no defined light or shade upon the earth that way, which I earnestly watched for; yet it was manifestly by degrees, and with oscillations, going back a little, and quickly advancing further; till at length upon the first lucid point appearing in the heavens, where the sun was, I could distinguish pretty plainly a rim of light running alongside of us a good while together, or sweeping by at our elbows from west to east. Just then, having good reason to suppose the totality ended with us, I looked on my watch, and found it to be full three minutes and a half more: now the hill-tops changed their black into blue again, and I could distinguish a horizon where the centre of darkness was before; the men cried out, they saw the copped hill again, which they had eagerly looked for: but still it continued dark to the south-east; yet I cannot say that ever the horizon that way was undistinguishable: immediately we heard the larks chirping and singing very briskly for joy of the restored luminary, after all things had been hushed into a most profound and universal silence: the heavens and earth now appeared exactly like morning before sun-rise, of a greyish cast, but rather more blue interspersed; and the earth, as far as the verge of the hill reached, was of a dark green or russet colour.

As soon as the sun emerged, the clouds grew thicker, and the light was very little amended for a minute or more, like a cloudy morning slowly advancing. After about the middle of the totality, and so after the emersion of the sun, we saw Venus very plainly, but no other star. Salisbury steeple now appeared. The clouds never removed, so that we could take no account of it afterward, but in the evening it lightened very much. I hasted home to write this letter; and the impression was so vivid upon my mind, that I am sure I could, for some days after, have wrote the same account of it, and very precisely. After supper I made a drawing of it from my imagination, upon the same paper I had taken a prospect of the country before.

I must confess to you, that I was (I believe) the only person in England that regretted not the cloudiness of the day, which added so much to the solemnity of the sight, and which incomparably exceeded, in my apprehension, that of 1715, which I saw very perfectly from the top of Boston steeple in Lincolnshire, where the air was very clear: but the night of this was more complete and dreadful. There indeed I saw both sides of the shade come from a great distance, and pass beyond us to a great distance; but this eclipse had much more of variety and majestic terror: so that I cannot but felicitate myself upon the opportunity of seeing these two rare accidents of nature, in so different a manner: yet I should willingly have lost this pleasure for your more valuable advantage of perfecting the noble theory of the celestial bodies, which last time you gave the world so nice a calculation of; and wish the sky had now as much favoured us for an addition to your honour and great skill, which I doubt not to be as exact in this as before. Amsbury, Wilts, May 10, 1724.

From the Itinerarium Curiosum *by William Stukeley, 2nd edition, 1776.*

33   THE WONDERS OF THE PEAK   before 1725

A little on the other Side of *Wirksworth*, begins a long Plain called *Brassington Moor*, which reaches full twelve Miles in Length another Way, (*viz.*) from *Brassington* to *Buxton*. At the beginning of it on this Side from Wirksworth, it is not quite so much. The *Peak* People, who are mighty fond of having Strangers shewed every Thing they can, and of calling every thing a Wonder, told us here of another high Mountain, where a Giant was buried, and which they called the *Giant's Tomb*.

This tempted our Curiosity, and we presently rode up to the Mountain in order to leave our Horses, Dragoon-like, with a Servant, and to clamber up to the top of it, to see this Giant's Tomb: Here we miss'd the imaginary Wonder, and found a real one; the Story of which I cannot but record, to shew the discontented part of the rich World how to value their own Happiness, by looking below them, and seeing how others live, who yet are capable of being easie and content, which content goes a great way towards being happy, if it does not come quite up to Happiness. The Story is this:

'As we came near the Hill, which seemed to be round, and a Precipice almost on every Side, we perceived a little parcel of Ground hedg'd in, as if it were a Garden, it was about twenty or thirty Yards long, but not so much broad, Parallel with the Hill, and close to it; we saw no House, but, by a Dog running out barking, we perceived some people were there-about; and presently after we saw two little Children, and then a third run out to see what was the Matter. When we came close up we saw a small opening, not a Door, but a natural opening into the Rock, and the Noise we had made brought a Woman out with a Child in her Arms, and another at her Foot. *N.B.* The biggest of these five was a Girl, about eight or ten Years old.

'We asked the Woman some Questions about the Tomb of the Giant upon the Rock or Mountain: She told us, there was a broad flat Stone of a great size lay there, which, she said, the People call'd *a Gravestone*; and, if it was, it might well be called a Giant's, for she thought no ordinary Man was ever so tall, and she describ'd it to us as well as she could, by which it must be at least sixteen or seventeen Foot long; but she could not give any Farther Account of it, neither did she seem to lay any Stress upon the Tale of a Giant being buried there, but said, if her Husband had been at home he might have shown it to us. I snatch'd at the Word, *at home!* says I, good Wife, why, where do you live. Here, Sir, says she, and points to the Hole in the Rock.

Here! says I; and do all these children live here too? Yes, Sir, says she, they were all born here. Pray how long have you dwelt here then? said I. My husband was born here, said she, and his Father before him. Will you give me leave, says one of our Company, as curious as I was, to come in and see your House, Dame? If you please, Sir, says she, but 'tis not a Place fit for such as you are to come into, calling him, your Worship, forsooth; but that by the by. I mention it, to shew that the good Woman did not want Manners, though she liv'd in a Den like a wild Body.

'However, we alighted and went in: There was a large hollow Cave, which the poor People by two Curtains hang'd cross, had parted into three Rooms. On one Side was the Chimney, and the Man, or perhaps his Father, being *Miners*, had found means to work a Shaft or Funnel through the Rock to carry the Smoke out at the Top, where the Giant's Tombstone was. The Habitation was poor, 'tis true, but Things within did not look so like Misery as I expected. Every Thing was clean and neat, tho' mean and ordinary: There were Shelves with Earthen Ware, and some Pewter and Brass. There was, which I observed in particular, a whole Flitch or Side of Bacon hanging up in the Chimney, and by it a good Piece of another. There was a Sow and Pigs running about at the Door, and a little lean Cow feeding upon a green Place just before the Door, and the little enclosed Piece of Ground I mentioned, was growing with good Barley; it being then near Harvest.

'To find out whence this appearance of Substance came, I asked the poor Woman, what Trade her Husband was? She said, he worked in the Lead Mines. I asked her, how much he could earn in a Day there? she said, if he had good luck he could earn about five pence a Day, but that he worked by the Dish (which was a Term of Art I did not understand, but supposed, as I afterwards understood it was, by the Great, in proportion to the Oar, which they measure in a wooden Bowl, which they call a Dish). I then asked, what she did? She said, when she was able to work she washed the Oar: But, looking down on her Children, and shaking her Head, she intimated, that they found her so much Business she could do but little, which I easily granted must be true. But what can you get at washing the Oar, said I, when you can work? She said, if she work'd hard she could gain Three-pence a Day. So that, in short, here was but Eight-pence a Day when they both worked hard, and that not always, and perhaps not often, and all this to maintain a Man, his Wife, and five small Children, and yet they seemed to live very pleasantly, the Children look'd plump and fat, ruddy and wholesome; and the Woman was tall, well shaped, clean, and (for the Place) a very well looking, comely Woman; nor was there any thing look'd like the Dirt and Nastiness of the miserable Cottages of the Poor; tho' many of them spend more Money on strong Drink than this poor Woman had to maintain five Children with.

'This moving Sight affected so us all, that, upon a short Conference at the

Door, we made up a little Lump of Money, and I had the honour to be Almoner for the Company; and though the Sum was not great, being at most something within a Crown, as I told it into the poor Woman's Hand, I could perceive such a Surprize in her Face, that, had she not given vent to her Joy by a sudden flux of Tears, I found she would have fainted away. She was some time before she could do any thing but Cry; but after that was abated, she expressed her self very handsomely (for a poor Body) and told me, she had not seen so much Money together of her own for many Months.

We asked her, if she had a good Husband; she smiled, and said, Yes, thanked God for it, and that she was very happy in that, for he worked very hard, and they wanted for nothing that he could do for them; and two or three times made mention of how contented they were: In a word, it was a Lecture to us all, and that such, I assure you, as made the whole Company very grave all the rest of the Day: And if it has no effect of that kind upon the Reader, the Defect must be in my telling the Story in a less moving manner than the poor Woman told it her self.

From hence enquiring no farther after the Giant, or his Tomb, we went, by the direction of the poor Woman, to a Valley on the Side of a rising hill, where there were several Grooves, so they call the Mouth of the Shaft or Pit by which they go down into a Lead Mine; and as we were standing still to look at one of them, admiring how small they were, and scarce believing a poor Man that shew'd it us, when he told us, that they went down those narrow Pits or Holes to so great a Depth in the Earth; I say, while we were wondering, and scarce believing the Fact, we were agreeably surprized with seeing a Hand, and then an Arm, and quickly after a Head, thrust up out of the very Groove we were looking at. It was the more surprizing as not we only, but not the Man that we were talking to, knew any thing of it, or expected it.

Immediately we rode close to the Place, where we see the poor Wretch working and heaving himself up gradually, as we thought, with difficulty; but when he shewed us that it was by setting his Feet upon Pieces of Wood fixt cross the Angles of the Groove like a Ladder, we found that the Difficulty was not much; and if the Groove had been larger they could not go up or down so easily, or with so much safety, for that now their Elbows resting on those Pieces as well as their Feet, they went up and down with great Ease and Safety.

Those who would have a more perfect Idea of those Grooves, need do no more than go to the Church of *St. Paul's*, and desire to see the square Wells which they have there to go down from the Top of the Church into the very Vaults under it, to place the Leaden Pipes which carry the Rain Water from the flat of the Roof to the Common-shore, which Wells are for the Workmen to set their Feet on, to go up and down to repair the Pipes; the manner of the Steps are thus describ'd:

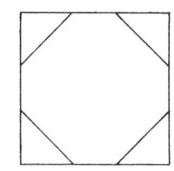

When this subterranean Creature was come quite out, with all his Furniture about him, we had as much Variety to take us up as before, and our Curiosity received full Satisfaction without venturing down, as we were persuaded to by some People, and as two of our Company were inclined to do.

First, the Man was a most uncouth Spectacle; he was cloathed all in Leather, had a Cap of the same without Brims, some Tools in a little Basket which he drew up with him, not one of the Names of which we could understand but by the help of an Interpreter. Nor indeed could we understand any of the Man's Discourse so as to make out a whole Sentence; and yet the Man was pretty free of his Tongue too.

For his Person, he was lean as a Skeleton, pale as a dead Corps, his Hair and Beard a deep Black, his Flesh lank, and, as we thought, something of the Colour of the Lead itself, and being very tall and very lean he look'd, or we that saw him ascend *ab Inferis*, fancied he look'd, like an Inhabitant of the dark Regions below, and who was just ascended into the World of Light.

Besides his Basket of Tools, he brought up with him about three quarters of a hundred Weight of Oar, which we wondered at, for the Man had no small Load to bring, considering the manner of his coming up; and this indeed made him come heaving and struggling up, as I said at first, as if he had great Difficulty to get out; whereas it was indeed the Weight that he brought with him.

If any Reader thinks this, and the past relation of the Woman and the Cave, too low and trifling for this Work, they must be told, that I think quite otherwise; and especially considering what a Noise is made of Wonders in this Country, which, I must needs say, have nothing in them curious, but much talked of, more trifling a great deal. See Cotton's *Wonders of the Peak*, Hobbes's *Chatsworth*, and several others; but I shall make no more apologies. I return to our subterranean Apparition.

We asked him, how deep the Mine lay which he came out of: He answered us in Terms we did not understand; but our Interpreter, as above, told us, it signified that he was at work 60 Fathoms deep, but that there were five Men of his Party, who were, two of them, eleven Fathoms, and the other three, fifteen Fathoms deeper: He seemed to regret that he was not at work with those three; for that they had a deeper Vein of Oar than that which he worked in and had a way out of the Side of the Hill, where they pass'd out without coming so high up as he was obliged to do.

If we blessed our selves before, when we saw how the poor Woman and her five Children lived in the Hole or Cave in the Mountain, with the

Giant's Grave over their Heads; we had to acknowledge to our Maker, that we were not appointed to get our Bread thus, one hundred and fifty Yards under Ground, or in a Hole as deep in the Earth as the Cross upon St. *Paul's Cupola* is high out of it: Nor was it possible to see these miserable People without such Reflections, unless you will suppose Man as stupid and senseless as the Horse he rides on. But to leave Moralizing to the Reader, I proceed.

We then look'd on the Oar, and got the poor Man's leave to bring every one a small Piece of it away with us, for which we gave him two small Pieces of a better Mettle, called Shillings, which made his Heart glad; and, as we understood by our Interpreter, was more than he could gain at sixty Fathoms under Ground in three Days; and we found soon after the Money was so much, that it made him move off immediately towards the Alehouse, to melt some of it into good *Pale Derby*; but, to his farther good Luck, we were gotten to the same Alehouse before him; where, when we saw him come, we gave him some Liquor too, and made him keep his Money, and promise us to carry it home to his Family, which they told us lived hard by.

From A Tour thro' the Whole Island of Great Britain *by Daniel Defoe, 1725.*

34   EFFECTS OF LIGHTNING IN NORTHAMPTONSHIRE   1725

On Saturday July 3. at *Mixbury*, a storm of thunder and lightning began about half past 1 in the afternoon, and lasted with intermissions for an hour. About 2. W. Hall, aged about sixty, was found dead in a hard gravelly field, together with five sheep which lay round him at about 30 yards Distance; but that only which lay nearest him had a visible Wound, through the head. The Shepherd lay partly upon his Side; the upper Part of his Head was terribly fractur'd, and his right knee was out of joint; He had a wound in the sole of his foot, towards the heel; his right Ear was cut off and beaten into his Skull, and blood flowed out of that Part upon the ground. All his Cloaths and Shirt were torn into small Pieces and hung about him; but from the Girdle downwards were carried away entirely, and scattered up and down the Field. Particularly, the Soles of a new strong Pair of Shoes were rent off. His Hat was driven to Pieces: I have a Hand-breadth of it full of irregular slits, and in some few Places cut as with a very sharp Pen-knife, and a little singed in the upper Part. His Beard and the Hair of his Head were for the most part close burnt off. The Iron Buckle of his belt was thrown 40 yards off, and a knife in the right Side Pocket of his Breeches. Near each Foot appear two round Holes five inches in diameter, but after that grew narrower; in both of them the matter divided into two parts, and formed horizontal cavities about three inches diameter. In one we found a hard glazed stone, about ten inches long, six wide, and four thick, cracked in two: others it could not pierce, but was turned here and there out of its course, yet left not the least blackness or other discolouring any where. I have seen an iron ball shot out of a mortar almost perpendicular which upon a like gravelly soil made not a greater impression. To make a gross estimate of the force, I took a cohorn charged with three quarters of a pound of very good powder wadded with thick paper, and fired it against a stone of the same dimensions, but not so hard, which it shattered to pieces at half an inch distance. But in the other blow we have above treble the effect, without any discoverable particles at all; and yet it seems to fly like small shot; pieces only here and there, and leaves a good many places quite untouch'd, as is evident from the hat which I have by me. To confirm this, J. Marshal of this town assures me that in the middle of the same storm he received a blow upon his hat, which rattled like shot through the branches of a tree: It beat in the crown a little without penetrating it; yet he staggered and was giddy for two days afterward. Two of his sons were at the same instant both knocked down to the ground, one of whom says he thought he had been felled with a beetle; they were stunn'd a little, but presently came to themselves and have no wound. May not this be accounted for by supposing the flame to rarefy the air and make a sort of vacuum about one; into which when it returns again, it gives a stroke as with a beetle? I fancy a wind-gun would have the same effect. About the time this accident happened, one in the same town observed a fire-ball as large as a man's head to burst in four pieces near the church. I my self heard the hiss of one which flew over my garden, from S.E. to N.W.

From an account by J. Wasse in Philosophical Transactions, *No.390.*

It is I think interesting to give the exact line of reasoning that leads to the inclusion of this image. It is this: when the 'bourgeoisie' took over in 1660, they began the final subjugation and exploitation of this island. They had amassed the necessary capital, 'fixed' the church on the laws of usury, tamed the power of the feudal monarchy.

The tasks that lay before them were the taking of the land from the people by the Enclosure Acts, the creation of the factory system and the invention of machines and means of power to run them. Before any of these things could be done it was necessary to make an analysis of the materials and forces existing in nature and in these islands which would contribute to the scheme. Hence the financial backing of the Royal Society.

Among these forces was electricity – not merely as a source of power but also as an essential part of the development of chemistry. Electricity was studied among other ways by the study of thunder and lightning. Before these phenomena could be studied a radically new attitude had to be developed towards them, and to all natural phenomena. One of strict realism.

In this image then we have a contributor to the papers of the Royal Society giving a cold, inch-by-inch analysis and reportage of the effects of a thunderstorm equally without reference to God or man. Without a trace of human feeling for the victim or on the other hand of the ancient awe with which 'the glance of God' had been regarded for centuries, even ages, past.

To do this required a new attitude. This new attitude is so clear and so marked as to constitute, I believe, a fundamental alteration of 'vision' parallel to that being developed by Defoe. Realism.

Here then is a case of an alteration in vision already being achieved not merely as the result *of changing means of production, but also making them possible.*

35   THE YORK BUILDINGS DRAGONS   1725

The York Buildings Dragons; or, a full and true account of a most horrid and barbarous murder intended to be committed next Monday, on the bodies, goods, and name of the greatest part of his Majesty's liege subjects dwelling and inhabiting between Temple Bar in the East, and St. James's in the West, and between Hungerford Market in the South, and St. Mary-la-bone in the North, by a set of evil minded persons, who do assemble twice a week, to carry their wicked purposes, in a private room over a stable by the Thames side, in a remote corner of the town.

Now these conspirators have purchased two enormous dragons from the deserts of Lybia of such monstrous size that the tail of one of 'em is a mile and a half long, which they have brought into this metropolis *incognito*, by the assistance of a conjurer, whom they have employed in that matter.

This conjurer, therefore, by the help of a hunting-whip that has a talisman in the handle of it, contrived a means to *run* these dragons without any duty to the government; for, by applying this talisman to the head of each dragon, he shut up all the life within one particular gland of the head, and then anatomically dissected the two monsters, so that they could easily be stowed in several ships, and be brought in as coming from different parts of the world. And accordingly most of the nerves and sinews came from Sweden; the greatest part of the head from Norway, by help of another conjurer who combined with the first; the joints, and veins, and arteries were brought from Derbyshire; the breast from Worcestershire; and the back and wings from Kent, Berkshire and Herefordshire; the belly from Cornwall; and the greatest part of the tail from the West country, except the thick end next to the body, which, together with the snout and teeth, came out of Sussex by the sea, and passed at the Custom House for some outlandish curiosity, imported by some virtuosos of Great Britain. *And you know natural knowledge is so much encouraged, that such things never pay any duty, but pass unexamined*; – witness Villette's great burning-glass, the Hugenian telescope, and the wax work anatomies. Now, if there had been any astrologers among the Custom House officers, nothing of this would have happened; for they are perfectly well acquainted with dragons' heads and dragons' tails. But what would you have men do that never saw a dragon in all their lives? Since there never was any in this kingdom before, but one, and that was at Wantley, almost two hundred miles distant from London, who was killed by More, of More Hall, before he could come southward; and he was but a little dragon in comparison; for he only devoured *three children*, whereas these dragons either have or will devour whole families.

But to return to our account. The conjurer and his abettors have concealed under a large tract of ground, the dreadful tail of one of these monsters, and are now vivifying the whole animal by the reunion of its parts; and diffusing its life from the *glandula pinealis* to the very extremities of the nostrils, wings, and tail.

On Monday, therefore, the 20th instant, at 14 minutes past 10 in the morning, a Lancashire wizzard, with long black hair and grim visage, will for some hours feed the eldest dragon with live coals; and a Welshman, bred on the top of Penmaenmaur, will lay hold of the bridle to direct the motion of the creature. Then on a sudden will the monster clap his wings several times successively with prodigious force, and so terrible will be the noise thereof, that it will be heard as far as Calais, if the wind set right. All those who have musical ears, within the bills of mortality, will be struck deaf; those *who have no ear* will become deaf; and all who were deaf before, will start up and run away.

The next disaster will be occasioned by the Welshman, who will cry 'Boh!' to make the dragon drink, who immediately dipping his two heads into the Thames, will suck out thence such a prodigious quantity of water, that barges will never after be able to go through bridges; the wharfs will become useless from the Steel Yard to Millbank; and the tide will not rise high enough to fill the basin of a set of good-natured gentlemen who have been at immense pains to serve the new buildings with water.

The next calamity will be this, – That, whereas, the dragon lives upon Newcastle and Scotch coal, (which, by the bye, will produce scarcity of coal, by reason of the great consumption,) and other bituminous substances, and is of himself of a *huffing, snuffing* temper, he will dart out of his nostrils perpendicularly up to the skies two such vast, dense, and opake columns of smoke, that those who live in the Borough will hardly see the sun at noon-day. Now this smoke being *ponderous*, will descend again upon all the neighbouring inhabitants; being *elastic*, will spread and fall upon all the evergreens within ten miles of London; and being *fuliginous*, will so discolor their hue, that it will puzzle a very nice botanist to determine concerning any leaf within that compass of ground whether it be of a *subfusc* or a downright *piceous* colour after this accident. *Happy* will then the ladies be who have papered up all their furniture before they went out of town! *Happy* the stationers who have timely shut up their shops to preserve their paper! And *thrice happy* the poor washer-women, who have closed up and pointed the garret-windows where they have hung up their linen clothes to dry. Besides all this, the sulphureous particles arising from the coals will be so pernicious to the lungs of all who suck them in, that they will break several blood-vessels with coughing. Add to all this, that upon the subsiding of this black pillar, the cities of London and Westminster will lose sight of one another, though in the clearest day; so that nobody can possibly receive any benefit by this contrivance, unless it be the link-boys, who will be absolutely necessary to conduct people through the smoke.

But the worst consequence of all, and which I almost dread to relate, is, *this dragon's way of poisoning*. Through a long proboscis, something like an elephant's trunk, this creature can at pleasure filtrate and suck in all the venomous effluvia out of the air, water, and other fluids. And, therefore, to make up the desolation of this poor city, he will from the Thames in great abundance draw in all the foetidcabbageous, deaddogitious, deadcatitious, Fish-streethillious, Drurylanious, issue-plasterious, excrementitious, and all common-shoreitious particles therein contained from time to time; and having therewith filled his stomach, this stygious compound will pass the pylorus, and being carried along the viscera by the peristaltic motion, will issue out at the anus, (which in this animal is the last joint of the tail) with great stench, in vast quantities, into a large receptacle prepared by the aforesaid conjuror for receiving and containing this hellish liquor. Now as this fluid is always to run in, and never go out, it is evident to all chemists and naturalists, and several other ingenious gentlemen besides, that there must be an intestine motion, because the fluid stands still, and this intestine motion will cause a fermentation, which fermentation will cast out *undequaque* such pestiferous steams and vapours, as will depopulate all the whole neighbourhood in such a manner that grass will grow in Queen Anne Street, Chandos Street, Mortimer Street, and all the adjacent streets, till the genius of architecture comes to the relief of the desolate place. And if it should so happen, that by the violent motion of the beast, it should receive any wounds in its tail, from every wound will issue with impetuosity rivers of this abominable liquor, which will inundate and render impassable the streets, drown all those that come within its vortex, and such as venture to look out of their chamber-windows will be suffocated with the putrid vapour.

To conclude my dismal story: I must let the world know that these conspirators are enemies to the souls as well as the bodies of all persons they can have any influence over, by setting up a new kind of Popery, and have already persuaded several families to worship these dragons. Among other things, they have a ceremony much like *Transubstantiation*; for, by the mixture of Ceres and Neptune, (*and what is the Popish Host but bread and water?*) they have contrived a *consigillated wafer*, which turns paper into money.

Now to give my reader a little hope, before I quit this melancholy tale, I must acquaint him that a set of honest and brave gentlemen intend to prosecute these *vile men*, who will find themselves deceived in trusting to the *Toleration Act*; for that act allows of no *image-worship* within ten miles of London, except it be in a foreign amb——r's chapel.

Written by a club of ingenious gentlemen.
Anodine Necklace, Secretary.

From Read's Weekly Journal, *December 18, 1725; reprinted in* Caricature History of the Georges *by Thomas Wright, 1867.*

36 THE CHILDREN OF IRELAND 1729

It is a melancholly Object to those, who walk through this great Town or travel in the Country, when they see the Streets, the Roads and Cabbin-doors crowded with Beggars of the Female Sex, followed by three, four or six Children, all in Rags, and importuning every Passenger for an Alms. These Mothers instead of being able to work for their honest livelyhood, are forced to employ all their time in Stroling to beg Sustenance for their helpless Infants, who, as they grow up, either turn Thieves for want of Work, or leave their dear Native Country, to fight for the Pretender in Spain, or sell themselves to the Barbadoes.

I think it is agreed by all Parties, that this prodigious number of Children in the Arms, or on the Backs, or at the Heels of their Mothers, and frequently of their Fathers, is in the present deplorable state of the Kingdom, a very great additional grievance; and therefore whoever could find out a fair, cheap and easy method of making these Children sound and useful Members of the Commonwealth, would deserve so well of the publick, as to have his Statue set up for a Preserver of the Nation.

But my Intention is very far from being confined to provide only for the Children of professed Beggers, it is of a much greater Extent, and shall take in the whole Number of Infants at a certain Age, who are born of Parents in effect as little able to support them, as those who demand our Charity in the Streets.

As to my own part, having turned my Thoughts, for many Years, upon this important Subject, and maturely weighed the several Schemes of other Projectors, I have always found them grossly mistaken in their computation. It is true, a Child just dropt from its Dam, may be supported by her Milk, for a Solar Year with little other Nourishment, at most not above the Value of two Shillings, which the Mother may certainly get, or the Value in Scraps, by her lawful Occupation of Begging; and it is exactly at one Year Old, that I propose to provide for them in such a manner, as, instead of being a Charge upon their Parents, or the Parish, or wanting Food and Raiment for the rest of their Lives, they shall, on the contrary contribute to the Feeding and partly to the Cloathing of many Thousands.

There is likewise another great Advantage in my Scheme, that it will prevent those voluntary Abortions, and that horrid practice of Women murdering their Bastard Children, alas! too frequent among us, Sacrificing the poor innocent Babes, I doubt, more to avoid the Expence than the Shame, which would move Tears and Pity in the most Savage and inhuman breast.

The number of Souls in this Kingdom being usually reckoned one Million and a half, Of these I calculate there may be about two hundred thousand Couple whose Wives are Breeders; from which number I substract thirty Thousand Couple, who are able to maintain their own Children, although I apprehend there cannot be so many, under the present Distresses of the Kingdom; but this being granted, there will remain an hundred and seventy thousand Breeders. I again Subtract fifty Thousand, for those Women who miscarry, or whose Children die by accident, or disease within the Year. There only remain an hundred and twenty thousand Children of poor Parents annually born: The question therefore is, How this number shall be reared, and provided for? which, as I have already said, under the present Situation of Affairs, is utterly impossible by all the Methods hitherto proposed; for we can neither employ them in Handicraft or Agriculture; we neither build Houses, (I mean in the Country) nor cultivate Land; They can very seldom pick up a Livelihood by Stealing till they arrive at six years Old; except where they are of towardly parts; although, I confess, they learn the Rudiments much earlier; during which time they can however be properly looked upon only as Probationers; as I have been informed by a principal Gentleman in the County of Cavan, who protested to me, that he never knew above one or two Instances under the Age of six, even in a part of the Kingdom so renowned for the quickest proficiency in that Art.

I am assured by our Merchants, that a Boy or a Girl before twelve years Old, is no saleable Commodity, and even when they come to this Age, they will not yield above three Pounds, or three Pounds and half a Crown at most, on the Exchange; which cannot turn to Account either to the Parents or Kingdom, the Charge of Nutriment and Rags having been at least four times that Value.

I shall now therefore humbly propose my own Thoughts, which I hope will not be liable to the least Objection.

I have been assured by a very knowing American of my acquaintance in London, that a young healthy Child well nursed is at a year Old a most delicious nourishing and wholesome Food, whether Stewed, Roasted, Baked, or Boiled; and I make no doubt that it will equally serve in a Fricasie, or a Ragoust.

I do therefore humbly offer it to publick consideration, that of the Hundred and twenty thousand Children, already computed, twenty thousand may be reserved for Breed, whereof only one fourth part to be

Males; which is more than we allow to Sheep, black Cattle, or Swine, and my Reason is, that these Children are seldom the Fruits of Marriage, a Circumstance not much regarded by our Savages, therefore, one Male will be sufficient to serve four Females. That the remaining Hundred thousand may at a year Old be offered in Sale to the Persons of Quality and Fortune, through the Kingdom, always advising the Mother to let them Suck plentifully in the last Month, so as to render them Plump, and Fat for a good Table. A Child will make two Dishes at an Entertainment for Friends, and when the Family dines alone, the fore or hind Quarter will make a reasonable Dish, and seasoned with a little Pepper or Salt will be very good Boiled on the fourth Day, especially in Winter.

From A Modest Proposal for Preventing the Children of Ireland from being a Burden to their Parents or Country *by Jonathan Swift, 1729.*

PART TWO

1730–1790
Exploitation

37 EXPERIMENT 1730

April 8. 1730. I made the following experiment on a boy between eight and nine Years of Age. His Weight with his Cloaths on was forty-seven pounds ten Ounces. I suspended him in a horizontal Position by two Hair-Lines, such as Cloaths are dried on, which were about thirteen Foot long with Loops at each End. There were drove into the Beam of my Chamber, which was a Foot thick, a Pair of Hooks opposite to each other, and two Foot from these another Pair in the same manner. Upon these Hooks the Lines were hung by their Loops so as to be in the Manner of two Swings, the lower Parts hanging within about two Foot of the floor of the Room. Then the Boy was laid on these Lines with his Face downwards, one of the lines being put under his Breast, the other under his Thighs. Then the Leaf-Brass was laid on a Stand, which was a round Board of a Foot Diameter with white Paper pasted on it, supported by a Pedestal of a Foot in Hight, which I often made use of in other Experiments. Upon the Tube's being rubbed and held near his Feet without touching them, the Leaf-Brass was attracted by the Boy's Face with such vigour, so as to rise to the Hight of eight, and sometimes ten Inches. I put a great many Pieces on the Board together, and almost all of them came up at the same Time. Then the Boy was laid with his Face upwards, and the hind Part of his Head which had short Hair on it attracted, but not at quite so great a Hight as his Face did. The Leaf-Brass being placed under his Feet, his Shoes and Stockings being on, and the Tube held near his Head his Feet attracted, but not altogether at so great a Hight as his Head: then the Leaf-Brass was again laid under his Head and the Tube held over it, but there was then no Attraction, nor was there any when the Leaf-Brass was laid under his Feet and the Tube held over them.

From 'A Letter to Cromwell Mortimer M.D. Sect. R.S. containing several Experiments concerning Electricity', by Stephen Gray, in Philosophical Transactions of the Royal Society, *No.417, January 1731.*

38 THE DERBY SILK-MILL c.1730

Some have earnestly wished to see this singular piece of mechanism, but I have sincerely wished I never had. I have lamented that, while almost every man in the world was born *out* of Derby, it should be my unhappy lot to be born *in*. To this curious, but wretched place, I was bound apprentice for seven years, which I always considered the most unhappy of my life. These I faithfully served, which was equalled by no other, in my time, except a worthy brother, then my companion in distress, and now my intelligent friend. It is therefore no wonder if I am perfectly acquainted with every movement in that superb work. My parents, through mere necessity, put me to labour before nature had made me able. Low as the engines were, I was too short to reach them. To remedy this defect, a pair of high pattens were fabricated and lashed to my feet, which I dragged after me till time lengthened my stature. The confinement and the labour were no burden, but the severity was intolerable, the marks of which I yet carry, and shall carry to the grave. The inadvertencies of an infant, committed without design, can never merit the extreme of harsh treatment. A love of power is predominant in every creature: a love to punish is often attendant upon that power. The man who delights in punishment is more likely to inflict it than the offender to deserve it. He who feels for another will not torture from choice. A merciful judge punishes with regret, a tyrant with pleasure. He who mourns over the chastisement he must inflict will endeavour to reduce it: one displays a great, the other a little mind. Hoisted upon the back of Bryant Barker, a giant approaching seven feet, was like being hoisted to the top of a precipice, when the wicked instrument of affliction was wielded with pleasure; but, alas, it was only a pleasure to one side. It was again my unhappy lot, at the close of this servitude, to be bound apprentice to a stocking-maker for a second seven years, so that, like Jacob, I served two apprenticeships, but was not, like him, rewarded either with wealth or beauty.

From the History of Derby *by William Hutton, 1817.*

The abstract horror of this image derives in part from the unspoken acknowledgement of the truth that as far as the 18th century poor were concerned

    1. the factory   3. the workhouse
    2. the school   4. the prison

were all the same building.

THE EAST PROSPECT OF DERBY

THE HOE-PLOW 1733

The making of the *Hoe-Plow* is not difficult for a good Workman; and a few of the Holes for setting the Beam are sufficient, provided they are made in their proper Places, which is impossible for me to describe exactly in a Number that is no more than necessary; because the Distance the Plow must go from the Horse-Path on either Side, is uncertain, as the Largeness or the Depth of the Furrow is; and for that Reason, 'tis as impossible for me to direct the Plowman to the particular Angles, at which his Beam must be set with the Plank, to keep the Share parallel to the Horse-Path; as it is to direct a Fidler, how far he must turn his Pegs to give his Strings their due Tension, for bringing them all in Tune, which without a Peg to each String could never be done; but when he has his just Number of Pegs, his Ear will direct him in turning them, 'till his Fiddle is in Tune; so the Plowman by his Eyes, his Feeling, and his Reason, must be directed in the setting his Plow; but without a competent Number of Holes, he can no more do it than a Musician can tune four Strings upon one Peg. And I am told that some Pretenders to making the *Hoe-Plow*, have fix'd its Bottom to the Plank immoveable, which makes it as useless for hoeing betwixt Rows, as a Violin with but one Peg to its four Strings, would be for playing a *Sonata*.

From Horse-Hoeing Husbandry *by Jethro Tull, Dublin, 1733.*

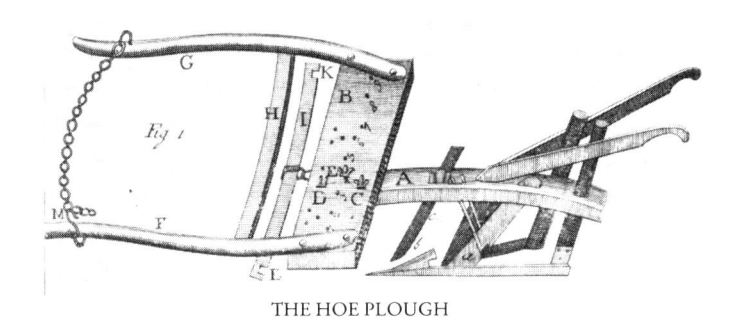

THE HOE PLOUGH

THE FIRST SPRINGS 1738

The admirable Secrets of Refraction were unknown to the Ancients. Notwithstanding its being before their Eyes, and their perpetual Use of it, they have not left us a single Tract, to induce us to believe that they had guessed the reason of it. Thus to this Day we still continue ignorant even of the Cause of the Motions of our Bodies, and of the Thoughts of our Souls; but this ignorance is of a different kind. We neither have nor ever shall have instruments of so exquisite a Frame, as to enable us to inspect the first springs, the vital Principles of ourselves; but human Industry has formed itself new Eyes, which has supplied us with the means of prying into the

Effects of Light, almost as far as it is permitted for Man to know concerning them.

From The Elements of Sir Isaac Newton's Philosophy *by Mr Voltaire, translated and revised by John Hanna, 1738.*

41	THE COLLIERS OF KINGSWOOD	November 1739

Few persons have lived long in the west of England who have not heard of the colliers of Kingswood; a people famous from the beginning hitherto, for neither fearing God nor regarding man: so ignorant of the things of God, that they seemed but one remove from the beasts that perish; and therefore utterly without desire of instruction, as well as without the means of it.

Many last winter used tauntingly to say of Mr Whitefield, 'If he will convert Heathens, why does not he go to the colliers of Kingswood?' In spring he did so. And as there were thousands who resorted to no place of public worship, he went after them into their own wilderness, 'to seek and save that which was lost.' When he was called away, others went into 'the highways and hedges, to compel them to come in.' And, by the grace of God, their labour was not in vain. The scene is already changed. Kingswood does not now, as a year ago, resound with cursing and blasphemy. It is no more filled with drunkenness and uncleanness, and the idle diversions that naturally lead thereto. It is no longer full of wars and fightings, of clamour and bitterness; of wrath and envyings: peace and love are there. Great numbers of the people are mild, gentle, and easy to be entreated. They 'do not cry, neither strive,' and hardly is their 'voice heard in the streets,' or, indeed, in their own wood; unless when they are at their usual evening diversion, singing praise unto God their Saviour.

From a letter to 'Mr D' by John Wesley, printed in Wesley's Journal, *edited by N. Curnock, 1909–16.*

HEATHENS. *In this phrase resides the whole truth on England. Britain was seen as a colony – its people the savages to be exploited – its wealth the property of the conquerors – and its preachers the missionaries to dope and convert the natives.*

42	EASTER	1742

April 1. Being Good Friday, I had a great desire to visit a little village called Placey, about ten measured miles north of Newcastle. It is inhabited by colliers only; and such as had been always in the first rank for savage ignorance and wickedness of every kind. Their grand assembly used to be on the Lord's Day, on which men, women, and children met together, to

dance, fight, curse, and swear, and play at chuck-ball, span-farthing, or whatever came next to hand. I felt great compassion for these poor creatures, from the time I heard of them first; and the more because all men seemed to despair of them. Between seven and eight I set out with John Heally, my guide. The north wind being unusually high, drove the sleet in our face, which froze as it fell, and cased us over presently. When we came to Placey we could very hardly stand. As soon as we were a little recovered, I went into the Square, and declared Him who 'was bruised for our sins, and wounded for our iniquities.' The poor sinners were quickly gathered together, and gave earnest heed to the things which were spoken. And so they did in the afternoon again, in spite of the wind and snow, when I besought them to receive Him for their King; to 'repent and believe in the Gospel.'

On Easter Monday and Tuesday, I preached there again, the congregation continually increasing; and as most of these had never in their lives pretended to any religion of any kind, they were the more ready to cry to God, as mere sinners, for the free redemption which is in Jesus.

From the Journal *of John Wesley, edited by N. Curnock, 1909–16.*

| 43 | A LOVE OF SYSTEM | August 9, 1750 |

... my Studies can not furnish a Recommendation of many new Books to you. there is Defense de l'Esprit des Loix by Montesquieu himself. it has some lively Things in it, but it is very short, & his Adversary appears to be so mean a Bigot, that he deserved no Answer. there are 3 V: in 4to of, Histoire du Cabinet du Roi, by Mess: Buffons, & D'Aubenton. the first is a Man of Character, but (I am told) has hurt it by this Work. it is all a Sort of Introduction to Natural History. the weak Part of it is a Love of System, wch runs thro' it, the most contrary Thing in the World to a Science, entirely grounded upon Experiments, & that has nothing to do with Vivacity of Imagination. there are some microscopical Observations, that seem'd curious to me, on those Animalcula to wch we are supposed to owe our Origin; and wch he has discover'd of like Figure in Females not pregnant, & in almost every Thing we use for Nourishment, even Vegetables, particularly in their Fruit & Seeds. not that he allows them to be animated Bodies, but *Molecules organisées.* if you ask what that is, I can not tell; no more than I can understand a new System of Generation wch he builds upon it. but what I was going to commend is a general View he gives of the Face of the Earth, follow'd by a particular one of all known Nations, their peculiar Figure & Manners, wch is the best epitome of Geography I ever met with, & wrote with Sense, & Elegance: in short these Books are well worth turning over....

From a letter of Thomas Gray to Dr Thomas Wharton.

44 ELECTRICAL FIRE — February 17, 1753

Sat. 17. From Dr. Franklin's Letters I learned; 1. That electrical fire (or aether) is a species of fire infinitely finer than any other yet known. 2. That it is diffused, and in nearly equal proportions, through almost all substances. 3. That as long as it is thus diffused, it has no discernible effect. 4. That if any quantity of it be collected together, whether by art or nature, it then becomes visible, in the form of fire, and inexpressibly powerful. 5. That it is essentially different from the light of the sun; for it pervades a thousand bodies which light cannot penetrate, and yet cannot penetrate glass, which light pervades so freely. 6. That lightning is no other than electrical fire collected by one or more clouds. 7. That all the effects of lightning may be performed by the artificial electric fire. 8. That any thing pointed, as a spire or tree, attracts the lightning, just as a needle does the electrical fire. 9. That the electrical fire, discharged on a rat or a fowl will kill it instantly; but discharged on one dipped in water, will slide off, and do it no hurt at all. In like manner, the lightning which will kill a man in a moment, will not hurt him if he be thoroughly wet. What an amazing scene is here opened for after ages to improve upon!

From the Journal *of John Wesley, edited by N. Curnock, 1909–16.*

45 PURE WARM AIR — 1757

The Princess will build a hot greenhouse, next spring at Kew, with a view to have exotics of the hottest climate, in which my pipes, to convey incessantly pure warm air, will probably be very serviceable. And as there will be several partitions in the greenhouse, I have proposed to have the glass of one of the rooms covered with shutters in winter to keep the cold out, which will make a perpetual spring and summer, with an incessant succession of pure warm air. What a scene is here opened for improvement in greenhouse vegetation!

From a contribution to the Gentleman's Magazine, *XXVII, 165, by Stephen Hales.*

46 TO THE DUKE OF BEDFORD, PRESIDENT OF THE FOUNDLING HOSPITAL — c.1758

My Lord,

As Beneficence is never exercised but at some expense of ease and leisure, your Grace will not be surprised that you are subjected as the general guardian of deserted infants and protector of their Hospital, to intrusion and importunity, and you will pardon in those who intend though perhaps unskilfully the promotion of the charity, the impropriety of their address for the goodness of their intention.

I therefore take the liberty of proposing to your Grace's notice a machine (for spinning cotton) of which I am the inventor and proprietor, as proper to be erected in the Foundling Hospital, its structure and operation being such that a mixed number of children from five to fourteen years may be enabled by it to earn their food and clothing. In this machine, thus useful and thus appropriated to the public, I hope to obtain from Parliament, by your Grace's recommendation, such a right as shall be thought due to the inventor.

I know, my Lord, that every project must encounter opposition, and I would not encounter it but that I think myself able to surmount it. Mankind has prejudices against every new undertaking, which are not always prejudices of ignorance. He that only doubts what he does not know may be satisfied by testimony. at least by that of his own eyes; but a projector, my Lord, has more dangerous enemies, the envious and the interested, who will neither hear reasons nor see facts, and whose animosity is more vehement as their conviction is more strong.

I do not implore your Grace's Patronage for a work existing only in possibility. I have a Machine erected which I am ready to exhibit to the view of your Grace, or of any proper judge of mechanical performances, whom you shall be pleased to nominate. I shall decline no trial; I shall seek no subterfuge; but shall shew, not by argument but by practical experience, that what I have here promised will be easily performed.

I am an old man oppressed with many infirmities, and therefore cannot pay the attention which your Grace's high quality demands and my respect would dictate, but whenever you shall be pleased to assign me an audience I shall explain my design with the openness of a man who desires to hide nothing, and receive your Grace's commands with the submission which becomes,

    My Lord,
    Your Grace's most obedient
    and most humble servant.

Draft of a letter from Lewis Paul to the Duke of Bedford, composed for him by Samuel Johnson; printed in an appendix to Life and Times of Samuel Crompton *by G.J. French, 1859.*

47   WESLEY IN CUMBERLAND   May 1759

Tues. 15. I rode over to Lorton, a little village at the foot of a high mountain. Many came from a considerable distance, and I believe did not repent of their labour; for they found God to be a God both of the hills and valleys, and no where more present than in the mountains of Cumberland.

Thurs. 17. I inquired into a signal instance of providence. When a coal-pit runs far under the ground, it is customary here to build a partition-wall, nearly from the shaft to within three or four yards of the end, in order to make the air circulate, which then moves down one side of the wall, turns at the end, and then moves briskly up on the other side. In a pit two miles from the town, (Whitehaven) which ran full four hundred yards under the ground, and had been long neglected, several parts of this wall were fallen down. Four men were sent down to repair it. They were about three hundred yards from the shaft, when the foul air took fire. In a moment it tore down the wall from end to end, and burning on till it came to the shaft, it then burst, and went off like a large cannon. The men instantly fell on their faces, or they would have been burnt to death in a few moments. One of them, who once knew the love of God, (Andrew English) began crying aloud for mercy: but in a very short time his breath was stopped. The other three crept on their hands and knees, till two got to the shaft and were drawn up; but one of them died in a few minutes: John M'Comlie was drawn up next, burnt from head to foot, but rejoicing and praising God. They then went down for Andrew, whom they found senseless, the very circumstance which saved his life: for, losing his senses, he lay flat on the ground, and the greatest part of the fire went over him; whereas had he gone forward on his hands and knees, he would undoubtedly have been burnt to death. But life or death was welcome; for God had restored the light of his countenance.

Sat.19. One was showing us the improvements, begun by Sir William Lowther. He had marked out places for new walks, and for tufts of trees, laid out a new plan for his gardens, begun to alter the house, and was preparing to make a little paradise round about it. But death came between. And how little loss was this, if it removed him to the paradise of God?

From the Journal *of John Wesley, edited by N. Curnock, 1909–16.*

48   PROVIDENCE   c.1760

Though fanners were used in mills as early as 1720, it was only about this time that our tenants got them for their barns. The winnowing of corn was of old a tedious and uncertain operation. Every mill had a sheiling hill, where it was performed in the open air. It is said the Anti-Burgher ministers testified against fanners, as a creating of wind and distrusting of Providence. They thought people should wait with patience for wind, as their fathers had done before them. But this scrupulosity being contrary to self-interest, made little impression on their followers.

From the note-books of John Ramsay of Ochtertye, printed in Scotland and Scotsmen in the Eighteenth Century, *1888.*

IX

For I am under the same accusation with my Saviour – for they said, he is besides himself.

For I pray God for the introduction of new creatures into this island.

For I pray God for the ostriches of Salisbury Plain, the beavers of the Medway & silver fish of Thames.

For Charity is cold in the multitude of possessions, & the rich are covetous of their crumbs.

For I pray to be accepted as a dog without offence, which is best of all.

For I wish to God and desire towards the most High, which is my policy.

For the tides are the life of God in the ocean, and he sends his angel to trouble the great DEEP.

For he hath fixed the earth upon arches & pillars, and the flames of hell flow under it.

For the grosser the particles the nearer to the sink, & the nearer to purity, the quicker the gravitation.

For MATTER is the dust of the Earth, every atom of which is the life.

For MOTION is as the quantity of life direct, & that which hath not motion, is resistance.

For Resistance is not of GOD, but he – hath built his works upon it.

For the Centripetal and Centrifugal forces are GOD SUSTAINING and DIRECTING.

For Elasticity is the temper of matter to recover its place with vehemence.

For Attraction is the earning of parts, which have a similitude in the life.

For the Life of God is in the Loadstone, and there is a magnet, which pointeth due EAST.

For the Glory of God is always in the East, but cannot be seen for the cloud of the crucifixion.

For due East is the way to Paradise, which man knoweth not by reason of his fall.

For the Longtitude is (nevertheless) attainable by steering angularly notwithstanding.

For Eternity is a creature & is built upon Eternity καταβολη επι τη διαβολη.

For Fire is a mixed nature of body & spirit, & the body is fed by that which hath not life.

For Fire is exasperated by the Adversary, who is Death, unto the detriment of man.

For an happy Conjecture is a miraculous cast by the Lord Jesus.

For a bad conjecture is a draught of stud and mud.

For there is a Fire which is blandishing, and which is of God direct.

For Fire is a substance and distinct, and purifyeth evn in hell.

For the Shears is the first of the mechanical powers, and to be used on the knees.

For if Adam had used this instrument right, he would not have fallen.

For the power of the Shears is direct as the life.

For the power of the WEDGE is direct as it's altitude by communication of Almighty God.

For the Skrew, Axle & Wheel, Pulleys, the Lever & inclined Plane are known in the Schools.

For the Centre is not known but by the application of the members to matter.

For I have shown the Vis Inertiae to be false, and such is all nonsense.

For the Centre is the hold of the Spirit upon the matter in hand.

For FRICTION is inevitable because the Universe is FULL of God's works.

For the PERPETUAL MOTION is in all the works of Almighty GOD.

For it is not so in the engines of man, which are made of dead materials, neither indeed can be.

For the Moment of bodies, as it is used, is a false term – bless God ye Speakers on the Fifth of November.

For Time and Weight are by their several estimates.

For I bless GOD in the discovery of the LONGTITUDE direct by the means of GLADWICK.

For the motion of the PENDULUM is the longest in that it parries resistance.

For the WEDDING GARMENTS of all men are prepared in the SUN against the day of acceptance.

For the Wedding Garments of all women are prepared in the MOON against the day of their purification.

For CHASTITY is the key of knowledge as in Esdras, Sir Isaac Newton & now, God be praised, in me.

For Newton nevertheless is more of error than of the truth, but I am of the WORD of GOD.

For WATER is not of solid constituents, but is dissolved from precious stones above.

For the life remains in its dissolvent state, and that in great power.

For WATER is condensed by the Lord's FROST, tho' not by the FLORENTINE experiment.

For GLADWICK is a substance growing on hills in the East, candied by the sun, and of diverse colours.

For it is neither stone nor metal but a new creature, soft to the ax, but hard to the hammer.

For it answers sundry uses, but particularly it supplies the place of Glass.

For it giveth a benign light without the fragility, malignity or mischief of glass.

For it attracteth all the colours of the GREAT BOW which is fixed in the EAST.

For the FOUNTAINS and SPRINGS are the life of the waters working up to God.

For they are in SYMPATHY with the waters above the Heavens, which are solid.

For the Fountains, springs and rivers are all of them from the sea, whose water is filtrated and purified by the earth.

For is Water above the visible surface in a spiritualizing state, which cannot be seen but by application of a CAPILLARY TUBE.

For the ASCENT of VAPOURS is the return of thanksgiving from all humid bodies.

For the RAIN WATER kept in a reservoir at any altitude, suppose of a thousand feet will make a fountain from a spout of ten feet of the same height.

For it will ascend in a stream two thirds of the way and afterwards prank itself into ten thousand agreeable forms.

For the SEA is a seventh of the Earth – the spirit of the Lord by Esdras.

For MERCURY is affected by the AIR because it is of a similar subtlety.

For the rising in the BAROMETER is not effected by pressure but by sympathy.

For it cannot be separated from the creature with which it is intimately & eternally connected.

For where it is stinted of air there it will adhere together & stretch on the reverse.

For it works by ballancing according to the hold of the spirit.

For QUICK-SILVER is spiritual and so is the AIR to all intents and purposes.

For the AIR-PUMP weakens & dispirits but cannot wholly exhaust.

For SUCKTION is the withdrawing of the life, but life will follow as fast as it can.

For there is infinite provision to keep up the life in all the parts of Creation.

X

For the AIR is contaminated by curses and evil language.

For poysonous creatures catch some of it & retain it or ere it goes to the adversary.

For IRELAND was without these creatures, till of late, because of the simplicity of the people.

For the AIR is purified by prayer which is made aloud and with all our might.

For loud prayer is good for weak lungs and for a vitiated throat.

For SOUND is propagated in the spirit and in all directions.

For the VOICE of a figure compleat in all its parts.

For a man speaks HIMSELF from the crown of his head to the sole of his feet.

For a LION roars HIMSELF compleat from head to tail.

For all these things are seen in the spirit which makes the beauty of prayer.
For all whispers and unmusical sounds in general are of the Adversary.
For 'I will hiss saith the Lord' is God's denunciation of death.
For applause or the clapping of the hands is the natural action of a man on the descent of the glory of God.
For EARTH which is an intelligence hath a voice and a propensity to speak in all her parts.
For ECHO is the soul of the voice exerting itself in hollow places.
For ECHO cannot act but when she can parry the adversary.
For ECHO is greatest in Churches and where she can assist in prayer.
For a good voice hath its Echo with it and it is attainable by much supplication.
For the VOICE is from the body and the spirit – and is a body and a spirit.
For the prayers of good men are therefore visible to second-sighted persons.
For HARPSICHORDS are best strung with gold wire.
For HARPS and VIOLS are best strung with Indian weed.
For the GERMAN FLUTE is an indirect – the common flute good, bless the Lord Jesus BENJAMIN HALLET.
For the feast of TRUMPETS should be kept up that being the most direct & acceptable of all instruments.
For the TRUMPET of God is a blessed intelligence & so are all the instruments in HEAVEN.
For GOD the father Almighty plays upon the HARP of stupendous magnitude and melody. .
For innumerable Angels fly out at every touch and his tune is a work of creation.
For at that time malignity ceases and the devils themselves are at peace.
For this time is perceptible to man by a remarkable stillness and serenity of soul.
For the Æolian harp is improveable into regularity.
For when it is so improved it will be known to be the SHAWM.
For it woud be better if the LITURGY were musically performed.
For the strings of the SHAWM were upon a cylinder which turned to the wind.
For this was spiritual musick altogether, as the wind is a spirit.
For there is nothing but it may be played upon in delight.
For the flames of fire may be blown thro musical pipes.
For it is so higher up in the vast empyrean.
For nothing is so real as that which is spiritual.
For an IGNIS FATUUS is either the fool's conceit or a blast from the adversary.
For SHELL-FIRE or ELECTRICAL is the quick air when it is caught.
For GLASS is worked in the fire till it partakes of its nature.
For the electrical fire is easily obtain'd by the working of glass.

For all spirits are of fire and the air is a very benign one.
For the MAN in VACUO is a flat conceit of preposterous folly.
For the breath of our nostrils is an electrical spirit.
For an electrical spirit may be exasperated into a malignant fire.
For it is good to quicken in paralytic cases being the life applied unto death.
For the method of philosophizing is in a posture of Adoration.
For the School-Doctrine of Thunder & Lightning is a Diabolical Hypothesis.
For it is taking the nitre from the lower regions and directing it against the Infinite of Heights.
For THUNDER is the voice of God direct in verse and musick.
For LIGHTNING is a glance of the glory of God.
For the Brimstone that is found at the times of thunder & lightning is worked up by the Adversary.
For the voice is always for infinite good which he strives to impede.
For the Devil can work coals into shapes to afflict the minds of those that will not pray.
For the coffin and the cradle and the purse are all against a man.
For the coffin is for the dead and death came by disobedience.
For the cradle is for weakness and the child of man was originally strong from ye womb.
For the purse is for money and money is dead matter with the stamp of human vanity.
For the adversary frequently sends these particular images out of the fire to those whom they concern.
For the coffin is for me because I have nothing to do with it.
For the cradle is for me because the old Dragon attacked me in it & I overcame in Christ.
For the purse is for me because I have neither money nor human friends.
For LIGHT is propagated at all distances in an instant because it is actuated by the divine conception.
For the Satellites of the planet prove nothing in this matter but the glory of Almighty God.
For the SHADE is of death and from the adversary.
For Solomon said vanity of vanities vanity of vanities all is vanity.
For Jesus says verity of verities, verity of verities all is verity.
For Solomon said THOU FOOL in malice from his own vanity.
For the Lord reviled not at all in hardship and temptation unutterable.
For the Fire hath this property that it reduces a thing till finally it is not.
For all the filth of wicked men shall be done away by fire in Eternity.
For the furnace itself shall come up at the last according to Abraham's vision.
For the Convex of Heaven shall work about on that great event.
For the ANTARCTICK POLE is not yet but shall answer in the Consummation.

From Rejoice in the Lamb *by Christopher Smart, written about 1761, first published, edited by W.F. Stead, 1939.*

The magnificent fragment of poetry of which this passage forms the ninth and tenth sections is a hymn of praise. It begins (Section 1):

Rejoice in God, O ye Tongues; give glory to the Lord, and the Lamb.

Then Smart proceeds through the Creation, through mythologies and catalogues and memories – through the mazes of his unhinged spirit – calling on each fragment however humble or queer or domestic or trivial or tremendous to praise the Lord. Then he asks God for his blessing upon the world – again the tortured world of fragmentary images and snatches which is in the poet's head. Including a prayer for his own deliverance:

For I am making to the shore day by day, the Lord Jesus take me.
For I bless the Lord Jesus upon RAMSGATE PIER – the Lord forward the building of harbours. (*Section 8*)

And so into the 'new creatures' which Science (Natural Philosophy) is bringing into the world. And he does not oppose them as later poets are to. He glories in the fulness of the earth and of the powers of creation (a 'new creature' is also a Methodist term – see Wesley's Journal, *Sunday May 3) – first for 'new creatures' in the sense of 'the ostriches of Salisbury Plain' and then in absolutely new creatures such as* GLADWICK:

For it is neither stone nor metal but a new creature. . . .

But he sees the action of all the new forms and discoveries around him as fulfilling the same laws as the ancient creation:

For an happy Conjecture is a miraculous cast by the Lord Jesus.
For the rising in the BAROMETER is not effected by pressure but by sympathy.
For QUICK-SILVER is spiritual . . .

Finally note the struggle between animism and materialism which this represents, including Smart's use of these scientific terms in poetry, thanks to his so-called madness. The so-called confusion is *revelation of the struggle.*

50   THE MATERIALIST CONCEPTION OF MUSIC   1761–6

A mason-lodge in Glasgow wanted an organ. The office-bearers were acquaintances of Mr Watt. We imagined that Mr Watt could do anything; and, though we all knew that he did not know one musical note from another, he was asked if he would build this organ. He had repaired one, and it had amused him. He said, 'Yes;' but he began by building a very small one for his intimate friend Dr Black, which is now in my possession. In doing this, a thousand things occurred to him which no organ-builder ever dreamed of, – nice indicators of the strength of the blast, regulators of it, &c. &c. He began to the great one. [*sic*]. He then began to study the philosophical theory of music. Fortunately for me, no book was at hand but the most refined of all, and the only one that can be said to contain any theory at all, – Smith's Harmonics. Before Mr Watt had half finished this organ, he and I were completely masters of that most refined and beautiful theory of the beats of imperfect consonances. He found that by these beats it would be possible for him, totally ignorant of music, to tune this organ according to any system of temperament; and he did so, to the delight and astonishment of our best performers. In prosecution of this, he invented a real monochord of continued tone; and, in playing with this, he made an observation which, had it been then known, would have terminated a dispute between the first mathematicians in Europe, – Euler and D'Alembert; which completely establishes the theory of Daniel Bernouilli, who differed from both of those gentlemen, about the mechanism of the vibration of musical chords; and as completely explains the harmonic notes [H.J.: tones?] which accompany all full musical notes, overturning the theories of Rameau and Tartini.

From a Narrative of Mr Watt's Invention of the Improved Engine *by Professor John Robison; printed in* The Life of James Watt *by J.P. Muirhead, 2nd edition, 1857.*

51   A PERFECT STEAM ENGINE   c.1765

At the breaking-up of the College (I think in 1765), I went to the country. About a fortnight after this, I came to town, and went to have a chat with Mr Watt, and to communicate to him some observations I had made on Desaguiliers' and Belidor's account of the steam-engine. I came into Mr Watt's parlour without ceremony, and found him sitting before the fire, having lying on his knee a little tin cistern, which he was looking at. I entered into conversation on what we had been speaking of at last meeting, – something about steam. All the while, Mr Watt kept looking at the fire, and laid down the cistern at the foot of his chair. At last he looked at me, and said briskly, 'You need not *fash* yourself any more about that, man; I have now got an engine that shall not waste a particle of steam. It shall be all boiling hot; – aye, and hot water injected if I please.' So saying, Mr Watt looked with complacency at the little thing at his feet, and, seeing that I observed him, he shoved it away under a table with his foot. I put a question to him about the nature of his contrivance. He answered me rather drily. I did not press him to a further explanation at that time, knowing that I had offended him a few days before by blabbing a pretty contrivance which he had hit on for turning the cocks of the engine. I had mentioned this in presence of an engine-builder who was going to erect one for a friend of mine; and this having come to Mr Watt's ears, he found fault with it.

I was very anxious, however, to learn what Mr Watt had contrived, but was obliged to go to the country in the evening. A gentleman who was going to the same house said he would give me a place in his carriage, and desired me to wait for him on the walk by the river-side. I went thither, and found Mr Alexander Brown, a very intimate acquaintance of Mr Watt's, walking with another gentleman, (Mr Craig, architect). Mr Brown immediately accosted me with, 'Well, have you seen Jamie Watt?' – 'Yes.' – 'He'll be in high spirits now with his engine, isn't he?' 'Yes,' said I, 'very fine spirits.' 'Gad,' says Mr Brown, 'the condenser's the thing: keep it but cold enough, and you may have perfect vacuum, whatever be the heat of the cylinder.' The instant he said this, the whole flashed on my mind at once. I did all I could to encourage the conversation, but was much embarrassed. I durst not appear ignorant of the apparatus, lest Mr Brown should find he had communicated more than he ought to have done. I could only learn that there was a vessel called a condenser, which communicated with the cylinder, and that this condenser was immersed in cold water, and had a pump to clear it of the water which was formed in it. I also learned that the great difficulty was to make the piston tight; and that leather and felt had been tried, and were found quite unable to stand the heat. I saw that the whole would be perfectly dry, and that Mr Watt had used steam instead of air to press up his piston, which I thought, by Mr Brown's description was inverted. We parted, and I went home, a very silent companion to the gentleman who had given me a seat. Next day, impatient to see the effects of the separate condensation, I sent to Paisley and got some tin things made there, in completion of the notion I had formed. I tried it as an air-pump, by making my steam-vessel communicate with a tea-kettle, a condenser, and a glass receiver. In less than two minutes I rarefied the air in a pretty large receiver more than twenty times. I could go no farther in this process, because my pump for taking out the air from my condenser was too large, and not tight enough; but I saw that when applied to the mere process of taking out the air generated from the water, the vacuum might be made almost complete. I saw, too, (in consequence of a conversation the preceding day with Mr Watt about the eduction-pipe in Beighton's engine), that a long suck-pipe, or syphon, would take off all the water. In short, I had no doubt that Mr Watt had really made a perfect steam-engine.

From a Narrative of Mr Watt's Invention of the Improved Engine *by Professor John Robison, written 1796; printed in* The Origin and Progress of the Mechanical Inventions of James Watt *by J.P. Muirhead, 1855.*

52 THE FORMING OF A TEA-POT c.1767

I sho^d be glad to know from some of you Gent^n learned in Natural History & Philosophy the most probable theory to account for these vegetables (as they once were) forming part of a stratum, which dips into the Earth to our knowledge 60 or 100 y^{ds} deep, & for ought we know to the Centre! These various strata, the Coals included, seem from various circumstances to have been in a Liquid state, & to have travel'd along what was then the surface of the Earth; something like the Lava from Mount Vesuvius. They wind & turn about, like a Serpentine River, and we have one under a Hill *Mole Cop*, which seems to have been formed by them, as the mines are all turned by it, some to the East and others to the West . . . . But I have done. I have got beyond my depth . . . . These wonderful works of Nature are too vast for my narrow microscopic comprehension. I must bid adieu to them for the present, & attend to what better suits my Capacity. The forming of a Jug or Teapot.

From a letter of Josiah Wedgwood to Thomas Bentley, printed in Eliza Meteyard, The Life of Wedgwood, *1865.*

53 THE WOODEN HORSE 1768

I was riding one day in a country, that was enclosed by walls of an uncommon height; and upon its being asserted, that it would be impossible for a person to leap such walls, I offered for a wager to produce a wooden horse, that should carry me safely over the highest wall in the country. It struck me, that, if a machine were made with eight legs, four only of which should stand upon the ground at one time; if the remaining body were divided into two parts, sliding, or rather rolling on cylinders, one of the parts, and the legs belonging to it, might in two efforts be projected over the wall by a person in the machine; and the legs belonging to this part might be let down to the ground, and then the other half of the machine might have its legs drawn up, and be projected over the wall, and so on, alternately. This idea by degrees developed itself in my mind, so as to make me perceive, that as one half of the machine was always a road for the other half, and that such a machine never rolled upon the ground, a carriage might be made, which should carry a road for itself. It is already certain, that a carriage moving on an iron rail-way may be drawn with a fourth part of the force requisite to draw it upon a common road.

After having made a number of models of my machine, that should carry and lay down its own road, I took out a patent to secure to myself the principle; but the term of my patent has long since expired, without my having been able to unite to my satisfaction in this machine strength with sufficient lightness, and with regular motion, so as to obtain the advantages I proposed.

From Memoirs of Richard Lovell Edgeworth Esq, begun by Himself and concluded by his Daughter, Maria Edgeworth. *Written 1808, published 1820.*

54   DÆMONS AT WORK   October 9, 1769

After dinner I went along the Milthrop turnpike four miles to see the falls, or force, of the river Kent, came to *Sizergh* (pronounce Siser) & turned down a lane to the left. The seat of the Stricklands an old Catholick family, is an ancient hall-house, with a very large tower embattled; the rest of the buildings added to this are of later date, but all is white & seen to advantage on a back ground of old trees; there is a small park also well-wooded. Opposite to this turning to the left, I soon came to the river; it works its way in a narrow and deep rocky channel overhung with trees. The calmness & brightness of the evening, the roar of the waters, and the thumping of huge hammers at an iron-forge not far distant, made it a singular walk, but as to the falls (for there are two) they are not four feet high. I went on down to the forge & saw the dæmons at work by the light of their own fires: the iron is brought in pigs to Milthrop by sea from Scotland &c. & is here beat into bars and plates. Two miles farther, at *Levens*, is the seat of Lord Suffolk, where he sometimes passes the summer. It was a favourite place of his late Countess: but this I did not see.

From Journal of a Tour of the Lakes *by Thomas Gray, first printed in* The Memoirs of his Life and Writings *by W. Mason and added to* The Poems of Mr Gray, *published in 1778.*

55   ON THE WYE   1770

Mines are frequent in rocky places; and they are full of ideas suited to such occasions. To these may sometimes be added the operations of engines; for machinery, especially when its powers are stupendous, or its effects formidable, is an effort of art, which may be accommodated to the extravagances of nature.

A scene at the New Weir on the Wye, which in itself is truly great and awful, so far from being disturbed, becomes more interesting and important, by the business to which it is destined. It is a chasm between two high ranges of hill, which rise almost perpendicularly from the water; the rocks on the sides are mostly heavy masses; and their colour is generally brown; but here and there a pale craggy shape starts up to a vast heighth above the rest, unconnected, broken, and bare: large trees frequently force out their way amongst them; and many of them stand far back in the covert, where their unnatural dusky hue is deepened by the shadow which overhangs them. The river too, as it retires, loses itself in woods which close immediately above, then rise thick and high, and darken the water. In the midst of all this gloom is an iron forge, covered with a black cloud of smoak, and surrounded with half-burned ore, with coal, and with cinders; the fuel for it is brought down a path, worn into steps, narrow and steep, and winding among precipices, and near it is an open space of barren moor, about which are scattered the huts of the workmen. It stands close to the cascade of the Weir, where the agitation of the current is encreased by large fragments of rocks, which have been swept down by floods from the banks, or shivered by the tempests from the brow; and the sullen sounds, at stated intervals, from the strokes of the great hammers in the forge, deadens the roar of the waterfall. Just below it, while the rapidity of the stream still continues, a ferry is carried across it; and lower down the fishermen use little round boats, called truckles, the remains perhaps of ancient British navigation, which the least motion will overset, and the slightest touch may destroy. All the employments of the people seem to require either exertion or caution; and the ideas of force or of danger which attend them, give to the scene an animation unknown to a solitary, though perfectly compatible with the wildest romantic situation.

From Observations on Modern Gardening Illustrated by Descriptions *by Thomas Whateley, 1770.*

56 THE ENCLOSURES 1770

Ill fares the land, to hast'ning ills a prey,
Where wealth accumulates, and men decay:
Princes or lords may flourish, or may fade;
A breath can make them, as a breath has made;
But a bold peasantry, the country's pride,
When once destroyed, can never be supply'd.
 A time there was, ere England's griefs began,
Where every rood of ground maintain'd its man;
For him light labour spread her wholesome store;
Just gave what life requir'd, but gave no more;
His best companions, innocence and health;
And his best riches, ignorance of wealth.
 But times are alter'd, trade's unfeeling train
Usurp the land, and dispossess the swain:
Along the lawn, where scatter'd hamlets rose,
Unwieldy wealth and cumb'rous pomp repose;
And every want to luxury ally'd,
And every pang that folly pays to pride.
Those gentle hours, that plenty bade to bloom:
Those calm desires, that ask'd but little room,
Those healthful sports, that grac'd the peaceful scene,
Liv'd in each look, and brighten'd all the green;

These, far departing seek a kinder shore,
And rural mirth and manners are no more.
From The Deserted Village *by Oliver Goldsmith, 1770.*

57   AN IMMENSE WILDERNESS   1770

London is literally new to me; new in its streets, houses, and even in its situation; as the Irishman said, 'London is now gone out of town.' What I left open fields, producing hay and corn, I now find covered with streets, and squares, and palaces, and churches. I am credibly informed, that in the space of seven years, eleven thousand new houses have been built in one quarter of Westminster, exclusive of what is daily added to other parts of this unwieldy metropolis. Pimlico and Knightsbridge are now almost joined to Chelsea and Kensington; and if this infatuation continues for half a century, I suppose the whole county of Middlesex will be covered with brick.

It must be allowed, indeed, for the credit of the present age, that London and Westminster are much better paved and lighted than they were formerly. The new streets are spacious, regular, and airy; and the houses generally convenient. The bridge at Black-friars is a noble monument of taste and public spirit – I wonder how they stumbled upon a work of such magnificence and utility. But, notwithstanding these improvements, the capital is become an overgrown monster; which, like a dropsical head, will in time leave the body and extremities without nourishment and support. The absurdity will appear in its full force, when we consider, that one sixth part of the natives of this whole extensive kingdom, is crowded within the bills of mortality. What wonder that our villages are depopulated, and our farms in want of day-labourers? The abolition of small farms is but one cause of the decrease of population. Indeed, the incredible increase of horses and black cattle, to answer the purposes of luxury, requires a prodigious quantity of hay and grass, which are raised and managed without much labour; but a number of hands will always be wanted for the different branches of agriculture, whether the farms be large or small. The tide of luxury has swept all the inhabitants from the open country. The poorest 'squire, as well as the richest peer, must have his house in town, and make a figure with an extraordinary number of domestics. The plough-boys, cow-herds, and lower hinds, are debauched and seduced by the appearance and discourse of those coxcombs in livery, when they make their summer excursions. They desert their dirt and drudgery, and swarm up to London, in hopes of getting into service, where they can live luxuriously and wear fine clothes, without being obliged to work; for idleness is natural to man. Great numbers of these being disappointed in their expectation, become thieves and sharpers; and London being an immense wilderness, in which there is neither watch nor ward of any signification, nor any order or police, affords them lurking-places as well as prey.

From The Expedition of Humphry Clinker *by Tobias Smollett, 1771.*

58 ALLOA 1770

About a fortnight is now elapsed, since we left the capital of Scotland, directing our course towards Stirling, where we lay. The castle of this place is such another as that of Edinburgh, and affords a surprising prospect of the windings of the river Forth, which are so extraordinary, that the distance from hence to Alloa by land, is but four miles, and by water it is twenty-four. Alloa is a neat thriving town, that depends in a great measure on the commerce of Glasgow, the merchants of which send hither tobacco and other articles, to be deposited in warehouses for exportation from the Firth of Forth. In our way hither we visited a flourishing iron-work, where instead of burning wood, they use coal, which they have the art of clearing in such a manner as frees it from the sulphur, that would otherwise render the metal too brittle for working. Excellent coal is found in almost every part of Scotland.

The soil of this district produces scarce any other grain but oats and barley; perhaps because it is poorly cultivated and almost altogether uninclosed. The few enclosures they have consist of paltry walls of loose stones gathered from the fields, which indeed they cover, as if they had been scattered on purpose. When I expressed my surprise that the peasants did not disencumber their grounds of these stones, a gentleman, well acquainted with the theory as well as the practice of farming, assured me that the stones, far from being prejudicial, were serviceable to the crop. This philosopher had ordered a field of his own to be cleared, manured, and sown with barley, and the produce was more scanty than before. He caused the stones to be replaced, and next year the crop was as good as ever. The stones were removed a second time, and the harvest failed; they were again brought back, and the ground retrieved its fertility. The same experiment has been tried in different parts of Scotland with the same success. Astonished at this information, I desired to know in what manner he accounted for this strange phenomenon; and he said there were three ways in which the stones might be serviceable. They might possibly restrain an excess in the perspiration of the earth, analogous to colliquative sweats, by which the human body is sometimes wasted and consumed. They might act as so many fences to protect the tender blade from the piercing winds of the spring; or, by multiplying the reflection of the sun, they might increase the warmth, so as to mitigate the natural chilness of the soil and climate. But surely this excessive perspiration might be more effectually checked by different kinds of manure, such as ashes, lime, chalk, or marl, of which last it seems there are many pits in this kingdom: as for warmth, it would be much more equally obtained by inclosures; one half of the ground which is now covered, would be retrieved; the cultivation would require less labour; and the ploughs, harrows, and horses, would not suffer half the damage which they now sustain.

From The Expedition of Humphry Clinker *by Tobias Smollett, 1771.*

59 INSPIRATION c.1770

In appearance and manners, as well as in acquirements, Mr Brindley was a mere peasant. Unlettered and rude of speech, it was easier for him to devise means for executing a design, than to communicate his ideas concerning it to others. Formed by nature for the profession he assumed, it was there alone that he was in his proper element; and so occupied was his mind with his business, that he was incapable of relaxing in any of the common amusements of life. As he had not the ideas of other men to assist him, whenever a point of difficulty in contrivance occurred, it was his custom to retire to his bed, where in perfect solitude he would lie for one, two, or three days, pondering the matter in his mind, till the requisite expedient had presented itself. This is that true *inspiration*, which poets have almost exclusively arrogated to themselves, but which men of original genius in every walk are actuated by, when from the operation of the mind acting upon itself, without the intrusion of foreign notions, they create and invent. A remarkably retentive memory was one of the essential qualities which Mr Brindley brought to his mental operations. This enabled him to execute all parts of the most complex machine in due order, without any help of models or drawings, provided he had once accurately settled the whole plan in his mind. In his calculations of the powers of machines, he followed a plan peculiar to himself; but, indeed, the only one he could follow without instructions in the rules of art. He would work the question some time in his head, and then set the result down in figures. Then taking it up at this stage, he would again proceed by a mental operation to another result; and thus he would go by stages till the whole was finished, only by making use of figures to mark the several results of his operations. But though, by the wonderful powers of native genius, he was thus enabled to get over his want of artificial method to a certain degree, yet there is no doubt, that when his concerns became extremely complicated, with accounts of various kinds to keep, and calculations of all sorts to form, he could not avoid that perplexity and embarrassment which a readiness in the processes carried on by pen and paper can alone obviate. His estimates of expense have generally proved wide of reality; and he seems to have been better qualified to be the contriver, than the manager, of a great design. His moral qualities were, however, highly respectable. He was far above envy and jealousy, and freely communicated his improvements to persons capable of receiving and executing them; taking a liberal satisfaction in forming a new generation of engineers able to proceed with the great plans in the success of which he was so deeply interested. His integrity and regard to the advantage of his employers were unimpeachable. In fine, the name of *Brindley* will ever keep a place among that small number of mankind, who form *eras* in the art or science to which they devote themselves, by a large and durable extension of their limits.

From A Description of the Country from Thirty to Forty Miles round Manchester *by John Aikin, 1795.*

60   SLEEP   c.1770

Another way of procuring sleep mechanically was related to me by Mr Brindley, the famous canal engineer, who was brought up to the business of a mill-wright; he told me, that he had more than once seen the experiment of a man extending himself across the large stone of a corn-mill, and that by gradually letting the stone whirl, the man fell asleep, before the stone had gained its full velocity, and he supposed would have died without pain by the continuance or increase of the motion. In this case the centrifugal motion of the head and feet must accumulate the blood in both those extremities of the body, and thus compress the brain.

From Zoonomia, *Sect.XVIII, 20, by Erasmus Darwin, written c.1785 and published 1796.*

61   THE ISLE OF RUM   1772

I

Notwithstanding this island has several streams, here is not a single mill; all the molinary operations are done at home: the corn is graddan'd, or burnt out of the ear, instead of being thrashed: this is performed two ways; first, by cutting off the ears, and drying them in a kiln, then setting fire to them on a floor, and picking out the grains, by this operation rendered as black as coal. The other method is more expeditious, for the whole sheaf is burnt, without the trouble of cutting off the ears: a most ruinous practice, as it destroys both thatch and manure, and on that account has been wisely prohibited in some of the islands. Graddaned corn was the parched corn of HOLY WRIT. Thus Boaz presents his beloved Ruth with parched corn; and Jesse sends David with an Ephah of the same to his sons in the camp of Saul. The grinding was also performed by the same sort of machine the quern, in which two women were necessarily employed: thus, it is prophesied two women shall be grinding at the mill, one shall be taken, the other left. I must observe too that the island lasses are as merry at their work of grinding of the Graddan, the καχρυς of the antients, as those of Greece were in the days of Aristophanes, who warbled as they ground their parched corn*.

The quern or bra is made in some of the neighboring countries, in the mainland, and costs about fourteen shillings. This method of grinding is very tedious: for it employs two pair of hands four hours to grind only a single bushel of corn. Instead of a hair sieve to sift the meal the inhabitants here have an ingenious substitute, a sheep's skin stretched round a hoop, and perforated with small holes made with a hot iron. They knead their bannock with water only, and bake or rather toast it, by laying it upright against a stone placed near the fire.

II

On my return am entertained with a rehearsal I may call it of the Luaghadh, or, walking of cloth, a substitute for the fulling-mill: twelve or fourteen women, divided into two equal numbers, sit down on each side of a long board, ribbed length-ways, placing the cloth on it: first they begin to work it backwards and forwards with their hands, singing at the same time as at the Quern: when they have tired their hands, every female uses her feet for the same purpose, and six or seven pair of naked feet are in the most violent agitation, working one against another: as by this time they grow very earnest in their labor, the fury of the song rises; at length it arrives to such a pitch, that without breach of charity you would imagine a troop of female dæmoniacs to have been assembled.

They sing in the same manner when they are cutting down the corn, when thirty or forty join in chorus. The subject of the songs at the Luaghadh, the Quern, and on this occasion, are sometimes love, sometimes panegyric, and often a rehearsal of the deeds of the antient heroes, but all the tunes slow and melancholy.

Singing at the Quern is now almost out of date since the introduction of water-mills. The laird can oblige his tenants, as in England, to make use of this more expeditious kind of grinding; and empowers his miller to search out and break any Querns he can find, as machines that defraud him of the toll.

From A Tour in Scotland, and Voyage to the Hebrides, 1772, *by Thomas Pennant.*

62   **THE SONG OF BIRDS**   January 10, 1773

Every poet, indeed, speaks with raptures of the harmony of the groves; yet those even, who have good musical ears, seem to pay little attention to it, but as a pleasing noise.

I am also convinced (though it may seem rather paradoxical), that the inhabitants of London distinguish more accurately, and know more on this

---

* Nubes, act v. scene ii. Gradden is derived from grad, quick, as the process is so expeditious.

head, than of all the other parts of the island taken together.

This seems to arise from two causes.

The first is, that we have not more musical ideas which are innate, than we have of language; and therefore those even, who have the happiness to have organs which are capable of receiving a gratification from this sixth sense (as it hath been called by some) require, however, the best instruction.

The orchestra of the opera, which is confined to the metropolis, hath diffused a good stile of playing over the other bands of the capital, which is, by degrees, communicated to the fidler and ballad-singer in the streets; the organs in every church, as well as those of the Savoyards, contribute likewise to this improvement of musical faculties in the Londoners.

If the singing of the ploughman in the country is therefore compared with that of the London blackguard, the superiority is infinitely on the side of the latter; and the same may be observed in comparing the voice of a country girl and London house-maid, as it is very uncommon to hear the former sing tolerably in tune.

I do not mean by this, to assert that inhabitants of the country are not born with as good musical organs; but only, that they have not the same opportunities of learning from others, who play in tune themselves.

The other reason for the inhabitants of London judging better in relation to the song of birds, arises from their hearing each bird sing distinctly, either in their own or their neighbours shops; as also from a bird continuing much longer in song whilst in a cage, than when at liberty; the cause of which I shall endeavour hereafter to explain.

'Experiments and Observations on the Singing of Birds' by the Hon. Daines Barrington, Vice-President R.S., in a letter to Mathew Maty M.D., Sec.R.S., printed in Philosophical Transactions, *Vol.LXIII, 1773.*

| 63 | TRADE | October 18, 1773 |

At breakfast, I asked, 'What is the reason that we are angry at a trader's having opulence?' – *Johnson*. 'Why, sir, the reason is, (though I don't undertake to prove that there is a reason,) we see no qualities in trade that should entitle a man to superiority. We are not angry at a soldier's getting riches, because we see that he possesses qualities which we have not. If a man returns from a battle, having lost one hand, and with the other full of gold, we feel that he deserves the gold; but we cannot think that a fellow, by sitting all day at a desk, is entitled to get above us.' – *Boswell*. 'But, sir, may we not suppose a merchant to be a man of an enlarged mind, such as Addison in the *Spectator* describes Sir Andrew Freeport to have been?' – *Johnson*. 'Why, sir, we may suppose any fictitious character. We may suppose a philosophical day-labourer, who is happy in reflecting that, by his labour, he contributes to the fertility of the earth, and to the support of his fellow-creatures; but we find no such philosophical day-labourer. A merchant may, perhaps, be a man of an enlarged mind; but there is nothing in trade connected with an enlarged mind.'

From The Journal of a Tour to the Hebrides with Samuel Johnson *by James Boswell, 1786.*

Note on 58, 59, 61 and 63. *In Smollett's* Expedition of Humphry Clinker *(published in 1771), Matthew Bramble describes a visit to Scotland (58). In 1772, Pennant went on a tour of the North including the Hebrides. The next year Johnson and Boswell followed roughly the same route. This intellectual penetration from the South corresponded to the finish of feudalism in Scotland. Following the suppression of the '45 rebellion, there was a phase of road and bridge building in the second half of the 18th century.*

In the quotations from Pennant (61), the economic sources of poetry are extraordinarily clearly shown. The reference to Ruth recalls the Book of Ruth, *chapter 2, verses 13 and 14:*

> Then she said, 'Let me find favour in thy sight, my lord; for that thou hast comforted me, and for that thou hast spoken friendly unto thine handmaid, though I be not like unto one of thy hand-maidens.' And Boaz said unto her, 'At mealtime come thou hither, and eat of the bread, and dip thy morsel in the vinegar.' And she sat beside the reapers: and he reached her parched corn, and she did eat, and was sufficed, and left.

The quotations also recall Wordsworth's 'The Solitary Reaper':

> Behold her, single in the field,
>   Yon solitary Highland Lass!
> Reaping and singing by herself;
>   Stop here, or gently pass!
> Alone she cuts and binds the grain,
> And sings a melancholy strain;
> O listen! for the Vale profound
> Is overflowing with the sound.
>
> No Nightingale did ever chaunt
>   More welcome notes to weary bands
> Of travellers in some shady haunt,
>   Among Arabian sands.
> A voice so thrilling ne'er was heard
> In spring-time from the Cuckoo-bird,
> Breaking the silence of the seas
> Among the farthest Hebrides.

And perhaps Keats[2] Ode to a Nightingale:

> Thou wast not born for death, immortal Bird!
> No hungry generations tread thee down;
> The voice I hear this passing night was heard
> In ancient days by emperor and clown;
> Perhaps the self-same song that found a path
> Through the sad heart of Ruth, when, sick for home,
> She stood in tears amid the alien corn ...

In the quotation from Aikin (59), the inspiration of the poet (the feudal creator) is arrogated to the engineer inventor (the modern creator). This modern creator himself comes directly from the dying peasantry. In 63, the purely literary critic Johnson compares economic man (existing by trade*) with the feudal soldier. 'Philosophic day-labourer' is Johnson's name for the peasant. Boswell takes it all a step further by arguing that the manufacturer has in fact purely feudal relations with his employees.*

64 AN IRON CHIEFTAIN 1776

Mr Hector was so good as to accompany me to see the great works of Mr Bolton, at a place which he has called Soho, about two miles from Birmingham, which the very ingenious proprietor showed me himself to the best advantage. I wish Johnson had been with us: for it was a scene which I should have been glad to contemplate by his light. The vastness and the contrivance of some of the machinery would have 'matched his mighty mind'. I shall never forget Mr Bolton's expression to me: 'I sell here, Sir, what all the world desires to have, – POWER.' He had about seven hundred people at work. I contemplated him as an iron chieftain, and he seemed to be a father to his tribe. One of them came to him, complaining grievously of his landlord for having distrained his goods. 'Your landlord is in the right, Smith, (said Bolton). But I'll tell you what: find you a friend who will lay down one half of your rent, and I'll lay down the other half; and you shall have your goods again.'

From The Life of Samuel Johnson *by James Boswell, 1799.*

65 GENIUS May 6, 1776

After preaching at Cockermouth and Wigton, I went on to Carlisle, and preached to a very serious congregation. Here I saw a very extraordinary genius, a man blind from four years of age, who could wind worsted, weave flowered plush on an engine and loom of his own making; who wove his own name in plush and made his own clothes and his own tools of every sort. Some years ago, being shut up in the organ-loft at church, he felt every part of it, and afterwards made an organ for himself which judges say is an exceeding good one. He then taught himself to play upon it psalm-tunes, anthems, voluntaries, or any thing which he heard. I heard him play several times with great accuracy and a complex voluntary: I suppose all Europe can hardly produce such another instance. His name is Joseph Strong. But what is he the better for all this, if he is still 'without God in the world?'

From the Journal *of John Wesley.*

66   MEMORANDUM   September 3, 1777

I promise to pay Dr Darwin of Lichfield one thousand pounds upon his delivering to me (within two years of date hereof) an Instrument calld an organ that is capable of pronouncing the Lord's prayer, the creed, and ten Commandments in the vulgar tongue and his ceding to me and me only the property of the sd invention with all the advantages thereunto appertaining,

M. BOULTON, Soho, Sep. 3rd. 1777

Witness: JAMES KEIR.   Witness: W. SMALL.

Quoted in Doctor Darwin *by Hesketh Pearson, 1930.*

67   SELBORNE ECHO   February 12, 1778

In a district so diversified as this, so full of hollow vales and hanging woods, it is no wonder that echoes should abound. Many we have discovered that return the cry of a pack of dogs, the notes of a hunting-horn, a tunable ring of bells, or the melody of birds, very agreeably: but we were still at a loss for a polysyllabical, articulate echo, till a young gentleman, who had parted from his company in a summer evening walk, and was calling after them stumbled upon a very curious one in a spot where it might least be expected. At first he was much surprised, and could not be persuaded but that he was mocked by some boy; but, repeating his trials in several languages, and finding his respondent to be a very adroit polyglot, he then discerned the deception.

This echo, in an evening, before rural noises cease, would repeat ten syllables most articulately and distinctly, especially if quick dactyls were chosen. The last syllables of

'Tityre, tu patulae recubans . . .'

were as audibly and intelligibly returned as the first: and there is no doubt, could trial have been made, but that at midnight, when the air is very elastic, and a dead stillness prevails, one or two syllables more might have been obtained; but the distance rendered so late an experiment very inconvenient.

Quick dactyls, we observed, succeeded best; for when we came to try its powers in slow, heavy, embarrassed spondees of the same number of syllables,

'Monstrum horrendum, informe, ingens . . .'

we could perceive a return of four or five.

All echoes have some one place to which they are returned stronger and more distinct than to any other; and that is always the place that lies at right angles with the object of repercussion, and is not too near, nor too far off. Buildings, or naked rocks, re-echo much more articulately than hanging woods or vales; because in the latter the voice is as it were entangled, and embarrassed in the covert, and weakened in the rebound.

The true object of this echo, as we found by various experiments, is the stone-built, tiled hop-kiln in *Gally-lane*, which measures in front 40 feet, and from the ground to the eaves 12 feet. The true *centrum phonicum*, or just distance, is one particular spot in the *King's-field*, in the path to *Nore-hill*, on the very brink of the steep balk above the hollow cart way. In this case there is no choice of distance; but the path, by meer contingency, happens to be the lucky, the identical spot, because the ground rises or falls so immediately, if the speaker either retires or advances, that his mouth would at once be above or below the object.

We measured this polysyllabical echo with great exactness, and found the distance to fall very short of Dr. *Plot's* rule for distant articulation: for the Doctor, in his history of *Oxfordshire*, allows 120 feet for the return of each syllable distinctly: hence this echo, which gives ten distinct syllables, ought to measure 400 yards, or 120 feet to each syllable; whereas our distance is only 258 yards, or near 75 feet, to each syllable. Thus our measure falls short of the Doctor's, as five to eight: but then it must be acknowledged that this candid philosopher was convinced afterwards, that some latitude must be admitted of in the distance of echoes according to time and place.

When experiments of this sort are making, it should always be remembered that weather and the time of day have a vast influence on an echo; for a dull, heavy, moist air deadens and clogs the sound; and hot sunshine renders the air thin and weak, and deprives it of all its springiness; and a ruffling wind quite defeats the whole. In a still, clear, dewy evening the air is most elastic; and perhaps the later the hour the more so.

Echo has always been so amusing to the imagination, that the poets have personified her; and in their hands she has been the occasion of many a beautiful fiction. Nor need the gravest man be ashamed to appear taken with such a phænomenon, since it may become the subject of philosophical or mathematical inquiries.

From The Natural History of Selborne *by Gilbert White, 1789.*

68 THE INVENTION OF ARTS April 29, 1779

In the most ancient Books, sacred as well as profane, the memory is preserved of a certain time when men lived upon the natural fruits of the

Earth, not prepared by fire; and these writers agree that it was a life infinitely happier than the life we now lead, subsisting upon the fruits of the Earth, raised by much art and labour, and prepared often with no less art, and strangely mixed and compounded before they are thought proper to be food for us. According to Hesiod, we were deprived of the happiness of this life, in punishment of Prometheus' theft of the fire from Heaven. But, according to Moses, we forfeited it by eating of the tree of Knowledge. If we are to understand both these accounts as allegorical, I think Moses' allegory is by far the best; for it is undoubtedly the improvement that men have made in Knowledge, by the invention of Arts, that has been the cause of all their misery.

From a letter of Lord Monboddo to John Hope, printed in Lord Monboddo and his Contemporaries *by William Knight, 1900.*

69   LETTER TO MATTHEW BOULTON   June 30, 1779

Birmingham.

Hallelujah! Hallelujee!
We have concluded with Hawkesbury,
217*l*. per annum from Lady-day last;
275*l*.5s. for time past; 157*l*. on account.
We make them a present of 100 guineas –
Peace and good-fellowship on earth –
Perrins and Evans to be dismissed –
3 more engines wanted in Cornwall –
Dudley repentant and amendant –

Yours rejoicing,
JAMES WATT.

Printed in Lives of Boulton and Watt *by Samuel Smiles, 1865.*

70   THE MOB   October 9, 1779

I wrote to my dear friend last from Bolton, and I mention'd the mob which had assembled in that neighbourhood; but they had not then done much mischief; they only destroyed a small engine or two near Chowbent. We met them on Saturday morning, but I apprehend what we saw were not the main body; for on the same day, in the afternoon, a capital engine or mill, in the manner of Arcrites, and in which he is a partner, near Chorley, was attacked; but from its peculiar situation they could approach to it by one passage only; and this circumstance enabled the owner, with the assistance of a few neighbours, to repulse the enemy and preserve the mill for that time. Two of the mob were shot dead upon the spot, one drowned, and several wounded. The mob had no fire-arms, and did not expect so warm a reception. They were greatly exasperated, and vowed revenge; accordingly they spent all Sunday and Monday morning in collecting fire-arms and ammunition and melting their pewter dishes into bullets. They were now join'd by the Duke of Bridgewater's colliers and others, to the number, we are told, of eight thousand, and march'd by beat of drum and with colours flying to the mill, where they met with a repulse on Saturday. They found Sir Richard Clayton guarding the place with fifty Invalids armed, but this handful were by no means a match for enraged thousands; they (the Invalids) therefore contented themselves with looking on, while the mob completely destroyed a set of mills valued at 10,000*l*.

This was Monday's employment. On Tuesday morning we heard their drum at about two miles distance from Bolton, a little before we left the place, and their professed design was to take Bolton, Manchester, and Stockport in their way to Crumford, and to destroy all the engines, not only on these places, but throughout all England. How far they will be able to put their threats into execution time alone can discover.

From a letter of Josiah Wedgwood to Thomas Bentley, published in A Group of Englishmen *by Eliza Meteyard, 1871.*

Here perhaps for the first time among these images there clearly appears the image of 'the mob'. I mention this not because it came into being now but because 'the mob' is one of the principal actors in the great struggles of the next seventy years – and the transformation of the mob into the ordered and disciplined demonstration of the 19th century is one of the clearest signs of increasing political consciousness. It is not too early to note here that the shooting begins on the side of the forces of so-called Law and Order: and that it produces immediate organisation, discipline, drum and colours etc.

71 BLIND JOHN METCALF 1782

With the assistance only of a long staff, I have several times met this man traversing the road, ascending precipices, exploring valleys and investigating their several extents, forms, and situations, so as to answer his designs in the best manner. The plans which he makes, and the estimates he prepares, are done in a method peculiar to himself; and of which he cannot well convey the meaning of to others. His abilities, in this respect, are, nevertheless, so great, that he finds constant employment. Most of the roads over the Peak in Derbyshire have been altered by his directions; particularly those in the vicinity of Buxton: and he at this time constructing a new one betwixt Wilmslow and Congleton to open a communication to the great London road, without being obliged to pass over the mountains. I have met this blind projector while engaged in making his survey. He was alone as usual, and, amongst other conversation, I made some enquiries respecting this new road. It was really astonishing to hear with what accuracy he described its course and the nature of the different soils through which it was conducted. Having mentioned to him a boggy piece of ground it passed through, he observed that 'that was the only place he had doubts concerning, and that he was apprehensive they had, contrary to his directions, been too sparing of their materials.'

From 'Observations on Blindness and on the Employment of the other Senses to supply the Loss of Sight' by Mr Bew, printed in Memoirs of the Literary and Philosophical Society of Manchester. *Paper read April 17, 1782.*

72   THE COMPOSITION OF WATER   April 26, 1783

The same ingenious philosopher (*Dr Priestley*) mixed together certain proportions of pure dry dephlogisticated air and of pure dry inflammable air in a strong glass vessel, closely shut, and then set them on fire by means of the electric spark. The first effect was the appearance of red heat or inflammation in the airs, which was soon followed by the glass vessel becoming hot. The heat gradually pervaded the glass, and was dissipated in the circumambient air, and as the glass grew cool, a mist or visible vapour appeared in it, which was condensed on the glass in the form of moisture or dew. When the glass was cooled to the temperature of the atmosphere, if the vessel was opened, with its mouth immersed in water or mercury, so much of these liquids entered as was sufficient to fill the glass within about 1/200th part of its whole contents; and this small residuum may safely be concluded to have been occasioned by some impurity in one or both kinds of air. The moisture adhering to the glass, after these deflagrations, being wiped off, or sucked up by a small piece of sponge paper, first carefully weighed, was found to be exactly, or very nearly, equal in weight to the airs employed. In some experiments, but not in all, a small quantity of a sooty-like matter was found adhering to the inside of the glass. The whole quantity of sooty-like matter was too small to be an object of consideration, particularly as it did not occur in all experiments.

Let us now consider what obviously happens in the case of the deflagration of the inflammable and dephlogisticated air. These two kinds of air unite with violence; they become red-hot, and upon cooling totally disappear. When the vessel is cooled a quantity of water is found in it equal to the weight of the air employed. The water is then the only remaining product of the process, and *water, light,* and *heat* are all the products.

Are we not, then, authorized to conclude that water is composed of dephlogisticated air and phlogiston, deprived of part of their latent or elementary heat; that dephlogisticated or pure air is composed of water deprived of its phlogiston, and united to elementary heat and light; and that the latter are contained in it in a latent state, so as not to be sensible to the thermometer or to the eye; and if light be only a modification of heat, or a circumstance attending it, or a component part of the inflammable air, then pure or dephlogisticated air is composed of water deprived of its phlogiston and united to elementary heat.

From a letter of James Watt, printed in Correspondence of the late James Watt, on his discovery of the Theory of the Composition of Water, *edited by J.P. Muirhead, 1846.*

The shape of this image is like a prelude and fugue – the prelude by Priestley, the fugue by Watt.

This classic discovery-experiment is an example of the repeatable, as a poem or piece of music is a recipe for a repeatable performance. Most scientific work is incompatible with poetic expression for one simple reason, that our interest in poetry does not lie in things, discoveries, inventions, formulae themselves but in their effect on people. In only a few pieces of purely scientific notation are the people *visible – often as here in the first account, in the first experiment, they are.*

Automatic notation – avoiding people, as in mathematics – and supposedly – 'Photogenic Drawing' – avoiding passing through the medium of a human being.

73 COALBROOK DALE 1783

Coalbrook Dale itself is a very romantic spot, it is a winding glen between two immense hills which break into various forms, and all thickly covered with wood, forming the most beautiful sheets of hanging wood. Indeed too beautiful to be much in unison with that variety of horrors art has spread at the bottom; the noise of the forges, mills, &c., with all their vast machinery, the flames bursting from the furnaces with the burning of the coal and the smoak of the lime kilns, are altogether sublime, and would unite well with craggy and bare rocks, like St. Vincent's at Bristol.

From Annals of Agriculture, *Vol.IV, by Arthur Young, 1785.*

74 THE EVIL ONE 1784

(At the time Mr Murdock was making his experiments with his locomotive engine, he greatly alarmed the clergyman of the parish of Redruth.) One night, after returning from his duties at the mine, he wished to put to the test the power of his engine; and, as railroads were then unknown, he had recourse to the walk leading to the church, which was situated about a mile from the town. This was rather narrow, but kept rolled like a garden walk, and bounded on each side by high hedges. The night was dark, and he alone sallied out with his engine. He lighted the fire or lamp under the boiler, and off started the locomotive with the maker in full chase after it. Shortly after he heard distant shouting, like that of despair; it was too dark to discern objects, but he soon found that the cries for assistance proceeded from the worthy pastor, who, going into the town, on business, was met in this lonely road by the fiery monster, whom he subsequently declared he took to be the Evil One *in propria persona*.

By William Buckle, quoted in Origin and Progress of the Mechanical Inventions of James Watt *by J.P. Muirhead, 1854.*

75 THE FIRST AËRIAL VOYAGE September 15, 1784

A little before two o'clock on Wednesday, Mr Biggin and myself were prepared for our expedition. His attention was allotted to the philosophical experiments and observations, mine to the conduct of the Machine, and the use of the vertical cars, in depressing the Balloon at pleasure.

The impatience of the multitude, made it unadviseable to proceed in filling the Balloon so as to give it the force it was intended to have: the process being therefore stopped, I retired for a few minutes to recollect and refresh myself previous to my departure, when a servant brought me a sudden account that by the falling of one of the masts which had been erected for the purpose of suspending the Balloon while filling, it had received a material injury which might possibly retard, if not prevent my voyage. I hastened instantaneously from the Armory House, where I then was, and though I was happy to find that the accident was prevented by giving the falling fixture an opposite direction, yet I was so extremely shocked at the danger that menaced me, and the word I had received, that I did not possess myself or recover the effect of my apprehension during the remainder of my stay on the earth. The consequence was, that in the convulsion of my ideas, I forgot to supply myself with those instruments of observation which had been appointed for the voyage. On ballancing the rising force of the Balloon, it was supposed incapable of taking up Mr Biggin with me, (whether he felt the most regret in relinquishing his design, or I in being deprived of his company it may be difficult to determine) but we were before a Tribunal, where an immediate decision was necessary, for hesitation and delay would have been construed into guilt, and the displeasure impending over us would have been fatal, if in one moment he had not the heroism to leave the gallery, and I the resolution to go alone. I now determined on my immediate ascension, being assured by the dread of any accident which might consign me and my Balloon to the fury of the populace, whose impatience had wrought them up to a degree of ferment. An affecting, because unpremeditated testimony of approbation and interest in my fate, was here given. The Prince of Wales, and the whole

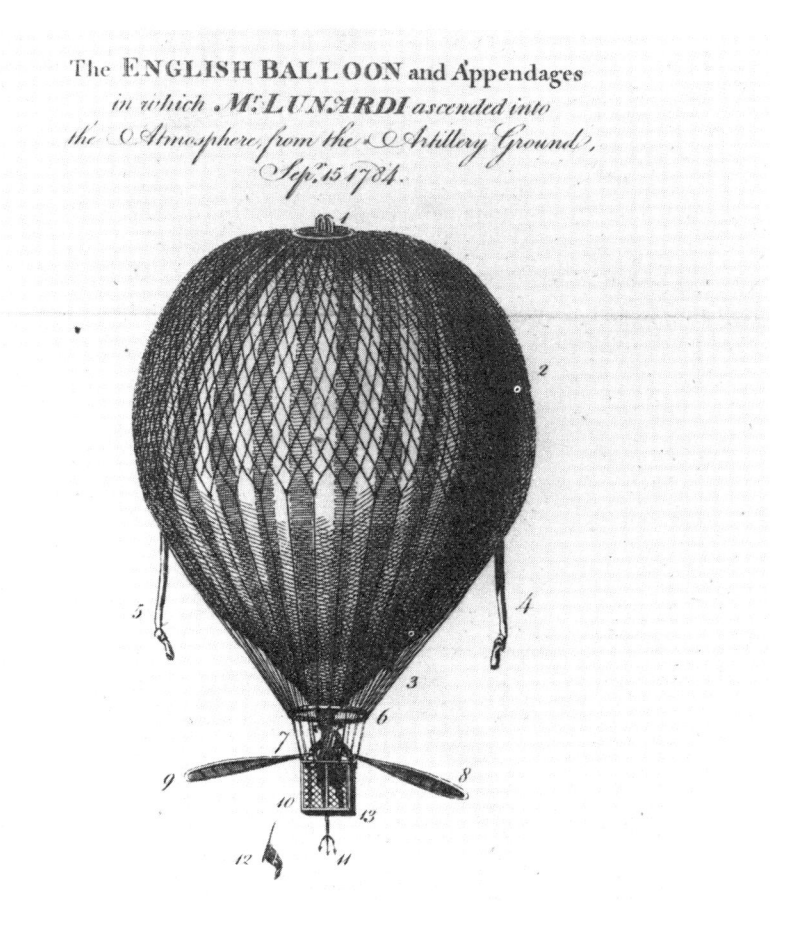

The ENGLISH BALLOON and Appendages in which Mr. LUNARDI ascended into the Atmosphere, from the Artillery Ground, Sep.r 15 1784.

surrounding assembly, almost at one instant, took off their hats, hailed my resolution, and expressed the kindest and most cordial wishes for my safety and success. At five minutes after two, the last gun was fired, the cords divided, and the Balloon rose, the company returning my signals of adieu with the most unfeigned acclamations and applauses. The effect was, that of a miracle, on the multitudes which surrounded the place; and they passed from incredulity and menace, into the most extravagant expressions of approbation and joy.

At the height of twenty yards, the Balloon was a little depressed by the wind, which had a fine effect; it held me over the ground for a few seconds, and seemed to pause majestically before its departure.

On discharging a part of the ballast, it ascended to the height of two hundred yards. As a multitude lay before me of a hundred and fifty thousand people, who had not seen my ascent from the ground, I had recourse to every stratagem to let them know I was in the gallery, and they literally rent the air with their acclamations and applause. In these stratagems I devoted my flag, and worked my oars, one of which was immediately broken, and fell from me, a pidgeon too escaped, which, with a dog, and cat, were the only companions of my excursion.

When the thermometer had fallen from 68°. to 61°. I perceived a great difference in the temperature of the air. I became very cold and found it necessary to take a few glasses of wine. I likewise eat the leg of a chicken, but my bread and other provisions had been rendered useless, by being mixed with the sand, which I carried as ballast.

When the thermometer was at fifty, the effect of the atmosphere and the combination of circumstances around, produced a calm delight, which is inexpressible, and which no situation on earth could give. The stillness, extent, and magnificence of the scene, rendered it highly awful. My horizon seemed a perfect circle; the terminating line several hundred miles in circumference. This I conjectured from the view of London; the extreme points of which, formed an angle of only a few degrees. It was so reduced on the great scale before me, that I can find no simile to convey an idea of it. I could distinguish Saint Paul's and other churches, from the houses. I saw the streets as lines, all animated with beings, whom I knew to be men and women, but which I should otherwise have had a difficulty in describing. It was an enormous bee-hive, but the industry of it was suspended. All the moving mass seemed to have no object but myself, and the transition from the suspicion, and perhaps contempt of the preceding hour, to the affectionate transport, admiration and glory of the present moment, was not without its effect on my mind. I recollected the puns* on my name, and was glad to find myself calm. I had soared from the apprehensions and anxieties of the Artillery Ground, and felt as if I had left behind me all the cares and passions that molest mankind.

From An Account of the First Aërial Voyage in England *by Vincent Lunardi, 1784.*

76 ELIZABETH BRETT, SPINSTER   September 16, 1784

The voluntary declaration and deposition on oath of ELIZABETH BRETT, Spinster, servant to Mr. THOMAS READ, Farmer, in the parish of Standon, in the county of Herts.

THIS Deponent on her oath saith, that on Wednesday, the 15th day of September, instant, between four and five o'clock in the afternoon, she, this Deponent, being then at work in her master's brew-house, heard an uncommon and loud noise, which on attending to it, she conceived to be the sound of men singing, as they returned from harvest home. That upon

---

* In some of the papers, witticisms appeared on the affinity of, Lunatic and Lunardi.

going to the door of the house she perceived a strange large body in the air, and on approaching it in a meadow-field near the house, called Long Mead, she perceived a man in it; that the person in the Machine, which she knew not what to make of, but which the person in it called an Air Balloon, called to her to take hold of the rope, which she did accordingly; that John Mills and George Philips, labourers with said Mr. Thomas Read, came up soon after, and being likewise requested to assist in holding the rope, both made their excuses, one of them, George Philips, saying he was too short, and John Mills saying that he did not like it; that this Deponent continued to hold the rope till some other harvest men of Mr. Benjamin Robinson, of High Cross came up, by whose assistance the machine was held down till the person got out of the machine; and this Deponent, further upon her oath saith, that the person now present, and shewn to her by William Baker, Esq. the justice of peace before whom this Deposition is taken, as Mr. Vincent Lunardi, was the person who called to me from the Machine, as above stated, and who descended therefrom in the said field, called Long Meadow.

her
ELIZABETH × BRETT
mark

Sworn before me this 16th day of September, 1784, at Barford Bury, in the County of Hertford, aforesaid.

WILLIAM BAKER.

From the Appendix to An Account of the First Aërial Voyage in England *by Vincent Lunardi, 1784.*

77   FARM SERVANTS   September 27, 1784

This morning, rode to 'POLESWORTH STATUTE:' a hiring place for farm servants; – the only one, of any note, in *this* part of the country; and, probably, the largest meeting of the kind, in England. Servants come (particularly out of Leicestershire) five and twenty or thirty miles to it, on foot! The number of servants collected together, in the 'statute yard,' has been estimated at two to three thousand. A number, however, which is the less extraordinary, as Polesworth being the only place, in this district, and this the only day, – farm servants, for several miles round, consider themselves as liberated from servitude, on this day.

Formerly, much rioting and disturbance took place, at this meeting; arising, principally, from gaming tables, which were then allowed, and for want of civil officers to keep the peace. But, by the spirited exertions of the present high constable, Mr. LAKING, these riots have been suppressed, and prevented.

The principal nuisance, at present, arises from groups of BALLADSINGERS, disseminating sentiments of dissipation, on minds which ought to be trained to industry and frugality. A ballad goes a great way towards forming the morals of rustics; and if, instead of the trash which is everywhere, at present, dealt out, at all their meetings, songs in praise of conjugal happiness, and a country life, were substituted, fortunate might be the effects.

If a Lord Chamberlain have the power of control, in the theatres, where the audience might, *now*, be presumed to be *themselves* sufficient judges, how much more requisite it appears, that a high constable, or a higher officer, should exercise a similar authority, over the productions to be delivered at a fair or a statute.

From The Rural Economy of the Midland Counties *by William Marshall, 2nd edition, 1796.*

78 THE PANTHEON December 1784

A dark day in December is not so well adapted for a view of the Pantheon, as a dark night; for, like other beauties, it is best seen by candle-light; yet even then, its grandeur might easily be discovered through the dark gloom of winter.

The lamps are ranged in curious devices; I was assured, that 20,000 lights are sometimes burning at once, though far from being the largest room I have seen. These, reflected from an immense number of looking-glasses, must have an astonishing effect. The sight, and the money for admittance, bear no proportion.

The first object which presented itself was Lunardi's balloon, suspended from the center of the dome, like a vast umbrella from Brobdignagg; and instead of the soft music of the place, a round bellied smith (for everything here seems executed in curve lines) who was altering it, sounded the hammer in the Birmingham tone.

Eleven beautiful ladies also, sat in a circle, repairing it with their needles, like the nymphs in Romance, fitting out their airy knight.

From A Journey from Birmingham to London *by William Hutton, 1785.*

79 YOUNG GEORGE CROMPTON c.1785

When I was quite a child my father removed from Hall-i'th'-Wood to Oldham, and there two brothers and a sister were born. I recollect that soon after I was able to walk I was employed in the cotton manufacture. My mother used to bat the cotton wool on a wire riddle. It was then put into a deep brown mug with a strong ley of soap suds. My mother then tucked up my petticoats about my waist, and put me in the tub to tread upon the cotton at the bottom. When a second riddleful was batted I was lifted out and it was placed in the mug, and I again trode it down. This process was continued until the mug became so full that I could no longer safely stand in it, when a chair was placed beside it, and I held on by the back. When the mug was quite full, the soap suds were poured off, and each separate dollop of wool well squeezed to free it from moisture. They were then placed on the bread-rack under the beams of the kitchen-loft to dry. My mother and my grandmother carded the cotton by hand, taking one of the dollops at a time on the simple hand-cards. When carded they were put aside in separate parcels ready for spinning.

From an interview given May 1854 in The Life and Times of Samuel Crompton *by G.J. French, 1860.*

80 OLD GEORGE BARWELL October 3, 1785

It having always appeared to me incomprehensible, how a common farm laborer, who perhaps does not earn more than six or seven shillings a week, rears a large family, as many a one does, – I desired old George Barwell, who has brought up five or six sons and daughters, to clear up the mystery.

He acknowledges that he has frequently been 'hard put to it'. He has sometimes barely had bread for his children: not a morsel for himself! having often made dinner off raw hog peas: saying, that he has taken a handful of peas, and ate them with as much satisfaction as, in general, he has eaten better dinners: adding, that they agreed with him very well, and that he was as able to work upon them, as upon other food: closing his remarks with the trite maxim – breathed out with an involuntary sigh – 'Ay, no man knows what he can do, till he's put to it.'

Since his children have been grown up, and able to support themselves, the old man has saved, by the same industry and frugality which supported his family in his younger days, enough to support himself in his old age! What a credit to the species!

From The Rural Economy of the Midland Counties *by William Marshall, 2nd edition, published 1796.*

81 RICHARD REYNOLDS c.1785

He was at that time residing in the beautiful valley of the Severn, in Coalbrook Dale. The large iron works carried on there, where the roaring of the blast furnaces, the long beds of glowing coke, the jets of flame and showers of sparks, and the stalwart forms of the various forgemen, mingled with the woods, the rocks, and caverns, or reflected in the broad waters of the Severn, gave it a peculiarity of appearance which I have never seen elsewhere. Nor were its moral less distinguished than its physical peculiarities.

The beautiful village of Madeley, the abode of the holy William Fletcher and of his equally remarkable wife, was only about a mile distant from the Dale. The clergyman of the parish was a devout and assiduous pastor of his flock, and all the firm of partners in the well-known company of Coalbrook Dale, with their families, were amongst the most strict, and excellent, and beneficent members of the Society of Friends. Perfect unanimity reigned amongst them: each and all seemed, before all other interests, to have it at heart to further the kingdom of Christ by self-consecration to God, and brotherly love.

From the Autobiography in The Life of Mary Anne SchimmelPenninck, *edited by Christiana Hankin, 1858.*

82 BANKS c.1785

I was surprised, and agreeably amused, with the following experiment. I covered a paper about four inches square with yellow, and with a pen filled with a blue colour wrote upon the middle of it the words BANKS in capitals, as in fig. 5, and sitting with my back to the sun, fixed my eyes for a minute exactly on the centre of the letter N in the middle of the word; after closing my eyes, and shading them somewhat with my hand, the word was distinctly seen in the spectrum in yellow letters on a blue field; and then, on opening my eyes on a yellowish wall at twenty feet distance, the magnified name of BANKS appeared written on the wall in golden characters.

BANKS.

From Zoonomia, *Vol.I, Section XL, 10, by Erasmus Darwin, 1796.*

83 THE LUNATICS c.1787

We had many interesting visitors at Barr. My father was a man of superior intellectual endowments; he had much taste for the exact sciences, in which he was eminently skilled. He was often deeply occupied in courses of experiments on optics and colours, and also on electricity and chemistry. He had long been a member of the Royal Society, and was one of the earliest members of the Linnaean Society. These tastes led to an intercourse with others of the like pursuits. My father belonged to a little society of gifted men, who, spending a day alternately once a month at the house of each of its members, were called the Lunar Society. Amongst them were Mr Boulton, the father of Birmingham, and the institutor of the Mint there; and his partner, Mr Watt, whose immense general knowledge was the delight of all who knew him, and whose discovery in the application of steam has revolutionized the process of manufactures and of land and ocean travel through the whole civilised world. Captain Keir, also, was one of this intellectual galaxy; he was the wit, the man of the world, the finished gentleman, who gave life and animation to the party. He often brought with him his intimate friends Mr Edgeworth and Mr Day. To this society also belonged the celebrated Dr Withering, distinguished alike in botany and medicine; and of whom it was said, years afterwards, when his life was terminating by a lingering consumption, 'The Flower of Physic is indeed Withering.' Then came Dr Stoke, profoundly scientific and eminently absent. On one occasion, when the Lunar meeting, or 'Lunatics,' as our butler called them, were seated at dinner, a blazing fire being in the room, we were astonished by hearing a sudden *hissing* noise, and seeing a large and beautiful yellow and black snake rushing about the room. My dear mother, who saw it was not venomous, said to me: 'Mary Anne go and catch that snake;' which, after some trouble, and thinking all the while of little Harry Sandford and Tommy Merton, I succeeded in accomplishing. We were wondering where it could have come from, when Dr Stoke said that, as he was riding along, he had seen the poor animal frozen on a bank, and put it in his pocket to dissect, but the snake had thawed, and escaped from his pocket. The doctor praised me very much for my prowess in the capture of the snake, and as a reward, he made me a present of my prisoner, which I long kept in a glass jar, and carefully tended every day; at last, however, I gave him his freedom.

From the Autobiography in The Life of Mary Anne SchimmelPenninck, *edited by Christiana Hankin, 1858.*

84   YEAR 1788   1788

It had been often remarked by ingenious men, that the Brawl burn, which ran through the parish, though a small, was yet a rapid stream, and had a wonderful capacity for damming, and to turn mills. From the time that the Irville water deserted its channel this brook grew into repute, and several mills and dams had been erected on its course. In this year a proposal came from Glasgow to build a cotton-mill on its banks, beneath the Witchlinn, which being on a corner of the Wheatrig, the property of Mr Cayenne, he not only consented thereto, but took a part in the profit or loss therein; and, being a man of great activity, though we thought him, for many a day, a serpent plague sent upon the parish, he proved thereby one of our greatest benefactors. The cotton-mill was built, and a spacious fabric it was – nothing like it had been seen before in our day and generation – and, for the people that were brought to work in it, a new town was built in the vicinity, which Mr Cayenne, the same being founded on his land, called Cayenneville, the name of the plantation in Virginia that had been taken from him by the rebellious Americans. From that day Fortune was lavish of her favours upon him; his property swelled, and grew in the most extraordinary manner, and the whole countryside was stirring with a new life. For, when the mill was set agoing, he got weavers of muslin established in Cayenneville; and shortly after, but that did not take place till the year following, he brought women all the way from the neighbourhood of Manchester in England, to teach the lassie bairns in our old clachan tambouring.

Some of the ancient families, in their turreted houses, were not pleased with this innovation, especially when they saw the handsome dwellings that were built for the weavers of the mills, and the unstinted hand that supplied the wealth required for the carrying on of the business. It sank their pride into insignificance, and many of them would almost rather have wanted the rise that took place in the value of their lands, than have seen this incoming of what they called o'er-sea speculation. But, saving the building of the cotton-mill, and the beginning of Cayenneville, nothing more memorable happened in this year, still it was a year of great activity. The minds of men were given to new enterprises; a new genius, as it were, had descended upon the earth, and there was an erect and outlooking spirit abroad that was not to be satisfied with the taciturn regularity of ancient affairs.

From The Annals of the Parish *by John Galt, written 1813, published 1821.*

85   IN THE CAVERN   1788

There is a bright spot seen in the corner of the eye, when we face a window, which is much attended to by portrait painters; this is the light reflected from the spherical surface of the polished corner, and brought to a focus; if the observer is placed in this focus, he sees the image of the window; if he is placed before or behind the focus, he only sees a luminous spot, which is more luminous and of less extent, the nearer he approaches to the focus. The luminous appearance of the eyes of animals in the dusky corners of a room, or in holes in the earth, may arise in some instances from the same principle; viz. the reflection of the light from the spherical cornea; which will be coloured red or blue in some degree by the morning, evening, or meridian light; or by the objects from which the light is previously reflected. In the cavern at Colebrook Dale, where the mineral tar exsudes, the eyes of the horse, which was drawing a cart from within towards the mouth of it, appeared like two balls of phosphorus, when he was above 100 yards off, and for a long time before any other part of the animal was visible. In this case I suspect the luminous appearance to have been owing to the light, which had entered the eye, being reflected from the back surface of the vitreous humour, and thence emerging again in parallel rays from the animal's eye, as it does from the back surface of the drops of the rainbow, and from the water-drops which lie, perhaps without contact, on cabbage-leaves, and have the brilliancy of quick silver. This accounts for this luminous appearance being seen in those animals which have large apertures in their iris, as in cats and horses, and is the only part visible in obscure places, because this is a better reflecting surface than any other part of the animal. If any of these emergent rays from the animal's eye can be supposed to have been reflected from the choroid coat through the semi-transparent retina, this would account for the coloured glare of the eyes of dogs or cats and rabbits in dark corners.

From Additional Note III to The Botanic Garden, *Part 1: The Economy of Vegetation, by Erasmus Darwin, 1791.*

86 THE FRENCH REVOLUTION   Summer 1789

It was one evening in this summer, towards the end of July, I well remember, the glorious sun was declining behind the distant hills, and the long shadows were spreading over the woods and meadows, when we saw at a distance a vehicle (usually employed to carry servants to town or church) returning at more than its usual speed. After some minutes the door of the drawing-room opened, and in burst Harry, William Priestley's brother, a youth of sixteen or seventeen, waving his hat, and crying out, 'Hurray! Liberty, Reason, brotherly love for ever! Down with kingcraft and priestcraft. The majesty of the People for ever! France is free, the Bastille is taken: William was there, and helping. I have just got a letter from him. He has put up the picture of the Bastille, and two stones from its ruins, for you,' (addressing himself to me,) 'which you will soon receive; but come, you must hear his letter.' We all stood thunderstruck.

From the Autobiography in The Life of Mary Anne SchimmelPenninck, *edited by Christiana Hankin, 1858.*

87   THE CHILDHOOD OF   Autumn 1789
MARY ANNE SCHIMMELPENNINCK

I

One other picture I will recall. It was a scene in the drawing-room. My cousin had been consulting Dr Darwin, and was joined there by my mother and Mr Berrington. I did not consider myself, a child, as part of the company. It would be impossible perhaps to select four persons of more strongly marked characters, and yet more dissimilar one to another. There was my mother, lofty in grandeur of heart, and in philosophic dignity of mind, eminent for beauty, and for a severe simplicity combined with richness of costume. Then my cousin Priscilla, almost ethereal in the expression of purity and holiness, her countenance continually growing upon the heart of the beholder, and replete with the charm which reveals a deep tranquillity in eternal things, while the surface is plastic to varying thought and emotion; like the immortal music of Palestrina, which flows on with one uniform soul-filling harmony, the fundamental bass continuing its uninterrupted stream, while the superficial parts display endless variety, grace, and adornment. Then came Mr Berrington's lofty, aristocratic figure, his intellectual and perhaps proud bearing, as he held up his glass, and looked, with a slightly sarcastic and yet playful air, on those around him. And I still seem to see Dr Darwin sitting on the sofa, as he gazed with almost a sneer on the beauty before him, beauty not merely physical, but yet more moral and intellectual; and never shall I forget the contrast between his figure and the fragile form of my cousin, who, as his patient, sat next him; fragile, indeed, she appeared, as though a breath might annihilate her; and yet there was that about her which seemed as a panoply of Divine strength, and before which the shafts of Dr Darwin's wit against Divine truth, aimed cautiously at first, but afterwards more openly, recoiled innocuous. 'My dear Madam,' said he, 'you have but one complaint; it is one ladies are very subject to, and it is the worst of all complaints; and that is, having a conscience. Do get rid of it with all speed; few people have health or strength enough to keep such a luxury, for utility I cannot call it.'

One of the party having expressed the hope that one day he would receive Christianity, he replied, 'Before I do that, you Christians must all be agreed. The other morning I received two parcels; one containing a work of Dr Priestley's, proving there is no spirit, the other a work by Berkeley, Bishop of Cloyne, proving there is no matter. What am I to believe amongst you all?' I shall never forget the look with which this was said.

II

Dr Darwin often used to say, 'Man is an eating animal, a drinking animal, and a sleeping animal, and one placed in a material world, which alone furnishes all the human animal can desire. He is gifted besides with knowing faculties, practically to explore and to apply the resources of this world to his use. These are realities. All else is nothing; conscience and sentiment are mere figments of the imagination. Man has but five gates of knowledge, the five senses; he can know nothing but through them; all else is a vain fancy, and as for the being of a God, the existence of a soul, or a world to come, who can know anything about them? Depend upon it, my dear Madam, these are only the bugbears by which men of sense govern fools; nothing is real that is not an object of sense.'

As I heard these things, and remembered the high esteem in which Dr Darwin's talents were held, and the respect with which his dicta were listened to, my mind seemed shaken to its centre. I felt perplexed and bewildered. My faith was disturbed even in the little I knew. Yet I had a latent misgiving that all these reasonings could not be true, and it sometimes occurred to me that the electric fluid, the magnetic attraction, and power of animal magnetism (then much in vogue), though imponderable and unseen forces, were the most powerful of agents; and that our perception of any substance depends not merely upon its being obvious to our senses, but upon our being gifted with those particular senses which enable us to receive its impressions. If a deaf man go into a ballroom, does the music cease to inspire the dancers because he hears it not? And are we not constantly subject to the power and operation of causes which we have not the faculties to investigate, though we are sensible of their effects? And may not the being of God, the spiritual world, the immortality of the soul, be as important spiritual realities to man as the equally unseen agency of the loadstone and electricity are in the natural world? Such were surmises which often presented themselves to my mind.

III

Even the excellent Dr Priestley, in those days, continually dwelt on the blessings of free inquiry and the overthrow of superstition, and on the coming time when all would be free to carry out their own opinions, and to be occupied in the search after truth, though all probably might come to a different result. Some others there were, not so devout, but more logical, who, taking up the matter where Dr Priestley left it, said that since no positive result could be obtained, the search might as well be spared. Child as I was at the time of the French Revolution, always accustomed to be with my parents and present in their social circle, I was full of intense interest in these things. How often, in a year or two after this period, while I listened to these philosophers, was I reminded of the tiger, which is at first playful as a kitten, but which, when once it has dipped its tongue in blood, assumes the glare of the eye, shoots forth its talons, exchanges its kind purr for a fierce growl or ominous spring, and spares neither friend nor foe in its cruel onslaught.

When I think of these sad times, it has often appeared to me that these philosophers were like ignorant children, who expect beautiful blossoms or fruit to grow if they merely stick severed stems into the ground; while my grandfather, and those who thought with him, were like wise gardeners, who, planting the root and leaving it to be watered by the dews from Heaven, are assured that the germ which contains the vital principle will grow and produce its proper fruit. Blessed is he that exercises himself day and night in the law of the Lord: he shall be like a tree planted by the living waters, that shall produce its fruit in its season, and even its leaves shall not wither.

From the Autobiography in The Life of Mary Anne SchimmelPenninck, *edited by Christiana Hankin, 1858.*

Part Three

1791–1850
Revolution

In consequence of all this preparation, we were informed that, though the trade of Birmingham had never been more brisk, so that hands could not be found to manufacture the goods that were ordered, many of the public-houses were that day full of people, whose horrid execrations against the Dissenters were heard into the streets; and it has been asserted, that some of the master manufacturers had shut up their work-shops, and thereby left their men at full liberty for any mischief.

It has since appeared, that besides the dinner at the hotel, there were also meetings of the opposite party on this fourteenth of July; and those not of the lower class of people, with whom the common ale-houses were filled. These meetings did not rise from their entertainment so early, or with such sobriety, as those who dined at the Hotel; and it was at the breaking up of *their* companies that the Riots commenced. Let the impartial, then, judge to which of the dinners the riot that followed is to be ascribed.

Mr Adam Walker, the ingenious and well-known lecturer in Natural Philosophy, was passing through the town with his wife and family, and dined with me at my own house, for the last time on that day. Before dinner, I had walked to the town with him, and they left me in the evening. Some time after this, three of my intimate friends, whose houses were situated near the same road, and farther from the town than mine, called upon me to congratulate me, and one another, on the dinner having passed over so well; and after chatting cheerfully some time on the subject, they left me just as it was beginning to be dark.

After supper, when I was preparing to amuse myself, as I sometimes did, with a game of backgammon, we were alarmed by some young men rapping violently at the door; and when they were admitted, they appeared to be almost breathless with running. They said that a great mob had assembled at the Hotel, where the company had dined; that after breaking the windows there, they were gone to the New Meeting and were demolishing the pulpit and pews, and that they threatened me and my house. That they should think of molesting *me*, I thought so improbable, that I could hardly give any credit to the story. However, imagining that perhaps some of the mob might come to insult me, I was prevailed upon to leave the house, and meant to go to some neighbour's at a greater distance from the town; but having no apprehension for the house itself, or anything in it, I only went up stairs, and put some papers and other things of value, where I thought that any persons getting into the house would not easily find them. My wife did the same with some things of hers. I then bade the servants keep the doors fastened; if any body should come, to say that I was gone, and if any stones should be thrown at the windows, to keep themselves out of danger, and that I did not doubt but they would go away again.

At this time, which was about half-past nine o'clock, Mr S. Ryland, a friend of mine, came with a chaise, telling us there was no time to lose, but that we must immediately get into it and drive off. Accordingly, we got in with nothing more than the clothes we happened to have on, and drove from the house. But hearing that the mob consisted only of people on foot, and concluding that when they found I was gone off in a chaise, they could not tell whither, they would never think of pursuing me, we went no farther than Mr Russell's, a mile on the same road, and there we continued several hours, Mr Russell himself, and other persons, being upon the road on horseback to get intelligence of what was passing. I also more than once walked about half way back to my own house for the same purpose; and then I saw the fires from the two meeting-houses, which were burning down.

About twelve we were told that some hundreds of the mob were breaking into my house, and that when they had demolished *it*, they would certainly proceed to Mr Russell's. We were persuaded, therefore, to get into the chaise again, and drive off; but we went no farther than Mr Thomas Hawkes's, on Moseley-Green, which is not more than half a mile farther from the town, and there we waited all the night.

It being remarkably calm; and clear moon-light, we could see to a considerable distance, and being upon a rising ground we distinctly heard all that passed at the house, every shout of the mob, and almost every stroke of the instruments they had provided for breaking the doors and furniture. For they could not get any fire, though one of them was heard to offer two guineas for a lighted candle; my son, whom we left behind us, having taken the precaution to put out all the fires in the house, and others of my friends got all the neighbours to do the same. I afterwards heard that much pains was taken, but without effect, to get fire from ny large electrical machine, which stood in the library.

From An Appeal to the Public on the Subject of the Riots in Birmingham *by Joseph Priestley, written and published in 1792.*

Note on 88–96. *In the year 1791 the Birmingham home of Joseph Priestley, scientist, democrat, dissenting minister, was sacked by a mob assembled under the slogan 'For Church and King'. Priestley's own account is given in 88. In the preceding years had grown up simultaneously an increasing consciousness of the brotherhood of man and mechanical inventions destined to alter fundamentally the means of production. This and the following images (88–96) describe, each in its own rhetoric, these developments. Some are apparently of the mind, theoretical, others apparently material, practical: but in fact such distinctions are far too simple. Priestley (88) and Galt (92) describe something of their true and more complex interaction. In Blake's 'London' (94) the fetters of man are hung upon him both inside and out. Tom Poole (95), Somerset yeoman, will take practical steps both towards his brother man and towards better production. He will deal bravely with both these tremendous problems in a few months of disguise. Alas! for the frontal attack: Hannah More (96) was not honest and it flatters her to imagine herself lowering the price of bread rather than writing the* Iliad. *She is not in danger of doing either.*

89 GLEANING 1791

Wilts Summer Assizes, August 6, 1791.
Edward Perry versus Thomas Abree and Margaret his Wife.

Whereas I Margaret Abree, wife of Thomas Abree, of the city of New Sarum, blacksmith, did, during the barley harvest, in the month of September last, many times wilfully and maliciously go into the fields of, and belonging to, Mr Edward Perry, at Clarendon Park, and take with me my children, and did there leaze, collect, and carry away a quantity of barley, in open defiance to, and notwithstanding my being repeatedly forbid, and ordered by the said Edward Perry to quit the said fields, by which the said Edward Perry sustained considerable damage, and very justly commenced his action against me and my husband, and a verdict was given against us, at this assizes, together with the costs of suit, by the judge's certificate.

And whereas the said Edward Perry did direct his counsel to declare in open court, that his only object in prosecuting this action against us was effectually to stop all such illegal and unjust practices in future; and that, notwithstanding the great trouble and expense attending the same, he had no wish to sue our execution, nor proceed further against us, in case he could be satisfied that sufficient has been done to accomplish this his only object with regard to us, and by our example to give others warning.

Now we do hereby declare, that we are fully convinced of the illegality of such proceedings, and that no person has a right to leaze any sort of grain, or to come on any field whatsoever, without the consent of the owner; and are also truly sensible of the obligation we are under to the said Edward Perry for his lenity towards us, inasmuch as the damages given, together with the heavy costs incurred, would have been much greater than we could possibly have discharged, and must have amounted to perpetual imprisonment, as even those who have least disapproved of our conduct, would certainly not have contributed so large a sum to deliver us from the legal consequences of it. And we do hereby faithfully promise never to be guilty of the same, or any like offence in future.

Witness	THOMAS ABREE,
THOMAS OAKFORD	MARGARET ABREE,
	Her x Mark.

'From a Hampshire newspaper', reprinted in The Annals of Agriculture, *Vol.17, 1792.*

90   Epitaph in Whitkirk Parish Church   1792

SACRED TO THE MEMORY
OF JOHN SMEATON, F.R.S.

A Man whom God had endowed with the most extraordinary abilities,
which he indefatigably exerted for the benefit
of Mankind in works of science
And Philosophical research:
More especially as an Engineer and Mechanic. His principal work, the Eddystone Lighthouse, erected on a rock in the open sea, (where one had been washed away by the violence of a storm, and another had been consumed by the rage of fire,) secure in its own stability, and the wise precautions for its safety, seems not unlikely to convey to distant ages, as it does to every Nation of the Globe, the Name of its constructor.

He was born at Austhorpe, June 8, 1724.
And departed this Life October 28, 1792.

Quoted in Lives of the Engineers *by Samuel Smiles, 1861.*

91   Panopticon   1791–92

The Building circular – an iron cage, glazed – a glass lantern about the size of Ranelagh – The Prisoners in their Cells, occupying the Circumference – The Officers, (Governor, Chaplain, Surgeon, &c.) the Centre.

By Blinds, and other contrivances, the Inspectors concealed (except in so far as they think fit to show themselves) from the observation of the Prisoners: hence the sentiment of a sort of invisible omnipresence. – The whole circuit reviewable with little, or, if necessary, without any, change of place.

One Station in the Inspection-Part affording the most perfect view of every Cell, and every part of every Cell, unless where a screen is thought fit occasionally and purposely to be interposed.

Against Fire (if, under a system of constant and universal inspection, any such accident could be apprehended), a pipe, terminating in a flexible hose, for bringing the water down into the central Inspection-Room, from a cistern, of a height sufficient to force it up again by its own pressure, on the mere turning of a cock, and spread it thus over any part within the Building.

For Visitors, at the time of Divine service, an Annular Gallery, rising from a floor laid immediately on the ceiling of the Central Dome, the superior surface of which serves, after descent, for the reception of Ministers, Clerk, and a select part of the Auditory: the Prisoners all round, brought forward, within perfect view and hearing of the Ministers, to the front of their respective Cells.

Solitude, or limited Seclusion, ad libitum. – But, unless for punishment, limited seclusion in assorted companies is preferable: an arrangement, upon this plan alone, exempt from danger. The degree of Seclusion fixed upon may be preserved, in all places, and at all times, inviolate. Hitherto, where solitude has been aimed at, some of its chief purposes have been frustrated by occasional associations.

The Approach, one only – Gates opening into a walled avenue cut through the area. Hence, no strangers near the building without leave, nor without being surveyed from it as they pass, nor without being known to come on purpose. The gates, of open work, to expose hostile mobs: On the other side of the road, a wall with a branch of the road behind, to shelter peaceable passengers from the fire of the building. A mode of fortification like this, if practicable in a city, would have saved the London Prisons, and prevented the unpopular accidents in St George's Fields.

From Panopticon *by Jeremy Bentham.*

Saint Paul's – Panopticon – The Crystal Palace: these three inventions were each symbolic of an epoch but also each the culmination of the period before: St Paul's the culmination of the protestantism of the 17th century; Panopticon the culmination of the rationalism of the 18th century; the Crystal Palace the culmination of the human energy and warmth of the 19th century. But each of course influencing the succeeding period.

1789 – the fall of the Bastille
1791 – Panopticon, the New Bastille

YEAR 1793

On the first night of this year I dreamt a very remarkable dream, which when I now recall to mind, at this distance of time, I cannot but think that there was a cast of prophecy in it. I thought that I stood on the tower of an old popish kirk, looking out of the window upon the kirkyard, where I beheld ancient tombs, with effigies and coats of arms on the wall thereof, and a great gate at the one side, and a door that led into a dark and dismal vault at the other. I thought all the dead, that were lying in the common graves, rose out of their coffins; at the same time, from the old and grand monuments, with the effigies and coats of arms, came the great men, and the kings of the earth with crowns on their heads, and globes and sceptres in their hands.

I stood wondering what was to ensue, when presently I heard the noise of drums and trumpets, and anon I beheld an army with banners entering in at the gate; upon which the kings and the great men came also forth in their power and array, and a dreadful battle was foughten; but the multitude, that had risen from the common graves, stood afar off, and were but lookers-on.

The kings and their host were utterly discomfited. They were driven with in the doors of their monuments, their coats of arms were broken off, and their effigies cast down, and the victors triumphed over them with the flourishes of trumpets and the waving of banners. But while I looked, the vision was changed, and I then beheld a wide and dreary waste, and afar off the steeples of a great city, and a tower in the midst, like the tower of Babel, and on it I could discern written in characters of fire, 'Public Opinion'. While I was pondering on the same, I heard a great shout, and presently the conquerors made their appearance, coming over the desolate moor. They were going in great pride and might towards the city, but an awful burning arose, afar as it were in the darkness, and the flames stood like a tower of fire that reached unto the heavens. And I saw a dreadful hand and an arm stretched from out of the storm, and it swept the fugitives like dust; and in their place I saw a churchyard, as it were cleared and spread around, the graves closed, and the ancient tombs, with their coats of arms and their effigies of stone, all as they were in the beginning. Then I awoke, and behold it was a dream.

This vision perplexed me for many days, and when the news came that the King of France was beheaded by the hands of his people, I received, as it were a token in confirmation of the vision that had been disclosed to me in my sleep, and I preached a discourse on the same, and against the French Revolution, that was thought one of the greatest and soundest sermons that I ever delivered in my pulpit.

On the Monday following, Mr Cayenne, who had been some time before appointed a justice of the peace, came over from Wheatrig House to the Cross Keys, where he sent for me and divers other respectable inhabitants of the clachan, and told us that he was to have a sad business, for a warrant was out to bring before him two democratic weaver lads, on a suspicion of high treason. Scarcely were the words uttered, when they were brought in, and he began asking them how they dared to think of dividing, with their liberty and equality of principles, his and every other man's property in the country. The men answered him in a calm manner, and told him they sought no man's property, but only their own natural rights; upon which he called them traitors and reformers. They denied they were traitors, but confessed they were reformers, and said they knew not how that should be imputed to them as a fault, for that the greatest men of all times had been reformers, – 'Was not,' they said, 'our Lord Jesus Christ a reformer?' 'And what the devil did He make of it?' cried Mr Cayenne, bursting with passion; 'was He not crucified?'

I thought, when I heard these words, that the pillars of the earth sunk beneath me, and that the roof of the house was carried away in a whirlwind.

The drums of my ears crackit, blue starns danced before my sight, and I was fain to leave the house and hie me home to the manse, where I sat down in my study, like a stupefied creature awaiting what would betide. Nothing, however, was found against the weaver lads; but I never from that day could look on Mr Cayenne as a Christian, though surely he was a true government man.

From The Annals of the Parish *by John Galt, written 1813, published 1821.*

93   TOM PAINE   c.1793

One Middleton wakes, as I remember, I, a mere child, sat on the steps of my father's dwelling, watching the holyday folks draw their rush-carts towards the church. They went close past our door; very grand and gaudy the drawers and carts were, with ribbons, and streamers, and banners, and garlands, and silver ornaments, and morrice bells, and other music, quite joyous and delightful. At length came a cart more richly decked than others, on the flake of which behind, was placed the figure of a man, which I thought was a real live being. A rabble which followed the cart, kept throwing stones at the figure, and shouting – 'Tum Pain a Jacobin' – 'Tum Pain a thief' – 'Deawn wi' o' th' Jacobins' – 'Deawn wi' th' Painites,' – whilst others with guns and pistols kept discharging them at the figure. They took care to stop when they came to the residence of a reformer; the shouting and the firing was renewed, and then they moved on. Poor Pain was thus shot in effigy on Saturday; repaired, re-embellished, and again set upright on Sunday; and 'murdered out-and-out' on Monday – being again riddled with shot, and finally burned. I, of course, became a friend of Tom Pain's. Such was one of the modes of annoyance and persecution to which the few, who dared to be honest, were subjected by the sires and grandsires of the present race of reforming Englishmen.

From Early Days *by Samuel Bamford, written 1848.*

94   LONDON   c.1793

> I wander thro' each charter'd street,
> Near where the charter'd Thames does flow,
> And mark in every face I meet
> Marks of weakness, marks of woe.
>
> In every cry of every Man,
> In every Infant's cry of fear,
> In every voice, in every ban,
> The mind-forg'd manacles I hear.

> How the Chimney-sweeper's cry
> Every black'ning Church appalls;
> And the hapless Soldier's sigh
> Runs in blood down Palace walls.
>
> But most thro' midnight streets I hear
> How the youthful Harlot's curse
> Blasts the new born Infant's tear,
> And blights with plagues the Marriage hearse.

From Songs of Experience *by William Blake, 1794.*

Just how much social and economic conditions do affect the poet's vision can be exceptionally well seen by comparing these lines of Blake not only with Wordsworth's London poems ('Earth has not anything to show more fair' etc.) but with the following lines by Sir Humphry Davy, written on his return from a semi-scientific, semi-picturesque tour of France and Italy and the Alps:

London, 1814

> Such art thou! mighty in thy power and pride:
> No city of the earth with thee can vie;
> Along thy streets still flows the unceasing tide
> Of busy thousands. E'en thy misty sky
> Breathes life and motion, and the subject waves,
> That wash thy lofty arches, bear the wings
> Of earthly commerce, where the winds, thy slaves,
> Speed the rich tribute to the ocean kings.

Davy's 'subject waves' are for Blake 'the charter'd Thames'. But then Davy was working directly for and with the ruling class (in the Royal Institution and through the Royal Society) – even if he was apparently in a year or two (1815–17) to give help to the workers underground with the invention of the Safety Lamp. The enormous fuss made of him by the mine-owners of the Northumberland and Durham coalfields suggests another interest in his invention: that it allowed the men to continue working in dangerous conditions and to go on winning coal in pits and at levels otherwise mortal. Of his own politics Davy has left the following intimations:

The unequal division of property and labour, the differences of rank and condition among mankind, are the sources of power in civilised life, its moving causes, and even its very soul.

The quotations above are from Memoirs of the Life of Sir Humphry Davy, *by John Davy, 1836.*
   Blake, however, lived with 'Poverty in Jesus' (see 169, 1827). Nearer to

Blake in many ways and contrasting well with the quotations from Davy is the poem of Clerk-Maxwell (275, 1853):

>In the dense entangled street,
>   Where the web of Trade is weaving ...

95   MY PLAN   June 27, 1793

I will only tell you that I shall set out on my peregrinations some time next week, therefore let me hear from you immediately, that your letter may reach Stowey before I leave it. My plan must be to offer myself to some one in the form of a common workman. This undertaking is, for me, odd, disagreeable, and romantick enough; yet I am convinced of the necessity of it, and I certainly shall attempt it. I expect some curious circumstances will occur, but I shall feel myself very comfortable under my mask, as I design not only changing my dress for the usual habit of a tanner, but my name also to Thomas Adams. When I am fixed at any place, which I shall first endeavour to be at Wantage, I shall write to you, and inform you how I support my new character. Do, in your letter, give me any hints you think will be useful to me in the progress of my undertaking, and also inform me of the yards which you know of in the kingdom, out of London, at all famous for their manufacture; so that, in case I should not be admitted in one, I should have others to apply to.

Your reflections on my emigration perhaps are various. First, you will smile at that transition which I certainly must experience; and, in the next place, you will shake your head at my having neglected acquiring what it was long since my indispensable duty to acquire. But I must tell you if my ideas were only to carry on the trade in the manner my father has done, I need not incur the risque of this adventure. My hope is to increase his trade; and I wish to see every variety of the manufacture, that I may appropriate to myself that which I conceive best. Having now a little leisure, and health and strength enough, I do not think I shall spend a few months unprofitably by applying them to this main object. At the close of my peregrinations, when I have washed my hands clean, and by due ablutions am fit to stand before you, I shall call at Brentford, and then I hope you will find I have not contaminated either mind or manners, by intercourse with those in the society of whom I necessarily must be; but that I have only stooped a little to acquire useful experience, and also to obtain a greater knowledge of that class of life, of which it is our duty to know most, inasmuch as that class most requires our assistance and protection.

From a letter of Tom Poole to S. Purkis, printed in Thomas Poole and his Friends *by Mrs Henry Sandford, 1888.*

Note on 94, 95 and 97. *In Tom Poole's letter (95) and in Blake's 'London' (94) and in the letter about 'Pantisocracy' (97) are presented three different ways of facing the world as it then was. Tom Poole explains to his friend that he is going on his adventure for the good of trade – but I suspect this is a genteel cover for an unformulated, unadmitted desire to go towards the people. This is also covered up by calling the idea 'romantick' and attempting to forestall criticism by laughing at himself and so on. What was there to be ashamed of? In this image it is not Tom Poole who is clearest, but the dim form of the class towards which his helm was pointed.*

Blake, Londoner, is in no such tangle. He has but to wander the streets of London, his native city, with eyes and ears open: in this poem most of all the visionary was seeing reality. He was clear too about the causes of the misery he saw: 'chartered street' – 'chartered Thames'. For the moment at least Blake was not escaping, as 'Coldridge' (i.e. Coleridge) and Southey were planning to do.

96   THE RIOT   November 1793

It has been no small support under the great labour of the Cheap Repository, that it has met with the warm protection of so many excellent persons, and has brought me to the acquaintance of many of the wise and good in very remote parts of the kingdom, who are anxiously catching at even the feeblest attempts to stem that headlong torrent of vice, and that spirit of licentiousness and insurrection, which is threatening to undo us. They would have me to believe, – but I ought not to tell you, it savours so much of arrogance and egotism, (and I should tell it hardly to any one else,) – that a very formidable riot among the colliers in the neighbourhood of Bath, was happily prevented by the ballad of *'The Riot'*. The plan was thoroughly settled; they were resolved to work no more, but to attack first the mills, and then the gentry. A gentleman of large fortune got into their confidence, and a few hundreds were distributed and sung with the effect, as they say, mentioned above. It is fresh proof by what weak instruments evils are now and then prevented. You will be so kind as to thank Mrs Theobald for the subscriptions to Mr Haggitt; and though I ought not to revert to the cheap publications, yet I wish her to know, that the object of the leading tract for the next month is the bad economy of the poor; and that I have been led to it by repeated applications in newspapers. I have endeavoured to show them that their distresses arise nearly as much from their own bad management as from the hardness of the times. It is called 'The Way to Plenty'. You, my dear Madam, will smile to see your friend figuring away in the new character of a cook, furnishing receipts for cheap dishes. It is not, indeed, a very brilliant career, but I feel that the value of a thing lies so much more in its usefulness than its splendour, that I have a notion I should derive more gratification from being able to lower the price of bread than from having written the Iliad.

From a letter of Hannah More to Mrs Boscawen, printed in Memoirs of the Life and Correspondence of Mrs Hannah More *by William Roberts, 3rd edition, 1835.*

97   PANTISOCRACY   September 22, 1794

Coldridge [Coleridge], whom I consider the Principal in the undertaking, and of whom I had heard much before I saw him, is about five and twenty, belongs to the University of Cambridge, possesses splendid abilities – he is, I understand, a shining scholar, gained the prize for the Greek verses the first or second year he entered the University, and is now engaged in publishing a selection of the best modern Latin poems with a poetical translation. He speaks with much elegance and energy, and with uncommon facility, but he, as it generally happens to men of his class, feels the justice of Providence in the want of those inferiour abilities which are necessary to the rational discharge of the common duties of life. His aberrations from prudence, to use his own expression, have been great; but he now promises to be as sober and rational as his most sober friends could wish. In religion he is a Unitarian, if not a Deist, in politicks a Democrat, to the utmost extent of the word.

Southey, who was with him, is of the University of Oxford, a younger man, without the splendid abilities of Coldridge, though possessing much information, particularly metaphysical, and is more violent in his principles than even Coldridge himself. In Religion, shocking to say in a mere Boy as he is, I fear he wavers between Deism and Atheism.

Thus much for the characters of two of the Emigrators. Their plan is as follows: –

Twelve gentlemen of good education and liberal principles are to embark with twelve ladies in April next. Previous to their leaving this country they are to have as much intercourse as possible, in order to ascertain each other's dispositions, and firmly to settle every regulation for the government of their future conduct. Their opinion was that they should fix themselves at – I do not recollect the place, but somewhere in a delightful part of the new back settlements; that each man should labour two or three hours a day, the produce of which labour would, they imagine, be more than sufficient to support the colony. As Adam Smith observes that there is not above one productive man in twenty, they argue that if each laboured the twentieth part of time, it would produce enough to satisfy their wants. The produce of their industry is to be laid up in common for the use of all; and a good library of books is to be collected, and their leisure hours to be spent in study, liberal discussion, and the education of their children. A system for the education of their children is laid down, for which, if this plan at all suits you, I must refer you to the authors of it. The regulations relating to the females strike them as the most difficult; whether the marriage contract shall be dissolved if agreeable to one or both parties, and many other circumstances, are not yet determined. The employments of the women are to be the care of infant children, and other occupations suited to their strength; at the same time the greatest attention is to be paid to the cultivation of their minds. Every one is to enjoy his own religious and political opinions, provided they do not encroach on the rules previously made, which rules, it is unnecessary to add, must in some measure be regulated by the laws of the state which include the district in which they settle. They calculate that each gentleman providing £125 will be sufficient to carry the scheme into execution. Finally, every individual is at liberty, whenever he pleases, to withdraw from the society.

These are the outlines of their plan, and such are their ideas. Could they realise them they would, indeed, realise the age of reason; but, however perfectible human nature may be, I fear it is not yet perfect enough to exist under the regulations of such a system, particularly when the Executors of the plan are taken from a society in a high degree civilised and corrupted. America is certainly a desirable country, so desirable in my eye that, were it not for some insuperable reasons, I would certainly settle there. At some future period I perhaps may. But I think a man would do well first to see the country and his future hopes, before he removes his connections or any large portion of his property there. I could live, I think, in America, much to my satisfaction and credit, without joining in such a scheme as I have been describing, though I should like well to accompany them, and see what progress they make.

From a letter of Tom Poole to Mr Haskins, printed in Thomas Poole and his Friends *by Mrs Henry Sandford, 1888.*

98   THE SONG OF THE KINGS OF ASIA   1795

'Shall not the King call for Famine from the heath,
Nor the Priest for Pestilence from the fen,
To restrain, to dismay, to thin
The inhabitants of mountain and plain,
In the day of full-feeding prosperity
And the night of delicious songs?

'Shall not the Councellor throw his curb
Of Poverty on the laborious,
To fix the price of labour,
To invent allegoric riches?

'And the privy admonishers of men
Call for fires in the City,
For heaps of smoking ruins
In the night of prosperity and wantonness?

'To turn man from his path,
To restrain the child from the womb,
To cut off the bread from the city,
That the remnant may learn to obey,

'That the pride of the heart may fail,
That the lust of the eyes may be quench'd,
That the delicate ear in its infancy
May be dull'd, and the nostrils clos'd up,
To teach mortal worms the path
That leads from the gates of the Grave?'

From The Song of Los *by William Blake, etched 1795.*

1795: the year of famine and unemployment; the year of Speenhamland and the systematisation of the dole, and in which was founded the 'Society for the Betterment of the Condition of the Poor'.
   In this year, as the J.P.s deliberated and the philanthropists worried and the working class suffered, one man – a London engraver – wrote a poem in which the whole situation, both its origins and its results, were made clear; a poem in which, seventy years before Marx, was shown the relationship of economics to the human situation and of the human situation to economics.

99   FOOD OF THE POOR OF INGLETON   1795

Troston, 26th. Dec. 1795.

DEAR SIR,
In writing to Ingleton, Yorkshire, upon another occasion, I made some queries relative to the subsistence of the poor on that border, and I send an extract of the answer with which the minister has favoured me.
   'Oat bread is the common bread in this country. They make it two ways, leavened and unleavened. It is mixed with no other kind of corn; very little bread made from wheat is used. The people are strong, vigorous, and healthy, as in any other part of the Kingdom, or perhaps even more so. In the neighbouring parishes great quantities of potatoes are planted; great quantities are exported yearly to our different settlements, especially to the West Indies: they are in general use at the table once, if not twice, a day. Indeed, oat bread, a little milk or tea, in the morning; potatoes, and sometimes a little flesh, but not often, at noon, with potatoes for supper, constitute the food of the lower classes of the people. The women, to their tea, buy, when they can afford it, bread made of wheat; but most of the opulent families eat oaten bread at all the other meals.'

I remain yours sincerely,
CAPELL LOFFT.

Letter to Arthur Young, editor of the Annals of Agriculture, *Vol.26, 1796.*

Note that 150 years earlier no one had heard of either tea or potatoes in England. Compare Dorothy Wordsworth, letters 38 and 39, April 1794, about potatoes, bread and tea at Keswick.

100   MR DALE'S COTTON-WORKS   October 7, 1796
           AT NEW LANARK

Some idea may be formed of the benefits which he has conferred upon the community, when it is mentioned, that 1800 persons derive employment under his auspices. His resources are all within himself; he cloathes, he feeds them, and large as the number of his dependants is, there is not an individual who does not partake of the attention of his benevolent and philanthropic master. Persons of all ages have the benefit of employment under him; old women, and even children afflicted with blindness, can obtain a subsistence by work. But above all, we were struck by the excellence of his arrangements with regard to the health, order, and morals of his work-people, in which his benevolence, not less than his good sense, was obvious. His plan must indeed be considered as a model, and it furnishes a convincing proof that most of the objections to manufactures on the score of their injurious influence on the persons employed in them, may be obviated by management and attention. There are several schools in the manufactory, adapted to the different ages of the children. A short time before we visited the works, Tom Paine's work had been circulated with much mischievous effect among the people. He informed us, that as his knowledge of the Scotch character gave him no hope of counteracting this mischief, but by argument, he had applied to the Bishop of Landaff for permission to print a cheap abridged edition of his lordship's 'Apology for the Bible.' This he had carefully circulated among the workmen, and had soon the satisfaction of finding them convinced by it, and restored to their quiet settled habits of thinking and acting.

From the Journal of a Tour in the Northern Parts of Great Britain *by the Duke of Rutland, published 1813.*

101   FACTS OF MIND   November 19, 1796

I am, & ever have been, a great reader – & have read almost everything – a library cormorant – I am *deep* in all out of the way books, whether of the monkish times, or of the puritanical aera – I have read & digested most of the Historical Writers; but I do not *like* history. Metaphysics & Poetry and 'Facts of Mind', (i.e. Accounts of all the strange phantasms that ever possessed your philosophy-dreamers; from Thoth, the Egyptian to Taylor the English pagan,) are my darling Studies. – In short, I seldom read except to amuse myself – & I am almost always reading – Of useful knowledge, I am a so-so chemist, & I love chemistry – all else is *blank* – but I *will* be (please God) an Horticulturalist and a Farmer.

From a letter of S.T. Coleridge to John Thelwall, quoted by Livingstone Lowes in The Road to Xanadu *and later printed in the* Collected Letters, *edited by E.L. Griggs, 1956.*

102   **THE REVERIE OF POOR SUSAN**   Spring 1797

At the corner of Wood Street, when daylight appears,
Hangs a Thrush that sings loud, it has sung for three years:
Poor Susan has passed by the spot, and has heard
In the silence of morning the song of the bird.

'Tis a note of enchantment; what ails her? she sees
A mountain ascending, a vision of trees;
Bright volumes of vapour through Lothbury glide,
And a river flows on through the vale of Cheapside.

Green pastures she views in the midst of the dale
Down which she so often has tripped with her pail;
And a single small cottage, a nest like a dove's,
The one only dwelling on earth that she loves.

She looks, and her heart is in heaven: but they fade,
The mist and the river, the hill and the shade;
The stream will not flow, and the hill will not rise,
And the colours have all passed away from her eyes!

By William Wordsworth, published 1800.

Note on 102–106. *Wood Street is a turning off Cheapside. In Wood Street there was at this period an Inn – The Swan with Two Necks – which was the terminus of the coaches from Cumberland and the North. We are told this in Smiles' life of George Moore who came up to town to seek and make his fortune. Poor Susan came from the lakes – even perhaps to the Swan with Two Necks – to seek employment in the great city. Her half-waking thoughts are expressed by the lake poet.*

In 105 the daughter of the banker John Gurney, at a tea party in Coalbrookdale, surrounded by the wives and daughters of great ironmasters, finds her life's work in the service of metropolitan man. Both poor Susan's and Elizabeth Fry's thoughts fly out to birds – thrush, dove, shadow of his wing.

In 106, the birds of Coleridge's tormented spirit are ghosts and starlings. Coleridge was himself a Londoner. He does not come to the great city, he looks out from it to Nature. He sees people only as phantasmagoria, and starlings as Euclidean shapes – the metamorphosis of the winged psyche into the manufactured balloon.

When the enclosures (103) forced the country-dwellers off the land they not only expropriated the people but also expropriated poetry, which has its roots in the emotional links of man to the land and of man to man in a common society. They also opened up *primitive land, cf. William Wordsworth. It is from this basis that Shelley spoke later of words quickening the earth ('Ode to the West Wind'). It is in this sense that poetry (and painting also) began in the 18th and 19th centuries to speak of the countryside as an area of holiness, connected with childhood – a garden of Eden which has been* lost. *It is the* recovery and saving *of this lost land that is behind very much of the imaginative writing of this period. It is in this way that the growing nostalgia for the country and the fading glory of childhood (compare Wordsworth's 'Ode: Intimations of Immortality from Recollections of Early Childhood') is connected with the political struggles of the expropriated working class: even when both sides are unaware of it. The cult of childhood – innocence etc. – is the same as the cult of the countryside: both were in danger. With the enclosures went the enclosure of the mind and the creation of* INFANT MAN *(104) for industrial purposes.*

The summer of 1798, when Davy joined Beddoes at Bristol just after the opening of the Pneumatic Institution, is the date of 'Kubla Khan'. With this poem, compare Davy's 'Researches Chemical and Philosophical; chiefly concerning Nitrous Oxide and its respiration'. Of course the two substances, opium *from the East and* nitrous oxide *from the chemist's laboratory, are precisely the two opposites which we are discussing, symbolic of two societies and two men and two methods of work and two sorts of results. Also note the paradox that opium and Coleridge and Kubla Khan are normally thought of as the* escape, *but the result today is reality, whereas nitrous oxide, its 'practical' origin, Davy the successful man, and so on, are today seen as the failure, even the escape. The common factor, who put up the money for both, and took both things, opium and nitrous oxide, was Tom Wedgwood.*

Xanadu is the palace of pleasure: the opposite of Pandæmonium. Now only a dream possibility, now only to be found in dreams or opium – only fragmentarily written down. It is the same palace as Blake's Jerusalem once builded on Pancras and Kentish-town, but now no more. Paradise Lost again.

| 103 | PETITION AGAINST ENCLOSURE | 1797 |

That the Petitioners beg Leave to represent to the House that, under Pretence of improving Lands in the said Parish; the Cottagers and other Persons entitled to Right of Common on the Lands intended to be inclosed, will be deprived of an inestimable Privilege, which they now enjoy, of turning a certain Number of their Cows, Calves, and Sheep, on and over the said Lands; a Privilege that enables them not only to maintain themselves and their Families in the Depth of Winter, when they cannot, even for their

Money, obtain from the Occupiers of other Lands the smallest Portion of Milk or Whey for such necessary Purpose, but, in addition to this, they can now supply the Grazier with young or lean Stock at a reasonable Price, to fatten and bring to Market at a more moderate Rate for general Consumption, which they conceive to be the most rational and effectual Way of establishing Public Plenty and Cheapness of Provision; and they further conceive, that a more ruinous Effect of this Inclosure will be the almost total Depopulation of their Town, now filled with bold and hardy Husbandmen, from among whom, and the Inhabitants of other open Parishes, the Nation has hitherto derived its greatest Strength and Glory, in the Supply of its Fleets and Armies, and driving them, from Necessity and Want of Employ, in vast Crowds, in to manufacturing Towns, where the very Nature of their Employment, over the Loom or the Forge, soon may waste their Strength, and consequently debilitate their Posterity, and by imperceptible Degrees obliterate that great Principle of Obedience to the Laws of God and their Country, which forms the Character of the simple and artless Villagers, more equally distributed through the Open Countries, and on which so much depends the good Order and Government of the State: These are some of the Injuries to themselves as Individuals, and of the ill Consequences to the Public, which the Petitioners conceive will follow from this, as they have already done from many Inclosures, but which they did not think they were entitled to lay before the House (the Constitutional Patron and Protector of the Poor) until it unhappily came to their own Lot to be exposed to them through the Bill now pending.

From the Petition of the Village of Raunds in Northamptonshire, printed in the House of Commons Journal, *June 19, 1797, and quoted in J.L. and Barbara Hammond's* The Village Labourer.

HORSE-HOEING HUSBANDRY

| 104 | INFANT MAN | 1798 |

And to what would they be indebted for this gentlest of revolutions? – To what, but to Economy? – Which dreads no longer the multiplication of man, now that she has shown by what secure and unperishable means infant man, a drug at present so much worse than worthless, may be endowed with an indubitable and universal value.

From a note by Jeremy Bentham in Annals of Agriculture, *Vol.XXXI.*

| 105 | AFTER TEA | September 4, 1798 |

(Colebrook Dale, September 4th.) – After tea, we went to the Darbys, accompanied by my dear friend Richard Reynolds, and still dearer Priscilla Gurney. We had spent a pleasant evening, when my heart began to feel itself silenced before God, and without looking at others, I found myself under the shadow of his wing, and I soon discovered that the rest were in the same state: I was persuaded that it must be *that* which I felt. After sitting a time in awful silence, Rebecca Young spoke most beautifully, she touched my heart, and I felt melted and bowed before my Creator. Deborah Darby then spoke; what she said was excellent, she addressed part of it to me; I only fear she says too much of what I am to be. A light to the blind; speech to the dumb; and feet to the lame; can it be? She seems as if she thought I was to be a minister of Christ. Can I ever be one? If I am obedient, I believe, I shall.

From the Journal of Elizabeth Fry, printed in the Life of Elizabeth Fry *by Susanna Corder, 1853.*

| 106 | COLERIDGE IN LONDON | November 27, 1799 |

Friday evening. The immoveableness of all things through which so many men were moving – a harsh contrast with the universal motion, the harmonious system of motions in the country, and everywhere in Nature. In the dim light London appeared to be a huge place of sepulchres through which hosts of spirits were gliding.

Soon after this I saw Starlings in vast Flights, borne along like Smoke, mist – like a body unendued with voluntary Power – now it shaped itself into a circular area inclined – now they formed a Square – now a Globe – now from a complete orb into an Ellipse – then oblongated into a Balloon with the Car suspended, now a concave semicircle, still expanding, or contracting, thinning or condensing, now glimmering and shivering, now thickening, deepening, blackening!

From the Notebooks *of S.T. Coleridge.*

(Jennings noted that the first of these paragraphs is quoted in Anima Poetae, *1895, the second in Humphrey House's edition of Gerard Manley Hopkins'* Notebooks, *without giving a source. In Kathleen Coburn's annotated edition of Coleridge's* Notebooks *the first draft of the second paragraph appears from the Notebooks of 1799, and Coburn links it with a transcription of earlier entries in the Notebooks which Coleridge rewrote as 'Images' in October 1803, the text of which is the whole extract quoted here.)*

107	THE POET AND THE MAN OF SCIENCE	September 13, 1800

If the labours of Men of Science should ever create any material revolution, direct or indirect, in our condition, and in the impressions which we habitually receive, the Poet will sleep then no more than at present, he will be ready to follow the steps of the Man of Science, not only in those general indirect effects, but he will be at his side, carrying sensation into the midst of the objects of the science itself. The remotest discoveries of the Chemist, the Botanist, or Mineralogist, will be as proper objects of the Poet's art as any upon which it can be employed, if the time should ever come when these things shall be familiar to us, and the relations under which they are contemplated by the followers of these respective sciences shall be manifestly and palpably material to us as enjoying and suffering human beings. If the time should ever come when what is now called science, thus familiarised to men, shall be ready to put on, as it were, a form of flesh and blood, the Poet will lend his divine spirit to aid the transfiguration, and will welcome the Being thus produced, as a dear and genuine inmate of the household of man.

From the Preface to the Second Edition of Lyrical Ballads *by William Wordsworth, 1800.*

108	BLAKE AT FELPHAM	September 21, 1800

We are safe arrived in our Cottage, which is more beautiful than I thought it, & more convenient. It is a perfect Model for Cottages &, I think, for Palaces of Magnificence, only Enlarging, not altering its proportions, & adding ornaments & not principals. Nothing can be more Grand than its Simplicity & Usefulness. Simple without Intricacy, it seems to be the Spontaneous Effusion of Humanity, congenial to the wants of Man. No other formed House can ever please me so well; nor shall I ever be perswaded, I believe, that it can be improved either in Beauty or Use.

    Mr. Hayley received us with his usual brotherly affection. I have begun to work. Felpham is a sweet place for Study, because it is more Spiritual than London. Heaven opens here on all sides her golden Gates; her windows are not obstructed by vapours; voices of Celestial inhabitants are more distinctly heard, & their forms more distinctly seen; & my Cottage is also a Shadow of their houses. My Wife & Sister are both well, courting Neptune for an embrace.

From a letter of William Blake to John Flaxman.

| 109 | COLERIDGE AT KESWICK November 1, 1800 |

The room in which I write commands six distinct Landscapes; the two Lakes, the Vale, the River, and Mountains, and Mists, and Clouds and Sunshine, make endless combinations, as if heaven & Earth were for ever talking to each other. Often when in a deep study, I have walked to the Window and remained there *looking without seeing*; all at once the lake of Keswick and the fantastic mountains of Borrowdale at the head of it have entered into my mind with a suddenness as if I had been snatched out of Cheapside & placed for the first time in the spot where I stood; and that is a delightful feeling, these Fits and Trances of *Novelty* received from a long known Object.

From a letter of S.T. Coleridge to Josiah Wedgwood, printed in Tom Wedgwood *by R.B. Litchfield, 1903.*

According to I.A. Richards in Coleridge on Imagination, *the move to Keswick in the summer of 1800, and the winter there, were the turning point in Coleridge's philosophy of poetry. J. Bronowski, in* Man Without a Mask, *says the same about Blake's move to Felpham in the same year (108).*

| 110 | THE DOMESTIC AFFECTIONS | January 14, 1801 |

It appears to me the most calamitous effect, which has followed the measures which have lately been pursued in this country, is a rapid decay of the domestic affections among the lower orders of society. This effect the present Rulers of this Country are not conscious of, or they disregard it. For many years past, the tendency of society amongst almost all the nations of Europe has been to produce it. But recently by the spreading of manufactures through every part of the country, by the heavy taxes upon postage, by workhouses, Houses of Industry, and the invention of Soup-shops &c. superadded to the encreasing disproportion between the price of labour and that of the necessaries of life, the bonds of domestic feeling among the poor, as far as the influence of these things has extended, have been weakened, and in innumerable instances entirely destroyed. The evil would be the less to be regretted, if these institutions were regarded only as palliatives to a disease; but the vanity and pride of their promoters are so subtly interwoven with them, that they are deemed great discoveries and blessings to humanity. In the mean time parents are separated from their children, and children from their parents; the wife no longer prepares with her own hands a meal for her husband, the produce of his labour; there is little doing in his house in which his affections can be interested, and but little left in it which he can love. I have two neighbours, a man and his wife, both upwards of eighty years of age; they live alone; the husband has been confined to his bed many months and has never had, nor till within these few weeks has ever needed, any body to attend to him but his wife. She has recently been seized with a lameness which has often prevented her from being able to carry him his food to his bed; the neighbours fetch water for her from the well, and do other kind offices for them both, but her infirmities encrease. She told my Servant two days ago she was afraid they must be boarded out among some other Poor of the parish (they have long been supported by the parish) but she said, it was hard, having kept house together so long, to come to this, and she was sure that 'it would burst her heart.' I mention this fact to shew how deeply the spirit of independence is, even yet, rooted in some parts of the country. These people could not express themselves in this way without an almost sublime conviction of the blessings of independent domestic life. If it is true, as I believe, that this spirit is rapidly disappearing, no greater curse can befal a land.

From a letter of William Wordsworth to Charles James Fox, published in The Early Letters of William and Dorothy Wordsworth, *edited by E. de Selincourt, 1935.*

111   LONDON   January 30, 1801

I ought before this to have reply'd to your very kind invitation into Cumberland. With you and your Sister I could gang anywhere. But I am afraid whether I shall ever be able to afford so desperate a Journey. Separate from the pleasure of your company, I don't much care if I never see a mountain in my life. I have passed all my days in London, until I have formed as many and intense local attachments, as any of your *Mountaineers* can have done with dead nature. The Lighted shops of the Strand and Fleet Street, the unnumerable trades, tradesmen and customers, coaches, waggons, playhouses, all the bustle and wickedness round about Covent Garden, the very women of the Town, the Watchmen, drunken scenes, rattles; – life awake, if you awake, at all hours of the night, the impossibility of being dull in Fleet Street, the crowds, the very dirt & mud, the Sun shining upon houses and pavements, the print shops, the old *Book* stalls, parsons cheap'ning books, coffee houses, steams of soup from kitchens, the pantomimes, London itself a pantomime and a masquerade, all these things work themselves into my mind and feed me without a power of satiating me. The wonder of these sights impells me into night walks about the crowded streets, and I often shed tears in the motley Strand from fulness of joy at so much *Life*. – All these emotions must be strange to you. So are your rural emotions to me. But consider, what must I have been doing all my life, not to have lent great portions of my heart with usury to such scenes? –

My attachments are all local, purely local –. I have no passion (or have had none since I was in love, and then it was the spurious engendering of poetry & books) to groves and vallies. – The rooms where I was born, the furniture which has been before my eyes all my life, a book case which has followed me about (like a faithful dog, only exceeding him in knowledge) wherever I have moved, old tables, streets, squares, when I have sunned myself, my old school, – these are my mistresses. Have I not enough, without your mountains? I do not envy you, I should pity you, did I not know, that the Mind will make friends of any thing. Your sun & moon and skies and hills & lakes affect me no more, or scarcely come to me in more venerable characters, than as a gilded room with tapestry and tapers, where I might live with handsome visible objects. –

From a letter of Charles Lamb to William Wordsworth, in The Letters of Charles Lamb, *edited by T.N. Talfourd.*

112   NEWTON   1801

Mock on, Mock on Voltaire, Rousseau:
Mock on, Mock on: 'tis all in vain!
You throw the sand against the wind,
And the wind blows it back again.

And every sand becomes a Gem
Reflected in the beams divine;
Blown back they blind the mocking Eye,
But still in Israel's paths they shine.

The Atoms of Democritus
And Newton's Particles of light
Are sands upon the Red sea shore,
Where Israel's tents do shine so bright.

From the 1800–1803 notebook of William Blake.

113   NEWTON   March 23, 1801

My opinion is thus: that deep Thinking is attainable only by a man of deep Feeling, and that all Truth is a Species of Revelation. The more I understand of Sir Isaac Newton's works, the more boldly I dare utter to my own mind, and therefore to you, that I believe the souls of 500 Sir Isaac Newtons would go to the making up of a Shakespere or a Milton. But if it please the Almighty to grant me health, hope, and a steady mind (always the 3 clauses of my hourly prayers), before my 30th year I will thoroughly understand the whole of Newton's Works. At present I must content myself with endeavouring to make myself entire master of his easier work, that on Optics. I am exceedingly delighted with the beauty and neatness of his experiments, and with the accuracy of his *immediate* deductions from them; but the opinions founded on these deductions, and indeed his whole Theory is, I am persuaded, so exceedingly superficial as without impropriety to be deemed false. Newton was a mere materialist. Mind, in his system, is always *passive*, – a lazy *Looker-on* on an external world. If the mind be not *passive*, if it be indeed made in God's Image, and that, too, in the sublimest sense, the Image of the *Creator*, there is ground for suspicion that any system built on the passiveness of the mind must be false, as a system. I need not observe, my dear friend, how unutterably silly and contemptible these Opinions would be if written to any but to another self. I assure you, solemnly assure you, that you and Wordsworth are the only men on Earth to whom I would have uttered a word on the subject.

From a letter of S.T. Coleridge to Tom Poole.

114   SOMERSET   April 9, 1801

Ever since the receipt of your last three letters (i.e. two metaphysical and one miscellaneous) we have been in a continued state of agitation and alarm by the riots concerning the price of provisions. It began in Devonshire, and has gradually travelled down to the Land's End and upwards to this neighbourhood, so that last week it might have been said that from the Land's End to Bridgwater the whole people had risen *en masse*. It is not now much otherwise, though there is a momentary calm. It is now, I understand, all in arms at Bristol, and among all the colliers, miners, and Pill-men of that neighbourhood. Here, for the present, the people have succeeded in lowering the price of provisions as follows: – the quartern loaf from 21d. to 10d.; butter, cheese, and bacon from 1s. and 14d. to 8d.; shambles meat from 9d. to 6d. per lb.

The people of Stogursey and the neighbourhood parishes joined the people here, and patrolled the country. They committed no violence, indeed they met with no opposition. I have been, as you may suppose, engaged enough by this business – a hundred people calling on me, being with the magistrates, etc. It is a curious phenomenon, but we see the people doing what Government dared not do, and Government permitting them to do it. Is Government timid, weak, or ignorant? One of the three it must be.

From a letter of Tom Poole to S.T. Coleridge, printed in Thomas Poole and his Friends *by Mrs Henry Sandford, 1888.*

115 THE CHILDREN 1801

August 22. – In the evening I walked to Cromford & saw the Children coming from their work out of one of Mr Arkwrights Manufactories. I was glad to see them look in general very healthy and many with fine, rosy, complexions. – These children had been at work from 6 or 7 oclock this morning, & it was now near or abt. 7 in the evening. The time allowed them for resting is at 12 oclock 40 minutes during which time they dine. One of them, a Boy of 10 or 11 years of age, told me his wages were 3s 6d a week, & a little girl said her wages were 2s 3d a week.

August 23. – We went to Church at Cromford where is a Chapel built abt. 3 years & ½ ago by Mr Arkwright. On each side the Organ a gallery in which about 50 Boys were seated. These children are employed in Mr Arkwrights work in the week-days, and on Sundays attend a school where they receive education. They came to Chapel in regular order and looked healthy & well & were decently cloathed & clean. They were attended by an Old Man their School Master. – To this school girls also go for the same purpose, and alternately with the Boys go to Church the Boys on one Sunday – the girls on the next following. – Whichever are not at Chapel are at the School, to which they both go every Sunday both morning and afternoon. The whole plan appears to be such as to do Mr Arkwright great credit.

From the Diary *of Joseph Farington, edited by James Greig, 1922.*

116 CHEMISTRY October 21, 1801

It is not *thinking* that will disturb a man's morals or confound the distinctions which to *think makes*. But it is *talking – talking – talking* that is the curse & the poison. I defy Davy to *think* half of what he *talks*: if indeed he talk what has been attributed to him. But I must see with my own eyes, and hear with my own ears. Till then I will be to Davy what Max was to Wallenstein. Yet I do agree with you that Chemistry is tending in its present state to turn its Priests into Sacrifices. One way, in which it does it – this however is an opinion, that would make Rickman laugh at me if you told it him – is this – it prevents or tends to prevent a young man from falling in love. We all have obscure feelings, that must be connected with something or other – the Miser with a guinea – Lord Nelson with a blue Ribbon, Wordsworth's old Molly with her washing Tub – Wordsworth with the Hills, Lakes and Trees – all men are poets in their way, tho' for the most part their ways are *damned bad ones*. Now Chemistry makes a young man associate these feelings with inanimate objects – & that without any moral revulsion, but on the contrary with complete self-approbation – and his distant views of Benevolence or his sense of immediate beneficence attach themselves either to Man as the whole human race, or to man, as a sick man, or a painter, as a manufacturer etc., and in no way to man as a Husband, Son, Brother, Daughter, Wife, Friend, &c. &c.

From a letter of S.T. Coleridge to Robert Southey, in Collected Letters, *edited by E.L. Griggs, 1956.*

117   THE CURSED BARBAULD   October 23, 1802
                            CREW

I am glad the snuff and Pi-po's Books please. 'Goody Two Shoes' is almost out of print. Mrs Barbauld's stuff has banished all the old classics of the nursery. . . . Knowledge insignificant and vapid as Mrs B.'s books convey, it seems, must come to a child in the *shape* of *knowledge*, and his empty noddle must be turned with conceit of his own powers, when he has learnt that a Horse is an animal, and Billy is better than a Horse, and such like; instead of that beautiful Interest in wild tales that made the child a man, while all the time he suspected himself to be no bigger than a child. . . . Hang them – I mean the cursed Barbauld Crew, those Blights and Blasts of all that is Human in man and child. . . .

Extract from a letter of Charles Lamb to S.T. Coleridge, in The Letters of Charles Lamb, *edited by T.N. Talfourd, 1848.*

118   SIMPLE NAKED SCOTLAND   August 19, 1803

We now felt indeed that we were in Scotland; there was a natural peculiarity in this place. In the scenes of the Nith it had not been the same as in England, but yet not simple, naked Scotland. The road led us down the hill, and now there was no room in the vale but for the river and the road; we had sometimes the stream to the right, sometimes to the left. The hills were pastoral, but we did not see many sheep; green smooth turf on the left, no ferns. On the right the heath-plant grew in abundance, of the most exquisite colour; it covered a whole hill-side, or it was in streams and patches. We travelled along the vale without appearing to ascend for some miles; all the reaches were beautiful, in exquisite proportion, the hills seeming very high from being so near to us. It might have seemed a valley which nature had kept to herself for pensive thoughts and tender feelings, but that we were reminded at every turning of the road of something beyond by the coal-carts which were travelling towards us. Though these carts broke in upon the tranquillity of the glen, they added much to the picturesque effect of the different views, which indeed wanted nothing, though perfectly bare, houseless, and treeless.

After some time our road took us upwards towards the end of the valley. Now the steeps were heathy all around. Just as we began to climb the hill we saw three boys who came down the cleft of a brow on our left; one carried a fishing-rod, and the hats of all were braided with honeysuckles; they ran after one another as wanton as the wind. I cannot express what a character of beauty those few honeysuckles in the hats of the three boys gave to the place: what bower could they have come from? We walked up the hill, met two well-dressed travellers, the woman barefoot. Our little lads before they had gone far were joined by some half-dozen of their companions, all without shoes and stockings. They told us they lived at Wanlockhead, the village above, pointing to the top of the hill; they went to school and learned Latin, Virgil, and some of them Greek, Homer, but when Coleridge began to enquire further, off they ran, poor things! I suppose afraid of being examined.

When, after a steep ascent, we had reached the top of the hill, we saw a village about half a mile before us on the side of another hill, which rose up above the spot where we were, after a descent, a sort of valley or hollow. Nothing grew upon this ground, or the hills above or below, but heather, yet round about the village – which consisted of a great number of huts, all alike, and all thatched, with a few larger slated houses among them, and a single modern-built one of a considerable size – were a hundred patches of cultivated ground, potatoes, oats, hay, and grass. We were struck with the sight of haycocks fastened down with aprons, sheets, pieces of sacking – as we supposed, to prevent the wind from blowing them away. We found afterwards that this practice was very general in Scotland. Every cottage seemed to have its little plot of ground, fenced by a ridge of earth; this plot contained two or three different divisions, kail, potatoes, oats, hay; the houses all standing in lines, or never far apart; the cultivated ground was all together also, and made a very strange appearance with its many greens among the dark brown hills, neither tree nor shrub growing; yet the grass and the potatoes looked greener than elsewhere, owing to the bareness of the neighbouring hills; it was indeed a wild and singular spot – to use a woman's illustration, like a collection of patchwork, made of pieces as they might have chanced to have been cut out by the mantua-maker, only just smoothed to fit each other, the different sorts of produce being in such a multitude of plots, and those of so small and of such irregular shapes. Add to the strangeness of the village itself, that we had been climbing upwards, though gently, for many miles, and for the last mile and a half up a steep ascent, and did not know of any village till we saw the boys who had come out to play. The air was very cold, and one could not help thinking what it must be in winter, when those hills, now 'red brown,' should have their three months' covering of snow.

The village, as we guessed, is inhabited by miners; the mines belong to the Duke of Queensberry. The road to the village, down which the lads scampered away, was straight forward. I must mention that we met, just after we had parted from them, another little fellow, about six years old, carrying a bundle over his shoulder; he seemed poor and half starved, and was scratching his fingers, which were covered with the itch. He was a

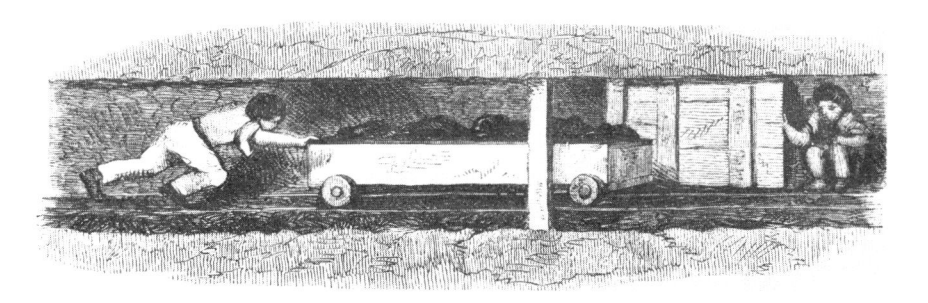

TRAPPER IN THE LANCASHIRE AND CHESHIRE COAL-PITS

miner's son, and lived at Wanlockhead; did not go to school, but this was probably on account of his youth. I mention him because he seemed to be a proof that there was poverty and wretchedness among these people, though we saw no other symptom of it; and afterwards we met scores of the inhabitants of this same village. Our road turned to the right, and we saw, at a distance of less than a mile, a tall upright building of grey stone, with several men standing upon the roof, as if they were looking out over battlements. It stood beyond the village, upon higher ground, as if presiding over it, – a kind of enchanter's castle, which it might have been, a place which Don Quixote would have gloried in. When we drew nearer we saw, coming out of the side of the building, a large machine or lever, in appearance like a great forge-hammer, as we supposed for raising water out of the mines. It heaved upwards once in half a minute with a slow motion, and seemed to rest to take breath at the bottom, its motion being accompanied with a sound between a groan and 'jike.' There would have been something in this object very striking in any place, as it was impossible not to invest the machine with some faculty of intellect; it seemed to have made the first step from brute matter to life and purpose, showing its progress by great power. William made a remark to this effect, and Coleridge observed that it was like a giant with one idea. At all events, the object produced a striking effect in that place, where everything was in unison with it – particularly the building itself, which was turret-shaped, and with the figures upon it resembled much one of the fortresses in the wooden cuts of Bunyan's *Holy War*.

From Recollections of a Tour made in Scotland *by Dorothy Wordsworth; written in 1803, first published in 1874.*

119 THE ENGINE February 22, 1804

Yesterday we proceeded on our journey with the engine; we carry'd ten tons of Iron, five waggons, and 70 Men riding on them the whole of the journey. Its above 9 miles which we perform'd in 4 hours & 5 Mints, but we had to cut down som trees and remove some Large rocks out of the road. The engine, while working, went nearly 5 miles pr hour; there was no water put into the boiler from the time we started untill we arriv'd at our journey's end. The coal consumed was 2 Hund^d. On our return home, abt 4 miles from the shipping place of the Iron, one of the small bolts that fastened the axel to the boiler broak, and let all the water out of the boiler, which prevented the engine returning untill this evening. The Gentleman that bet five Hund^d Guineas against it, rid the whole of the journey with us and is satisfyde that he have lost the bet. We shall continue to work on the road, and shall take forty tons the next journey. The publick untill now call'd mee a schemeing fellow but now their tone is much alter'd.

From a letter of Richard Trevithick to Davies Giddy, printed in Richard Trevithick *by H.W. Dickinson and A. Titley, 1934.*

120   PORTSMOUTH   March 24, 1804

While I was writing, Mottley, a dashing bookseller, a booted, buck-skin-breeched Jockey to whom Stuart gave me a Letter of most urgent recommendation (he is their Portsmouth Correspondent) called – he is a man of wealth & influence here, & a knowing Fellow. He took me thro' the Dock-yards & I was lucky enough to be present at a HEAT, *i.e.* at the welding a huge *faggot* of small laths of red hot Iron into the Shaft of the Anchor of a Man of War. It was truly sublime – the enormous Blaze, the regular yet complex intertwisted Strokes of between 20 & 30 men, with their huge Flail-hammers – the astonishment how they could throw them about, with such seeming wildness without dashing out each other's Brains, and how they saved their eyes amidst the shower of Sparks – the Iron *dripping* like a Millwheel from the intense white Heat – verily it was an unforgettable Scene! The poor men are pitiable Slaves – from 4 in the morning they work till 9 at night, & yet are payed less than any other in the yard. They all become old men in the prime of manhood. So do the Rope-makers who yet only work from 7 till noon. The Rope room is a VERY LOW board room, of a length far too great for the Eye to see from one end to the other – it gave me a grand idea of an Hindostan Cavern. A pin machine has been lately introduced, after a rebellion among the men & but for the same deplorable Delusion 2 thirds of that Labor might be done by machines, which now eats up the Rope-men like Giant in a fairy tale.

From a letter of S.T. Coleridge to Robert Southey, in Collected Letters, *edited by E.L. Griggs, 1956.*

121   CANDLE-POWER OF VENUS   April 1, 1804

On Sunday the first of April, 1804, at 9 o'clock at night, the air being very calm & clear & Venus appearing to be full (I had no ephemeris by me), I took a lens from a small telescope & receiving the light of the planet full upon it & condensed it till it became barely visible upon white paper from the general light of other stars illuminating the atmosphere. I then placed a mould candle (well snuffed, 4 in the pound, of tallow, burning nine hours) in a room with the window open, but far enough from it not to disturb the flame. Having then gone to different distances in an adjoining field & compared the condensed light of the candle with that of the star, as near as I could observe the lights were equally visible under the same condensation when the candle was at 195 or 200 yards distance.

From the Aeronautical and Miscellaneous Notebook *of Sir George Cayley, printed by the Newcomen Society, 1933.*

122 OMNIPRESENCE March 1805

What comfort in the silent eye upraised to God! 'Thou knowest.' O! what a thought! Never to be friendless, never to be unintelligible! The omnipresence has been generally represented as a spy, a sort of Bentham's Panopticon. O to feel what the pain is to be utterly unintelligible and then – 'O God, thou understandest!'

From the Notebooks of S.T. Coleridge, printed in Anima Poetae, *edited by E.H. Coleridge, 1895.*

123 NIGHT IMAGES April 14, 1805

In looking at objects of Nature while I am thinking, as at yonder moon dim-glimmering thro' the dewy window-pane, I seem rather to be seeking, as it were *asking*, a symbolical language for something within me that already and forever exists, than observing anything new. Even when that latter is the case, yet still I have always an obscure feeling as if that new phenomenon were the dim Awaking of a forgotten or hidden truth of my inner nature. . . .

From the Notebooks of S.T. Coleridge, printed in Anima Poetae, *edited by E.H. Coleridge, 1895.*

On the night-images of Coleridge recorded in Anima Poetae, *the thing, for us, is how they are half way (roughly) between the scientific weather-descriptions of natural history or astronomical reports of the 18th century –* Halley, Philosophical Transactions, Gray, White *– where always the struggle was to be objective only and to omit all personal feelings, and the soul-diary of Jefferies or the Journal of Hopkins in the 19th century. The fact of course is that the objective and subjective descriptions over both centuries divided, one line being science, the other poetry or meditation, one for the use of the body, the other for the use of the soul, and in the end were to* *become so clear of each other that they were to forget their common origin and clash. Compare Tylor on animism, 1871 (338).*

There would also appear to be a connection between the fact that very many images are of the moon and attendant stars – compare Livingston Lowes, The Road to Xanadu, *on moon-passages and the Ancient Mariner – and the 'Lunar Theory' in navigation, the use of the moon for finding longitude. It was for this that the observations at sea (e.g. by Halley) and at Greenwich (e.g. by Maskelyne) were made, of which Coleridge was undoubtedly aware.*

124   THE SMOKE OF LONDON   1806

I had now to part from my ladye-love, and I shall say nothing on the subject beyond confessing that on the road to London I cried for the first twenty miles as if my heart was quite broken. However, about the thirtieth mile, I caught myself laughing at a charming little creature at an inn where we changed horses. I dozed and dreamed of her pretty dimpled face until I scented the London smoke, when all these rustic whims and fancies gave way to deep reflection on High Art and a fearless confidence in my own ambition.

So far from the smoke of London being offensive to me, it has always been to my imagination the sublime canopy that shrouds the City of the World. Drifted by the wind or hanging in gloomy grandeur over the vastness of our Babylon, the sight of it always filled my mind with feelings of energy such as no other spectacle could inspire.

'Be Gode,' said Fuseli to me one day, 'it's like de smoke of de Israelites making bricks.' 'It is grander,' said I, 'for it is the smoke of a people who have made the Egyptians make bricks for them.' 'Well done, John Bull,' replied Fuseli.

Often have I studied its peculiarities from the hills near London, whence in the midst of its drifted clouds you catch a glimpse of the great dome of St Paul's, announcing at once civilisation and power.

From the Autobiography and Journal *of B.R. Haydon, edited by Tom Taylor. Written about 1840–41 and published 1847.*

125   THE EXTREME DELIGHT   October 1806

This discovery, it would appear from his MS. lectures, was made in the beginning of October; potassium on the 6th of that month, and sodium a few days later. It was effected by acting on moistened potash and soda, by means of several voltaic batteries combined, – one consisting of twenty-four plates of copper and zinc of twelve inches square, one of one hundred plates of six inches, and a third of one hundred and fifty of four inches.

The extreme delight which he felt, when he first saw the metallic basis of potash, can only be conceived by those who are familiar with the operations of the laboratory, and the exciting nature of original research; who can enter into his previous views, and the analogies by which he was guided, and can comprehend the vast importance of the discovery, in its various relations to chemical doctrine; and, perhaps, not least, who can appreciate the workings of a young mind with an avidity for knowledge and glory commensurate. I have been told by Mr Edmund Davy, his relation and then assistant, now professor of Chemistry to the Dublin Society, that when he saw the minute globules of potassium burst through the crust of potash, and take fire as they entered the atmosphere, he could not contain his joy – he actually bounded about the room in extatic delight; and that some little time was required for him to compose himself sufficiently to continue the experiment.

From Memoirs of the Life of Sir Humphry Davy *by John Davy, 1839.*

126   RATIONAL TOYS   1806

It requires but slight observation to be satisfied of the utter inutility of the articles with which the Toyshop is usually replenished. And on close reflection, it may possibly appear neither strained nor severe to condemn most play-things as worse than useless. Their gay appearance, and the movements which they are sometimes contrived to perform, doubtless raise strong and sudden desires in the mind of children. But satiety as quickly follows. The flush of delight, arising from the first impression, cannot but be transitory; and no sooner does the little possessor examine into the structure of his new acquisition, than he flings it aside, or breaks it to pieces and tramples it under foot, as if to revenge himself upon it for belying the promise of its exterior.

This succession of longing and loathing is a more serious evil than may at first be apprehended. If it be true that youthful curiosity cannot be frequently baulked with impunity, every such disappointment may be considered as some advance toward dullness.

We often meet with a species of toy calculated to excite surprize. This, if not liable to the same objection as the unmeaning toy, may be suspected of fostering a disposition for petty stratagems, by which a connexion between pleasure in the individual who plays them off, and pain in others is almost inevitably established.

Ten years ago, the idea of substituting models of machines in the place of ordinary toys suggested itself to one of the persons whose names are subjoined to the present paper.

Every quality, he conceived, which distinguishes models, would secure them against neglect and destruction, the merited fate of toys. The knowledge conveyed by the mutual dependency of the parts, and by the purpose of the whole would be laid up with advantage and might be revived with pleasure. Whatever improvement the understanding derives from mathematics would more agreeably flow from well-constructed models. And mathematics would be studied with more success by children accustomed to such models. They would rouse the faculty of invention, and confer the habit of pursuing trains of thought to a great extent. To girls, by conveying information without awakening their sensibility, they would be particularly serviceable. From this statement, the utility of a set of models in schools and private families is obvious. It is equally obvious that their utility would not be confined to young people.

This scheme has been generally approved by those to whom it has been mentioned. Different persons, long since, offered to advance money towards its execution. Indeed, in 1796, it was partially carried into execution, when the whole design was announced under the title of Rational Toys, in a letter prefixed to Mr. Donne's explanation of his elementary mathematical models. Towards its complete execution, however, there was wanting a person well informed concerning machines, and of ready mechanical invention. This difficulty is now removed by the offer of Mr. Robert Weldon, to conduct a manufactory of Rational Toys.

Committee

Thomas Beddoes James Stephens
John Billingsley John Wedgwood
Wm. Clayfield Wm. Wynch
Benj. Hobhouse MP

Printed as an Appendix to Memoirs of the Life of Thomas Beddoes M.D. *by John Edmonds Stock, 1811.*

127   THE ISLAND OF BRITAIN   c.1808

O! place before your eyes the island of Britain in the reign of Alfred, its unpierced woods, its wide morasses and dreary heaths, its blood-stained and desolated shores, its untaught and scanty population; behold the monarch listening now to Bede, and now to John Erigena; and then see the same realm, a mighty empire, full of motion, full of books, where the cotter's son, twelve years old, has read more than archbishops of yore, and possesses the opportunity of reading more than our Alfred himself; and then finally behold this mighty nation, its rulers and its wise men listening to – Paley and to – Malthus! It is mournful, mournful.

From 'Rationalism is not Reason' by S.T. Coleridge, in Omniana, *1812.*

128   JERUSALEM   1804–08

And did those feet in ancient time
Walk upon England's mountains green?
And was the holy Lamb of God
On England's pleasant pastures seen?

And did the Countenance Divine
Shine forth upon our clouded hills?
And was Jerusalem builded here
Among these dark Satanic Mills?

Bring me my Bow of burning gold:
Bring me my Arrows of desire:
Bring me my Spear: O clouds unfold!
Bring me my Chariot of fire.

I will not cease from Mental Fight,
Nor shall my Sword sleep in my hand
Till we have built Jerusalem
In England's green & pleasant Land.

From Milton *by William Blake, written between 1804 and 1808.*

129   ENCAGED   May 16, 1808

O that sweet bird! where is it? It is encaged somewhere out of sight; but from my bedroom at the *Courier* office, from the windows of which I look down on the walls of the Lyceum, I hear it at early dawn, often alas! lulling me to late sleep – again when I awake and all day long. It is in prison, all its instincts ungratified, yet it feels the influence of spring, and calls with unceasing melody to the Loves that dwell in field and greenwood bowers, unconscious, perhaps, that it calls in vain. O are they the songs of a happy, enduring day-dream? Has the bird hope? or does it abandon itself to the joy of its frame, a living harp of Eolus? I would that I could do so!

From the Notebooks of S.T. Coleridge, printed in Anima Poetae, *edited by E.H. Coleridge, 1895.*

130   THE ENGINE IS THE FAVORITE   July 8, 1808

We are credibly informed that there is a Steam Engine now preparing to run against any mare, horse, or gelding that may be produced at the next October Meeting at Newmarket; the wagers at present are stated to be 10,000 *l*; the engine is the favourite. The extraordinary effects of mechanical power is already known to the world; but the novelty, singularity and powerful application against time and speed has created admiration in the minds of every scientific man. – TREVITHICK, the proprietor and patentee of this engine, has been applied to by several distinguished personages to exhibit this engine to the public, prior to its being sent to Newmarket; we have not heard this gentleman's determination yet; its greatest speed will be 20 miles in one hour, and its slowest rate will never be less than 15 miles.

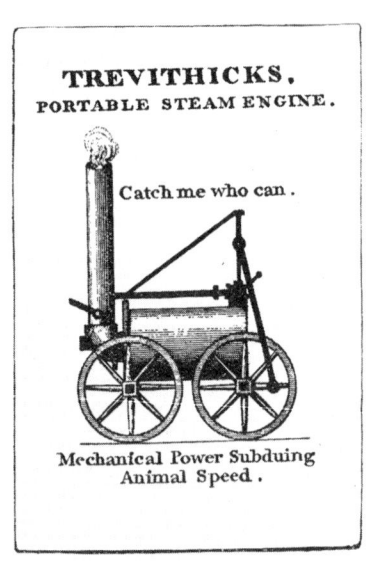

ADMISSION CARD TO THREVITHICK'S RAILWAY

From The Times, *quoted in* Richard Trevithick *by H.W. Dickinson and A. Titley, 1934.*

131   MY FIRST SIGHT OF THE ELGIN MARBLES   Summer 1808

To Park Lane then we went, and after passing through the hall and thence into an open yard, entered a damp, dirty pent-house where lay the marbles ranged within sight and reach. The first thing I fixed my eyes on was the wrist of a figure in one of the female groups, in which were visible, though in a feminine form, the radius and ulna. I was astonished, for I had never seen them hinted at in any female wrist in the antique. I darted my eye to the elbow, and saw the outer condyle visibly affecting the shape as in nature. I saw that the arm was in repose and the soft parts in relaxation. That combination of nature and idea which I had felt was so much wanting for high art was here displayed to midday conviction. My heart beat! If I had seen nothing else I had beheld sufficient to keep me to nature for the rest of my life. But when I turned to the Theseus and saw that every form was altered by action or repose, – when I saw that the two sides of his back varied, one side stretched from the shoulder-blade being pulled forward, and the other side compressed from the shoulder-blade being pushed close to the spine as he rested on his elbow, with the belly flat because the bowels fell into the pelvis as he sat, – and when, turning to the Ilyssus, I saw the belly protruded, from the figure lying on its side, – and again, when in the figure of the fighting metope I saw the muscle shown under the one arm-pit in that instantaneous action of darting out, and left out in the other arm-pits because not wanted – when I saw, in fact, the most heroic style of art combined with all the essential detail of actual life, the thing was done at once and for ever.

Here were principles which the common sense of the English people would understand; here were principles which I had struggled for in my first picture with timidity and apprehension; here were the principles which the great Greeks in their finest time established, and here was I, the most prominent historical student, perfectly qualified to appreciate all this by my own determined mode of study under the influence of my old friend the watchmaker – perfectly comprehending the hint at the skin by knowing well what was underneath it!

From the Autobiography and Journals *of B.R. Haydon, edited by Tom Taylor; written about 1840 and published 1847.*

| 132 | **WHEN THE SUN RISES** | c.1810 |

'What,' it will be Question'd, 'When the Sun rises, do you not see a round disk of fire somewhat like a Guinea?' O no, no, I see an Innumerable company of the Heavenly host crying, 'Holy, Holy, Holy is the Lord God Almighty.' I question not my Corporeal or Vegetative Eye any more than I would Question a Window concerning a Sight. I look thro' it & not with it.

From A Vision of the Last Judgment *by William Blake, written c.1810.*

133 COTTLE'S FREE VERSION OF THE PSALMS 1810

Diamond + oxygen = charcoal. Even so on the fire-spark of his zeal did Cottle place the King-David diamonds, and caused to pass over them the oxygenous blast of his own inspiration, and lo! the diamond becomes a bit of charcoal.

From the Notebooks of S.T. Coleridge, printed in Anima Poetae, *edited by E.H. Coleridge, 1895.*

If the above is the right date (as given by E.H. Coleridge), it must refer to Allen and Pepys 'On the Quantity of Carbon in Carbonic Acid, and on the Nature of the Diamond', Philosophical Transactions, *1807. But Davy published, also in* Philosophical Transactions, *1814, 'Some Experiments on the Combustion of the Diamond and other Carbonaceous Substances'. Compare also the work of Smithson Tennant (d.1815). Probably the clue is 'oxygenous blast'.*

134 MACHINE FOR COPYING SCULPTURE 1811

Bust of Sappho, January, 1811

Date	Task	Hour
Jan. 28	Making pedestal, 1 hour	1
29	Soaking in a strong coat of oil-varnish, and cementing the bust on pedestal	1
30	Cutting out the stone, cementing it and the bust to the moveable plates, and fixing the centres	3
31	Roughing the stone with the tearing-drills to within the thickness of a halfpenny of the truth	9
Feb. 1	Going over it with the quarter-inch drill to within the thickness of a thin sixpence	5
Saturday 2	Doing the face with the 1-8th drill to the truth, from the outer corner of one eye to do. of the other (went too slow)	5
3	Doing her breast with do.	1
Monday 4	Do. one side of the head	4
Tuesday 5	Do. round to within 1-4th of the whole	4
6	Quite round, finished the shoulders, removed some of the steps, or plaits	3
7	Cut the crown of the head, undercut the neck and cut it off from the centre-piece, repaired the most of it	3
		39

From The Life of James Watt *by J.P. Muirhead, 1858.*

135   SEARCH FOR BEAUTIFUL FORMS   May 11, 1811

I was much gratifyed by the particulars you mentioned concerning your new Invention, as to wch. my Lips were ever sealed till lately that I perceived you had imparted it to the excellent Dr. Herschel when with you at Heathfield last Summer. We then, under your patent, talked about it confidentially when I was pleased your contrivances had been admired by that Friend who certainly is an excellent judge. The first thought of making a cutting or gnawing point eat its way, according to three Dimensions, with next to mathematical precision too, by the turning of a Winch, so as to search for beautiful Forms, into the heart of marble and bring them out into full day light, is no mean instance of human sagacity.

From a letter of Dr Patrick Wilson to James Watt, printed in The Garret Workshop of James Watt *by H.W. Dickinson, 1929.*

136   SPIDER-WORK   February 27, 1812

To enter into any detail of the riots would be superfluous: the House is already aware that every outrage short of actual blood shed has been perpetrated, and that the proprietors of the frames obnoxious to the rioters, and all persons supposed to be connected with them, have been liable to insult and violence. During the short time I recently passed in Nottinghamshire, not twelve hours elapsed without some fresh act of violence; and on the day I left the county I was informed that forty frames had been broken the preceding evening, as usual, without resistance and without detection.

    Such was then the state of that county, and such I have reason to believe it to be at this moment. But whilst these outrages must be admitted to exist to an alarming extent, it cannot be denied that they have arisen from circumstances of the most unparalleled distress: the perseverance of these miserable men in their proceedings tends to prove that nothing but absolute want could have driven a large, and once honest and industrious, body of the people, into the commission of excesses so hazardous to themselves, their families, and the community. At the time to which I allude, the town and county were burdened with large detachments of the military; the police was in motion, the magistrates assembled; yet all the movements, civil and military, had led to – nothing. Not a single instance had occurred of the apprehension of any real delinquent actually taken in the fact, against whom there existed legal evidence sufficient for conviction. But the police, however useless, were by no means idle: several notorious delinquents had been detected, – men, liable to conviction, on the clearest evidence, of the capital crime of poverty; men, who had been nefariously guilty of lawfully begetting several children, whom, thanks to the times! they were unable to maintain. Considerable injury has been done to the proprietors of the improved frames. These machines were to them an advantage, inasmuch as they superseded the necessity of employing a number of workmen, who were left in consequence to starve. By the adoption of one species of frame in particular, one man performed the work of many, and the superfluous labourers were thrown out of employment. Yet it is to be observed, that the work thus executed was inferior in quality; not marketable at home, and merely hurried over with a view to exportation. It was called, in the cant of the trade, by the name of 'Spider-work'. The rejected workmen, in the blindness of their ignorance, instead of rejoicing at these improvements in arts so beneficial to mankind, conceived themselves to be sacrificed to improvements in mechanism. In the foolishness of their hearts they imagined that the maintenance and well-doing of the industrious poor were objects of greater importance than the enrichment of a few individuals by any improvement, in the implements of trade, which threw the workmen out of employment, and rendered the labourer unworthy of his hire.

From the Lord Byron's maiden speech in the House of Lords, in the debate on the Frame-Work Bill, printed in The Works of Lord Byron, *edited R.E. Prothero, 1898.*

In a letter to Lord Holland on February 25 in which he outlines the argument he hopes to make in his speech, Byron adds, 'I am a little apprehensive that your Lordship will think me too lenient towards these men, & half a framebreaker myself.'

137 THE FELLING COLLIERY DISASTER May 25, 1812

About half past eleven o'clock in the morning of the 25th May, 1812, the neighbouring villages were alarmed by a tremendous explosion in this colliery. The subterraneous fire broke forth with two heavy discharges from the John Pit, which were, almost instantaneously, followed by one from the William Pit. A slight trembling, as from an earthquake, was felt for about half a mile around the workings; and the noise of the explosion, though dull, was heard to three or four miles distance, and much resembled an unsteady fire of infantry. Immense quantities of dust and small coal accompanied these blasts, and rose high into the air, in the form of an inverted cone. The heaviest part of the ejected matter, such as corves, pieces of wood, and small coal, fell near the pits; but the dust, borne away by a strong west wind, fell in a continued shower from the pit to the distance of a mile and a half. In the village of Heworth, it caused a darkness like that of early twilight, and covered the roads so thickly, that the foot-steps of passengers were strongly imprinted in it. The heads of both the shaft-frames were blown off, their sides set on fire, and their pullies shattered in pieces; but the pullies of the John Pit gin, being on a crane not within the influence of the blast, were fortunately preserved. The coal dust, ejected from the William Pit into the drift or horizontal parts of the tube, was about three inches thick, and soon burnt to a light cinder. Pieces of burning wood, driven off the solid stratum of the mine, were also blown up this shaft.*

As soon as the explosion was heard, the wives and children of the workmen ran to the working-pit. Wildness and terror were pictured in every countenance. The crowd from all sides soon collected to the number of several hundreds, some crying out for a husband, others for a parent or a son, and all deeply affected with an admixture of horror, anxiety, and grief.

The machine being rendered useless by the eruption, the rope of the gin was sent down the pit with all expedition. In the absence of horses, a number of men, whom the wish to be instrumental in rescuing their neighbours from their perilous situation, seemed to supply with strength proportionate to the urgency of the occasion, put their shoulders to the starts or shafts of the gin, and wrought it with astonishing expedition. By twelve o'clock, 32 persons, all that survived this dreadful calamity, were brought to day-light. The dead bodies of two boys, numbers one and four, who were miserably scorched and shattered, were also brought up at this time: three boys, viz. numbers two, three, and five, out of the 32 who escaped alive, died within a few hours after the accident. Only twenty-nine persons were, therefore, left to relate what they observed of the appearances and effects of this subterraneous thundering.

One hundred and twenty-one were in the mine when it happened, and eighty-seven remained in the workings. One overman, two wastemen, two deputies, one headsman or putter, (who had a violent toothache) and two

---

* This eruption, though a very feeble representation of the subterranean labours of Mount Ætna, naturally enough brings to mind the description of that volcano by Pindar†, Lucretius‡, Virgils§, Aulus Gellius§§, and others. The poets tell us that Jupiter having conquered the Giants, threw Enceladus, the son of Titan and Terra, upon the island of Trinacria, or Sicily, and, to prevent his future rebellion, loaded him with Mount Ætna. Virgil's description is taken from Pindar's, and the following is nearly a literal translation of it.

> From frightful ruins Ætna's thunders rise,
> Now sable clouds discharging to the skies;
> Smoking with pitchy wheel and red hot coals,
> It licks the skies or casts out flaming balls;
> Now belching lifts up rocks, and bowels torn
> Of mountain; melted stones, with heavy groan,
> It rolleth out, and roaring boils below.
> They say Enceladus, by lightning's blow
> Half-burned, had Ætna cast upon his frame,
> Which since through rugged chimnies breatheth flame,
> And, as he changes still his weary side,
> Trinacria murmuring shakes, and fumes the zenith hide.

† Pythia i. Str. 2.   ‡ De Nat. Rer. lib. vi.   § Geo. 1.472. Aen. iii. 555, 570.   §§ Noc. Atticae xvi. 10.

masons, in all *eight persons*, came up at different intervals, a short time before the explosion.

From The Funeral Sermon of the Felling Colliery Sufferers *by the Rev. John Hodgson, published 1813 in Newcastle.*

It was this disaster that ultimately led Sir Humphry Davy to invent his Safety Lamp. But it was more important than that. In the fantastic symphony of the Industrial Revolution from the beginnings up to today – yes, today – the dull subterranean explosions of the great and horrible pit disasters return (precisely like the periodic activities of a volcano) like a Fate theme, like reminders from the unconscious (as in dreams) of this work that goes on, out of sight, night and day. Yet these 'accidents' are unnecessary, and the idea that they are due to 'Fate' is a conception à la Calvin to depress the people. And with each explosion, the reverberations drown for a time all the petty squabbles on the surface – Felling (1812), Wallsend (1829), Haslam (1844), Risca (1862), Gresford (1934).

138   Davy in Paris   October 30, 1813

On the 30th he was conducted by Mr Underwood to the Louvre. The English philosopher walked with a rapid step along the gallery, and, to the great astonishment and mortification of his friend and *cicerone*, did not direct his attention to a single painting; the only exclamation of surprise that escaped him was – 'What an extraordinary collection of fine frames!' – On arriving opposite to Raphael's picture of the Transfiguration, Mr Underwood could no longer suppress his surprise, and in a tone of enthusiasm he directed the attention of the philosopher to that most sublime production of art, and the chef d'oeuvre of the collection. Davy's reply was as laconic as it was chilling – 'Indeed I am glad I have seen it;' and then hurried forward, as if he were desirous of escaping from any critical remarks upon its excellencies.

They afterwards descended to a view of the statues in the lower apartments: here Davy displayed the same frigid indifference towards the higher works of art. A spectator of the scene might have well imagined that some mighty spell was in operation, by which the order of nature had been reversed: – while the marble glowed with more than human passion, the living man was colder than stone! The apathy, the total want of feeling he betrayed on having his attention directed to the Apollo Belvedere, the Laocoön, and the Venus de Medicis, was as inexplicable as it was provoking; but an exclamation of the most vivid surprise escaped him at the sight of an Antinous, treated in the Egyptian style, and sculptured in *Alabaster.* – 'Gracious powers,' said he, 'what a beautiful stalactyte!'

From The Life of Sir Humphry Davy *by J.A. Paris, 1831.*

139   A REFORM   1813

The awe which his admirers had of Bentham was carried so far as to make them think everything he said or thought a miracle. Once, I remember, he came to see Hunt in Surrey Gaol, and played battledore and shuttlecock with him. Hunt told me after of the prodigious power of Bentham's mind. 'He proposed,' said Hunt, 'a reform in the handle of battledores!' 'Did he?' said I with awful respect. 'He did,' said Hunt, 'taking in everything, you see, like the elephant's trunk, which lifts alike a pin or twelve hundredweight. Extraordinary mind!' 'Extraordinary,' I echoed; and then Hunt would regard me, the artist, the mere artist, with the laurelled superiority becoming the poet – the Vates, as Byron called him.

From the Autobiography and Journals *of B.R. Haydon, edited by Tom Taylor; written about 1840–41, published 1847.*

140   ALMOST ORGANIC   November 29, 1814

Our Journal of this day presents to the public the practical result of the greatest improvement connected with printing since the discovery of the art itself. The reader of this paragraph now holds in his hand one of the many thousand impressions of The Times newspaper which were taken off last night by a mechanical apparatus. A system of machinery almost organic has been devised and arranged, which, while it relieves the human frame of its most laborious efforts in printing, far exceeds all human powers in rapidity and dispatch. That the magnitude of the invention may be justly appreciated by its effects, we shall inform the public that after the letters are placed by the compositors, and enclosed in what is called the forme, little more remains for man to do than to attend upon and to watch this unconscious agent in its operations. The machine is then merely supplied with paper: itself places the forme, inks it, adjusts the paper to the forme newly inked, stamps the sheet, and gives it forth to the hands of the attendant, at the same time withdrawing the forme for a fresh coat of ink, which itself again distributes, to meet the ensuing sheet now advancing for impression; and the whole of these complicated acts is performed with such a velocity, and simultaneousness of movement, that no less than 1100 sheets are impressed in one hour.

From The Times.

141   DEMONSTRATION   c.1814

Then left the Sons of Urizen the plow & harrow, the loom,
The hammer & the chisel & the rule & compasses; from London fleeing,
They forg'd the sword on Cheviot, the chariot of war & the battle-ax,
The trumpet fitted to mortal battle, & the flute of summer in Annandale;

And all the Arts of Life they chang'd into the Arts of Death in Albion.
The hour-glass contemn'd because its simple workmanship
Was like the workmanship of the plowman, & the water wheel
That raises water into cisterns, broken & burn'd with fire.
Because its workmanship was like the workmanship of the shepherd;
And in their stead, intricate wheels invented, wheel without wheel,
To perplex youth in their outgoings & to bind to labours in Albion
Of day & night the myriads of eternity: that they may grind
And polish brass & iron hour after hour, laborious task,
Kept ignorant of its use: that they might spend the days of wisdom
In sorrowful drudgery to obtain a scanty pittance of bread,
In ignorance to view a small portion & think it All,
And call it Demonstration, blind to all the simple rules of life.

From Jerusalem *by William Blake, written and etched 1804–20.*

142 THE ROAD TO PUTNEY c.1815

On arriving near the top of this road, I obtained a distinct view of a phenomenon, which can be seen no where in the world but at this distance from London. The Smoke of nearly a million of coal fires, issuing from the two hundred thousand houses which compose London and its vicinity, had been carried in a compact mass in the direction which lay at a right angle from my station. Half a million of chimneys, each vomiting a bushel of smoke per second, had been disgorging themselves for at least six hours of the passing day, and they now produced a sombre tinge, which filled an angle of the horizon equal to 70°, or in bulk twenty-five miles long, by two miles high. As this cloud goes forward it diverges like a fan, becoming constantly rarer; hence it is seldom perceived at its extremity, though it has been distinguished near Windsor. As the wind changes, it fills by turns the whole country within twenty or thirty miles of London; and over this area it deposits the volatilized products of three thousand chaldrons, or nine millions of pounds of coals per day, producing peculiar effects on the country. In London this smoke is found to blight or destroy all vegetation; but, as the vicinity is highly prolific, a smaller quantity of the same residua may be salutary, or the effect may be counteracted by the extra supplies of manure which are afforded by the metropolis. Other phenomena are produced by its union with fogs, rendering them nearly opaque, and shutting out the light of the sun; it blackens the mud of the streets by its deposit of tar, while the unctuous mixture renders the foot-pavement slippery; and it produces a solemn gloom whenever a sudden change of wind returns over the town the volume that was previously on its passage into the country. One of the improvements of this age, by which the next is likely to benefit, has been its contrivances of more perfect combustion; and for the condensation and sublimation of smoke. The general adoption of a system of consuming smoke would render the London air as pure as that of the country, and diminish many of the nuisances and inconveniences of a town residence. It must in a future age be as difficult to believe that the Londoners could have resided in the dense atmosphere of coal-smoke above described, as it is now hard to conceive that our ancestors endured houses without the contrivance of chimneys, from which consequently the smoke of fires had no means of escape but by the open doors and windows, or through a hole in the roof!

A Morning's Walk from London to Kew *by Sir Richard Phillips, 1817, but originally published in parts 1813–16.*

143   MECHANIC POWERS   c.1815

At a few yards from the toll-gate of the bridge, on the Western side of the road, stand the work-shops of that eminent, modest, and persevering mechanic, Mr. BRUNEL; a gentleman of the rarest genius, who has effected as much for the Mechanic Arts as any man of his time. The wonderful apparatus in the dock-yard at Portsmouth, by which he cuts blocks for the navy, with a precision and expedition that astonish every beholder, secures him a monument of fame, and eclipses all rivalry. In a small building on the left, I was attracted by the solemn action of a steam-engine of a sixteen-horse or eighty-men power, and was ushered into a room, where it turned, by means of bands, four wheels fringed with fine saws, two of eighteen feet in diameter, and two of them nine feet. These circular saws were used for the purpose of separating veneers, and a more perfect operation was never performed. I beheld planks of mahogany and rose-wood sawed into veneers the sixteenth of an inch thick, with a precision and grandeur of action which really was sublime! The same power at once turned these tremendous saws, and drew their work upon them. A large sheet of veneer, nine or ten feet long by two feet broad, was thus separated in about ten minutes, so even, and so uniform, that it appeared more like a perfect work of Nature than one of human art! The force of these saws may be conceived when it is known that the large ones revolve sixty-five times in a minute; hence, $18 \times 3,14 = 56, 5 \times 65$ gives 3672 feet, or two thirds of a mile in a minute; whereas, if a sawyer's tool give thirty strokes of three feet in a minute, it is but ninety feet, or only the fortieth part of the steady force of Mr Brunel's saws!

In another building, I was shown his manufactory of shoes, which like the other, is full of ingenuity, and, in regard to subdivision of labour, brings this fabric on a level with the oft-admired manufactory of pins. Every step in it is effected by the most elegant and precise machinery; while as each operation is performed by one hand, so each shoe passes through twenty-five hands, who complete from the hide, as supplied by the currier, a hundred pair of strong and well-finished shoes per day. All the details are performed by ingenious application of the mechanic powers, and all the parts are characterized by precision, uniformity, and accuracy. As each man performs but one step in the process, which implies no knowledge of what is done by those who go before or follow him, so the persons employed are not shoemakers, but wounded soldiers, who are able to learn their respective duties in a few hours. The contract at which these shoes are delivered to government is 6s.6d. per pair, being at least 2s. less than what was paid previously for an unequal and cobbled article.

While, however, we admire these triumphs of mechanics, and congratulate society on the prospect of enjoying more luxuries at less cost of human labour, it ought not to be forgotten, that the general good in such cases is productive of great partial evils, against which a paternal government ought to provide. No race of workmen being proverbially more industrious than shoemakers, it is altogether unreasonable, that so large a portion of valuable members of society should be injured by improvements which have the ultimate effect of benefitting the whole.

From A Morning's Walk from London to Kew *by Sir Richard Phillips, 1817.*

144   PERSONIFICATION OF FICTIONS   1815

Amongst the instruments of delusion employed for reconciling the people to the dominion of the one and the few, is the device of employing for the designations of persons, and classes of persons, instead of the ordinary and appropriate denominations, the names of so many abstract fictitious entities, contrived for the purpose. Take the following examples:

Instead of Kings, or the King – the Crown and the Throne.
Instead of a Churchman – the Church, and sometimes the Altar.
Instead of Lawyers – the Law.
Instead of Judges, or a Judge – the Court.
Instead of Rich men, or the Rich – Property.

Of this device, the object and effect is, that any unpleasant idea that in the mind of the hearer or reader might happen to stand associated with the idea of the person or the class, is disengaged from it: and in the stead of the more or less obnoxious individual or individuals, the object presented is a creature of the fancy, by the idea of which, as in poetry, the imagination is tickled – a phantom which, by means of the power with which the individual or class is clothed, is constituted an object of respect and veneration.

In the first four cases just mentioned, the nature of the device is comparatively obvious.

In the last case, it seems scarcely to have been observed. But perceived, or not perceived, such, by the speakers in question, has been the motive and efficient cause of the prodigious importance attached by so many to the term property: as if the value of it were intrinsic, and nothing else had any value: as if man were made for property, not property for man. Many, indeed, have gravely asserted, that the maintenance of property was the only end of government.

From 'Constitutional Code' by Jeremy Bentham, first published in 1815, and in Works, *edited by John Bowring, published 1843, Vol.IX Chap.XI: Delusion.*

This passage is quoted by C.K. Ogden in the introduction to Theory of Fictions *(1932). Bentham's animist-materialist conception may be compared with Wordsworth and Coleridge's theory of Poetic Diction, and with Tylor on animism in 338 (1871). It illustrates the relation of logic to poetry – and to politics.*

Realism, at any given moment, equals the next step in historical development.

Bentham's ideas on neutralising *language are developed by Halévy in* The Growth of Philosophic Rationalism *(1928). In Jennings' copy of the book he has underlined the passage where Halévy says that 'since the fundamental error which vitiates the language is its sentimentalism, which attributes a good or evil valuation to motives in themselves, motives should no longer be designated by* sentimental *or passionate* terms, *but instead by terms which are* neutral *and do not connote praise or blame. . . . In this way it will be possible to talk of morals no longer in the manner of a* littérateur *or a satirist, but as a scientist, that is impartially and objectively. . . .' Jennings notes in the margin: 'Attempts at "non-animist" language (hence Ogden etc.)'. In Chapter IV of* Mencius on the Mind *(1932), I.A. Richards deals with the problems of ambiguity and argues for the exercise of Multiple Definition and the need to develop word-consciousness in the absence of a neutral language. In* The Meaning of Meaning *(C.K. Ogden and I.A. Richards, 1946) the fictitious entities introduced by language are examined. As '. . . in Photography it is not uncommon for effects due to the processes of manipulation to be mistaken by amateurs for features of the objects depicted . . . In a similar fashion language is full of elements with no representative or symbolic functions, due solely to its manipulation; these are similarly misinterpreted or exploited by metaphysicians and their friends greatly to exercise one another – and such of the laity as are prepared to listen to them.'*

145   **TEREDO NAVALIS**   1816

At the time when Mr Hawkins's project was put forward, Brunel was completing his works at Chatham, and one day, as he himself related to me, when passing through the dockyard, his attention was attracted to an old piece of ship timber which had been perforated by that well-known destroyer of timber – the *Teredo navalis*. He examined the perforations, and afterwards the animal. He found it armed with a pair of strong shelly valves which enveloped its anterior integuments, and that, with its foot as a fulcrum, a rotatory motion was given by powerful muscles to the valves, which, acting on the wood like an auger, penetrated gradually but surely, and that as the particles were removed, they were passed through a longitudinal fissure in the foot, which formed a canal to the mouth, and were so engorged. To imitate the action of this animal became Brunel's study.

From Memoir of the Life of Sir Marc Isambard Brunel *by Richard Beamish, 1862.*

146   THE GREATNESS OF GREAT BRITAIN   September 13, 1816

Rode through a most beautiful country to Otley. The roads in many places for a mile or two scarcely passable, the first four mile from Rochdale excessively bad, two miles in the middle between Halifax and Bradford very bad, a mile down to the bridge over the Aire between Bradford and Otley, these parts are the worst, but it is matter of great surprize that the whole of the road should be in such indifferent repair and some execrably bad through the whole of this manufacturing district, that the whole and sole cause where the road is not pitched is the not letting the water off or breaking the stones and that the whole distance from Congleton to Otley there were not 20 persons employed in either of these occupations, notwithstanding they tell you half the people are out of employ and every three mile at the furthest there is a shilling turnpike for a chaise and pair. The environs of Rochdale, Ripponden, Halifax, Bradford, the bridges over the Aire and Otley are beautiful in the extreme and were it not for the reflection that the greatness of Great Britain depended I may say principally on the defacing of the hand of nature in these parts by the hand of man, which produces not only riches in every way from exploitation and taxation at home and raises in time of war an innumerable population which is seen over the whole district for the armies, one could not help regretting that scenes so romantic and lovely, should be impaired and destroyed by the black steam engines, by the yarn, the cloth, the cotton, the morals of the people destroyed by being crowded together and the hammer of the water engines perpetually affrighting quiet and comfort from vallies which at first view one would imagine were placed by nature in the most remote and sequestred situations for the peculiar residence of innocence and peace. The seats or rather the villas of the manufacturers like the citizens in the neighbourhood of London have neatness to recommend them but scarcely any character through the whole district that distinguishes one very much from another.

From the Diary *of Benjamin Newton, edited by C.P. Fendall and E.A. Crutchley, 1933.*

147   FRANKENSTEIN   1816

Everything must have a beginning, to speak in Sanchean phrase; and that beginning must be linked to something that went before. The Hindoos give the world an elephant to support it, but they make the elephant stand upon a tortoise. Invention, it must be humbly admitted, does not consist in creating out of void, but out of chaos; the materials must, in the first place, be afforded: it can give form to dark, shapeless substances, but cannot bring into being the substance itself. In all matters of discovery and invention, even of those that appertain to the imagination, we are continually reminded of the story of Columbus and his egg. Invention consists in the capacity of seizing on the capabilities of a subject, and in the power of moulding and fashioning ideas suggested to it.

Many and long were the conversations between Lord Byron and Shelley, to which I was a devout but nearly silent listener. During one of these, various philosophical doctrines were discussed, and among others the nature of the principle of life, and whether there was any probability of its ever being discovered and communicated. They talked of the experiments of Dr Darwin, (I speak not of what the Doctor really did, or said that he did, but, as more to my purpose, of what was then spoken of as having been done by him,) who preserved a piece of vermicelli in a glass case, till by some extraordinary means it began to move with voluntary motion. Not thus, after all, would life be given. Perhaps a corpse would be reanimated; galvanism had given token of such things: perhaps the component parts of a creature might be manufactured, brought together, and endued with vital warmth.

Night waned upon this talk, and even the witching hour had gone by, before we retired to rest. When I placed my head upon my pillow, I did not sleep, nor could I be said to think. My imagination, unbidden, possessed and guided me, gifting the successive images that arose in my mind with a vividness far beyond the usual bounds of reverie. I saw – with shut eyes, but acute mental vision, – I saw the pale student of unhallowed arts kneeling beside the thing he had put together. I saw the hideous phantasm of a man stretched out, and then, on the working of some powerful engine, show signs of life, and stir with an uneasy, half vital motion. Frightful it must be; for supremely frightful would be the effect of any human endeavour to mock the stupendous mechanism of the Creator of the world. His success would terrify the artist; he would rush away from his odious handy-work, horror-stricken. He would hope that, left to itself, the slight spark of life which he had communicated would fade; that this thing, which had received such imperfect animation, would subside into dead matter; and he might sleep in the belief that the silence of the grave would quench for ever the transient existence of the hideous corpse which he had looked upon as the cradle of life. He sleeps; but he is awakened; he opens his eyes; behold the horrid thing stands at his bedside, opening his curtains, and looking at him with yellow, watery, but speculative eyes.

From the Standard Novels edition of Frankenstein, *written by Mary Shelley in 1816; the Introduction written in 1831.*

| 148 | THE PRODUCE OF THE MIND | November 30, 1816 |

By machines mankind are able to do that which their own bodily powers would never effect to the same extent. Machines are the produce of the *mind* of man; and, their existence distinguishes the civilized man from the savage. The savage has no machines, or, at least, nothing that we call machines. But, his life is a very miserable life. He is ignorant; his mind has no powers; and therefore, he is feeble and contemptible. To shew that machines are not naturally and necessarily an evil, we have only to suppose the existence of a patriarchal race of a hundred men and their families, all living in common, *four men* of which are employed in *making cloth by hand*. Now, suppose some one to discover a machine, by which all the cloth wanted can be made by *one man*. The consequence would be that the great family would (having enough of everything else) use *more cloth*; or, if any part of the labour of the three cloth-makers were much wanted in any other department, they would be employed in that other department. Thus, would the *whole* be benefitted by the means of the invention.

From A Letter to the Luddites *by William Cobbett, published in his* Political Register, *XXXI, C, 561.*

| 149 | LETTER FROM VENICE | December 24, 1816 |

>What are you doing now,
>   Oh Thomas Moore?
>What are you doing now,
>   Oh Thomas Moore?
>Sighing or suing now,
>Rhyming or ruing now,
>Billing or cooing now,
>   Oh Thomas Moore?

Are ye not near the Luddites? By the Lord! if there's a row, but I'll be among ye! How go on the weavers – the breakers of frames – the Lutherans of politics – the reformers?

>As the Liberty lads o'er the sea
>Bought their freedom, and cheaply, with blood,
>   So we, boys, we
>   Will *die* fighting, or *live* free,
>And down with all kings but King Ludd!
>
>When the web that we weave is complete,
>And the shuttle exchanged for the sword,
>   We will fling the winding-sheet
>   O'er the despot at our feet,
>And dye it deep in the gore he has pour'd.
>
>Though black as his heart its hue,
>Since his veins are corrupted to mud,
>   Yet this is the dew
>   Which the plant shall renew
>Of Liberty, planted by Ludd!

There's an amiable *chanson* for you – all impromptu. I have written it principally to shock your neighbour ****, who is all clergy and loyalty – mirth and innocence – milk and water.

>But the Carnival's coming,
>   Oh Thomas Moore,
>The Carnival's coming,
>   Oh Thomas Moore;
>Masking and mumming,
>Fifing and drumming,
>Guitarring and strumming,
>   Oh Thomas Moore.

From a letter of Lord Byron to Thomas Moore, printed in Moore's Letters and Journals of Lord Byron, 1830.

150 THE MACHINE-WRECKERS OF ARMATA   before 1817

'... be assured no greater delusion ever existed than that the matchless ingenuity of your people, in the construction of mechanical aids, can in any possible sense be an evil. I was shocked, indeed, to hear of outrages, which I should have expected only to have existed amongst the very dregs of a civilized people. The mistaken or rather the *delirious* incitement, is when numbers are unemployed; but how many more would be without employment, or rather how many thousands, and tens and hundreds of thousands would be starving, if the machinery they attack were overthrown? In the present condition of the country you could not send a single bale of your manufactures into a foreign market, if they were to be worked up only by manual labour, and *then* not only the turbulent destroyers, but the most diligent of your people must perish. Having been blessed with religious parents, my mind was directed from my earliest youth, to contemplate the benevolent dispensations of an offended God; and in nothing have they inspired a more constant and grateful admiration than that when the first and greatest of his works had been cast down for disobedience into the most forlorn and helpless condition, he should not only be gifted to subdue to his use and dominion all inferior things, but that, fashioned after the image of Heaven, he should be enabled to scan its most distant worlds, and to augment his own strength in mitigation of his appointed labour, by engines so tremendously powerful as would crush, with a single stroke, his weak frame to atoms, whilst they form, under his directing skill, the smallest and most delicate things for the uses and ornaments of the world.

'You must beat down those insane outrages by the whole strength and vigour of your laws. Select the *guiltiest* for condign punishment; but *let no such guilt be spared.*'

Morven here expressed his highest satisfaction. Taking me by the hand, he assured me that the very *existence* of Armata depended upon the most unremitting execution of the laws in this respect; and I was glad to find that her government had acted with the greatest promptitude and firmness in stigmatizing and punishing this opprobrium of a civilized world.

From Armata: A Fragment *by Thomas, Lord Erskine, published 1817, 2nd edition.*

151   SUNDAY IN THE   December, 1817
                         BREW-HOUSE

On Saturday last, in consequence of an almost obsolete promise to sleep in town when all the other partners were absent, I slept at Brick Lane. S. Hoare had complained to me that several of our men were employed on the Sunday. To inquire into this, in the morning I went to the brew-house, and was led to the examination of a vat containing 170 ton weight of beer. I found it in what I considered a dangerous situation, and I intended to have it repaired the next morning. I did not anticipate any immediate danger, as it has stood so long. When I got to Wheeler Street Chapel, I did as I usually do in cases of difficulty – I craved the direction of my heavenly Friend, who will give rest to the burdened, and instruction to the ignorant.

From that moment I became very uneasy, and instead of proceeding to Hampstead, as I had intended, I returned to Brick Lane. On examination I saw, or thought I saw, a still further declension of the iron pillars which supported this immense weight; so I sent for a surveyor; but before he came, I became apprehensive of immediate danger, and ordered the beer, though in a state of fermentation, to be let out. When he arrived, he gave it as his decided opinion that the vat was actually sinking, that it was not secure for five minutes and that if we had not emptied it, it would probably have fallen. Its fall would have knocked down our steam-engine, coppers, roof, with two great iron reservoirs full of water – in fact the whole Brewery.

From the Commonplace Book of Thomas Fowell Buxton, quoted in Memoirs of Sir T.F. Buxton, Bart., *edited by Charles Buxton, 1848.*

152 THE IMMORTAL DINNER — December 28, 1817

On December 28th the immortal dinner came off in my painting-room, with Jerusalem towering up behind us as a background. Wordsworth was in fine cue, and we had a glorious set-to – on Homer, Shakespeare, Milton and Virgil. Lamb got exceedingly merry and exquisitely witty; and his fun in the midst of Wordsworth's solemn intonations of oratory was like the sarcasm and wit of the fool in the intervals of Lear's passion. He made a speech and voted me absent, and made them drink my health. 'Now,' said Lamb, 'you old lake poet, you rascally poet, why do you call Voltaire dull?' We all defended Wordsworth, and affirmed that there was a state of mind when Voltaire would be dull. 'Well,' said Lamb, 'here's Voltaire – the Messiah of the French nation, and a very proper one too.'

He then, in a strain of humour beyond description, abused me for putting Newton's head into my picture; 'a fellow,' said he, 'who believed nothing unless it was as clear as the three sides of a triangle.' And then he and Keats agreed he had destroyed all the poetry of the rainbow by reducing it to the prismatic colours. It was impossible to resist him, and we all drank 'Newton's health, and confusion to mathematics.' It was delightful to see the good humour of Wordsworth in giving in to all our frolics without affectation and laughing as heartily as the best of us.

From the Autobiography and Journals *of B.R. Haydon, edited by Tom Taylor; written about 1840–41, published 1847.*

153 KEATS IN THE LAKES — June 26, 1818

June 26 – I merely put *pro forma*, for there is no such thing as time and space, which by the way came forcibly upon me on seeing for the first time the Lake and mountain of Winander – I cannot describe them – they surpass any expectation – beautiful water – shores and islands green to the marge – mountains, all round up to the clouds. We set out from Endmoor this morning, breakfasted at Kendal with a soldier who had been in all the wars for the last seventeen years – then we have walked to Bowne's to dinner – said Bowne's situated on the Lake where we have just dined, and I am writing at this present. I took an oar to one of the islands to take up some trout for our dinner, which they keep in porous boxes. I enquired of our waiter for Wordsworth – he said he knew him, and that he had been here a few days ago, canvassing for the Lowthers. What think ye of that – Wordsworth versus Brougham!! Sad – sad – sad – and yet the family has been his friend always. What can we say? We are now about seven miles from Rydale, and expect to see him tomorrow. You shall hear all about our visit.

There are many disfigurements to the Lake – not in the way of land or water. No; the two views we have had of it are of the most noble tenderness – they can never fade away – they make one forget the divisions of life; age, youth, poverty and riches, and refine one's sensual vision into a sort of north star which can never cease to be open lidded and stedfast over the wonders of the great Power. The disfigurement I mean is the miasma of London. I do suppose it contaminated with bucks and soldiers, and women of fashion – and hatband ignorance. The border inhabitants are quite out of keeping with the romance about them, from a continual intercourse with London rank and fashion. But why should I grumble? They let me have a prime glass of soda water – O they are as good as their neighbours. But Lord Wordsworth, instead of being in retirement, has himself and his house full in the thick of fashionable visitors, quite convenient to be pointed at all the summer long.

From a letter of John Keats to Thomas Keats, printed in Poetical Works and Other Writings, *edited by H.B. Forman, 1883.*

A postscript to a letter of William Godwin to Mary Shelley dated July 7, 1818, reads: 'Mr Brougham has just lost his election for Westmoreland; but he appears to be sanguine of success at the next opportunity. He had 900 votes; his competitors 1,100 and 1,200.' Printed in Shelley Memorials, *edited by Lady Shelley, 1859.*

154   PETERLOO   August 16, 1819

By eight o'clock on the morning of Monday, the 16th of August, 1819, the whole town of Middleton might be said to be on the alert: some to go to the meeting, and others to see the procession, the like of which for such a purpose, had never before taken place in that neighbourhood.

First were selected twelve of the most comely and decent-looking youths, who were placed in two rows of six each, with each a branch of laurel presented in his hand, as a token of amity and peace; then followed the men of several districts in fives; then the band of music, an excellent one; then the colours: a blue one of silk, with inscriptions in golden letters,

'Unity and Strength', 'Liberty and Fraternity'; a green one of silk, with golden letters, 'Parliaments Annual', 'Suffrage Universal'; and betwixt them, on a staff, a handsome cap of crimson velvet with a tuft of laurel, and the cap tastefully braided, with the word 'Libertas' in front. Next were placed the remainder of the men of the districts in fives.

Every hundred men had a leader, who was distinguished by a sprig of laurel in his hat; others similarly distinguished were appointed over these, and the whole were to obey the directions of a principal conductor, who took his place at the head of the column, with a bugleman to sound his orders. Such were our dispositions on the ground at Barrowfields. At the sound of the bugle not less than three thousand men formed a hollow square, with probably as many people around them, and, an impressive silence having been obtained, I reminded them that they were going to attend the most important meeting that had ever been held for Parliamentary Reform, and I hoped their conduct would be marked by a steadiness and seriousness befitting the occasion, and such as would cast shame upon their enemies, who had always represented the reformers as a mob-like rabble; but they would see they were not so that day. I requested they would not leave their ranks, nor show carelessness, nor inattention to the orders of their leaders; but that they would walk comfortably and agreeably together. Not to offer any insult or provocation by word or deed; not to notice any persons who might do the same by them, but to keep such persons as quiet as possible; for if they began to retaliate, the least disturbance might serve as a pretext for dispersing the meeting. If the peace officers should come to arrest myself or any other person, they were not to offer any resistance, but suffer them to execute their office peaceably. When at the meeting, they were to keep themselves as select as possible, with their banners in the centre, so that if individuals straggled, or got away from the main body, they would know where to find them again by seeing their banners; and when the meeting was dissolved, they were to get close around their banners and leave the town as soon as possible, lest, should they stay drinking or loitering about the streets, their enemies should take advantage, and send some of them to the New Bailey. I also said that, in conformity with a rule of the committee, no sticks, nor weapons of any description, would be allowed to be carried in the ranks; and those who had such were requested to put them aside, or leave them with some friend until their return. In consequence of this order many sticks were left behind; and a few only of the oldest and most infirm amongst us were allowed to carry their walking staves. I may say with truth that we presented a most respectable assemblage of labouring men; all were decently though humbly attired; and I noticed not even one who did not exhibit a white Sunday's shirt, a neck-cloth, and other apparel in the same clean, though homely condition. My address was received with cheers; it was heartily and unanimously assented to. We opened into column, the music struck up, the banners flashed in the sunlight, other music was heard, it was that of the Rochdale party coming to join us. We met, and a shout from ten thousand startled the echoes of the woods and dingles. Then all was quiet save the breath of music; and with intent seriousness we went on.

Our whole column, with the Rochdale people, would probably consist of six thousand men. At our head were a hundred or two of women, mostly young wives, and mine own was amongst them. A hundred or two of our handsomest girls, sweethearts to the lads who were with us, danced to the music, or sung snatches of popular songs; a score or two children were sent back, though some went forward; whilst on each side of our line walked thousands of stragglers. And thus, accompanied by our friends and our dearest and most tender connections, we went slowly towards Manchester.

At Blackley the accession to our ranks and the crowd in the road had become much greater. At Harpurhey we halted, whilst the band and those who thought proper, refreshed with a cup of prime ale from Sam Ogden's tap. When the bugle sounded every man took his place, and we advanced.

From all that I had heard of the disposition of the authorities, I had scarcely expected that we should be allowed to enter Manchester in a body. I had thought it not improbable that they, or some of them, would meet us with a civil and military escort; would read the Riot Act, if they thought proper, and warn us from proceeding, and that we should then have nothing to do but turn back and hold a meeting in our town. I had even fancied that they would be most likely to stop us at the then toll-gate, where the roads forked towards Collyhurst and Newtown; but when I saw both these roads open, with only a horseman or two prancing before us, I began to think that I had over-estimated the forethought of the authorities, and I felt somewhat assured that we should be allowed to enter the town quietly, when, of course, all probability of interruption would be at an end.

We had got a good length on the higher road towards Collyhurst, when a messenger arrived from Mr Hunt with a request that we would return, and come the lower road; and lead up his procession into Manchester. I at first determined not to comply. I did not like to entangle ourselves and the great mass now with us in the long hollow road through Newtown, where, whatever happened, it would be difficult to advance or retreat or disperse, and I kept moving on. But a second messenger arrived, and there was a cry of 'Newtown', 'Newtown', and so I gave the word, 'left shoulders forward,' and running at the charge step we soon gained the other road, and administered to the vanity of our 'great leader', by heading his procession from Smedley Cottage.

A circumstance interesting to myself now occurred. On the bank of an open field on our left I perceived a gentleman observing us attentively. He beckoned me, and I went to him. He was one of my late employers. He took my hand, and rather concernedly, but kindly, said he hoped no harm was intended by all those people who were coming in. I said 'I would pledge my life for their entire peaceableness.' I asked him to notice them, 'did they look like persons wishing to outrage the law? were they not, on the contrary, evidently heads of decent working families? or members of such families?' 'No, no,' I said, 'my dear sir, and old respected master, if any wrong or violence take place, they will be committed by men of a very different stamp from these.' He said he was very glad to hear me say so; he was happy he had seen me, and gratified by the manner in which I had expressed myself. I asked, did he think we should be interrupted at the meeting? he said he did not believe we should; 'then', I replied, 'all will be well'; and shaking hands, with mutual good wishes, I left him, and took my station as before.

At Newtown we were welcomed with open arms by the poor Irish weavers, who came out in their best drapery, and uttered blessings and words of endearment, many of which were not understood by our rural patriots. Some of them danced, and others stood with clasped hands and tearful eyes, adoring almost, that banner whose colour was their national one, and the emblem of their green island home. We thanked them by the band striking up, 'Saint Patrick's day in the morning.' They were electrified; and we passed on, leaving those warm-hearted suburbans capering and whooping like mad.

Having squeezed ourselves through the gully of a road below St Michael's church, we traversed Blackley Street and Miller's Lane, and went along Swan Street and Oldham Street, frequently hailed in our progress by the cheers of the towns-people. We learned that other parties were on the field before us, and that the Lees and Saddleworth Union had been led by Doctor Healey, walking before a pitch-black flag, with staring white letters, 'Equal Representation or Death', 'Love' – two hands joined and a heart, all in white paint, and presenting one of the most sepulchral looking objects that could be contrived. The idea of my diminutive friend leading a funeral procession of his own patients, such it appeared to me, was calculated to force a smile even at that thoughtful moment.

We now perceived we had lost the tail of our train, and understood we had come the wrong way, and should have led down Shudehill, and along Hanging Ditch, the Market-place, and Deansgate; which route Hunt and his party had taken. I must own I was not displeased at this separation. I was of opinion that we had tendered homage quite sufficient to the mere vanity of self-exhibition, too much of which I now thought was apparent.

Having crossed Piccadilly, we went down Mosley Street, then almost entirely inhabited by wealthy families. We took the left side of St Peter's Church, and at this angle we wheeled quickly and steadily into Peter Street, and soon approached a wide unbuilt space, occupied by an immense multitude, which opened and received us with loud cheers. We walked into that chasm of human beings, and took our station from the hustings across the causeway of Peter Street, and so remained, undistinguishable from without, but still forming an almost unbroken line, with our colours in the centre.

My wife I had not seen for some time; but when last I caught a glimpse of her, she was with some decent married females; and thinking the party quite safe in their own discretion, I felt not much uneasiness on their account, and so had greater liberty in attending to the business of the meeting.

In about half an hour after our arrival the sounds of music and reiterated shouts proclaimed the near approach of Mr Hunt and his party; and in a minute or two they were seen coming from Deansgate, preceded by a band of music and several flags. On the driving seat of a barouche sat a neatly dressed female, supporting a small flag, on which were some emblematical drawings and an inscription. Within the carriage were Mr Hunt, who stood up, Mr Johnson, of Smedley Cottage; Mr Moorhouse, of Stockport; Mr Carlile, of London; Mr John Knight, of Manchester; and Mr Saxton, a sub-editor of the *Manchester Observer*. Their approach was hailed by one universal shout from probably eighty thousand persons. They threaded their way slowly past us and through the crowd, which Hunt eyed, I thought, with almost as much of astonishment as satisfaction. This spectacle could not be otherwise in his view than solemnly impressive. Such a mass of human beings he had not beheld till then. His responsibility must weigh on his mind. Their power for good or evil was irresistible, and who should direct that power? Himself alone who had called it forth. The task was great, and not without its peril. The meeting was a tremendous one. He mounted the hustings; the music ceased; Mr Johnson proposed that Mr Hunt should take the chair; it was seconded, and carried with acclamation; and Mr Hunt, stepping towards the front of the stage, took off his white hat, and addressed the people.

Whilst he was doing so, I proposed to an acquaintance that, as the speeches and resolutions were not likely to contain anything new to us, and as we could see them in the papers, we should retire awhile and get some refreshment, of which I stood much in need, being not in very robust health. He assented, and we had got to nearly the outside of the crowd, when a noise and strange murmur arose towards the church. Some persons said it was the Blackburn people coming, and I stood on tip-toe and looked in the direction whence the noise proceeded, and saw a party of cavalry in blue and white uniform come trotting, sword in hand, round the corner of the garden-wall, and to the front of a row of new houses, where they reined up in a line.

'The soldiers are here,' I said; 'we must go back and see what this means.' 'Oh,' some one made reply, 'they are only come to be ready if there should be any disturbance in the meeting.' 'Well, let us go back,' I said, and we forced our way towards the colours.

On the cavalry drawing up they were received with a shout of good-will, as I understood it. They shouted again, waving their sabres over their heads;

and then, slackening rein, and striking spur into their steeds, they dashed forward and began cutting the people.

'Stand fast,' I said, 'they are riding upon us; stand fast.' And there was a general cry in our quarter of 'Stand fast.' The cavalry were in confusion: they evidently could not, with all the weight of man and horse, penetrate that compact mass of human beings; and their sabres were plied to hew a way through naked held-up hands and defenceless heads; and then chopped limbs and wound-gaping skulls were seen; and groans and cries were mingled with the din of that horrid confusion. 'Ah! Ah!' 'for shame! for shame!' was shouted. Then, 'Break! break! they are killing them in front, and they cannot get away'; and there was a general cry of 'break! break!' For a moment the crowd held back as in a pause; then was a rush, heavy and resistless as a headlong sea, and a sound like low thunder, with screams, prayers, and imprecations from the crowd moiled and sabre-doomed who could not escape.

By this time Hunt and his companions had disappeared from the hustings, and some of the yeomanry, perhaps less sanguinarily disposed than others, were busied in cutting down the flag-staves and demolishing the flags at the hustings.

On the breaking of the crowd the yeomanry wheeled, and, dashing whenever there was an opening, they followed, pressing and wounding. Many females appeared as the crowd opened; and striplings or mere youths also were found. Their cries were piteous and heart-rending, and would, one might have supposed, have disarmed any human resentment: but here their appeals were in vain. Women, white-vested maids, and tender youths, were indiscriminately sabred or trampled; and we have reason for believing that few were the instances in which that forbearance was vouchsafed which they so earnestly implored.

In ten minutes from the commencement of the havoc the field was an open and almost deserted space. The sun looked down through a sultry and motionless air. The curtains and blinds of the windows within view were all closed. A gentleman or two might occasionally be seen looking out from one of the new houses before mentioned, near the door of which a group of persons (special constables) were collected, and apparently in conversation; others were assisting the wounded or carrying off the dead. The hustings remained, with a few broken and hewed flag-staves erect, and a torn and gashed banner or two dropping; whilst over the whole field were strewed caps, bonnets, hats, shawls, and shoes, and other parts of male and female dress, trampled, torn, and bloody. The yeomanry had dismounted – some were easing their horses' girths, others adjusting their accoutrements, and some were wiping their sabres. Several mounds of human beings still remained where they had fallen, crushed down and smothered. Some of these still groaning, others with staring eyes, were gasping for breath, and others would never breathe more. All was silent save those low sounds, and the occasional snorting and pawing of steeds. Persons might sometimes be noticed peeping from attics and over the tall ridgings of houses, but they quickly withdrew, as if fearful of being observed, or unable to sustain the full gaze of a scene so hideous and abhorrent.

From Passages in the Life of a Radical *by Samuel Bamford, 1840–44.*

Note on 154. *G.M. Trevelyan, in* British History in the Nineteenth Century and After, *describes Peterloo like this:*
In 1819 ... since Habeas Corpus was no longer suspended, monster meetings of working-men were held in the industrial districts to demand universal suffrage. It would have been better if the authorities had prohibited such meetings altogether, according to their usual custom; rather than act as they acted in St Peter's Fields, Manchester, on 16 August. An orderly and unarmed crowd of about 60,000 men, women and children was permitted to assemble; but then the magistrates, stricken with alarm at the sight of so great a multitude, sent in the yeomanry to arrest the speaker, the notorious Radical Hunt, after the meeting had fairly begun. When the horsemen, pushing their way through the throng on such an errand, were shouted at and hustled, the cavalry in reserve were ordered by the magistrates to charge. Their impact drove the dense mass of human beings, cursing and shrieking, off the field, while the yeomanry, who were Tory partisans, used their sabres with gusto. In the disturbances of that day some eleven persons, including two women, were killed or dead of their injuries; over a hundred were wounded by sabres and several hundred more injured by horse-hoofs or crushed in the stampede. The women injured were over a hundred.

J.L. Hammond and Barbara Hammond, in The Town Labourer, *fill in the background:*
The town they met in, though almost the largest in England, was unrepresented in a Parliament that gave two seats to Old Sarum. Of the eighty thousand, the vast mass were voteless men and women, whom Parliament had handed over to their employers by the Combination Laws, while it had taxed their food for the benefit of the landowners by a most drastic Corn Law. The classes that controlled Parliament and their lives were represented by the magistrates, who were landlords or parsons, and by the yeomanry, who were largely manufacturers. Between these classes must be shared the responsibility for the sudden and unprovoked charge on a defenceless and unresisting crowd, for if the magistrates gave the orders, the yeomanry supplied the zeal.'

In a letter to his publisher, Ollier, dated Leghorn, September 6, 1819, the poet Shelley wrote:
The same day that your letter came, came the news of the Manchester work, and the torrent of my indignation has not yet done boiling in my veins. I

wait anxiously to hear how the country will express its sense of this bloody, murderous oppression of its destroyers. 'Something must be done. What, yet I know not.'

The quotation is from Act III, Scene 1, of his play, The Cenci, *written earlier in 1819, where it is spoken by Beatrice:*

> Ay, something must be done;
> What, yet I know not . . . something which shall make
> The thing that I have suffered but a shadow
> In the dread lightning which avenges it. . . .'

In the autumn of 1819, Shelley composed his Mask of Anarchy written on the occasion of the massacre at Manchester, *a poem in ninety-one verses, and 372 lines:*

> As I lay asleep in Italy
> There came a voice from over the Sea,
> And with great power it forth led me
> To walk in the visions of Poesy.
>
> I met Murder on the way –
> He had a mask like Castlereagh . . .
>
> Next came Fraud, and he had on,
> Like Eldon, an ermined grown . . .
>
> Like Sidmouth, next, Hypocrisy
> On a crocodile rode by . . .'

Castlereagh, as Prime Minister, Eldon, as Lord Chancellor, and Sidmouth, as Home Secretary, could all fairly be blamed for the situation which led to the Peterloo massacre. In addition it was Eldon who had ruled that Shelley was not a fit person to be in charge of his two children by his first wife Harriet. The poem continues:

> And many more Destructions played
> In this ghastly masquerade,
> All disguised, even to the eyes,
> Like Bishops, lawyers, peers or spies.
>
> Last came Anarchy: he rode
> On a white horse, splashed with blood;
> He was pale, even to the lips,
> Like Death in the Apocalypse.
>
> With a pace stately and fast,
> Over English land he passed,
> Trampling to a mire of blood
> The adoring multitude.

And a mighty troop around,
With their trampling shook the ground,
Waving each a bloody sword,
For the service of their Lord.

And with glorious triumph they
Rode through England proud and gay,
Drunk as with intoxication
Of the wine of desolation.

O'er fields and towns, from sea to sea,
Passed the Pageant swift and free,
Tearing up and trampling down;
Till they came to London town . . .

Then all cried, with one accord,
'Thou art King, and God, and Lord . . .'

And Anarchy, the Skeleton,
Bowed and grinned to everyone, . . .

For he knew the Palaces
Of our kings were rightly his . . .

So he sent his slaves before
To seize upon the Bank and Tower,
And was proceeding with intent
To meet his pensioned Parliament

When one fled past, a maniac maid
And her name was Hope, she said:
But she looked more like Despair,
And she cried out in the air:

'My Father Time is weak and gray
With waiting for a better day;
See how idiot-like he stands,
Fumbling with his palsied hands!' . . .

Then she lay down in the street,
Right before the horses' feet,
Expecting, with a patient eye,
Murder, Fraud and Anarchy.

When between her and her foes
A mist, a light, an image rose,
Small at first, and weak, and frail
Like the vapour of a vale:

Till as clouds grow on the blast,
Like tower-crowned giants striding fast,
And glare with lightnings as they fly,
And speak in thunder to the sky,

It grew – a Shape arrayed in mail
Brighter than the viper's scale,
And upborne on wings whose grain
Was as the light of sunny rain . . .

And Anarchy, the ghastly birth
Lay dead earth upon the earth;
The Horse of Death tameless as wind
Fled, and with his hoofs did grind
To dust the murderers thronged behind.

A rushing light of clouds and splendour,
A sense awakening and yet tender
Was heard and felt – and at its close
These words of joy and fear arose

As if their own indignant Earth
Which gave the sons of England birth
Had felt their blood upon her brow,
And shuddering with a mother's throe

Had turn'd every drop of blood
By which her face had been bedewed
To an accent unwithstood, –
As if her heart had cried aloud:

'Men of England, heirs of Glory,
Heroes of unwritten story,
Nurslings of one mighty Mother,
Hopes of her, and one another;

'Rise like Lions after slumber
In unvanquishable number,
Shake your chains to earth like dew
Which in sleep had fallen on you, –
Ye are many – they are few . . .'

This speech of the voice of the Earth continues to the end of the poem – and fifty-two verses of it are still to come – ending with the repetition of the five lines above.

UTOPIA September 28, 1819

After breakfast we walked to New Lanark, which is about a mile from the town. The approach to this establishment reminded me of the descent upon the baths of Monchique, more than any other scene which I could call to mind. The hills are far inferior in height, neither is there so much wood about them; but the buildings lie in such a dingle, and in like manner surprize you by their position, and their uncommon character. There is too a regular appearance, such as belongs to a conventual or eleemosynary establishment. The descent is very steep: such as is implied by saying you might throw a stone down the chimnies.

A large convent is more like a cotton-mill than it is like a college – that is to say, such convents as have been built since the glorious age of ecclesiastical architecture, and these are by far the greater number. They are like great infirmaries, or manufactories; and these mills which are three in number, at a distance might be mistaken for convents, if in a Catholic country. There are also several streets, or rather rows of houses for the persons employed there; and other buildings connected with the establishment. These rows are cleaner than the common streets of a Scotch town, and yet not quite so clean as they ought to be. Their general appearance is what might be looked for in a Moravian settlement.

I had written to Owen from Inverary; and he expected us, he said, to stay with him a week, or at least three days; it not without difficulty that we persevered in our purpose of proceeding the same evening to Douglas Mill.

He led us thro' the works with great courtesy, and made as full an exhibition as the time allowed. It is needless to say anything more of the Mills than that they are perfect of their kind, according to the present state of mechanical science, and that they appeared to be under admirable management; they are thoroughly clean, and so carefully ventilated, that there was no unpleasant smell in any of the apartments. Everything required for the machinery is made upon the spot, and the expence of wear and tear is estimated at 8000£ annually. There are stores also from which the people are supplied with all the necessaries of life. They have a credit there to the amount of sixteen shillings a week each, but may deal elsewhere if they chuse. The expences of what he calls the moral part of the establishment, he stated at 700£ a year. But a large building is just compleated, with ball and concert and lecture rooms, all for 'the formation of character'; and this must surely be set down to Owen's private account, rather than to the cost of the concern.

In the course of going thro' these buildings, he took us into an apartment where one of his plans, upon a scale larger than any of the Swiss models, was spread upon the floor. And with a long wand in his hand he explained the plan, while Willy and Francis stood by, with wondering and longing eyes, regarding it as a plaything, and hoping they might be allowed to amuse themselves with it. Meantime the word had been given: we were conducted into one of the dancing rooms; half a dozen fine boys, about nine or ten years old, led the way, playing on fifes, and some 200 children, from four years of age till ten, entered the room and arranged themselves on three sides of it. A man whose official situation I did not comprehend gave the word, which either because of the tone or the dialect I did not understand; and they turned to right or left, faced about, fell forwards and backwards, and stamped at command, performing manoeuvres the object of which was not very clear, with perfect regularity. I remembered what T. Vardon had told me of the cows in Holland. When the cattle are housed, the Dutch in their spirit of cleanliness, prevent them from dirtying their tails by tying them up (to the no small discomfort of the cows) at a certain elevation, to a cross string which extends the whole length of the stalls: and the consequence is that when any one cow wags her tail, all the others must wag theirs also. So I could not but think that these puppet-like motions might, with a little ingenuity, have been produced by the great water-wheel, which is the *primum mobile* of the whole Cotton-Mills. A certain number of the children were then drawn out, and sung to the pipe of six little pipers. There was too much of all this, but the children seemed to like it. When the exhibition was over, they filed off into the adjoining school room.

I was far better pleased with a large room in which all the children of the establishment who are old enough not to require the constant care of their mothers, and too young for instruction of any kind, were brought together while their parents were at work, and left to amuse themselves. They made a glorious noise, worth all the concerts of New Lanark, and of London to boot. It was really delightful to see how the little creatures crowded about Owen to make their bows and their curtesies, looking up and smiling in his face; and the genuine benignity and pleasure with which he noticed them, laying his hand on the head of one, shaking hands with another, and bestowing kind looks and kind words upon all.

Owen in reality deceives himself. He is part-owner and sole Director of a large establishment, differing more in accidents than in essence from a plantation: the persons under him happen to be white, and are at liberty by law to quit his service, but while they remain in it they are as much under his absolute management as so many negro-slaves. His humour, his vanity, his kindliness of nature (all these have their share) lead him to make these *human machines* as he calls them (and literally believes them to be) as happy as he can, and to make a display of their happiness. And he jumps at once to the monstrous conclusion that because he can do this with 2210 persons, who are totally dependent upon him – all mankind might be governed with the same facility. *Et in Utopia ego*. But I never regarded man as a machine; I never believed him to be merely a material being; I never for one moment could listen to the nonsense of Helvetius, nor suppose, as Owen does, that men may be cast in a mould (like the other parts of his mill) and take the impression with perfect certainty. Nor did I ever disguise from myself the difficulties of a system which took for its foundation the principle of a community of goods. On the contrary I met them fairly, acknowledged them, and rested satisfied with the belief (whether erroneous or not) that the evils incident in such a system would be infinitely less than those which stare us in the face under the existing order. But Owen reasons from Cotton Mills to the whole empire. He keeps out of sight from others, and perhaps from himself, that his system, instead of aiming at perfect freedom, can only be kept in power by absolute power. Indeed, he never looks beyond one of his own ideal square villages, to the rules and proportions of which he would square the whole human race. *The formation of character*! Why the end of his institutions would be, as far as possible, the destruction of all character. They tend directly to destroy individuality of character and domesticity – in the one of which the strength of men consists, and in the other his happiness. The power of human society, and the grace, would both be annihilated.

Yet I admire the man, and like him too. And the Yahoos who are bred in our manufacturing towns, and under the administration of our Poor Laws are so much worse than the Chinese breed which he proposes to raise, that I should be glad to see his regulations adopted, as the Leeds people have proposed, for a colony of paupers. Such a variety in society would be curious; and might as well be encouraged as Quakerism and Moravianism.

From Journal of a Tour in Scotland in 1819 *by Robert Southey, published 1829.*

This apparently chance remark that the appearance of New Lanark was like that of a Moravian settlement is in fact extremely profound. The Moravian Church – or rather the Moravian settlement of Herrnhut in Saxony – was visited and studied by John Wesley the founder of Methodism in 1738. Its rules and systems of life are recorded in his Journal and show the relationship of methodism to the factory system.

Note that Edward Baines and Robert Oastler (Richard's father) were on an official visit to New Lanark in August, 1819. Also that the Oastlers were, precisely, Moravian methodists. There was a Moravian school near Leeds which Richard went to. These were 'the Leeds people' referred to by Southey. They were the 'Guardians of the Poor' at Leeds.

| 156 | THE BIRTH OF THE CYLINDER | November 12–17, 1819 |

November 12, 1819. The event is now past – both the steam cylinder and air-pump were cast at three o'clock this afternoon. At two o'clock this morning I repaired to the mill to see that the preliminary operations, upon which the ultimate success of a *fount* greatly depends, were conducted with proper attention. The moulds are buried in a pit, made close, before the mouth of the furnace, so that the melted metal, when the plug is driven in, may run easily into them, and fill up the vacant space left between the core and the shell, in order to form the desired cylinders. The fire was lighted in the furnace at nine, and in three hours the metal was fused. At three o'clock it was ready to cast, the fusion being remarkably rapid, owing to the perfection of the furnace. The metal was also heated to an extreme degree, boiling with fury, and seeming to dance with the pleasure of running in its proper form. The plug was struck, and a massy stream of a bluish dazzling whiteness filled the moulds in the twinkling of a shooting star. The castings will not be cool enough to be drawn up till to-morrow afternoon; but to judge from all appearances, I expect them to be perfect.

Saturday, Nov. 13. They have been excavated and drawn up. I have examined them and found them really perfect; they are massive and strong to bear any usage and sea-water, *in sæcula sæculorum*. I am now going on gently with the brasswork, which does not require any immediate expenses, and which I attend to entirely myself. I have no workmen about me at present.

Henry Reveley to P.B. Shelley

November 17, 1819. Your volcanic description of the birth of the cylinder is very characteristic both of you, and of it. One might imagine God when he made the earth, and saw the granite mountains & flinty promontories flow into their craggy forms, & the splendour of their fusion filling millions of miles of the void space, like the tail of a comet, so looking, & so delighting in his work. God sees his machine spinning round the sun, & delights in its success, and has taken out patents to supply all suns in space with same manufacture. Your boat will be to the Ocean of Water, what this earth is to the Ocean of Æther – a prosperous and swift voyager.

P.B. Shelley to Henry Reveley

From letters of Henry Reveley to P.B. Shelley, and of Shelley to Reveley, printed in The Letters of Percy Bysshe Shelley, *edited by Roger Ingpen, published 1915.*

157   PROFESSIONAL FANCIES   December 1820

My dear Sarah,   Royal Institution: Thursday evening

It is astonishing how much the state of the body influences the powers of the mind. I have been thinking all the morning of the very delightful and interesting letter I would send you this evening, and now I am so tired, and yet have so much to do, that my thoughts are quite giddy, and run round your image without any power of themselves to stop and admire it. I want to say a thousand kind and, believe me, heartfelt things to you, but am not master of words fit for the purpose; and still, as I ponder and think on you, chlorides, trials, oil, Davy, steel, miscellanea, mercury, and fifty other professional fancies swim before and drive me further and further into the quandary of stupidness.

From your affectionate
Michael

Being a letter from Michael Faraday to Sarah Barnard, printed in The Life and Letters of Faraday *by H. Bence Jones, published 1870.*

158 THE WIND OF HEAVEN May 19, 1821

We intended to stop a day here [Sheffield], to look about us, and survey the curiosities of this great city of Vulcan, and well should we have been repaid for the delay no doubt, but as important events not only frequently arise from small causes, but are baffled by them, our dreams of all the shining jewels of this wondrous cave, shrouded in smoke and sulphur, and glaring fire, were quickly annihilated by a very significant object. As I sat up in bed, I was almost startled by a sudden exclamation of my wife, who discovered one of those noisome flat insects so common in the beds of towns and crowded places, crawling up my shirt. This determined her. 'She would not stop in that place,' she said, 'for the world – she would not eat in it – and we must set off directly;' and suiting the action to the word, she was dressed in quick time, and fidgeting to be gone – to get out 'into the green lanes', and to 'breathe the sweet country air'. I rather thought, however, that the wish to see her child affected her; perhaps she had been dreaming of her; at all events, I am sure the anticipated pleasure of embracing my dear little girl once more had considerable influence in my acquiescence to quit the town thus suddenly.

Well, we soon paid the shot, and were on our way out of the town. We got, however, on the wrong route, and, before we were aware of that, we found ourselves climbing the foot of the great hills which divide Yorkshire from Derbyshire. For several miles we continued to ascend, and everywhere we came to a small flat, and hoped we had surmounted all, when a few paces discovered to us another eminence. I wondered how my little woman stood it, but she this morning showed me her light foot indeed, and with all cheerfulness we breasted the hill, anon looking back, to see how far we had travelled towards home. At length we entered on a broad wild moor, where for miles and miles towards Yorkshire all was a scene of dun heath and shelterless plain; whilst downwards, over Derbyshire and Cheshire, the eye commanded what seemd an almost illimitable expanse of mountain land.

'But where the vision began to fail
There seemed to be hills of a cloudy pale.'

In the valley we had left – now as we could discover of a beautifully undulating surface, and gaily green in the sun – lay the town of Sheffield, shrouded in its furnace clouds. On our right and left were the wild and boundless districts I have mentioned, and before us was the wrinkled front of Mam Tor, frowning like an eld, in witch-land.

We walked to the height of Hathersage Grange, and there stopped to survey the vast, solitary, yet pleasing scenes. My wife was seated on a grassy knoll, whilst I stood beside her with my stick and bundle over my shoulder, my back towards the sun, whose beams were somewhat mitigated by light clouds, and my looks directed over the wold towards the Yorkshire border.

'Well, I am convinced now,' I said, breaking a long silence, 'that Burke was not so far wide of the truth after all.'

'What did Burke say?' she asked; 'for my part, I never heard him say much of either truth or falsehood.'

She thought I was alluding to one of the simplest of my Radical comrades, whom we had nicknamed 'Burke'.

'Pho! it's Edmund Burke, the great orator and political apostate, that I mean.'

'And what did he say?' she asked.

'Say? He called the people "the swinish multitude"; and I am convinced he was right, for I have discovered I am one of them.'

'What do you mean?' she asked again, now more interested.

'I can see the wind,' I said, 'and that's a sure sign I'm one of the swinish herd.'

'See the wind! And what's it like?' asked she, looking up and laughing.

'It's the most beautiful thing I ever saw,' I said, 'and if thou'll come here, thou shall see it also.'

I will suppose that the curiosity natural to the sex was excited, for she instantly was at my side.

'Now look over the top of the brown heath with a steady eye, and see if thou canst discern a remarkably bright substance, brighter than glass or pearly water, deeply clear and lucid, swimming, not like a stream, but like a quick spirit, up and down, and forward, as if hurrying to be gone.'

'Nonsense!' she said, 'there is not anything.'

'Look again, steady, for a moment,' I said; 'I still behold it.'

'There is,' she said, 'there is; I see it! Oh! what a beautiful thing!'

I gave her a kiss, and said I loved her better than ever. She was the first woman who, I believed, had ever seen the vital element, the life-fraught wind.

'Is that the wind?' she asked.

'That is the wind of heaven,' I said, 'now sweeping over the earth and visible. It is the great element of vitality, water quickened by fire, the spirit of life!'

I know not whether I was quite right in my philosophy, but we bowed our hearts, and adored the Creator; and in that we were both right, I hope.

We stood gazing in wonder and admiration; for still, like a spirit-stream, it kept hurrying past – or as a messenger in haste; and so we left it glittering and sweeping away. This was on the morning of the 19th day of May, 1821.

From Passages in the Life of a Radical *by Samuel Bamford, 1840–44.*

| 159 | THE DEATH-BED OF HERSCHEL | August 15, 1822 |

Aug. 15th. – I hastened to the spot where I was wont to find him with the newspaper which I was to read to him. But instead I found Mrs. Morson, Miss Baldwin, and Mr Bulman, from Leeds, the grandson of my brother's earliest acquaintance in this country. I was informed my brother had been obliged to return to his room, whither I flew immediately. Lady H. and the housekeeper were with him, administering everything which could be thought of for supporting him. I found him much irritated at not being able to grant Mr Bulman's request for some token of remembrance for his father. As soon as he saw me, I was sent to the library to fetch one of his last papers and a plate of the forty-feet telescope. But for the universe I could not have looked twice at what I had snatched from the shelf, and when he faintly asked if the breaking up of the Milky Way was in it, I said 'Yes,' and he looked content. I cannot help remembering this circumstance, it was the last time I was sent to the library on such an occasion. That the anxious care for his papers and workrooms never ended but with his life was proved by his frequent whispered inquiries if they were locked and the key safe, of which I took care to assure him that they were, and the key in Lady Herschel's hands.

From the Recollections *of Caroline Lucretia Herschel, printed in* Memoir and Correspondence of Caroline Herschel *by Mrs John Herschel, published 1876.*

| 160 | WILLIAM BLAKE | August 1823 |

Some persons of a scientific turn were once discoursing pompously, and, to him, distastefully, about the incredible distance of the planets, the length of time light takes to travel to the earth, etc., when he burst out: 'It is false. I walked the other evening to the end of the earth, and touched the sky with my finger'; perhaps with a little covert sophistry, meaning that he thrust his stick out into space, and that, had he stood upon the remotest star, he could do no more; the blue sky itself being but the limit of our bodily perceptions of the infinite which encompasses us. Scientific individuals would generally make him come out with something outrageous and unreasonable. For he had an indestructible animosity towards what, to his devout, old-world imagination, seemed the keen polar atmosphere of modern science. In society, once, a cultivated stranger, as a mark of polite attention, was showing him the first number of the *Mechanic's Magazine*. 'Ah, sir,' remarked Blake, with bland emphasis, 'these things we artists HATE!' The latter years of Blake's life was an era when universal homage was challenged for mechanical science – as for some new evangel; with a triumphant clamour on the part of superficial enthusiasts, which has since subsided.

From the Life of William Blake *by Alexander Gilchrist, 1863.*

161   EXTRACT FROM A PLAY   1823

The Devil
(Going to the timepiece)
Half after midnight! these mute moralizers,
Pointing to the unheeded lapse of hours,
Become a tacit eloquent reproach
Unto the dissipation of this Earth.
There is a clock in Pandemonium,
Hard by the burning throne of my great grandsire,
The slow vibrations of whose pendulum,
With click-clack alternation to and fro,
Sound *'Ever, Never'* thro' the courts of Hell,
Piercing the wrung ears of the damned that writhe
Upon their beds of flame, and whenso'er
There may be short cessation of their wails,
Through all the boundless depth of fires is heard
The shrill and solemn warning *'Ever, Never'*:
Then bitterly, I trow, they turn and toss
And shriek and shout to drown the thrilling noise.
(Looking again at the timepiece)
Half after midnight! Wherefore stand I here?
Methinks my tongue runs twenty knots an hour:
I must unto mine office.
(Exit abruptly)

By Alfred Tennyson, aged 14, *in* Tennyson, A Memoir *by Hallam, Lord Tennyson, 1897.*

162   SAINT PAUL'S   June 25, 1824

I was hurrying along Cheapside into Newgate-Street among a thousand bustling pigmies and the innumerable jinglings and rollings and crashings of many-coloured labour, when all at once in passing from the abode of John Gilpin, stunned by the tumult of his restless compeers, I looked up from the boiling throng through a little opening at the corner of the street – and there stood St. Paul's – with its columns and friezes, and massy wings of bleached yet unworn stone; with its statues and its graves around it; with its solemn dome four hundred feet above me, and its gilded ball and cross gleaming in the evening sun, piercing up into the heaven through the vapours of our earthly home! It was silent as Tadmor of the Wilderness: gigantic, beautiful, enduring; it seemed to frown with a rebuking pity on the vain scramble which it overlooked: at its feet were tombstones, above it was the everlasting sky, within priests perhaps were chanting hymns; it seemed to transmit with a stern voice the sounds of Death, Judgment, and Eternity through all the frivolous and fluctuating city. I saw it oft and from various points, and never without new admiration.

From a letter of Thomas Carlyle to Alexander Carlyle, printed in Early Letters of Thomas Carlyle, *edited by C.E. Norton, 1886.*

163 USE OF THE CAMERA OBSCURA August 7, 1824

An occurrence originated in a Camera Obscura exhibited here during the Fair week, which shows the important use to which this amusing optical apparatus may be applied. A person happened to be examining, with great interest, the various lively and ever shifting figures which were pourtrayed upon the white tablet during the exhibition, when he beheld, with amazement, the appearance of one man picking another man's pocket. Perfectly aware of the reality of this appearance, he opened the door, and recognizing the culprit at a short distance, ran up and seized him in the very act of depredation. It is, perhaps, unnecessary to add, that he was immediately handed over to the Police. From this circumstance, the utility of placing such apparatus in all places of public amusement and exhibitions, must be obvious. Whether it might be proper to erect it in the streets of a populous city like this, and to place it under the inspection of an officer for the detection of mischief and crime, is a matter worthy of the consideration of the local authorities. Would it not be an eligible plan, indeed, to employ the Camera Obscura of the Observatory, (which is not otherwise in use) to take a view of what is passing in the streets in town, and communicate the result, if necessary, to the Police Office, or the Jail, by means of a telegraph? If the Observatory be considered too far off, the apparatus could be fixed up near the top of the Tron or Cross Steeple. By this means, the necessity of sending out emissaries to reconnoitre the conduct of the lieges would be superseded, since every thing would then take place, as it were, under the eye of the Police; and, if any impropriety or misconduct were observed, it would only be necessary to send a *posse* to the particular spot where it happened.

From The Glasgow Mechanics' Magazine, *No.XXXII.*

164 THE BLACK COUNTRY August 11, 1824

I was one day through the iron and coal works of this neighbourhood, – a half-frightful scene! A space perhaps of 30 square miles to the north of us, covered over with furnaces, rolling-mills, steam-engines and sooty men. A dense cloud of pestilential smoke hangs over it for ever, blackening even the grain that grows upon it; and at night the whole region burns like a volcano spitting fire from a thousand tubes of brick. But oh the wretched hundred and fifty thousand mortals that grind out their destiny there! In the coal-mines they were literally naked, many of them, all but trousers; black as ravens; plashing about among dripping caverns, or scrambling amid heaps of broken mineral; and thirsting unquenchably for beer. In the iron-mills it was little better: blast-furnaces were roaring like the voice of many whirlwinds all around; the fiery metal was hissing thro' its moulds, or sparkling and spitting under hammers of a monstrous size, which fell like so many little earthquakes. Here they were wheeling charred coals, breaking their ironstone, and tumbling all into their fiery pit; there they were turning and boring cannon with a hideous shrieking noise such as the earth could hardly parallel; and through the whole, half-naked demons pouring with sweat and besmeared with soot were hurrying to and fro in their red nightcaps and sheet-iron breeches rolling or hammering or squeezing their glowing metal as if it had been wax or dough. They also had a thirst for ale. Yet on the whole I am told they are very happy: they make forty shillings or more per week, and few of them will work on Mondays. It is in a spot like this that one sees the sources of British power.

From a letter of Thomas Carlyle to Alexander Carlyle, printed in Early Letters of Thomas Carlyle, *edited by C.E. Norton, 1886.*

165 CARLYLE IN LONDON December 14, 1824

Of this enormous Babel of a place I can give you no account in writing: it is like the heart of all the universe; and the flood of human effort rolls out of it and into it with a violence that almost appals one's very sense. Paris scarcely occupies a quarter of the ground, and does not seem to have the twentieth part of the business. O that our father sey [*saw*] Holborn in a fog! with the black vapour brooding over it, absolutely like fluid ink; and coaches and wains and sheep and oxen and wild people rushing on with bellowings and shrieks and thundering din, as if the earth in general were gone distracted. To-day I chanced to pass thro' Smithfield, when the market was three-fourths over. I mounted the steps of a door, and looked abroad upon the area, an irregular space of perhaps thirty acres in extent, encircled with old dingy brick-built houses, and intersected with wooden pens for the cattle. What a scene! Innumerable herds of fat oxen, tied in long rows, or passing at a trot to their several shambles; and thousands of graziers, drovers, butchers, cattle-brokers with their quilted frocks and long goads pushing on the hapless beasts; hurrying to and fro in confused parties, shouting, jostling, cursing, in the midst of rain and *shairn* [*dung*], and braying discord such as the imagination cannot figure. – Then there are stately streets and squares, and calm green recesses to which nothing of this abomination is permitted to enter. No wonder Cobbett calls the place a Wen. It is a monstrous Wen! The thick smoke of it beclouds a space of thirty square miles; and a million of vehicles, from the dog- or cuddy-barrow to the giant waggon, grind along its streets for ever. I saw a six-horse wain the other day with, I think, Number 200,000 and odds upon it!

There is an excitement in all this, which is pleasant as a transitory feeling, but much against my taste as a permanent one. I had much rather visit London from time to time, than live in it. There is in fact no *right* life in it that I can find: the people are situated here like plants in a hot-house, to which the quiet influences of sky and earth are never in their unadulterated state admitted. It is the case with all ranks: the carman with his huge slouch-hat hanging half-way down his back, consumes his breakfast of bread and tallow or hog's lard, sometimes as he swags along the streets, always in a hurried and precarious fashion, and supplies the deficit by continual pipes, and pots of beer. The fashionable lady rises at three in the afternoon, and begins to live towards midnight. Between these two extremes, the same false and tumultuous manner of existence more or less infests all ranks. It seems as if you were for ever in 'an inn', the feeling of *home* in our acceptation of the term is not known to one of a thousand. You are packed into paltry shells of brick-houses (calculated to endure for forty years, and then fall); every door that slams to in the street is audible in your most secret chamber; the necessaries of life are hawked about through multitudes of hands, and reach you, frequently adulterated, always at rather more than *twice* their cost elsewhere; people's friends must visit them by rule and measure; and when you issue from your door, you are assailed by vast shoals of quacks, and showmen, and street sweepers, and pick-pockets, and mendicants of every degree and shape, all plying in noise or silent craft their several vocations, all in their hearts like 'lions ravening for their prey.' The blackguard population of the place is the most consummately blackguard of anything I ever saw.

From a letter of Thomas Carlyle to Alexander Carlyle, printed in Early Letters of Thomas Carlyle, *edited by C.E. Norton, 1886.*

166   HARRY AND LUCY   Autumn 1826

Harry knew very well what it was and went on with his drawing but Lucy soon called him away and bid him observe a great black cloud from the north which seemed rather electrical. Harry ran for an electrical apparatus which his father had given him and the cloud electrified his apparatus positively after that another cloud came which electrified his apparatus negatively and then a long train of smaller ones but before this cloud came a great cloud of dust rose from the ground and followed the positive cloud and at length seemed to come in contact with it and when the other cloud came a flash of lightning was seen to dart through the cloud of dust upon which the negative cloud spread very much and dissolved in rain which presently cleared the sky. After this phenomenon was over and also the surprise Harry began to wonder how electricity could get where there was so much water but he soon observed a rainbow and a rising mist under it which his fancy soon transformed into a female form. He then remembered the witch of the waters of the Alps who was raised from them by takeing some water in the hand and throwing it into the air pronouncing some unintelligable words. And though it was a tale it affected Harry now when he saw in the clouds something like it.

From a book written by John Ruskin, aged 7, and printed by him in Praeterita, *published 1886.*

167   Rays of Darkness   October 6, 1827

A beautiful aereal phenomenon observed about St. Paul's Church, from the shadow of the dome and the part above cast on very thin clouds moving at that height. The moon at the full and rising. On looking at St. Paul's cross from Ludgate hill, about stationers' Court and the opposite side a stream of darkness seemed to issue from the part above the dome, and expanding seemed to pass over the head of the spectator; by moving a little to the north or south so as to get under the edge of the shadow it was exceedingly well defined and distinct. Each of the turrets in front threw a similar shadow, but more faintly. As the moon rose and moved towards the south the shadows or rays also changed their directions, and at last they were best seen from the corner of Ludgate Hill and St. Paul's Church Yard. The mist or cloud was very faint, for the stars could be well seen. Whilst looking at it my companion thought she saw a black ray in another direction; this however proved to be the clear space between one thin cloud and another, and watching this and by it tracing the motion of the cloud in the wind, we were able to account for the increase and diminution in strength of the shadow of the church spire as the cloud came up and afterwards passed over. The effect was very beautiful. Many persons went away fully convinced that rays of darkness were issuing from the Church. Time about 8 o'clock.

From the Diary *of Michael Faraday, edited by Thomas Martin, 1932.*

The Beautiful Road to Hades December 1827

Since last you heard from me I have seen the great West India Dock and the Thames Tunnel. Oh, H—, 'que c'est une jolie chose que l'homme!' Annihilated by any one of the elements if singly opposed to its power, he by his genius yet brings their united forces into bondage, and compels obedience from all their manifold combined strength. We penetrate the earth, we turn the course of rivers, we exalt the valleys and bow down the mountains; and we die and return to our dust, and they remain and remember us no more. Often enough, indeed, the names of the great inventors and projectors have been overshadowed or effaced by mere finishers of their work or adaptors of their idea, who have reaped the honor and emolument due to an obscure originator, who passes away from the world, his rightful claim to its admiration and gratitude unknown or unacknowledged. But these obey the law of their being; they cannot but do the work God's inspiration calls them to.

But I must tell you what this tunnel is like, or at least try to do so. You enter, by flights of stairs, the first door, and find yourself on a circular platform which surrounds the top of a well or shaft, of about two hundred feet in circumference and five hundred in depth. This well is an immense iron frame of cylindrical form, filled in with bricks; it was constructed on level ground, and then, by some wonderful mechanical process, sunk into the earth. In the midst of this is a steam engine, and above, or below, as far as your eye can see, huge arms are working up and down while the creaking, crashing, whirring noises, and the swift whirling of innumerable wheels all around you, make you feel for the first few minutes as if you were going distracted. I should have liked to look much longer at all these beautiful, wise, working creatures, but was obliged to follow the last of the party through all the machinery, down little wooden stairs and along tottering planks, to the bottom of the well. On turning round at the foot of the last flight of steps through an immense dark arch, as far as sight could reach stretched a vaulted passage, smooth earth underfoot, the white arches of the roof beyond one another lengthening on and on in prolonged vista, the whole lighted by a line of gas lamps, and as bright, almost, as if it were broad day. It was more like one of the long avenues of light that lead to the abodes of the genii in fairy tales, than anything I had ever beheld. The profound stillness of the place, which was first broken by my father's voice, to which the vaulted roof gave extraordinary and startling volume of tone, the indescribable feeling of subterranean vastness, the amazement and delight I experienced, quite overcame me, and I was obliged to turn from the friend who was explaining everything to me, to cry and ponder in silence. How I wish you had been with us, dear H—! Our name is always worth something to us: Mr Brunel, who was superintending some of the works, came to my father and offered to conduct us to where the workmen were employed – an unusual favour, which of course delighted us all. So we left our broad, smooth path of light, and got into dark passages, where we stumbled among coils of ropes and heaps of pipes and piles of planks, and where ground springs were welling up and flowing about in every direction, all which was very strange. As you may have heard, the tunnel caved in once, and let the Thames in through the roof; and in order that, should such an accident occur again, no lives may be lost, an iron frame has been constructed – a sort of cage, divided into many compartments, in each of which a man with his lantern and his tools is placed – and as they clear the earth away this iron frame is moved onward and advances into new ground. All this was wonderful and curious beyond measure, but the appearance of the workmen themselves, all begrimed, with their brawny arms and legs bare, some standing in black water up to their knees, others laboriously shovelling the black earth in their cages (while they sturdily sung at their task), with the red, murky light of links and lanterns flashing and flickering about them, made up the most striking picture you can conceive. As we returned I remained at the bottom of the stairs last of all, to look back at the beautiful road to Hades, wishing I might be left behind, and then we reascended, through wheels, pulleys, and engines, to the upper day. After this we rowed down the river to the docks, lunched on board a splendid East Indiaman, and came home again. I think it is better for me, however, to look at the trees, and the sun, moon, and stars, than at tunnels and docks; they make me too humanity proud.

From a letter of Fanny Kemble to a friend, printed in her Records of a Girlhood, *published 1878.*

169   THE LORD'S PRAYER   1827

Doctor Thornton's Tory Translation, Translated out of its disguise in the Classical & Scotch languages into the vulgar English.

Our Father Augustus Caesar, who art in these thy Substantial Astronomical Telescopic Heavens, Holiness to thy Name or Title, & reverence to thy Shadow. Thy Kingship come upon Earth first & then in Heaven. Give us day by day our Real Taxed Substantial Money bought Bread; deliver from the Holy Ghost whatever cannot be taxed; for all is debts & Taxes between Caesar & us & one another; lead us not to read the Bible, but let our Bible be Virgil & Shakespeare; & deliver us from Poverty in Jesus, that Evil One. For thine is the Kingship, [or] Allegoric Godship, & the Power, or War, & the Glory, or Law, Ages after Ages in thy descendants; for God is only an Allegory of Kings & nothing Else.

Amen.

From the Marginalia to Dr Thornton's New Translation of the Lord's Prayer *1827, by William Blake.*

170   LONDON LIFE   May 1, 1829

I am in very good health: London life suits me excellently. I think the town and the streets are beautiful. Again I was struck with awe when I drove in an open cabriolet yesterday to the City, along a different road, and everywhere found the same flow of life, everywhere green, yellow, red bills stuck on the houses from top to bottom, or gigantic letters painted on them, everywhere noise and smoke, everywhere the ends of the streets lost in fog. Every few moments I passed a church, or a market-place, or a green square, or a theatre, or caught a glimpse of the Thames, on which the steamers can now go right through the town under all the bridges, because a mechanism has been invented for lowering the large funnels like masts. To see, besides, the masts from the West India Docks looking across, and to see a harbour as large as Hamburg's treated like a pond, with sluices, and the ships arranged not singly but in rows, like regiments – all that makes one's heart rejoice over the great world.

From a letter of Felix Mendelssohn to his family, in Letters, *edited by G. Selden-Gott, published 1946.*

171   THIS SHEFFIELD   January 31, 1830

All the way along, from Leeds to Sheffield, it is coal and iron, and iron and coal. It was dark before we reached Sheffield; so that we saw the iron furnaces in all the horrible splendour of their everlasting blaze. Nothing can be conceived more grand or more terrific than the yellow waves of fire that incessantly issue from the top of these furnaces, some of which are close by the way-side. Nature has placed the beds of iron and the beds of coal alongside of each other, and art has taught man to make one operate upon the other, as to turn the iron-stone into liquid matter, which is drained off from the bottom of the furnace, and afterwards moulded into blocks and bars, and all sorts of things. The combustibles are put into the top of the furnace, which stands thirty, forty, or fifty feet up in the air, and the ever-blazing mouth of which is kept supplied with coal and coke and iron-stone, from little iron wagons forced up by steam, and brought down again to be refilled. It is a surprising thing to behold; and it is impossible to behold it without being convinced that, whatever other nations may do with cotton and with wool, they will never equal England with regard to things made of iron and steel. This Sheffield, and the land all about it, is one bed of iron and coal. They call it black Sheffield, and black enough it is; but from this town and its environs go nine-tenths of the knives that are used in the whole world.

From the Northern Tour *of William Cobbett, 1832.*

On leaving Coalbrookdale I trudged my way towards Wolverhampton. I rested at Shiffnal for the night. Next day I was in the middle of the Black Country. I had no letters of introduction to employers in Wolverhampton; so that, without stopping there, I proceeded at once to Dudley. The Black Country is anything but picturesque. The earth seems to have been turned inside out. Its entrails are strewn about; nearly the entire surface of the ground is covered with cinder-heaps and mounds of scoriae. The coal, which has been drawn from below ground, is blazing on the surface. The district is crowded with iron furnaces, puddling furnaces and coal-pit engine furnaces. By day and by night the country is glowing with fire, and the smoke of the ironworks hovers over it. There is a rumbling and clanking of iron forges and rolling mills. Workmen covered with smut, and with fierce white eyes, are seen moving about amongst the glowing iron and dull thud of forge-hammers.

Amidst these flaming, smoky, clanging works, I beheld the remains of what had once been happy farmhouses, now ruined and deserted. The ground underneath them had sunk by the working out of the coal, and they were falling to pieces. They had in former times been surrounded by clumps of trees but only the skeletons of them remained, dilapidated, black, and lifeless. The grass had been parched and killed by the vapours of sulphureous acid thrown out by the chimneys; and every herbaceous object was of a ghastly gray – the emblem of vegetable death in its saddest aspect. Vulcan had driven out Ceres. In some places I heard a sort of chirruping sound, as of some forlorn bird haunting the ruins of the old farmsteads. But no! the chirrup was a vile delusion. It proceeded from the shrill creaking of the coal-winding chains, which were placed in small tunnels beneath the hedgeless road.

I went into some of the forges to see the workmen at their labours. There was no need of introduction; the works were open to all, for they were unsurrounded by walls. I saw the white-hot iron run out from the furnace; I saw it spun, as it were, into bars and iron ribbands, with an ease and rapidity which seemed marvellous. There were also the ponderous hammers and clanking rolling-mills. I wandered from one to another without restraint. I lingered among the blast furnaces, seeing the flood of molten iron run out from time to time, and remained there until it was late. When it became dark the scene was still more impressive. The workmen within seemed to be running about amidst the flames as in a pandemonium; while around and outside the horizon was a glowing belt of fire, making even the stars look pale and feeble. At last I came away with reluctance, and made my way towards Dudley. I reached the town at a late hour. I was exhausted in mind and body, yet the day had been most interesting and exciting. A sound sleep refreshed me, and I was up in the morning early, to recommence my journey of inquiry.

I made my way to the impressive ruins of Dudley Castle, the remnant of a very ancient stronghold, originally built by Dud, the Saxon. The castle is situated on a finely wooded hill; it is so extensive that it more resembles the ruins of a town than of a single building. You enter through a treble gateway, and see the remnants of the moat, the court, and the keep. Here are the central hall, the guard-rooms and the chapel. It must have been a magnificent structure. In the Midlands it was known as the 'Castle of the Woods'. Now it is abandoned by its owners, and surrounded by the Black Country. It is undermined by colleries, and even penetrated by a canal. The castle walls sometimes tremble when a blast occurs in the bowels of the mountain beneath. The town of Dudley lies quite close to the castle, and was doubtless protected by it in ancient times.

The architectural remains are of various degrees of antiquity, and are well worthy of study, as embodying the successive periods which they represent. Their melancholy grandeur is rendered all the more impressive by the coal and iron works with which they are surrounded – the olden type of buildings confronting the modern. The venerable trees struggle for existence under the destroying influence of sulphureous acid; while the grass is withered and the vegetation everywhere blighted. I sat down on an elevated part of the ruins, and looking down upon the extensive district, with its roaring and blazing furnaces, the smoke of which blackened the country as far as eye could reach; and as I watched the decaying trees I thought of the price we had to pay for our vaunted supremacy in the manufacture of iron. We may fill our purses, but we pay a heavy price for it in the loss of picturesqueness and beauty.

From James Nasmyth, Engineer, An Autobiography, *edited by* Samuel Smiles, 1883.

173   MR STEPHENSON   August 26, 1830
                                  Liverpool
MY DEAR H—,

A common sheet of paper is enough for love, but a foolscap extra can alone contain a railroad and my ecstasies. There was once a man, who was born at Newcastle-upon-Tyne, who was a common coal-digger; this man had an immense constructiveness, which displayed itself in pulling his watch to pieces and putting it together again; in making a pair of shoes when he happened to be some days without occupation; finally – here there is a great gap in my story – it brought him in the capacity of an engineer before a committee in the House of Commons, with his head full of plans for constructing a railroad from Liverpool to Manchester. It so happened that to the quickest and most powerful perceptions and conceptions, to the most indefatigable industry and perseverance, and the most accurate knowledge of the phenomena of nature as they affect his peculiar labours, this man joined an utter want of the 'gift of the gab;' he could no more explain to others what he meant to do and how he meant to do it, than he could fly; and therefore members of the House of Commons, after saying, 'There is rock to be excavated to a depth of more than sixty feet, there are embankments to be made nearly to the same height, there is a swamp of five miles in length to be traversed, in which if you drop an iron rod it sinks and disappears: how will you do all this?' and receiving no answer but a broad Northumbrian 'I can't tell you how I'll do it, but I can tell you I *will* do it,' dismissed Stephenson as a visionary. Having prevailed upon a company of Liverpool gentlemen to be less incredulous, and having raised funds for his great undertaking, in December of 1826 the first spade was struck into the ground. And now I will give you an account of my yesterday's excursion. A party of sixteen persons was ushered into a large court-yard, where, under cover, stood several carriages of a peculiar construction, one of which was prepared for our reception. It was a long-bodied vehicle with seats placed across it, back to back; the one we were in had six of these benches, and was a sort of uncovered *char à banc*. The wheels were placed upon two iron bands, which formed the road, and to which they are fitted, being so constructed as to slide along without any danger of hitching or becoming displaced, on the same principle as a thing sliding on a concave groove. The carriage was set in motion by a mere push, and, having received this impetus, rolled with us down an inclined plane into a tunnel, which forms the entrance to the railroad. This tunnel is four hundred yards long (I believe), and will be lighted by gas. At the end of it we emerged from darkness, and, the ground becoming level, we stopped. There is another tunnel parallel with this, only much wider and longer, for it extends from the place which we had now reached, and where the steam-carriages start, and which is quite out of Liverpool, the whole way under the town, to the docks. This tunnel is for waggons and other heavy carriages; and as the engines which are to draw the trains along the railroad do not enter these tunnels, there is a large building at this entrance which is to be inhabited by steam-engines of a stationary turn of mind, and different constitution from the travelling ones, which are to propel the trains through the tunnels to the terminus in the town, without going out of their houses themselves. The length of the tunnel parallel to the one we passed through is (I believe) two thousand two hundred yards. I wonder if you are understanding one word I am saying all this while! We were introduced to the little engine which was to drag us along the rails. She (for they make these curious little fire-horses all mares) consisted of a boiler, a stove, a small platform, a bench, and behind the bench a barrel containing enough water to prevent her being thirsty for fifteen miles, – the whole machine not bigger than a common fire-engine. She goes upon two wheels, which are her feet, and are moved by bright steel legs called pistons; these are propelled by steam, and in proportion as more steam is applied to the upper extremities (the hip-joints,

I suppose) of these pistons, the faster they move the wheels; and when it is desirable to diminish the speed, the steam, which unless suffered to escape would burst the boiler, evaporates through a safety-valve into the air. The reins, bit, and bridle of this wonderful beast is a small steel handle, which applies or withdraws the steam from its legs or pistons, so that a child might manage it. The coals, which are its oats, were under the bench, and there was a small glass tube affixed to the boiler, with water in it, which indicates by its fulness or emptiness when the creature wants water, which is immediately conveyed to it from its reservoirs. There is a chimney to the stove, but as they burn coke there is none of that dreadful black smoke which accompanies the progress of a steam-vessel. This snorting little animal, which I felt rather inclined to pat, was then harnessed to our carriage, and Mr Stephenson having taken me on the bench of the engine with him, we started at about ten miles an hour. The steam-horse being ill adapted for going up and down hill, the road was kept at a certain level, and appeared sometimes to sink below the surface of the earth, and sometimes to rise above it. Almost at starting it was cut through the solid rock, which formed a wall on either side of it, about sixty feet high. You can't imagine how strange it seemed to be journeying on thus, without any visible cause of progress other than the magical machine, with its flying white breath and rhythmical, unvarying pace, between these rocky walls, which are already clothed with moss and ferns and grasses; and when I reflected that these great masses of stone had been cut asunder to allow our passage thus far below the surface of the earth, I felt as if no fairy tale was ever half so wonderful as what I saw. Bridges were thrown from side to side across the top of these cliffs, and the people looking down upon us from them seemed like pigmies standing in the sky. I must be more concise, or I shall want room. We were to go only fifteen miles, that distance being sufficient to show the speed of the engine, and to take us on to the most beautiful and wonderful object on the road. After proceeding through this rocky defile, we presently found ourselves raised upon embankments ten or twelve feet high; we then came to a moss, or swamp of considerable extent, on which no human foot could tread without sinking, and yet it bore the road which bore us. This had been the great stumbling-block in the minds of the committee of the House of Commons; but Mr Stephenson has succeeded in overcoming it. A foundation of hurdles, or as he called it, basket-work, was thrown over the morass, and the interstices were filled with moss and other elastic matter. Upon this the clay and soil were laid down, and the road *does* float, for we passed over it at the rate of five and twenty miles an hour, and saw the stagnant swamp water trembling on the surface of the soil on either side of us. I hope you understand me. The embankment had gradually been rising higher and higher, and in one place, where the soil was not settled enough to form banks, Stephenson had constructed artificial ones of wood-work, over which the mounds of earth were heaped, for he calculated that though the wood-work would rot, before it did so the banks of earth which covered it would have been sufficiently consolidated to support the road.

We had now come fifteen miles, and stopped where the road traversed a wide and deep valley. Stephenson made me alight and led me down to the bottom of this ravine, over which, in order to keep his road level, he has thrown a magnificent viaduct of nine arches, the middle one of which is seventy feet high, through which we saw the whole of this beautiful little valley. It was lovely and wonderful beyond all words. He here told me many curious things respecting this ravine: how he believed the Mersey had once rolled through it; how the soil had proved so unfavourable for the foundation of his bridge that it was built upon piles, which had been driven into the earth to an enormous depth; how, while, digging for a foundation, he had come to a tree bedded in the earth fourteen feet below the surface of the ground; how tides are caused, and how another flood might be caused; all of which I have remembered and noted down at much greater length than I can enter upon it here. He explained to me the whole construction of the steam-engine, and said he could soon make a famous engineer of me, which, considering the wonderful things he *has* achieved, I dare not say is impossible. His way of explaining himself is peculiar, but very striking, and I understood, without difficulty, all that he said to me. We then rejoined the rest of the party, and the engine having received its supply of water, the carriage was placed behind it, for it cannot turn, and was set off at its utmost speed, thirty-five miles an hour, swifter than a bird flies (for they tried the experiment with a snipe). You cannot conceive what that sensation of cutting the air was; the motion is as smooth as possible, too. I could either have read or written; and as it was, I stood up, and with my bonnet off 'drank the air before me.' The wind, which was strong, or perhaps the force of our thrusting against it, absolutely weighed my eyelids down. When I closed my eyes this sensation of flying was quite delightful, and strange beyond description; yet, strange as it was, I had a perfect sense of security, and not the slightest fear. At one time, to exhibit the power of the engine, having met another steam-carriage which was unsupplied with water, Mr Stephenson caused it to be fastened in front of ours; moreover, a waggon laden with timber was also chained to us, and thus propelling the idle steam-engine, and dragging the loaded wagon which was beside it, and our own carriage full of people behind, this brave little she-dragon of ours flew on. Farther on she met three carts, which being fastened in front of her, she pushed on before her without the slightest delay or difficulty; when I add that this pretty little creature can run with equal facility either backwards or forwards, I believe I have given you an account of all her capacities.

Now for a word or two about the master of all these marvels, with whom I am most horribly in love. He is a man of from fifty to fifty-five years of age; his face is fine, though careworn, and bears an expression of deep thoughtfulness; his mode of explaining his ideas is peculiar and very original, striking, and forcible; and although his accent indicates strongly his north-country birth, his language has not the slightest touch of vulgarity or coarseness. He has certainly turned my head.

Four years have sufficed to bring this great undertaking to an end. The railroad will be opened upon the 15th of next month. The Duke of Wellington is coming down to be present on the occasion, and, I suppose, what with the thousands of spectators and the novelty of the spectacle, there will never have been a scene of more striking interest. The whole cost of the work (including the engines and carriages) will have been eight hundred and thirty thousand pounds; and it is already worth double that sum.

From a letter of Fanny Kemble to a friend, printed in her Records of a Girlhood, *1878.*

174   OPENING OF THE RAILWAY   September 15, 1830

The Northumbrian was appointed to take the lead of the procession, drawing a splendid carriage, appropriated to the reception of the Duke of Wellington, Sir Robert Peel, and about thirty other distinguished individuals, who honoured the ceremony with their presence. Each of the other locomotives drew four carriages, containing between eighty and ninety persons. So that the total number of individuals accommodated with seats in the procession, must have been about 600. It fell to our lot to make part of the train to the Arrow, the seventh engine in the line of procession.

At twenty minutes to eleven o'clock the procession commenced its progress towards Manchester, the Northumbrian taking exclusively one of the two lines of rail, and the rest of the engines the other. The brilliancy of the *cortège*, the novelty of the sight, considerations of the almost boundless advantages of the stupendous power about to be put in operation, gave to the spectacle an interest unparalleled. On every side the tumultuous voice of praise was heard, and countless thousands waved their hats to cheer on the sons of enterprise in this their crowning effort. The engines proceeded at a moderate speed towards Wavertree-lane, when increased power having been added, they went forward with great swiftness, and thousands fell back, whom all the previous efforts of a formidable police could not move from the road. Numerous booths and vehicles lined the various roads, and were densely crowded. After passing Wavertree-lane, the procession entered the deep ravine at Olive Mount, and the eye of the passenger could scarcely find time to rest on the multitudes that lined the roads, or admire the various bridges thrown across this great monument of human labour. Shortly afterwards Rainhill bridge was neared, and the inclined plane of Sutton began to be ascended at a more slackened rate. The summit was soon gained, and twenty-four miles an hour became the maximum of the speed. About noon the procession passed over the Sankey viaduct. The scene at this part was particularly striking. The fields below were occupied by thousands, who cheered us as we passed over the stupendous edifice: carriages filled the narrow lanes, and vessels in the water had been detained, in order that their crews might gaze up at the gorgeous pageant passing far above their mast heads. Shortly after we passed the borough of Newton, and reached Parkside, 17 miles from Liverpool. Here the engines stopped to take in a supply of water and fuel, and many of the company having alighted in the interval, were walking about congratulating each other on the truly delightful treat they were enjoying, all hearts bounding with joyous excitement, and every tongue eloquent in the praise of the gigantic work now completed, and the advantages and pleasures it afforded. A murmur and an agitation at a little distance now betokened something alarming, and too soon we learnt particulars of an accident which has justly created the deepest sorrow throughout the Empire.

The Phoenix and North Star having taken in their supplies of water and fuel, had resumed their journey, and passed the Northumbrian, which remained stationary on the other line, in order that the whole train of carriages might here pass in review before the Duke of Wellington and his party. Several gentlemen embraced the opportunity to alight from the state carriage, and were walking about on the road; among the number was Mr Huskisson, who caught the eye of the Duke of Wellington. A recognition immediately followed, when the duke extended his hand, which Mr Huskisson advanced to take. At this moment the Rocket came rapidly forward upon the other line, and a cry of danger was raised. Several gentlemen succeeded in regaining the state carriage, but Mr Huskisson, who was in a weak state of health, and one of whose limbs was somewhat tender, became flurried, and, after making two attempts to cross the road upon which the Rocket was moving, ran back, in a state of great agitation, to the side of the duke's carriage. White, the engineer, saw the unfortunate gentleman, as the engine approached, in a position of imminent danger, and immediately endeavoured to arrest its progress, but without success. Mr Holmes, M.P., who had not been able to get into the carriage, stood next to Mr Huskisson, and, perceiving that he had altogether lost his presence of mind, seeming like a man bewildered, cried out, 'For God's sake, Mr Huskisson, be firm!' – The space between the two lines of rails is just four feet; but, the state car being eight feet wide, extended two feet beyond the rail on which it moved, thus diminishing the space to *two feet* between its side and the rail on which the Rocket was moving. The engine, besides, projected somewhat over the rail on which it ran, still farther diminishing the standing room to not more, perhaps, than *one foot and a half*, when the vehicles were side by side on the opposite rails. To make matters worse the door of the state car happened to be *three feet* broad, and, when on the full swing, extended *one foot beyond* the rail on which the Rocket moved; so that it was impossible for that engine to pass without striking it. Of this door Mr Huskisson had grasped hold, when he stepped back, after his vain attempts to cross the road, when warned of the approach of the Rocket. Mr Littleton, M.P. for Staffordshire, who had sprung into the state car, had just 'pulled in' (to use his own expression) Prince Esterhazy, when he saw Mr Huskisson, alarmed and agitated, with his hand on the door, which he seemed to grasp with a kind of trembling or convulsive hold. At this moment the Rocket struck the door, and Mr Huskisson was thrown to the ground, across one of the rails of the line on which the engine was advancing, the wheels of which went over his leg and thigh, and fractured them in so dreadful a manner as to produce death, before the lapse of many hours.

The Duke of Wellington and Sir Robert Peel now with great propriety of feeling, expressed a wish that the procession, instead of going forward to Manchester, should return to Liverpool, and the directors acquiesced in the proposition. The directors, however, on reconsideration, thought the policy of this course was doubtful. Another consultation was accordingly held, in the midst of which, Mr Hulton, of Hulton, a magistrate, came up, and stated to his grace, that if the procession did not reach Manchester, where an unprecedented concourse of people would be assembled, and would wait for it, he should be fearful of the consequences to the peace of the town. The duke remarked, 'There is something in that.' Sir Robert Peel then said, 'Where are these directors? Let us see them;' and his grace and the right honourable baronet moved to the spot where the directors were in deliberation. A circle was formed round the group, and the point was discussed at much length. Some of the directors observed, that they were but trustees for property to an immense amount; that the value of that property might be affected, if the procession did not go on, and thus demonstrate the practicability of locomotive travelling on an extensive scale; and that, though the illustrious duke and his *cortège* might not deem it prudent to proceed, it was the duty of the directors to complete the ceremony of opening the road. The Boroughreeve of Manchester repeated and enforced the arguments respecting the difficulty of preserving the public peace, if the assembled thousands were not gratified by a sight of the procession at Manchester. This reasoning having great weight, the Duke of Wellington acquiesced in the opinion of the directors. His grace then proposed, that the whole party should proceed, but return as soon as possible, and refrain from all festivity at Manchester.

The procession accordingly resumed its onward progress, and reached Manchester at a quarter before three. Neither the Duke of Wellington nor any of his party alighted, but the greater portion of the company in the other carriages descended as they arrived, and were shown into the large upper rooms of the company's warehouses, where they hastily partook of a cold collation.

From the Mechanics' Magazine, *Saturday, September 25, 1830.*

| 175 | A REPRESENTATIVE MAN | September 15, 1830 |

After this disastrous event the day became overcast, and as we neared Manchester the sky grew cloudy and dark, and it began to rain. The vast concourse of people who had assembled to witness the triumphant arrival of the successful travellers was of the lowest order of mechanics and artisans, among whom great distress and a dangerous spirit of discontent with the Government at that time prevailed. Groans and hisses greeted the carriage, full of influential personages, in which the Duke of Wellington sat. High above the grim and grimy crowd of scowling faces a loom had been erected, at which sat a tattered, starved-looking weaver, evidently set there as a *representative man*, to protest against this triumph of machinery, and the gain and glory which the wealthy Liverpool and Manchester men were likely to derive from it. (The contrast between our departure from Liverpool and our arrival at Manchester was one of the most striking things I ever witnessed. The news of Mr Huskisson's fatal accident spread immediately, and his death, which did not occur till the evening, was anticipated by rumour. A terrible cloud covered this great national achievement, and its success, which in every respect was complete, was atoned for to the Nemesis of good fortune by the sacrifice of the first financial statesman of the country.)

From Records of a Girlhood *by Fanny Kemble, 1878.*

| 176 | A GLOSS | September 1830 |

'Let the great world spin for ever down the ringing grooves of change.'

When I went by the first train from Liverpool to Manchester (1830), I thought that the wheels ran in a groove. It was a black night and there was such a vast crowd round the train at the station that we could not see the wheels. Then I made this line.

A gloss on 'Locksley Hall' by Alfred Tennyson, quoted in Tennyson, a Memoir *by Hallam, Lord Tennyson, 1897.*

| 177 | COPY OF UNION CLUB OATHS | c.1830 |

Prepare, prepare, for dust thou art, and unto dust thou shalt return. So, therefore, fall down on your knees, and lay your right hand on this Holy Book, and your left hand on your heart, and say after me this solemn obligation:

Question: What is your name?

Is it of your free will that you come here to join this Friendly Society of Coal Mining? I do.

1. I most solemnly and sincerely swear, with my hand on the Holy Book and on my bended knees, that I never will tell who gives me this solemn obligation, or these witnesses present as long as I live. So help me God.

2. I will enter this Society and will pay according to the rules, or as the Committee thinks proper, or as far as lies in my power.
So help me God.

3. I will never instruct any person into the art of coal mining, tunnelling, or boring, or engineering, or any other department of my work, except to an obliged brother or brothers, or an apprentice. So help me God.

4. I will never work any work where an obliged brother has been unjustly enforced off for standing up for his price, or in defence of his trade.
So help me God.

5. I will never take any more work than I can do myself in one day, except necessity requires me to do so; and if I do, I will employ none but an obligated brother, and will pay him according to the master's price, or according to his work. So help me God.

6. I never will leave my work to be supported by this Society, without first having acquainted the Committee, and will pay my share down justly and truly, and will act accordingly. So help me God.

7. I never will injure an obligated brother, or anything belonging to him, before I acquaint him of his foreseen danger. So help me God.

8. I will never in a boasting manner make known how much money I get, or in how short a time. So help me God.

10. I will never make known any signs, tokens, passwords, or guess, or write them on stones, sand, wood, tin, lead, or anything visible or invisible to the eye. So help me God.

11. I will never make these obligations known to either master, manager, or underkeeper, overlooker, book-keeper, or any person, except to a legal obligated brother. So help me God.

If a man vow a vow unto the Lord, or swear an oath to bind his soul with a bond, he shall not break his word; he shall do according to all that proceedeth out of his mouth. Deuteronomy, chap.xxiii., verses 21–23.

From the Cambrian *newspaper, November 11, 1831.*

178   MR TOOGOOD   1831

Next to him is Mr Toogood, the co-operationist, who will have neither fighting nor praying; but wants to parcel out the world into squares like a chess-board, with a community on each, raising everything for one another, with a great steam-engine to serve them in common for tailor and hosier, kitchen and cook. . . .

From Crotchet Castle *by Thomas Love Peacock, 1831.*

179   CRISPATIONS   June 30, 1831

Saw last night a Brewer's caravan going along over the stones. It contained empty Butts upon end and rain had fallen on to them. As the vehicle proceeded it rumbled over the stones and the upward jerks frequently threw the water up into heaps quite of the nature of the crispations.

From the Diary *of Michael Faraday, edited by Thomas Martin, 1932.*

180   GALVANISM   August 8, 1831

Galvanism is the union of electricity and magnetism, and, by being continuous, it exhibits an image of life; – I say, an image only; it is life in death.

From the Table Talk *of Samuel Taylor Coleridge, 1835.*

181   THE SALVATION OF THE TRIATARSOSTINUS 1831–32

I was spending the winter of 1831 as usual in London: – the Pestilence came just in time to drive me thence into Somerset for the salvation of the Triatarsostinus.

Listen reader.
December gave up the ghost amidst a thousand frightful rumours of the coming cholera: if I remember right, the 1st of January, 32, is mournfully distinguished as the day in which one of the morning papers announced 'the Scourge' present in Southwark: who will ever forget the panic that followed; London was comparatively deserted within twenty-four hours. Tuesday six cases were bulletined as having occurred since its breaking out – a distinguished physician assured me that six hundred were nearer the truth: along the Borough bank of the Thames – in those crowded lanes, where so many Irish people herd, pent up as in a lazar-house; where is Defoe? – what havoc and death!

    Wednesday fatal cases trebled – about twenty publicly acknowledged – at least a hundred and twenty known to the observant few. Ah! I was smoking cigars on the box of the Bath mail all the night and at ten o'clock Thursday galloping over the Mendips – the British Alps – on the Exeter.

The first thing that I ever do when I come to Glastonbury is to call on my friend – my Pythias – there: the second to drink a cup of coffee as sedative after my hundred-and-forty-mile journey: the third is to dash over to the lias quarries at a neck-hazard tangent.

Now it happened that a person of Street by name Creese – a quarrier – a worthy man enow – came across the Triatarsostinus a few days before, and as I had given him no inconsiderable monies for the bones that he had met with in the course of his business, he was at pains of taking it home in hopes of getting more.

The Philistines from Dan and Beersheba know what a vile tendency to mischief every beautiful object that he can set his paw upon, disgraces John Bull. Oh! that the pillory should have been sent a packing before the last brute that is fond of marring the sacred works of nature and art had his Esquimaux thing-of-a-soul tamed by it and the eggs and yellow cucumbers its excellent adjuncts. I blush for the truth that points my pen, but I will tell one of my many chapters of accident – 'tis characteristic.

A COLLOQUY BETWEEN TWO QUARRY-MEN,
OVER THE TRIATARSOSTINUS.

'I wonder what tes.'
'O a viery dragern a-maa-be.'
'One that stinged Moses a-maa-be: hae.'
'Here's at 'un.' A tremendous blow with the mallet.
'How he do zound: I wonder if the stwoone be holler.'
Another tremendous blow.
' 'Tes vire-stwoone – vire stwoone is terrible hard – het 'un agean Jack.'
Oh my Triatarsostinus! broke in half.
'There's hes baak-bwoone.'
'An ther's hes ribs.'
'Have her got a head?' A blow follows the question that breaks the head and neck – or rather the slab as the skeleton was buried in the centre of the stone – to eleven pieces.
'No – nore bet o' a hed – noo zine o' one o' hes iys.'
'Dosten het 'un in the right pleaze.'
'Hang the twood.' Another miserable blow which separates the tail part.
'What ell Measter Haakins say?'
'Oh we can tell 'un we didn't know what 'twere and waanted to zee a bit.'

May heaven forgive me – 'Magna componere parvis,' – I have never forgiven the Goths that sacked 'the Eternal City,' the infamous Caliph that destroyed the Alexandrian library, nor these men: when I came to Street so opportunely, they had thrown away nearly the whole of the two anterior paddles and the whole of the posterior right one – they had reduced the fine flagstone to nearly thirty pitiful pieces and stabbed the bones as a Spanish mata-dore does a bull – all over. But I should congratulate myself upon such fortune as fell to my lot and thank the stars and Cholera that it was no worse as (– had I not arrived at that very four of the clock in the afternoon, how unhappy –) Bruin had resolved to chisel away the surface of the stone, never dreaming that the process would have swept away the bone too!

Creese paid a severe penalty for his temerity: instead of giving him as much as my conscience told me was the worth of it – a rule that I have never departed from but in this deserving instance – I was content to pay him liberally for the trouble he had been at in noticing it: the rest of the chapter is short.

Some parts of the three ruined paddles are recovered.
I forgot the Pestilence.
Sat up at work all day and all night over and over.
And in about two months,
The Triatarsostinus,
My hewn-god,
Was finished.

From the Memoirs of the Ichthyosauri and Plesiosauri *by Thomas Hawkins, 1834.*

182   OASTLER ON THE TEN HOURS' BILL   August 27, 1832

Silence ye hissers. I tell ye, ye cowards, and ye may go and tell the tyrants by whom ye are employed, that ye may do your worst – that the Bill is safe – that WE WILL HAVE IT – that IT SHALL PASS! (*Loud cheers.*) Tell me not of your hypocritical supporters. Look at Manchester and its hundred thousand or more. Look at this meeting – look everywhere. Who's for us? Every father, every mother, every Christian. I tell ye again that we will have it – God in Heaven is for it, and who have we against it? A few hissers here, who skulk back in the dark and are ashamed to show their faces. (*Cheers.*) Go back, ye contemptible hissers, ye vipers, – go back and tell your gang what I say. – Go back to your dens and there feed on the blood of your own cruelty. (*Immense cheering.*) Did you see that banner to-day? Here I stand the Factory King, declared King by the most contemptible enemies of the Cause. Yorkshire is mine! (*Cheers.*) Lancashire is mine! (*Cheers.*) Scotland is mine! (*Cheers.*) All Christendom is mine! (*Cheers.*) WE WILL HAVE THE BILL. . . .

From the speech of Richard Oastler at Bradford on August 27, 1832, quoted in The Life of Richard Oastler *by Cecil Driver, 1946.*

I had requested the younger members of the staff, charged with the visitation of the out-patients of the infirmary, to give me the earliest information of the occurrence of any cases indicating the approach of cholera. I had a scientific wish to trace the mode of its propagation, and to ascertain if possible by what means it would be introduced into the town. My purpose also was to discover whether there was any, and if so what, link or connection between the physical and social evils, to which my attention had been so long directed.

A loop of the river Medlock swept round by a group of houses lying immediately below Oxford Road, and almost on the level of the black, polluted stream. This was a colony of Irish labourers and consequently known as Irishtown. I was requested by one of the staff of the out-patients of the infirmary to visit a peculiar case in one of these cottages. He gave me no description of it as we walked thither. On my arrival in a two-roomed house, I found an Irishman lying on a bed close to the window. The temperature of his skin was somewhat lower than usual, the pulse was weak and quick. He complained of no pain. The face was rather pale, and the man much dejected. None of the characteristic symptoms of cholera had occurred, but his attendant told me that the strength had gradually declined during the day, and that, seeing no cause for it, he had formed a suspicion of contagion. I sat by the man's bed for an hour, during which the pulse became gradually weaker. In a second hour it was almost extinct, and it became apparent that the patient would die. His wife and three children were in the room, and she was prepared by us for the too probable event. Thus the afternoon slowly passed away, and as evening approached I sent the young surgeon to have in readiness the cholera van not far away. We were surrounded by an excitable Irish population, and it was obviously desirable to remove the body as soon as possible, and then the family, and to lock up the house before any alarm was given. As twilight came on the sufferer expired without cramp or any other characteristic symptom. The wife had been soothed and she readily consented to be removed with her children to the hospital. Then suddenly the van drew up at the door, and in one minute, before the Irish were aware, drove away with its sad burden.

No case of Asiatic cholera had occurred in Manchester, yet notwithstanding the total absence of characteristic symptoms in this case, I was convinced that the contagion had arrived, and the patient had been its victim. The Knott Hill Hospital was a cotton factory stripped of its machinery, and furnished with iron bedsteads and bedding on every floor. On my arrival here I found the widow and her three children with a nurse grouped round a fire at one end of a gloomy ward. I ascertained that all necessary arrangements had been made for their comfort. They had an evening meal; the children were put to bed near the fire, except the infant which I left lying upon its mother's lap. None of them showed any sign of disease, and I left the ward to take some refreshment. On my return, or at a later visit before midnight, the infant had been sick in its mother's lap, had made a faint cry and had died. The mother was naturally full of terror and distress, for the child had had no medicine, had been fed only from its mother's breast, and, consequently, she could have no doubt that it perished from the same causes as its father. I sat with her and the nurse by the fire very late into the night. While I was there the children did not wake, nor seem in any way disturbed, and at length I thought I might myself seek some repose. When I returned about six o'clock in the morning, another child had severe cramps with some sickness, and while I stood by the bedside, it died. Then, later, the third and eldest child had all the characteristic symptoms of cholera and perished in one or two hours. In the course of the day the mother likewise suffered from a severe and rapid succession of the characteristic symptoms and died, so that within twenty-four hours the whole family was extinct, and it was not known that any other case of cholera had occurred in Manchester or its vicinity. . . .

From a MS written in 1877 by James Kay-Shuttleworth and quoted in The Life and Work of Sir James Kay-Shuttleworth *by Frank Smith, 1923.*

184   MAN AND MACHINE   1832

Whilst the engine runs the people must work – men, women, and children are yoked together with iron and steam. The animal machine – breakable in the best case, subject to a thousand sources of suffering – is chained fast to the iron machine, which knows no suffering and no weariness. . . .

From The Moral and Physical Conditions of the Working Classes employed in the Cotton Manufacture in Manchester *by James Phillips Kay, later Sir James Kay-Shuttleworth, published 1832.*

185   WHEN THE SAVAGE SETTLES DOWN   April 13, 1833

. . . Perhaps, in a perfectly rational state of society, there would be little poetry; very certainly, there would be much less than now there is. The state of mind which usually produces poetry, is a feverish one. Poets, with a very few happy exceptions, are excitable if not irritable, and of unequal if not unhappy tempers. And there is much of plausible at least in the argument, that the genius of poetry, like the spirit of romance, flourishes best in a rude soil. The uncultivated Indian is, almost in his every expression, a poet. He speaks of 'burying the red tomahawk under the spreading tree of peace.' The lake, the forest, the exciting sports of the hunter, or the yet more stirring adventures of the warrior – all these furnish forth similies to enrich not only the 'talk' of the sylvan council, but even the conversation of the wigwam. And when the savage settles down into habits of steady industry, the romance of his language subsides into the plainer matter-of-fact phrases of ordinary life.

From The Crisis, or the Change from Error and Misery to Truth and Happiness, *Vol.11, No.13, edited by Robert Owen and Robert Dale Owen.*

186   THE ASPECT AND CHARACTER   June 1833

On entering Huddersfield I found that in respect of fairs, I was out of the frying pan into the fire; for before my inn door, the George, there was a prodigious assemblage of people at a market; and I had to wait some time ere I could get a room for the evening. The crowd was vastly augmented by there being furthermore a political meeting in the open air, and the whole of the spacious market-place was filled with the multitude. Mr Oastler held forth on the sufferings of the factory children, and was enthusiastically cheered. I saw from my window, but heard not. Then followed, to me an original scene, the burning of the Factory Commissioners, and Captain Fenton, one of their obnoxious members of Parliament, and another unpopular master-manufacturer, in effigy. The figures were fearfully like men; and being now dark, the conflagration lighted up the whole square, and revealed the faces of the yelling myriads, so as to give the aspect and character of Pandemonium to the scene. The burning figures were tossed ferociously into the air; and to renew their combustion were dashed into a bonfire from time to time. The spectacle I am sure is a depraving one, and fitted to prepare the actors for burning the originals instead of the copies.

From a letter of Thomas Chalmers to his sister, printed in Memoirs of Thomas Chalmers *by William Hanna, 1844.*

187   THE STEAM-CARRIAGES   June 10, 1833

Liverpool. *June 10th*. At twelve Mr Armon and myself placed ourselves upon an *Omnibus*, and were driven up a steep hill to the place whence the steam-carriages start. And at 12 we embarked. We travelled in the second class of carriages. There were five trams linked together on each of which were placed open seats for the traveller, four and four facing each other & of these twenty four in each tram – but not all were full – And, besides, there was a close carriage, and one other machine for luggage. The fare 4/- for the thirty one miles. Everything went on so rapidly that I had scarcely the power of observation. The road begins at an excavation thro' rock, and is generally to a certain extent insulated from the adjacent country. It is occasionally placed on bridges, and is frequently intersected by ordinary roads. Not quite a perfect level is preserved. On setting off there is a slight jolt, arising from the chain catching each tram, but, once in motion we proceeded as smoothly as possible. For a minute or two the pace is gentle, and is constantly varying. The machine produces little smoak or steam. First in order is the tall chimney – then the boiler – barrel-like vessel. Then an oblong reservoir of water. Then a vehicle for coals. And then comes, of a length infinitely extendible, the trams on which are the carriages. Our train would have carried if all the seats had been filled, abt. 150 passengers; but Mr — assured me at Chester that he went with a thousand persons to *Newton* fair. There must have been two engines then. I have heard since that there went to and from the fair that day, two thousand persons and more. But only two thousand at 3/- each way, would have produced £600! But, after all, the expense is so great, that it is considered uncertain whether the establishment will ultimately remunerate the proprietors. Yet I have heard that it already yields the shareholders a nine per cent dividend. And bills have already been passed for making rail roads between London and Birmingham, and Birmingham and Liverpool. And what a change it will produce in the intercourse! One conveyance will take between 100 and 200 passengers, and in a forenoon the journey will be made. Of the rapidity with which the journey will be made I had better experience on my return; but I may say now – that it is certain that stoppages included, the journey may be made 20 miles an hour!

I should have remarked before that the most remarkable movements of the journey are those when trains pass one another. The rapidity is such, that there is no recognizing the features of a traveller. The noise on several occasions, of the passing engine was like the whizzing of a rocket. On the road are stationed guards who hold flags at the station to give notice to the drivers when to stop. Near Manchester I noticed an inscription on marble recording the memorable death of Huskisson.

From the manuscript diary of Henry Crabb Robinson, later printed in part in the Diary, Reminiscences and Correspondence *edited by Thomas Sadler, 1869.*

VILLE UNIVERSELLE July 8, 1833

Bath
dimanche. 8 Juillet 1833.

Mon cher Scholl,

Je gage que les beaux changemens qui ont eu lieu au pays de Vaud me déplairont souverainement – ennuyeuses longues rues, grands chemins, jardins anglais, maisons parisiennes (mauvaises copies d'originaux médiocres) – bâtimens qui se ressemblent tous, et qui ne font pour ainsi dire, qu'une espèce de ville universelle qui s'étend d'un bout à l'autre de l'Europe et même en Asie et sur les côtes de l'Afrique grâce à Mehemet Ali.

Il n'y a plus de Campagne nulle part – on abat les forêts, on viole les montagnes – on ne veut que des canaux – on se fiche des rivières – partout le Gaz et la vapeur – la même odeur, les mêmes tourbillons d'exécrable fumée épaisse et fétide – le même coup d'oeil commun et mercantile de quel côté qu'on se trouve – une monotonie assommante, et un artifice impie crachant à chaque minute au visage de la Mère Nature, qui bientôt trouvera ses enfans changés en Automates et en Machines.

Draft of a letter of William Beckford to Dr Scholl of Geneva, in the Hamilton papers, printed in Life of Beckford *by John W. Oliver, 1932.*

189 THIS NEW DESCRIPTION OF PROPERTY Summer 1834

The sound of the engines, on the Stockton and Darlington railroad, may be distinctly heard on a still day at the Dinsdale Hotel, like the flapping of mighty wings, as they pass along; and the line being in many parts circuitous, the puffs of smoke appear here and there among the trees in a thickly wooded country, enabling the spectator to mark the progress of the trains and trace their direction. In one part of the railroad the rails are laid straight for more than a mile together. Here I used to feel much gratification, by seating myself to watch the approach of the several heavy trains of coal-waggons, on their way backwards and forwards, laden and unladen, between the Darlington coal-field, and the staiths at Middleborough or Stockton.

The general order of things on a railroad is curious from its novelty; in this new description of property, the vested right of the public in the way and footpath is not acknowledged, yet their advantages are increased by rapidity of locomotion, while the disadvantages of the thoroughfare to the proprietors of the soil, in comparison with those attendant on highways in general, are diminished in an equal proportion. On the banks of a canal navigators and loiterers infest the towing-paths and create a nuisance, but all descriptions of travellers on a railroad may rather be compared to a flock of pigeons or swallows, that confine their flight to the regions of the air, and leave neither track nor trace behind. Silence and stillness reign within its precincts, and harmonize with the grandeur of the spectacle; the rails converging in perspective form the track of a terrestrial zodiac, – lines terminating in points in the horizon, whence at prescribed periods earthly objects rise and perform their transit, while many a muscular arm toils in preparation for the phenomenon, which appears and passes away. As train after train of rolling wagons approached, a black speck first appeared in the distance, gradually and by slow degrees extending its dimensions; meanwhile the sound, like the roaring of the sea, became as a heavy gust of winds, and then, as the carriages receded, grew again less and less audible, till it expired in a low gentle murmur.

I remarked especially one train, consisting of upwards of a score of laden coal-waggons, on their way for shipment at the mouth of the Tees. As they glided onwards, steadily but rapidly, the attitudes of the two engine-men in front were in striking contrast with the stupendous momentum of the advancing body. Impelled by a power called by themselves into action, their arms folded on their bosoms, as if either lost in their own reflections, or dozing life away, they passively reclined in an easy posture, whirled along with an equable velocity.

Behind the coal-waggons, on the last carriage of all, a low truck, stood an old cart-horse quietly eating hay out of a basket. The sagacious animal, thus left to himself, on a bare platform of boards, within a couple of feet of the ground, and without side-rail or guard of any description, displayed a consciousness of the danger of jumping out, by the mode in which he cautiously rested on his haunches, prepared by his attitude against the sudden possible contingency of a halt.

From A Home Tour through the Manufacturing Districts and other parts of England, Scotland and Ireland, *by Sir George Head, 1835.*

THE COUNTRY OF THE IGUANODON

August 27, 1834

27. Saturday. – Among the host of visitors who have besieged my house today was Mr John Martin (and his daughter) the celebrated, most justly

THE COUNTRY OF THE IGUANODON

celebrated, artist, whose wonderful conceptions are the finest productions of modern art. Mr Martin was deeply interested in the remains of the Iguanodon etc. I wish I could induce him to portray the country of the Iguanodon: no other pencil but his should attempt such a subject. . . .

From the Journal *of Gideon Mantell, edited by E. Cecil Curwen, 1940.*

| 191 | THE PHILOSOPHER'S OPINION OF THE WHITBY SNAKES | 1834 |

Gentlemen – These snakes are nothing more than a simple production of nature, and have not the least appearance of the animal so named, and you will find none of them with their heads on. If these were petrified snakes, as is falsely represented, the head would be found, and the impression of the scales also, which not being the case, it is evident that they never were alive. These natural productions are not found in any other part but Whitby, and at the alum-works, which are two or three miles from it. This is a sufficient proof that they are nothing but a production of nature's laws – AIR.

I understand some people, through ignorance, think it was once a shell-fish, and possessed life; but I will refute that. If it were once a shell-fish, the shell would be found there also. But instead of a shell, it has got a cover of stone, which proves such assertions to be foolishness.

Gentlemen – I am a philosopher, and not a disciple of any man's, and can prove that air is the cause of all nature's laws, and of all effects under the sun; if it is not the atmospheric air, it is another, down to the very centre of the earth. If any man begins to lecture on any subject under the sun, it is a false lecture, and not worth anything, if he leaves out the cause – AIR. He would not be there to expose his ignorance, if he had not air to breathe; neither would he have any to hear his ignorant nonsense – even lecturing on education, or on eloquence of speech, or any thing under the sun.

From a pamphlet entitled The Christian Philosopher's Explanation of the General Deluge *by William Martin, Newcastle, 1834.*

The interesting thing is that at exactly this period, John Martin, brother of William, was illustrating Mantell's and Hawkins's Plesiosauri *etc. Ruthven Todd has written about these brothers, and the insanity which haunted the family, in his essay on 'The Imagination of John Martin' in* Tracks in the Snow *(1946).*

| 192 | LETTER TO FRANCIS PLACE | February 1835 |

My dear Sir:

I am very much obliged to you for the tables, & for the trouble you have taken; I desired a Guinea to be left with this letter at your sons. Am I to understand that the other tables will come? Pray employ the person again for me, if he can complete them.

It is very odd that you wise men in *Lunnon* cannot understand that what we Chew-bacons in the country mean by reform, is more bread, beer & bacon; but we have not got one mouthfull more; & you have given us a *bill*, & nothing but a *bill*: so we think that you conjurors have humbugged us; & we do not believe that your bills about pensions or about the church, will be one whit better than the other, or give us more to eat. You are too philosophic to like ale & rashers, but the march of mind has not got so far with us, & so we bellow for reform still; that is, [*for the*] *spunge* – which is the only reform worth a farthing.

Your very truly,

HENRY DRUMMOND

From a letter of Henry Drummond to Francis Place, printed in Place on Population, *edited by Norman E. Himes, 1930.*

For the phrase 'march of mind', compare Thomas Peacock's Crochet Castle *(1831), Chap.11: 'I am out of all patience with this march of mind'; and earlier, Chap.1: 'a numerous detachment from the advanced guard of the "march of intellect" often marched down to Crotchet Castle', and 'many young soldiers of fortune, who were marching with the march of mind'. And in Chap.X there is: 'thus all nature marches with march of mind'.*

Compare Burke On Conciliation with America: *'The march of the human mind is slow' (1775).*

Also compare Tennyson, 'Locksley Hall' (written c. 1830):
'There methinks would be enjoyment more than in this march of mind
In the steamship, in the railway, in the thoughts that shake mankind.'

There is no doubt that these phrases belong, as clichés, to the early '30s. For example The Casket, *August 17, 1832, has a cross-head,* March of Intellect.

193 THE IRON MAN c.1835

In the factories for spinning coarse yarn for calicoes, fustians, and other heavy goods, the mule-spinners have also abused their powers beyond endurance, domineering in the most arrogant manner, as we have shown, over their masters. High wages, instead of leading to thankfulness of temper and improvement of mind, have, in too many cases, cherished pride and supplied funds for supporting refractory spirits in strikes, wantonly inflicted upon one set of mill-owners after another throughout the several districts of Lancashire and Lanarkshire, for the purpose of degrading them into a state of servitude. During a disastrous turmoil of this kind at Hyde, Stayley-bridge, and the adjoining factory townships, several of the capitalists, afraid of their business being driven to France, Belgium, and the United States, had recourse to the celebrated machinists Messrs. Sharp and Co., of

Manchester, requesting them to direct the inventive talents of their partner, Mr Roberts, to the construction of a self-acting mule, in order to emancipate the trade from galling slavery and impending ruin. Under assurances of the most liberal encouragement in the adoption of his inventions, Mr Roberts, who was then little versed in spinning-machines, suspended his professional pursuits as an engineer, and set his fertile genius to construct a spinning automaton.

The drawing, stretching, and twisting of the yarn had been rendered in a great measure the result of self-acting mechanism by the labours of Crompton and Kelly, the first inventor and first improver of the mule; but to back off the spiral-coil from the tip of the spindle, and then wind the thread upon it in a shapely conoid, was the Gordian knot left for Mr Roberts to untie. The problem did not puzzle him long, for to the delight of the mill-owners who ceased not to stimulate his exertions by frequent visitations, he produced, in the course of a few months, a machine apparently instinct with the thought, feeling, and tact of the experienced workman – which even in its infancy displayed a new principle of regulation, ready in its mature state to fulfil the functions of a finished spinner. Thus, the *Iron Man*, as the operatives fitly call it, sprung out of the hands of our modern Prometheus at the bidding of Minerva – a creation destined to restore order among the industrious classes, and to confirm to Great Britain the empire of art. The news of this Herculean prodigy spread dismay through the union, and even long before it left its cradle, so to speak, it strangled the Hydra of misrule.

From The Philosophy of Manufactures *by Andrew Ure M.D., F.R.S., 1835.*

194   THE PHILOSOPHY OF MANUFACTURES   c.1835

Our legislators, when bewailing, not long ago, the fate of their fellow-creatures doomed to breathe the polluted air of a factory, were little aware how superior the system of ventilation adopted in many cotton-mills was to that employed for their own comfort in either house of Parliament. The engineers of Manchester do not, like those of the metropolis, trust for a sufficient supply of fresh air into any crowded hall, to currents physically created in the atmosphere by the difference of temperature excited by chimney draughts, because they know them to be ineffectual to remove with requisite rapidity the dense carbonic acid gas generated by many hundred powerful lungs. The factory plan is to extract the foul air, in measureable volumes, by mechanical means, of the simplest but most unfailing kind, especially by excentric fans made to revolve with the rapidity of nearly 100 feet per second; and thereby to ensure a constant renewal of the atmosphere in any range of apartments however large or closely pent they may be. The effect of one of Fairbairn and Lillie's four-guinea fans upon a large factory is truly admirable; it not only sweetens the interior space immediately, but renders the ingress of odorous nuisance from without altogether impossible. In a weaving-mill near Manchester, where the ventilation was bad, being dependent on currents of equilibration, as in the House of Lords, the proprietor lately caused the fan apparatus to be mounted. The consequence soon became apparent in a curious manner. The work-people, little remarkable for olfactory refinement, instead of thanking their master for his humane attention to their comfort and health, made a formal complaint to him, that the ventilator had increased their appetites, and therefore entitled them to a corresponding increase of wages! The weekly pay of these attendants on steam-going looms, being nearly double of that received by labourers on the breezy plains of Sussex and Kent, could admit of no augmentation under the low rate of profits of trade. But the master made an ingenious compromise with his servants; by stopping the fan during half the day, he adjusted the ventilation and the voracity of his establishment to a medium standard, after which he heard no complaint either on the score of health or appetite.

From The Philosophy of Manufactures *by Andrew Ure M.D., F.R.S., 1835.*

Note on 193 and 194. *I make these quotations from this notorious book because whereas it is often referred to and the facts in it are cited, I do not think people now will believe the attitude of mind which it presents. It reads of course like a satire: indeed the relationship of actual documents on the mind of the capitalist to social satire is far from clear. To which pray do the Sherlock Holmes stories belong? And Jane Austen? And Kipling?*

195   CARLYLE IN LONDON   July 1835

The world looks often quite spectral to me; sometimes, as in Regent Street the other night (my nerves being all shattered), quite hideous, discordant, almost infernal. I had been at Mrs. Austin's, heard Sydney Smith for the first time guffawing, other persons prating, jargoning. To me through these thin cobwebs Death and Eternity sate glaring. Coming homewards along Regent Street, through street-walkers, through – *Ach Gott!* unspeakable pity swallowed up unspeakable abhorrence of it and of myself. The moon and the serene nightly sky in Sloane Street consoled me a little. Smith, a mass of fat and muscularity, with massive Roman nose, piercing hazel eyes, huge cheeks, shrewdness and fun, not humour or even wit, seemingly without soul altogether. Mrs. Marcet ill-looking, honest, rigorous, commonplace. The rest babble, babble. Woe's me that I in Meshech am! To work.

From the Journal of Thomas Carlyle, quoted in Thomas Carlyle, a History of His Life in London, *by J.A. Froude, 1884.*

196   THE POWERS OF THE MACHINE   July 12, 1835

From church we went, by his special invitation, to see Babbage's calculating machine; and I must say, that during an explanation which lasted between two and three hours, given by himself with great spirit, the wonder at its incomprehensible powers grew upon us every moment. The first thing that struck me was its small size, being only about two feet wide, two feet deep, and two and a half high. The second very striking circumstance was the fact that the inventor himself does not profess to know all the powers of the machine; that he has sometimes been quite surprised at some of its capabilities; and that without previous calculation he cannot always tell whether it will, or will not work out a given table. The third was that he can set it to do a certain regular operation, as, for instance, counting 1,2,3,4; and then determine that, at any given number, say the 10,000th, it shall *change* and take a different ratio, like triangular numbers, 1,3,6,9,12, etc.; and afterwards at any other given point, say, 10,550, change again to another ratio. The whole, of course, seems incomprehensible, without the exercise of volition and thought.

From the Journal of George Ticknor quoted in the Life, Letters and Journals of George Ticknor, *1876.*

197   PHOTOGENIC DRAWING   1835

But perhaps the most curious application of this art is the one I am now about to relate. At least it is that which has appeared the most surprising to those who have examined my collection of pictures formed by solar light.

Everyone is acquainted with the beautiful effects which are produced by a *camera obscura*, and has admired the vivid picture of external nature which it displays. It had often occurred to me, that if it were possible to retain upon the paper the lovely scene which thus illumines it for a moment, or if we could but fix the outline of it, the lights and shadows divested of all *colour*, such a result could not fail to be most interesting. And however much I might be disposed at first to treat this notion as a scientific dream, yet when I had succeeded in fixing the images of the solar microscope by means of a peculiarly sensitive paper, there appeared no longer any doubt that an analogous process would succeed in copying the objects of external nature, although indeed they are much less illuminated.

Not having with me in the country a *camera obscura* of any considerable size, I constructed one out of a large box, the image being thrown upon it by a good object glass fixed in the opposite end. This apparatus being armed with a sensitive paper, was taken out in a summer afternoon and placed about a hundred yards from a building favourably illuminated by the sun. An hour or two afterwards I opened the box, and I found depicted on the paper a very distinct representation of the building, with the exception of those parts of it which lay in the shade. A little experience in this branch of the art showed me that with smaller *camerae obscurae* the effect would be produced in a smaller time. Accordingly I had several small boxes made, in which I fixed lenses of shorter focus, and with these I obtained very perfect but extremely small pictures; such as without great stretch of imagination might be supposed to be the work of some Lilliputian artist. They require indeed examination with a lens to discover all their minutiae.

In the summer of 1835 I made in this way a great number of representations of my house in the country, which is well suited to the purpose, from its ancient and remarkable architecture. And this building I believe to be the first that was ever yet known *to have drawn its own picture.*

From Some Account of the Art of Photogenic Drawing, or the Process by which Natural Objects may be made to delineate themselves without the aid of the Artist's Pencil, *by Henry Fox Talbot F.R.S., 1834.*

198 QUALITY AND QUANTITY 1835

But the sight, or rather sound, of all others which created upon my mind the strongest impression was that of the air-blast driven by two powerful steam-engines through the main furnaces; the two furnaces about twenty feet distant from each other – the engines in the rear of these. A cylindrical trunk, of a couple of feet diameter, extends from the engines sending forth at right angles two smaller branches, decreasing gradually in size to four or five inches at the extremities, which enter one at the bottom of each furnace, like the nozzles of bellows. No verbal description can do justice to the awful effect produced by the air rushing through these iron tubes; and I was involuntarily led to the reflection to what extraordinary extent such a power might be applied in the production of musical sounds: for, combining the volume of air at command with the thrilling softness of tone already attained in the key bugle, the effect with which these two elements, – quality and quantity may, by and bye, be blended together, is almost indefinite. Not a word, though delivered with the utmost effort, was heard, spoken at the same time close to the ear. I have listened to a storm on the Atlantic, I have stood on the Table Rock at Niagara, yet never did I hear a sound in nature equal to this, – so terrific, or of so stunning a din.

From A Home Tour through the Manufacturing Districts and other parts of England, Scotland and Ireland, *by Sir George Head, 1835.*

199 THE ICHTHYOSAURUS 1835

The mere indices of these things, because they have a silent moral, are interesting for that very reason. The sublime discloses itself only in the silence of which we speak, when, by the most stupendous Efforts of Intellect, by the revivification of the Worlds, by the inhabitation thereof by all the Creatures which the laboring Soul can re-articulate, we stand in a Presence which has not, nor ever shall have one sympathy with ourselves; those Worlds, those antipodal Populations, that Presence passionless, and silent dead; I say the instruments of a few bones verify a Sublimity before which no man can stand unappalled.

The present is so absolutely little when compared with the dread Past, that these Reliquiae derive an Attribute from that circumstance to our Faculties as absolutely infinite. The sight expires in the distance, our minds are lost in the sweeping landscape, eternity for an horizon, and the god of the scene silence all.

The Philosophic Ancients lived and acted under this impression, carrying it on to the Unknown Future, in which alone they could substantially realize a Personality. And in this mood did they achieve for themselves that Greatness which leaves the Moderns pigmies, because we lack the mental dignity by which it was accomplished. For this reason, likewise, have the Moderns, although studious of forms, overlooked the Living Soul of Things, disenchanting Life, and encumbering the Earth with the most uninteresting Automatons imaginable. No Fawn, no Satyr now, no shy Nymph frequents the grove, no Dian courses the resounding hills; all, all is unfrequent, and desolate all. Enthusiasm, without which there can be no sense of Truth, nor of fitness and beauty, seems as extinct as the Sea-Dragons which here inspire it: their strange eloquent Remains bespeak a Chord in our breast, which vibrates only to the Master Touch: the subtle and jealous gods of the vast Promontory of Time start at the well-known sound, They seize, They seize me wholly, and if the oracle, O Reader, be ambiguous, blame thy Fortune in escaping the Pythonic furor, with its extatic but exhausting delirium, its shiver, and wild excentric fate.

Io. Io. Io.
A long grey Cloud in the far-west, covering many a Rood.
A golden Sun Autumnal.
Golden Islands in the Deep Skies.
O my voluptuous heart, gushing soft music.
O life! so profoundly felt.
Heaven above, around, beneath, Eternal.
See! in the long grey Cloud a Tanin in the Empyreal Ocean.
Suns, Systems, Time and Eternity cluster around him.
Io. Io. Chase him on Wings of the Mighty Spheres.

Flee away, Time. I follow.
Both fledged to the same Stroke.
Across Desert Skies.
A million years. A million Essays of Wing. Each from one Vortice to another.

O weary Wings, and Space dreary ever.
Sea-dragons! Chase them in the Expanse of Heavens.
Wild Lucifer Spirits our Companions through all Immensity.

The Spirit of Prophecy is not dead. Nor do I consider it at all remarkable, that these waking dreams preceded the discovery of Two Taninim, about to be introduced. A subject must be esteemed for its consequences, and who can sum the Legions of thoughts, which these Sea-dragons evoked, and shall yet evoke in our own and many other breasts? Were we to abandon ourselves to all the more occult influences of the mind, it would be elevated to a pitch of sensibility, and an acuteness of perception unspeakable; nor do I shun to avow a habit, which raises one above the moral conditions of Earth, if indulged in a right Royal Heart. And what, quotha, are the Skeletons which interest us so much, stripped of the habiliments of Eld, or what is Kingly Power without the symbols, or the Heavens themselves without the Dominions which rule them withal.

But we must refer our reader to the Paramecostinus of Plate XVII, which supersedes a former one, (Vide Memoirs,) rejected because the right paddle of the subject it was taken from is improperly reversed. This beautiful Skeleton was found in our neighbouring Street, and the following extracts, copied from my note-book, explain the attendant circumstances.

'1835, June. John Steel announced a fossil, lying in Mogs quarry, in the thick marl, twenty-feet from the surface.

'Proceeding to extricate it, we ascertained that the tail was covered by one of the facets of the quarry, which cannot be removed for some months.

'John Mog, personally, not unlike Æsop, hobbling into the pit, and touching his hat with a useful crutch, requested to speak. "Your Sarvant, Zir, how much be I to have vor the faussil?"

' "You know, John, I always give the master one half, and his man who chances to find it the other."

' "Very well, Zir. – Thank'ee, Zir."

' "We must leave the tail here, until we work out the ground."

' "Yes, Zir."

'Thursday, Friday, Tuesday. Dissected the Skull and Snout, laying bare an eye deeply sunk in his socket, and identifying it with the Paramecostinus in the British Museum, by the shape and number of the teeth, the well-defined nasal Foramen, and the general outline.

'Wednesday. The Cervix, if indeed Ichthyosauri have any, rather the Atlas, axis, and a few succeeding vertebrae, are in their right place: but the subvertebral wedges are overlaid.

'Thursday. Encountered a stubborn group of the marginal rays of the anterior paddles, heretofore thought to be spines of a Cidaris, which I greatly regretted, but was obliged to sacrifice.

'Friday. Developed that beautiful pectoral paddle.

'Monday, Tuesday, to Saturday. The Seventh and five succeeding dorsal vertebrae are twisted round, presenting the spinous fossae, although luckily the apophyses themselves continue almost in their proper place: the entire twelve are but little distinguished from one another in shape, but they decrease somewhat in size receding from the occiput. The Sternal arch and the whole subsidiary Apparatus is remarkably strong, and perfect.

'July, Tuesday, Wednesday. The anterior long ribs dive right through the matrix, an unusual accident; and the phalanges of the left paddle are dislocated by the superincumbent pressure which occasioned it.

'Saturday, Monday to Wednesday night. Now then the Spine enlarges, the apophyses spread, the ribs resume their order, and chocolate colored laminae indicate the once abdominal fluids. The gradually emerging beauty of this Tanin so possesses me, that I shall order my lamp, to enjoy another sight of it before I go to bed.

Thursday. Fortieth vertebra, forty first, second, third, superb!

'Friday and Saturday. There are the posterior paddles, like all that preceded them, perfect. The Pelvis maintains its articulation, as did the Sternum before it. Here also the spine acquires its maximum long diameter.'

The quarry having been at length worked farther back, the journal continues,

'Oct. Friday. An entirely new feature presents itself: the receding caudal vertebrae disclose double spinous apophyses, mounting the twenty bones anterior to the first break of the tail. No suspicion of any such thing ever occurred to us; no Ichthyosaurus ever indicated such a fact before. All the other individuals known have these spines a little thicker perhaps than any of their relations, but the difference leads to a mere nothing. Here we have bifid spines, for what purpose? to support a fin? Now a fin comprises, besides its erector and compressor muscles, at least a cartilaginous, if not an osseous frame, upon which to exercise them: other more perishable substances than cartilage have left marks behind them in this very marl. On one or two Saurians we have even fancied that their skin, their mere outline of Form were indicated, if not to the eye, to that manual touch with which they certainly came in contact.'

In the elaboration of several tails we have been unable to detect the least proof of a fin. Nothing due to our chisel ever advanced pretension to any such member.

The multiplication of these apophyses then was manifestly appointed as a balance, the cushion of flesh which clothed them assisting its consequence, mounted probably by a cuticular fringe, which may have been lengthened and widened out upon the tail, as shown in our frontispiece.

We have remarked the nearly equal size of the first twelve vertebrae of the back. In the several genera, nay even in all other Species, it will most

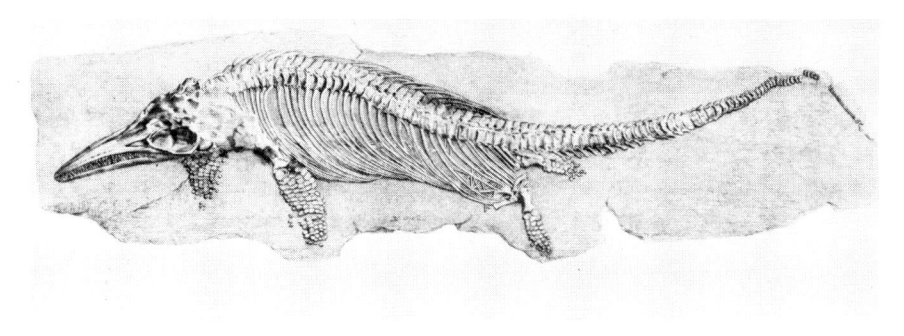

ICHTHYOSAURUS CHIROPAREMEKOSTINUS

probably be found, that the so-called neck is more attenuated than that of the Person now before us. His Cranium is very enlarged, as is also the other fore-part of the Skeleton. His aspect is stiff, fore-right, and heavy, demanding a compensation of some decided sort. These double processes afford it at once, while the whole tail, auxiliary by its just proportions of chevron and other joints, refute the idea of a proper fin, by the equilibrium in which it holds the dependant whole, as well as supersede the necessity of one by the curious rudder-like provision which we have demonstrated in it before.

Here then we have another Ichthyosaurus with a novelty of contrivance particularly his own; so marked a difference is itself sufficient to particularize him from all others upon Record. There are individuals which at first blush appear to be the same identical Species, disproved by this very singularity. In truth, it has never occurred to us to find a Saurian undistinguished from any preceding one, either in the number or figure of certain bones. A Species starts forth in every new individual, or at least differences, which belong, no doubt, occasionally to the Sexes themselves, about which we can of course only speculate.

The skeleton before us is altogether unique: he is the longest ever found in Somerset, and lacks not one the least joint. His color remains unchanged by the lapse of many Ages; his Animus survives in his attitude, discoursing most eloquent things. The Profound, the Solitary Seas he haunted, the appetites he accomplished, the brassy Skies he saw, the Soulless World he ruled, the unjoyous Times, the unchecked lusts this dragon knew, crowd their Memories into his ribbed boat, which, tracking the wide Oceans of years, lands them at last on our Modern Shores.

The fleeting Generations of Men shall pass away and be forgotten, while the Lessons which these awful retrospections teach them will continue until the absorption of all Truth by the ONE, innate, adorable Being, the Almighty Lord and Father of us all.

From The Book of the Great Sea-Dragons *by Thomas Hawkins, 1840.*

The word TANIN *is Hebrew for dragon, plural* TANINIM. *Thus Hawkins:*

These unparalleled phenomena demand a Style and Title of their own. Throughout the Greek, and Latin, and all the derivative Languages living, float traditional notices of a supposed Chimaera, under the term Dragon. Backing this word through the more ancient Semitic Tongues, we come at last to its root in the most ancient of all, the blessed Hebrew. There, in the inspired Annals of Earth, we read of the Gedolim Taninim, the Great Sea-Serpents, the frightful Dragons of the Dead Times, the long-lost Ichthyosauri and Plesiosauri, of which we treat.

200 THOSE BEAUTIFUL FACES June 7, 1836

Throughout England, Scotland, and Ireland, there is in every town and village an institution for the education of the poor and orphan children. One day in the year, which is the 7th of June, all these children come from every direction to the city of London, accompanied by their teachers and superintendents. Each party have different coloured dresses, the children march two by two, both male and female, all in perfect order; they are beautifully arranged in their way, like a disciplined army. This great church, where they assemble, is a lofty edifice, magnificently built, the sight of it dazzles the mind; there are in it a number of splendid statues cut in marble, with most beautiful figures of animals and birds; in short, if a man does not see it, he could not believe any description of it. The outside of this church all round, and the inside consists of four quarters; each of them is two hundred feet long, and fifty feet broad; the church is three hundred feet high. Around the four parts of the church there are seats beautifully arranged; from the one end to the other there are forty ranks of seats, and all see alike; all of them are made of fine wood, elegantly worked, and cushioned with rich woollen cloth: besides these, there are other places expensively fitted up with beautiful chairs: these are seats for the royal family and their attendants. All these poor children, in regiments and beautiful order, were seated on benches round the church, each company by itself; the seats raised one above the other from the ground up into the dome, so wonderfully, that it could not be described but by a drawing. When all these children took their seats the visitors came into the church. At the gate stood some priests and persons of their religion, dressed in a strange costume. These priests gave the permission for entrance, and held in their hands plates of gold, and every person, who entered the church, put into the plates some charitable money for the support of these children; every one gave according to his ability and zeal. After all came in and sat down, then the very large organ, which they have in this church, began to play, and the children followed by singing. The high tune of the organ and the singing of the children could not be distinguished; all their hymns were composed with reference to this charity, and what the prophets had ordered for this purpose. Everyone in the church was quite silent while all this was going on. Afterwards, one of their great iskofs, a follower of Christ, went up into the pulpit, which was beautifully dressed with rich woollen cloth; he opened the books of the Gospel and Psalms, and read some chapters relating to charity, and gave a sermon to that effect. When the preaching was over, they began singing again so pleasantly, that it nourished the heart. On the whole, it was a most brilliant sight to see those beautiful faces who attended the feast. There must have been at this day in the streets near this church, about 40,000 carriages, beside many who came on horse-back and on foot. The money which is collected, is regularly distributed for the support and education of the children; these children are kept in the parishes till they arrive at the age of maturity.

From Journal of a Residence in England . . . of their Royal Highnesses Reeza Koolee Meerza, Najaf Koolee Meerza, and Taymoor Meerza, of Persia, *by H.R.H. Najaf Koolee Meerza. Printed for private circulation only. No date.*

201 THE REAL SIGHTS July 9, 1836

After we had gazed at all these different kinds of inventions, we asked whether there were other things to be seen. They said, 'all that you have already seen are old inventions, and their glory is passing away, but the real sights you have not seen.' 'Well,' said we, 'where shall we go?' They invited us up stairs into a large room, half of which was furnished with seats for visitors to sit on, who have to pay some money for entrance. We sat on these seats, and a number of men and women were also seated. The wall opposite to our face was made most elegantly white with paint, so much so, that in the place although dark, yet the face of a man might be seen in this wall; opposite this wall there is another which was just behind us, which had several holes in it, where there are several instruments, which had such a power, a thousand times more than the lustre of the sun. Whenever they touched this apparatus, the array of the loadstone came out of the holes, and gave out such a ray and light that no one dared to look at the wall; but when they moderated the power of the instrument, a man might look at it. The light was so great as to lead any one to say that all the power of the sun, or the sun itself was in this room. Afterwards the master brought some water in a glass, which he placed against this light. This drop of water suddenly (praise be to God!) looked as if it were a great sea; in which we observed myriads of animals of different kinds, in forms of leopards, and some as large as elephants, and camels, they were mingled together, and eating each other. All of them had several thousand feet and hands; such a thing had never been thought of, nor would it enter the mind. Indeed, all those that came to see this, had no courage to look at these dreadful beasts. The operator was standing by the wall with a stick in his hand, explaining the nature of every one of these animals, and said in the English language, 'This is the pure water that you drink every day, without being sensible of the wonderful power of God of the universe displayed in it; and what food he has given you which you do not understand.'

From Journal of a Residence in England . . . of their Royal Highnesses Reeza Koolee Meerza, Najaf Koolee Meerza, and Taymoor Meerza, of Persia, *by H.R.H. Najaf Koolee Meerza. Printed for private circulation only. No date.*

Note on 200, 201 and 208. *The service for children in St Paul's which the Persian princes attended (200) is the same as the one described by William Blake in his 'Holy Thursday' (from* Songs of Innocence, *1789):*

'Twas on a Holy Thursday, their innocent faces clean,
The children walking two and two, in red and blue and green,
Grey-headed beadles walk'd before, with wands as white as snow,
Till into the high dome of Paul's they like Thames' waters flow.

O what a multitude they seem'd, these flowers of London town!
Seated in companies they sit with radiance all their own.
The hum of multitudes was there, but multitudes of lambs,
Thousands of little boys & girls raising their innocent hands.

Now like a mighty wind they raise to heaven the voice of song,
Or like harmonious thunderings the seats of Heaven among.
Beneath them sit the aged men, wise guardians of the poor;
Then cherish pity, lest you drive an angel from your door.

The service in St Paul's was also attended by Hector Berlioz (in 1851, see 268) and described by him in his Les Soirées de L'Orchestre.

The microscope projections witnessed by the Princes were probably at that date exhibited at the Gallery of Practical Science in the Lowther Arcade. Two Indian visitors saw the same thing two years later (208) at the Polytechnic which opened in that year, and which was the third such institution to be promoted by John Martin, after the failure of the Adelaide Gallery and of another venture, known as the 'Panopticon'. (See Mary Pendered, John Martin, Painter: His Life and Times, *1923.)*

That these sights were the vogue in London in the '30s is borne out by Hallam Tennyson's Memoir *(1892) Vol 1, where the young Tennysons do a tour very similar to the Persians' and Indians', and look through microscopes 'at moths' wings, gnats' heads and at all the lions which lie perdus in a drop of spring water.' Both here, and again later Tennyson discusses the religious implications of these shows and (unquoted) tells the story of a Brahmin who destroyed a microscope because of the strife he saw taking place (compare, by the way, Tennyson's 'Nature red in tooth and claw . . .').*

From the Persian account it is clear that 'the operator' of the show pointed the moral. Probably this is why the Indians (208) appear spontaneously to consider the religious implications and also Tennyson. Ruskin refers to this also, but much later.

BLACK SWANS — Summer 1836

When you get into the Bishopric of Durham, going northward as I have observed in the Visit to Houghton-le-Spring, you begin to see tall engine-houses, and vastly tall chimneys, breathing into the sky long black clouds of smoke. You hear groans, and whistlings, and numerous unearthly sounds about you. These engine-houses contain those great steam-engines that work the coal-mines; and those noises proceed from pulleys, and gins, and railways, and other industrious instruments for raising and conveying away the coals. As you get into the country nearer Newcastle, all these operations – these groanings and wailings – these smokes and fires – increase upon you. Here you pass one of those tall engine-houses that you saw in the distance, with its still taller chimney hoisting into the sky its slanting column of turbid smoke. You now see a huge beam, protruding itself from the upper part of the engine-house, like a giant's arm, and alternatively lifting itself up, and then falling again. To this beam is attached the rod and bucket of a pump, which probably, at the depth of some hundred yards or more, is lifting out the water from the mine, and enabling the miners to work, where otherwise it would be all drowned in subterranean floods. Or you see a great beam suspended from its centre, and elevated aloft on a proper support, wagging its ends alternately up and down, and up and down, with that busy and whimsical air which has obtained for it the name of a whimsey. This is performing a similar operation by a different contrivance. Then, again, those huge engines are at work whirling buckets down into the deep shafts for coal, or whirling colliers themselves down to get the coal. For two or three hundred yards down a hideous gulf into the bowels of the earth are they sent, with a rapidity which to the stranger is frightful, to their labour, and pulled up again, after its performance, to day light as fast. All this time these great engines, of perhaps 200 horse power, are groaning and crying over their toils like condemned Titans; and the wheels and pulleys that they put in motion are singing and whistling lamentably, like so many lesser spirits doomed to attend upon their labours. Then you see buckets of coal emerge from the mouth of the pit, and immediately by self-agency run away, empty themselves into a waggon or boat, and come back empty and ready for a fresh exploit. Then, as you advance over the plain, you see a whole train of waggons loaded with coal, careering by themselves, without horse, without steam-engine, without man, except that there sits one behind, who, instead of endeavouring to propel these made waggons on their way, seems labouring hopelessly by his weight to detain them.

But what is your amazement when you come in sight of the river Tyne, and see these waggons still careering on to the very brink of the water! – to see a railway carried from the high bank and supported on tall piles, horizontally above the surface of the river, and to some distance into it, as if to allow those vagabond trains of waggons to run right off, and dash themselves down into the river. There they go, all mad together! Another moment, and they will shoot over the end of the lofty railway, and go headlong into the Tyne, helter-skelter! But behold, these creatures are instinct with sense. They have a principle of self-preservation as well as of speed in them. See, as they draw near the river, they pause – they stop; one by one they detach themselves, and as one devoted waggon runs on, like a victim given up for the salvation of the rest, to perform a wild summerset into the water below – what do we see? It is caught. A pair of gigantic arms separate themselves from the end of the railway. They catch the waggon; they hold it suspended in the air; they let it softly and gently descend, ay, softly and gently as an angel dropping to earth with some heavenly message, (I fear the angel of coal comes the other way,) – and whither? Into the water? No; we see now that a ship already lies below the end of the railway. The waggon descends to it; a man standing there strikes a bolt – the bottom falls, and the coals which it contains are nicely deposited in the hold of the vessel! Up again soars the empty waggon in that pair of gigantic arms. It reaches the railway; it glides like a black swan into its native lake, upon it, and away it goes as of its own accord, to a distance to await its brethren, who successively perform the same exploit, and then, joining it, all scamper back again as hard as they can over the plain to the distant pit.

From Visits to Remarkable Places *by William Howitt, 1842. Date of visit from Mary Howitt's* Autobiography, *published 1889.*

203   OUR ORIGIN   1837

If we choose to let our conjecture run wild, then animals, our fellow brethren in pain, disease, death, suffering and famine – our slaves in the most laborious works, our companions in our amusements – they may partake [of?] our origin in one common ancestor – we may be all melted together.

From the Note-Book of 1837 by Charles Darwin, printed in Life and Letters of Charles Darwin, *edited by Francis Darwin, 1887.*

204   COAL-PIPES   c.1837

In a colliery near Newcastle, say the authors of the Fossil Flora, a great number of *Sigillariae* were placed in the rock as if they had retained the position in which they grew. Not less than thirty, some of them 4 or 5 feet in diameter, were visible within an area of 50 yards square, the interior being sandstone, and the bark having been converted into coal. The roots of one individual were found imbedded in shale; and the trunk, after maintaining a perpendicular course and circular form for the height of about 10 feet, was then bent over so as to become horizontal. Here it was distended laterally, and flattened so as to be only one inch thick, the flutings being comparatively distinct. Such vertical stems are familiar to our miners, under the name of coal-pipes. One of them, 72 feet in length, was discovered, in 1829, near Gosforth, about five miles from Newcastle, in coal-grit, the strata of which it penetrated. The exterior of the trunk was marked off at intervals with knots, indicating the points at which branches had shot off. The wood of the interior had been converted into carbonate of lime; and its structure was beautifully shown by cutting transverse slices, so thin as to be transparent.

These 'coal-pipes' are much dreaded by our miners, for almost every year in the Bristol, Newcastle, and other coal-fields, they are the cause of fatal accidents. Each cylindrical cast of a tree, formed of solid sandstone, and increasing gradually in size towards the base, and being without branches, has its whole weight thrown downwards, and receives no support from the coating of friable coal which has replaced the bark. As soon, therefore, as the cohesion of this external layer is overcome, the heavy column falls suddenly in a perpendicular or oblique direction from the roof of the gallery whence coal has been extracted, wounding and killing the workman who stands below. It is strange to reflect how many thousands of these trees fell originally in their native forests in obedience to the law of gravity; and how the few which continued to stand erect, obeying, after myriads of ages, the same force, are cast down to immolate their human victims.

From Elements of Geology *by Sir Charles Lyell, 1838.*

205   IMAGINATION   June 1837

June 1st–5th. – Lecturing till I am sick. I am not happy in Manchester. The associations of these hideous mill-prisons for children destroy my enjoyment in society. The people are quite insensible to it; but how they can go on as they do in all luxurious enjoyments with those huge factories overhanging them, is most extraordinary.

17th, 18th. – This was imagination. I have since examined large factories – 2000 in one room, and found the children healthy and strong, and the room well aired and wholesome.

From the Autobiography and Journals *of B.R. Haydon, edited by Tom Taylor; written 1840–41, published 1847.*

I will embody these inductions in a more impressive form, by employing the metaphor of an Arabian writer, and imagining some higher intelligence from another sphere to describe the physical mutations of which he may be supposed to have taken cognizance, from the period when the forests of Portland were flourishing, to the present time.

'Countless ages ere man was created,' he might say, 'I visited these regions of the earth, and beheld a beautiful country of vast extent, diversified by hill and dale, with its rivulets, streams, and mighty rivers flowing through fertile plains. Groves of tall ferns and forests of coniferous trees clothed its surface; and I saw monsters of the reptile tribe, so huge that nothing among the existing races can compare with them, basking on the banks of its rivers, and roaming through its forests; while in its marshes and lagoons thousands of crocodiles and turtles crept and swam. Winged reptiles of strange forms shared with birds the dominion of the insect-teeming air, and the waters abounded with fishes, shells, and crustacea. – And after the lapse of many ages I again visited the earth; the beautiful country, and its innumerable dragon-forms, its rivers, and its tropical forests, all had disappeared, and an ocean had usurped their place. And its waters teemed with nautili, ammonites, and other cuttle-fishes, of races now extinct, and with innumerable fishes and marine reptiles. – And thousands of centuries rolled by, and I returned, and, lo! the ocean was gone, and dry land had again appeared, and it was covered with groves and forests; but these were wholly different in character from those of the vanished country of the Iguanodon. And I beheld herds of deer of enormous size, quietly browsing, and groups of elephants, mastodons, and other herbivorous animals of colossal magnitude. And I saw in its rivers and marshes the hippopotamus, tapir, and rhinoceros; and I heard the roar of the lion and the tiger, and the yell of the hyena and the bear. – And another epoch passed away, and I came again to the scene of my former contemplations; and all the mighty forms which I had left had disappeared, the face of the country no longer presented the same aspect: it was broken into islands, and the bottom of the sea had become dry land, and what before was dry land had sunk beneath the waves. Herds of deer were still to be seen on the plains, with swine, and horses, and oxen; and bears and wolves in the woods and forests. And I beheld human beings, clad in the skins of animals, and armed with clubs and spears; and they had formed themselves habitations in caves, constructed huts for shelter, and enclosed pastures for cattle, and were endeavouring to cultivate the soil. – And a thousand years elapsed, and I revisited the country, and a village had been built upon the sea-shore, and its inhabitants supported themselves by fishing; and they had erected a temple on the neighbouring hill, and dedicated it to their patron saint. And the adjacent country was studded with towns and villages; and the downs were covered with flocks, and the valleys with herds, and the cornfields and pastures were in a high state of cultivation, denoting an industrious and peaceful community. – And lastly, after the interval of many centuries, I arrived once more, and the village was swept away, and its site covered by the waves; but in the valley and on the hills above the cliffs a beautiful city appeared; with its palaces, its temples, and its thousand edifices, and its streets teeming with a busy population in the highest state of civilization; the resorts of the nobles of the land, the residence of the monarch of a mighty empire. And I perceived many of its intelligent inhabitants gathering together the vestiges of the beings which had lived and died, and whose very forms were now obliterated from the face of the earth, and endeavouring, by these natural memorials, to trace the succession of those events of which I had been the witness and which had preceded the history of their race.'

From The Wonders of Geology *by Gideon Mantell, 1838.*

207   SEDGWICK AT NEWCASTLE   August 7, 1838

All the show here is over. It has been by far the most brilliant meeting of the Association, and in all the public proceedings perfect good taste has reigned. Sedgwick wound up on Saturday with a burst of eloquence (something in the way of a sermon) of astonishing beauty and grandeur.

But this, I am told, was nothing compared to an out-of-door speech, address, or lecture, which he read on the sea-beach at Tynemouth to some 3000 or 4000 colliers and rabble (mixed with a sprinkling of their employers), which has produced a sensation such as is not likely to die away for years. I am told by ear and eye witnesses that it is impossible to conceive the sublimity of the scene, as he stood on the point of a rock a little raised, to which he rushed as if by sudden impulse, and led them on from the scene around them to the wonders of the coal-country below them, thence to the economy of a coal-field, then to their relations to the coal-owners and capitalists, then to the great principles of morality and happiness, and last to their relation to God, and their own future prospects. . . .

From a letter of Sir John Herschel printed in The Life and Letters of Adam Sedgwick *by J.W. Clark and T.M. Hughes, 1890.*

208   INDIANS AT THE POLYTECHNIC   late 1838

We saw in the lecture room numerous living animalculae in water, exhibited through Cary's Oxyhydrogen Microscope, upon a screen containing four hundred and twenty-five square feet, and to see the hundreds of monsters of *horrid* shapes in a *drop of water* magnified so as to appear several feet long, and to see a flea made to look as large almost as an Elephant, and the myriads of live eels in a bit of sour paste no bigger than a pin's head filled us with wonder and awe of that Being, who has created the most minute living things with all the air vessels and all the functions of life similar to the larger objects of his creation; and when we remembered to have heard it said, that there were men who say there is no God, we could only wish that such men, *if any such there be*, could be brought here to see these things, and then surely if they were not devoid of reason they would say these things cannot have been the effect of chance; there must have been, and now is a great, a good God who created all things for some wise and good purpose, and if we cannot penetrate all his designs, if there are some things for which we cannot account, let us bow with awe before our Creator, and acknowledge that all his productions are good, and let all human beings upon the face of the earth praise the Lord their God.

From Journal of a Residence of Two Years and a half in Great Britain *by Jehangeer Nowrojee and Hirjeebhoy Merwanjee, of Bombay, 1841.*

209   PAUPER CHILDREN FARMED OUT   1838

What struck me most was the pallor, the subdued mien, and listless demeanour of the children. They were decently but scantily clad. The rooms were generally clean and the windows wide open in the day time. The counterpanes and sheets were unsoiled. The beds did not seem too near together, though the rooms were low, and had no means of ventilation except through the windows. But when I measured the capacity of the bedrooms, and counted the numbers of the children and the beds, I found that each bed must receive at least two inmates at night, and that other beds must be brought into the rooms in the evening. It was only by special visits that I could verify this suspicion. These visits disclosed to me the secret of the discipline, for I found children chained to logs of wood, and I soon discovered that harsh punishments were not spared. But the sudden dissolution of a system which had grown up gradually in the preceding fifty years and had become an accredited part of the parochial arrangement, was impossible. The children could not be sent back to ill-constructed workhouses, often in unhealthy parts of London. Nor was there any other place ready to receive them. Some ameliorations could be effected. The number of children in certain establishments could be limited. The dietary could be improved. Means of cheerful recreation could be devised. The instruction in industry could be modified. But every change cost money. The contractors had friends on the board who could make a formidable resistance to improvements, however obvious, which involved a new and more costly contract. Consequently the ameliorations were imperfect. Even that which seemed imperative for the health of the children was obtained only with difficulty.

From a MS written in 1877 by James Kay-Shuttleworth and quoted in

The Life and Work of Sir James Kay-Shuttleworth *by Frank Smith, 1923.*

| 210 | TWO HEARTS | c.1839 |

It was a curious contrast to see how the timid country girl shrunk through the crowd that hurried up and down the streets, giving way to the press of people, and clinging closely to Ralph as though she feared to lose him in the throng; and how the stern and hard-featured man of business went doggedly on, elbowing the passengers aside, and now and then exchanging a gruff salutation with some passing acquaintance, who turned to look back upon his pretty charge, with looks expressive of surprise, and it seemed to wonder at the ill-sorted companionship. But, it would have been a stranger contrast still, to have read the hearts that were beating side by side; to have laid bare the gentle innocence of the one, and the rugged villainy of the other; to have hung upon the guileless thoughts of the affectionate girl, and been amazed that, among all the wily plots and calculations of the old man, there should not be one word or figure denoting thought of death or of the grave. But so it was; and stranger still – though this is a thing of every day – the warm young heart palpitated with a thousand anxieties and apprehensions, while that of the old worldly man lay rusting in its cell, beating only as a piece of cunning mechanism, and yielding no one throb of hope, or fear, or love, or care, for any living thing.

From The Life and Adventures of Nicholas Nickleby *by Charles Dickens, written c.1839.*

| 211 | FROM AN OLD JOURNAL | May 24, 1839 |

Friday, May 24th. Rose at six to pack, and left Liverpool for London at half-past nine by the railway. Fares, £2 11s. 3d. each; Jane, the servant, £1, 8s. 0d. Before Warrington the country very flat, but rich-looking and prettily diversified with trees. Long stop at Warrington, with steam puffing loudly; afterwards undulating country. Now we pass through a deep cutting – now a tunnel! Now trees flying past! A pretty country – a canal – across a valley; rushing at the rate of thirty-three miles an hour on an embankment high above the surrounding country – Father holding his watch in hand marking speed by the mile posts. Now running over a tedious, tame district – level and bleak; greatly prefer the land of the mountain and the flood. Stopped at Hartford. Not a hill! Just a boundless plain of fields and trees and hedges. Now a lovely little blue hill far away in Derbyshire! Stopping often – pretty undulating country. Going twenty-eight miles an hour. Stopping at a very pretty village – picturesque church with two towers – bells chiming most musically. Going at a tremendous rate – no less than thirty-six miles an hour! Stopped at Wolverhampton –

many tall chimneys. Passing through a long tunnel near Birmingham. Stopped there an hour – took a walk in the busy streets – paid 9d. each for a glass of wine. Off again, flew past many towns which cannot name, and pretty villages looking sweet in evening light. Dark when we reached London. Drove to hotel recommended to us at station – no room. Tried another – no room. At last, after driving by lamp light through interminable streets, we got very handsome rooms in Ragget's Hotel, Dover Street, an elegant drawing-room with three windows down to the floor, and bedrooms to match. The name was appropriate, for there were holes in some of the sheets, so we called it the 'Ragged Hotel' after we saw them, though everything else was very fine – silver tea urn, etc., at breakfast and tea, and stylish waiters to attend; but everything stiff and formal.

From 'an old journal' of Elizabeth King, sister of William Thompson, Lord Kelvin, then aged 21. In Lord Kelvin's Early Home, *edited by Elizabeth Thomson King, 1909.*

212 KERSALL MOOR May 25, 1839

8th June. – Too busy to keep my journal for a month. From the 10th of May my time has been constantly employed, and the various reports which came in from all quarters, to the effect that the intended meeting would decide the fate of the country, were harassing. All the best informed of the rich people, and the magistrates, asserted that this district could easily turn out three hundred thousand people on Kersall Moor; and the Chartist newspapers asserted that they would turn out five hundred thousand. I did not believe this, but secretly thought one hundred thousand might be assembled: – quite enough to render my position dangerous. My two hundred thousand men and four guns were indeed enough, if well handled, but not enough to afford mistakes. I had been long out of practice myself, my troops had been but lately brought together, were all young soldiers, and not a dozen of the officers had ever seen a shot fired: all this was awkward. But allowing that no error occurred, what a slaughter! Good God what work! to send grape-shot from four guns into a helpless mass of fellow-citizens; sweeping the streets with fire and charging with cavalry, destroying poor people whose only crime is that they have been ill-governed, and reduced to such straits that they seek redress by arms, ignorant that of all ways that is the most certain to increase the evils they complain of.

On one side we have an ill-used people suffering want, and thinking, justly, that if they had their rights the want would be relieved. But how are those rights to be gained? By changing our government into a republic say the vagabonds who want power, and do not want to see their countrymen fed; who like Daniel O'Connell delight in seeing them poor and miserable, as a means of continuing their popularity and power: keep the people aggrieved and we will keep power by declaiming against those grievances.

On the other hand, what do the Whigs and Tories do? Madly refuse the people's rights, thereby convincing them the democrats speak truly, and that aristocracy will yield nothing; that the people are lost if they trust to anything but arms. Madness on both sides. One seeking right in a wrong way, the other wrong in a wrong way. Hence not only slaughter might have occurred, but the example of one rising might be followed throughout England; for the agitation is so general no one can tell the effect of a single shot: all depended upon avoiding collision. I met the magistrates every week and impressed on them to the utmost of my power the necessity of not attacking the people, of letting them meet, and speak also, as they have a perfect right to do. That if an orator excited them to overt acts of treason, burning, murder, he should be arrested after the crowd dispersed; that if any went armed we could seize them as being armed. Otherwise to let the people alone. In all this Mr Foster agreed with me, and this line we pursued.

The redoubted 25th May came and not three hundred thousand but thirty thousand assembled. At this meeting Wemyss addressed a few of the people in high Tory oratory, and argued with a drunken old pensioner, fiercely Radical and devilish sharp; in ten minutes an eighth of the whole crowd collected round Wemyss and cheered him! These certainly were not Chartists. Some days before this I had a meeting with a gentleman, intimate with the Chartist leaders if not one himself, and begged him to shew them how impossible it would be to feed and move three hundred thousand men; that armed, starving, interspersed with villains they must commit horrid excesses; that I would never allow them to charge me with their pikes, or even march ten miles without mauling them with cannon and musketry, and charging them with cavalry when they dispersed to seek food: finally that the country would rise on them and they would be destroyed in three days!

He said peace had put us out of practice, and we could not use our artillery: but he was soon convinced that was nonsense, and reported my observations to the leaders. I offered him no abuse, said many Chartists who acted on principle were to be honoured, others to be pitied as acting from ignorance, and certain to bitterly repent when they saw the terrible mischief that would ensue. This I believe had a good effect, and saying only what in my conviction was true it is probable I spoke well, for he seemed struck with the evils pointed out as inevitably attending even a disciplined army. At all events my meaning was good, urged by my dread of the havoc impending, for every one believed that three hundred thousand men would assemble. Such a force in one mass had never met my eyes, and I was resolved not to let them come near me, but to fight with my guns, keeping cavalry on their flanks to prevent small parties foraging.

How small accidents affect men's minds and decide events. The 1st Dragoons and 10th Foot came from Ireland with the 79th but the last being in kilts terrified the Chartists more than a brigade of other troops. Again.

Not being sure if the first outbreak would not be at Birmingham, where the mulcibers are bolder than the weavers, the 10th were kept at Liverpool as a reserve. Birmingham was quiet and the 10th came to Manchester by wings, one with the band, the other marching with drums and fifes: so I had ordered. The Chartists thought two regiments had joined, and Mr B— says that supposed increase of force decided them not to attack: thus the kilt, which was no force at all; and the division of the 10th, which was weakness, contributed largely to our security.

From the Journal of General Sir Charles Napier, quoted in The Life and Opinions of Gen. Sir Charles Napier *by Lieut.-Gen. Sir W. Napier, published 1857.*

213   THE DEVIL   August 9, 1839

Spanked along the road to Liverpool. It is quite a just remark that the Devil, if he travelled, would go by train.

From the Journal of Lord Shaftesbury, quoted in The Life and Work of the Seventh Earl of Shaftesbury *by Edwin Hodder, 1888.*

214   FAUST'S FLIGHT   September 13, 1839

The whirl through the confused darkness, on those steam wings, was one of the strangest things I have experienced – hissing and dashing on, one knew not whither. We saw the gleam of towns in the distance – unknown towns. We went over the tops of houses – one town or village I saw clearly, with its chimney heads vainly stretching up towards us – *under* the stars; not under the clouds, but among them. Out of one vehicle into another, snorting, roaring we flew: likest thing to a Faust's flight on the Devil's mantle; or as if some huge steam night-bird had flung you on its back, and was sweeping through unknown space with you, most probably towards London. At Birmingham, an excellent breakfast, with deliberation to eat it, set us up surprisingly; and so, with the usual series of phenomena, we were safe landed at Euston Square, soon after one o'clock. We slept long and deep. It was a great surprise the first moment to find one did not waken at Scotsbrig. Wretched feelings of all sorts were holding carnival within me. The best I could do was to keep the door carefully shut on them. I sate dead silent all yesterday, working at 'Meister;' and now they are gone back to their caves again.

From a letter of Thomas Carlyle to John Carlyle, quoted in Thomas Carlyle, A History of His Life in London, *by J.A. Froude, 1884.*

215   MIND AND MATTER   May 8, 1840

Attended Carlyle's second lecture. It was on 'The Prophetic Character,' illustrated by Mahomet. It gave great satisfaction, for it had uncommon thoughts, and was delivered with unusual animation. He declared his conviction that Mahomet was no mere sensualist, or vulgar impostor, but a real reformer. His system better than the Christianity current in his day in Syria. Milnes there, and Mrs Gaskell, with whom I chatted pleasantly. In the evening heard a lecture by Faraday. What a contrast to Carlyle! A perfect experimentalist – with an intellect so clear. Within his sphere, '*un uomo compito*'. How great would that man be who could be as wise on Mind and its relations as Faraday is on Matter!

From the Diary of Henry Crabb Robinson, in The Diary, Reminiscences and Correspondence of Henry Crabb Robinson, *edited by Thomas Sadler, 1869.*

216   **THE MONSTER**   June 15, 1840

Except on compulsion, I go little into the town, call on nobody there. They can come here if they want me; if not I shall like it still better. Our old wooden Battersea bridge takes me over the river; in ten minutes' swift trotting I am fairly away from the monster and its bricks. All lies behind me like an enormous world-filling *pfluister*, infinite potter's furnace, sea of smoke, with steeples, domes, gilt crosses, high black architecture swimming in it, really beautiful to look at from some knoll-top while the sun shines on it. I ply away, away, some half-dozen miles out. The monster is then quite buried, its smoke rising like a great dusky-coloured mountain melting into the infinite clear sky. All is green, musical, bright. One feels that it is God's world this; and not an infinite Cockneydom of *stoor* and din after all.

From a letter of Thomas Carlyle to his sister, quoted in Thomas Carlyle, A History of His Life in London, *by J.A. Froude, 1884.*

217   **CARLYLE AT LEEDS**   April 17, 1841

I was much entertained with the new mill yesterday, with the thousands of men, lasses and boys and girls, all busy there. It is not nothing, but something, we here live amidst. At six o'clock here a general muster of the Spring Rices and Marshalls, Mrs Henry Taylor among them, awaited us to dinner, and we had a reasonable enough evening, one of the best I have yet had. Beautiful room where I now sit writing, with Leeds lying safe in the hollow of the green knolls; its steeple-chimneys all dead to-day (Sunday), its very house-smoke cleared away by the brisk wind that is rattling in all windows, growling mystically through all the trees. Nothing that art, aided by wealth, good sense, and honest kindness, can do for me is wanting.

From a letter of Thomas Carlyle to Jane Welsh Carlyle, printed in

Thomas Carlyle, A History of His Life in London, *by J.A. Froude, 1884.*

| 218 | A TOO MUCH DIVIDED HEART | December 20, 1841 |

When I contemplated the engagements of my three dear sons during this day, my heart's desire was that they should all be employed as my first born (John) at Oxford Select Quarterly Meeting, but my second (Joseph) was at Newcastle respecting Coals; my third (Henry) at Wolsingham respecting Railways – these latter may be needful and useful engagements, but a too much divided heart ruffles the tide of peace.

From the Diaries of Edward Pease, The Father of the English Railways, *edited by A.E. Pease, 1907.*

| 219 | A YORKSHIRE CHILDHOOD | c.1842 |

My father's native place was Honley, about 7 miles from Huddersfield. His parents were poor working people – so much so that they had to get rid of their children as best they could; so my father was a town's apprentice to a farmer – he got his food but no wages at a village, Crossland Hill, his master finding him what clothing he thought useful, while he was of age. After his apprenticeship he went to work in the stone quarries. In due time he got maryed, and there was a family of 3 children. I was the second, and had 2 sisters. Poor mother died when I was between 2 and 3. My eldest sister went to work in the factory very early. I soon had to follow, I think about 9 years of age. What with hunger and hard usage I bitterly got it burned into me – I believe it will stay while life shall last. We had to be up at 5 in the morning to get to the factory, ready to begin work at 6, then work while 8, when we stopped ½ an hour for breakfast, then work to 12 noon; for dinner we had 1 hour, then work while 4. We then had ½ an hour for tee, and tee if anything was left, then commenced work again on to 8.30. If any time during the day had been lost, we had to work while 9 o'clock, and so on every night till it was all made up. Then we went to what was called home. Many times I have been asleep when I had taken my last spoonful of porige – not even washed, we were so overworked and underfed. I used to curs the road we walked on. I was so weekley and feeble I used to think it was the road would not let me go along with the others. We had not always the kindest of masters. I remember my master's strap, 5 or 6 feet long, about ¾ in. broad, and ¼ in. thick. He kept it hung on the ginney at his right hand, so we could not see when he took hould of it. But we could not mistake its lessons; for he got hold of it nearly in the middle, and it would be a rare thing if we did not get 2 cuts at one stroke. I have reason to believe on one occasion he was somewhat moved to compassion, for the end of his strap striped the skin of my neck about 3 in. long. When he saw the blood and cut, he actually stopped the machine, came and tied a handkerchief round my neck to cover it up. I have been fell'd to the floor many times by the ruler on the top of the carding, about 8 or 9 feet long, iron hoop at each end. This was done as a change for the strap. For a time I could not tell whether living or dead.

From an account by George Oldfield written in 1904, published in The Hungry Forties: Life under the Bread Tax, *with an introduction by Mrs Cobden Unwin, 1904.*

220   SHAFTESBURY'S MINES BILL   June 7, 1842

As I stood at the table, and just before I opened my mouth, the words of God came forcibly to my mind, 'Only be strong and of a good courage' – praised be His Holy Name, I was as easy from that moment as though I had been sitting in an arm-chair. Many men, I hear, shed tears – Beckett Denison confessed to me that he did, and that he left the House lest he should be seen. Sir G. Grey told William Cowper that he 'would rather have made that speech than any he ever heard.' Even Joseph Hume was touched. Members took me aside, and spoke in a *very serious* tone of thanks and admiration. I must and will sing an everlasting 'non nobis.' – Grant, oh blessed God, that I may not be exalted above measure, but that I may ever creep close to the ground, knowing and joyfully confessing that I am Thy servant, that without Thee I am nothing worth, and that from Thee alone cometh all counsel, wisdom, and understanding, for the sake of our most dear and only Saviour, God manifest in the flesh, our Lord Jesus Christ! It has given me hopes for the Empire, hopes for its permanence, hopes for its services in the purposes of the Messiah. God prosper the issue!

From the Journal of Lord Shaftesbury, quoted in The Life and Work of the Seventh Earl of Shaftesbury *by Edwin Hodder, 1888.*

221   CIVILITY TO VULCAN   Summer 1842

Herculaneum and Pompeii were also visited, but, more than all, the crater of Vesuvius. During my visit the mountain was in its normal state. I mounted the volcanic ashes with which it is strewn, and got to the top. There I could look down into the pit from which the clouds of steam are vomited forth. I went down to the very edge of the crater, stood close to its mouth, and watched the intermittent uprushing of the blasts of vapour and sulphureous gases. To keep clear of these I stood to the windward side, and was thus out of harm's way.

What struck me most was the wonderfully brilliant colours of the rugged lava rocks forming the precipitous cliffs of the interior walls of the crater. These brilliant colours were the result of the sublimation and condensation on their surfaces of the combinations of sulphur and chloride of iron, quite as bright as if they had been painted bright red, chrome, and all the most brilliant tints. Columns of all manner of chemical vapours ascended from the clefts and deep cracks, at the bottom of which I saw clearly the bright hot lava.

I rolled as big a mass of cool lava as I could, to the edge of the crater and heaved it down; but I heard no sound. Doubtless the depth was vast, or it might probably have fallen into the molten lava and thus make no noise. On leaving this horrible pit edge, I tied a card of the Bridgewater Foundry to a bit of lava and threw it in, as a token of respectful civility to Vulcan, the head of our craft.

From James Nasmyth, an Autobiography, *edited by Samuel Smiles, 1883.*

222 POEMS September 1842

Milnes brought Carlyle to the railway, and showed him the departing train. Carlyle looked at it and then said, 'These are our poems, Milnes.' Milnes ought to have answered, 'Aye, and our histories, Carlyle.'

From the Journals *of R.W. Emerson, edited by E.W. Emerson and Waldo Emerson Forbes, 1909–14.*

It was in this year 1842 that J.C. Doppler noticed the differing pitch of train whistles – advancing and retiring – and proposed, by analogy, the Doppler effect in the spectra of certain stars.

223 THE CONDITION OF ENGLAND January 1843

The condition of England, on which so many pamphlets are now in the course of publication, and many thoughts unpublished are going on in every reflective head, is justly regarded as one of the most ominous, and withal one of the strangest, seen in this world. England is full of wealth, of multifarious produce, supply for human want in every kind; yet England is dying of inanition. With unabated bounty the land of England blooms and grows; waving with yellow harvests; thick-studded with workshops, industrial implements, with fifteen millions of workers, understood to be the strongest, the cunningest and the willingest our Earth ever had; these men are here; the work they have done, the fruit they have realised is here, abundant, exuberant on every hand of us: and behold, some baleful fiat as of Enchantment has gone forth, saying, 'Touch it not, ye workers, ye master-workers, ye master idlers; none of you can touch it, no man of you shall be the better for it; this is enchanted fruit!' On the poor workers such fiat falls first, in its rudest shape; but on the rich master-workers too it falls; neither can the rich master-idlers, nor any richest or highest man escape, but all are like to be brought low with it, and made 'poor' enough, in the money-sense or a far fataler one.

Of these successful skilful workers some two millions, it is now counted, sit in Workhouses, Poor-law Prisons; or have 'outdoor relief' flung over the wall to them, – the workhouse Bastille being filled to bursting, and the strong Poor-law broken asunder by a stronger.* They sit there, these many months now; their hope of deliverance as yet small. In workhouses, pleasantly so named, because work cannot be done in them. Twelve hundred thousand workers in England alone; their cunning right-hand lamed, lying idle in their sorrowful bosom; their hopes, outlooks, share of this fair world, shut-in by narrow walls. They sit there, pent up, as in a kind of horrid enchantment; glad to be imprisoned and enchanted, that they may not perish starved. The picturesque Tourist, in a sunny autumn day, through this bounteous realm of England, describes the Union workhouse on his path. 'Passing by the workhouse of St. Ives in Huntingdonshire, on a bright day last autumn,' says the picturesque Tourist, 'I saw sitting on wooden benches, in front of their Bastille and within their ring-wall and its railings, some half-hundred or more of these men. Tall robust figures, young mostly or of middle age; of honest countenance, many of them thoughtful or even intelligent-looking men. They sat there, near by one another; but in a kind of torpor, especially in a silence, which was very striking. In silence: for alas, what word was to be said? An Earth all lying around, crying, Come and till me, come and reap me, – yet we here sit enchanted! In the eyes and brows of these men hung the gloomiest expression, not of anger, but of grief and shame and manifold inarticulate distress and weariness; they returned my glance with a glance that seemed to say, "Do not look at us. We sit enchanted here, we know not why. The Sun shines and the Earth calls; and, by the governing Powers and Impotences of this England, we are forbidden to obey. It is impossible, they tell us!" There was something that reminded me of Dante's Hell in the look of all this; and I rode swiftly away.'

From Past and Present, *by Thomas Carlyle, written January–February 1843.*

224   THE COMPANY'S ENTERPRISE AND TASTE   1843

The new Cemetery Companies have perpetrated the grossest absurdities in the buildings they have erected. Of course there are a superabundance of inverted torches, cinerary urns, and pagan emblems, tastefully disposed by the side of neat ground walks, among cypress trees and weeping willows.

The central chapel is generally built in such a comprehensive plan as to be

---

* The Return of Paupers for England and Wales, at Ladyday, 1842, is, 'In-door 221,687, Out-door 1,207,402, Total 1,429,089.' – (Official Report.)

ENTRANCE GATEWAY FOR A NEW CEMETERY

adapted (in the modern sense) for each sect and denomination in turn, as they may require its temporary use; but the entrance gateway is usually selected for the grand display of the company's enterprise and taste, as being well calculated from its position to induce persons to patronize the undertaking by the purchase of shares or graves. – This generally Egyptian, probably from some association between the word catacombs, which occurs in the prospectus of the company, and the discoveries of Belzoni on the banks of the Nile; and nearly opposite the Green Man and Dog public-house, in the centre of a dead wall (which serves as a cheap medium of advertisement for blacking and shaving-strop manufacturers), a cement miniature of the entrance to an Egyptian temple, $2\frac{1}{2}$ inches to the foot, is erected, with convenient lodges for the policeman and his wife, and a neat pair of cast iron hieroglyphical gates, which would puzzle the most learned to decipher; while, to prevent any mistake, some such words as 'New Economical Compressed Grave Cemetery Company' are inscribed in *Grecian* capitals along the frieze, interspersed with hawk-headed divinities and surmounted by a huge representation of the winged Osiris bearing a gas lamp.

From the Apology for the Revival of Christian Architecture in England *of A.W. Pugin, 1843.*

Two shillings a-week for lads twelve and fourteen years old. From two and sixpence to three and sixpence a-week for lads fourteen to sixteen years old. Four shillings and five shillings a-week for young men seventeen, eighteen, nineteen, and twenty years old! And by those youths and young men two-thirds of all the ploughing and carting of the farm is done. They are hired from a distance in almost all cases; are hired by the year; provide themselves with food and clothing out of their wages; sleep in a stable-loft or barn, having no fireside to go to; no hot dinners, but everlasting bread and lard, bread and lard, bread and lard!

Here is a conversation with one of them on a large farm near Abingdon:
'You hold the plough, you say; how old are you?'
'I bees sixteen a'most.'
'What wages have you?'
'Three shillin' a-week.'
'Three shillings! Have you nothing else? Don't you get victuals, or part of them, from your master?'
'No, I buys them all.'
'All out of three shillings?'
'Ees, and buys my clothes out of that.'
'And what do you buy to eat?'
'Buy to eat! Why, I buys bread and lard.'
'Do you eat bread and lard always? What have you for breakfast?'
'What have I for breakfast? Why, bread and lard.'
'And what for dinner?'
'Bread and lard.'
'What for supper, the same?'
'Ees, the same for supper – bread and lard.'
'It seems to be always bread and lard; have you no boiled bacon and vegetables?'
'No, there be no place to boil 'em; no time to boil 'em; none to boil.'
'Have you never a hot dinner nor supper; don't you get potatoes?'
'Ees, potatoes, an we pay for 'em. Master lets us boil 'em once a-week an we like.'
'And what do you eat to them; bacon?'
'No.'
'What then?'
'Lard; never has nothing but lard.'
'Can't you boil or cook your victuals any day you choose?'
'No; has no fire.'
'Have you no fire to warm you in cold weather?'
'No, we never has fire.'
'Where do you go in the winter evenings?'

'To bed, when it be time; an it ben't time, we goes to some of the housen as be round about.'

'To the firesides of some of the cottagers, I suppose?'

'Ees, an we can get.'

'What if you cannot get; do you go into the farmhouse?'

'No, mustn't; never goes nowhere but to bed an it be very cold.'

'Where is your bed?'

'In the *tollit*,' (stable loft.)

'How many of you sleep there?'

'All on us as be hired.'

'How many are hired?'

'Four last year, five this.'

'Does any one make the beds for you?'

'No, we make 'em ourselves.'

'Who washes your sheets?'

'Who washes 'em?'

'Yes; they are washed, I suppose?'

'No, they ben't.'

'What, never washed? Do you mean to say you don't have your sheets washed?'

'No, never since I comed.'

'When did you come?'

'Last Michaelmas.'

'Were your bedclothes clean then?'

'I dare say they was.'

'And don't you know how long they are to serve until they are changed again?'

'To Michaelmas, I hear tell.'

'So one change of bedclothes serves a year! Don't you find your bed disagreeable?'

'Do I! I bees too sleepy. I never knows nought of it, only that I has to get up afore I be awake, and never get into it afore I be a'most asleep. I be up at four, and ben't done work afore eight at night.'

'You don't go so long at the plough as that?'

'No; but master be always having summat for we to do as be hired; we be always at summat.'

From The Whistler at the Plough *by Alexander Somerville, published in book form 1852, but originally published as letters in the* Morning Chronicle. *This is from letter XXIV.*

226   IN BEDLAM   October 23, 1843

Methinks I see a hieroglyphic bat
Skim o'er the zenith in a slipshod hat,
And to shed infants' blood with horrid strides
A damned potato on a whirlwind rides.

Fabulously attributed to Nat Lee in Bedlam; composed, I imagine, by John Sterling, who gave it me yesterday.

From The Journal of Thomas Carlyle, quoted in Thomas Carlyle, a History of His Life in London, *by J.A. Froude, 1884.*

227   PROSE   November 14, 1843

The poets of our day have a glorious prospect before them, if they will pursue their own interests through the wants of the age, and write in prose. I should have written few verses if, before I had acquired the bad habit of rhyming, I had been honest enough to confess to myself that my thoughts were not good enough for prose. The best poetry of the age – the only poetry that is read – is written in prose, and to be found in the prose of Scott, Dickens, Richter, Thomas Carlyle, and others. Verse is a trick which the age has seen through and despises. It is utterly unsaleable, and absolutely unread. . . .

From a letter of Ebenezer Elliott to Ebenezer Hingston, printed in Life, Poetry and Letters of Ebenezer Elliott *by John Watkins, 1850.*

228   CHRISTMAS DAY   December 25, 1843

'This is the day that the Lord hath made; let us rejoice and be glad in it.' Rose before six to prayer and meditation. Ah, blessed God, how many in the mills and factories have risen at four, on this day even, to toil and suffering!

From the Journal of Lord Shaftesbury, quoted in The Life and Work of the Seventh Earl of Shaftesbury *by Edwin Hodder, 1888.*

229   SCROOGE AND THE SECOND SPIRIT   as for Christmas 1843

Much they saw, and far they went, and many homes they visited, but always with a happy end. The Spirit stood beside sick beds, and they were cheerful; on foreign lands, and they were close at home; by struggling men, and they were patient in their greater hope; by poverty, and it was rich. In almshouse, hospital, and jail, in misery's every refuge, where vain man in his little brief authority had not made fast the door, and barred the Spirit out, he left his blessing, and taught Scrooge his precepts.

It was a long night, if it were only a night; but Scrooge had his doubts of this, because the Christmas Holidays appeared to be condensed into the space of time they passed together. It was strange, too, that while Scrooge remained unaltered in his outward form, the Ghost grew older, clearly older. Scrooge had observed this change, but never spoke of it, until they left a children's Twelfth Night party, when, looking at the Spirit as they stood together in an open place, he noticed that its hair was gray.

'Are spirits' lives so short?' asked Scrooge.

'My life upon this globe, is very brief,' replied the Ghost. 'It ends to-night.'

'To-night!' cried Scrooge.

'To-night at midnight. Hark! The time is drawing near.'

The chimes were ringing the three quarters past eleven at that moment.

'Forgive me if I am not justified in what I ask,' said Scrooge, looking intently at the Spirit's robe, 'but I see something strange, and not belonging to yourself, protruding from your skirts. Is it a foot or a claw?'

'It might be a claw, for the flesh there is upon it,' was the Spirit's sorrowful reply. 'Look here.'

From the foldings of its robe, it brought two children; wretched, abject, frightful, hideous, miserable. They knelt down at its feet, and clung upon the outside of its garment.

'Oh, Man! look here. Look, look, down here!' exclaimed the Ghost.

They were a boy and girl. Yellow, meagre, ragged, scowling, wolfish; but prostrate too, in their humility. Where graceful youth should have filled their features out, and touched them with its freshest tints, a stale and shrivelled hand, like that of age, had pinched, and twisted them, and pulled them into shreds. Where angels might have sat enthroned, devils lurked, and glared out menacing. No change, no degradation, no perversion of humanity, in any grade, through all the mysteries of wonderful creation, has monsters half so horrible and dread.

Scrooge started back, appalled. Having them shown to him in this way, he tried to say they were fine children, but the words choked themselves, rather than be parties to a lie of such enormous magnitude.

'Spirit! are they yours?' Scrooge could say no more.

'They are Man's,' said the Spirit, looking down upon them. 'And they cling to me, appealing from their fathers. This boy is Ignorance. This girl is Want. Beware them both, and all of their degree, but most of all beware this boy, for on his brow I see that written which is Doom, unless the writing be erased. Deny it!' cried the Spirit, stretching out its hand towards the city. 'Slander those who tell it ye! Admit it for your factious purposes, and make it worse! And bide the end!'

'Have they no refuge or resource?' cried Scrooge.

'Are there no prisons?' said the Spirit, turning on him 'for the last time with his own words. 'Are there no work-houses?'
The bell struck twelve.
Scrooge looked about him for the Ghost and saw it not.
From A Christmas Carol *by Charles Dickens, 1843.*

Thomas Hood's famous 'Song of the Shirt' occurs in the Christmas Supplement to Punch, *1843, i.e. at exactly the same moment as* A Christmas Carol.

230   CLASSIC SOIL   before 1844

If we cross Blackstone Edge or penetrate it with the railroad, we enter upon that classic soil on which English manufacture has achieved its master-work and from which all labour movements emanate, namely South Lancashire with its central city Manchester. Again we have beautiful hill country, sloping gently from the watershed westwards towards the Irish Sea, with the charming green valleys of the Ribble, the Irwell, the Mersey, and their tributaries, a country which, a hundred years ago chiefly swamp land, thinly populated, is now sown with towns and villages, and is the most densely populated strip of country in England. In Lancashire, and especially in Manchester, English manufacture finds at once its starting point and its centre. The Manchester Exchange is the thermometer for all the fluctuations of trade. The modern art of manufacture has reached its perfection in Manchester. In the cotton industry of South Lancashire, the application of the forces of Nature, the superseding of hand labour by machinery (especially by the power loom and the self-acting mule), and the division of labour, are seen at the highest point; and, if we recognise in these three elements that which is characteristic of modern manufacture, we must confess that the cotton industry has remained in advance of all other branches of industry from the beginning down to the present day. The effects of modern manufacture upon the working-class must necessarily develop here most freely and perfectly, and the manufacturing proletariat present itself in its fullest classic perfection. The degradation to which the application of steam-power, machinery, and the division of labour reduce the working-man, and the attempts of the proletariat to rise above this abasement, must likewise be carried to the highest point and with the fullest consciousness.

From Friedrich Engels, The Condition of the Working-Class in England in 1844, *published in German 1845, English translation published New York, 1886.*

This passage is of quite extraordinary interest as an image, *over and above what it says politically. In it Engels presents South Lancashire as a unity – a new unity – 'classic soil' – created by the Industrial Revolution. Created not destroyed. Almost everywhere else in these images, particular places in Britain are referred to as holy because of surviving the Industrial Revolution or being destroyed by it. Ruskin later speaks of 'the sacred places of the Earth.' Engels is speaking in strictly neutral terms both of the Earth and of the human consumers: the historical process does not consecrate – it brings to 'classic perfection'. 'Classic' as being at a given moment the most perfect example or specimen, in a scientific sense, as a natural organism (plant or animal) might be selected for discussion.*

231   THE MORAL MACHINERY   February 1844

A few words may here be added concerning what we may term the *social* or *moral* machinery of the place. Where the operations are extended over so wide an area, and partake of so varied a character, the number of persons employed must be very great. We believe that in busy times it amounts to nearly two thousand. As there are no large towns near, these workpeople form a sort of community, having not much intercourse with others, and this isolation gives to them many characteristic features. They have seldom shown a tendency to join in the outbreaks which have from time to time disturbed the manufacturing districts, and there seems to exist between the employers and the employed a kind of mutual confidence, productive of many good consequences. Nearly all the houses inhabited by the workmen belong to the Company, excepting, perhaps, those at Ripley. At the spot formerly spoken of, called Golden Valley, there is a village entirely occupied by the workmen; and nearer to Codnor Park there is another, presenting many interesting features. It is called, appropriately enough, Ironville, and presents, with all due loyalty, its 'King William Street,' 'Victoria Row,' 'Albert Row' &c. The houses are neatly built of brick; and are of such a character that a four-roomed house, with a neat little garden either before or behind, is let at about 4£ a year.

In the mode of paying the workmen, precautions are taken against abuses, which are too apt to occur where the employers do not keep a watchful eye. Most of the operations in an iron-work are conducted by 'piece-work,' that is, the men are paid according to the quantity of their produce. Where four or more are employed on the same mass of iron, one man is generally master over the rest, and receives payment for the whole, giving to each man the amount of his earnings. In such a case it is required by the Company that the wages shall not be paid in a public-house, and that the payment shall be in money; the reason for the former rule is obvious, and the latter is to avoid the evils and injustice of the 'truck-system.' As an incentive to frugality, a Savings' Bank has been established at the works, where the Company allow four per cent. on all deposits from the workmen. There is also a sick-fund established, through which, by a small monthly subscription, the workmen ensure medical attendance, medicines, and a monthly allowance in money, when ill.

The little folks, too are not neglected. It is a standing rule of the Company that no apprentice shall be received until he can read, write, and perform the earlier processes of arithmetic; and as this rule would press heavily on those who have not the means of acquiring education, the proprietors have built a large, commodious, and even elegant school at Ironville, for the education of the workmen's children; and it is, we believe, in contemplation to build a church there likewise – the school being at present licensed for the Church of England service on Sundays. The school-house has two school-rooms; one for boys, and the other for girls. There about a hundred of each sex attend the school, under the superintendence of a master and mistress, engaged expressly for the purpose. The usual and most useful branches of education are taught, and, in addition, vocal music is taught on the system of Mr Hullah. In every large group of children there must of course be a considerable number who cannot make the least approach to correct singing; but there are in this school many who go through concerted pieces with an accuracy which would do credit to 'children of larger growth'; some of them, too, being able to sing off a piece of moderately difficult music at sight. To hear a song adapted to the tune of Auber's 'Prayer' in Masaniello, and such a glee as Webbe's 'When winds breathe soft', sung, in three or four parts, by a little group of incipient miners or smelters – some in blue pinafores, and some in whitey-brown, and accompanied by their sisters (for both schools join occasionally in the singing lessons) – is as novel as it is pleasant, as creditable to those who teach, as it is welcome and beneficial to those who are taught.

From 'A Day at the Butterly Ironworks, Derbyshire', in a supplement to The Penny Magazine, *February 24, 1844.*

232 THE DUE REWARD June 1844

I have just received your letter with a rejoinder to my anti-non-interference philippic. Of course I do not mean that if a labourer has at present his proper proportion for twelve hours work, he should have the same sum for ten. But I do believe that he has not his proper proportion, that capital tyrannises over labour, and that Government is bound to interfere to prevent such bullying; and I do believe, too, that in some way or other the problem now solved by universal competition or the devil-take-the-hindmost may receive a more satisfactory solution. It is manifestly absurd that, to allow me to get my stockings a halfpenny a pair cheaper, the operative stocking-weaver should be forced to go barefoot. It is, surely, not wholly Utopian to look for some system which will apportion the due reward to the various sets of workmen, and evade this perpetual struggle for securing (each man to the exclusion of his neighbour) the whole market.

I have got two beautiful white water-lilies floating in a green dessert dish beside me. Enviest thou not, O Sicilian Shepherd? Or hast thou thyself also such treasures?

From a letter of A.H. Clough to the Rev. T. Burbidge, written at Oxford, and printed in his Poems and Prose Remains, *1869.*

233   HALF-TIMERS   1844

They are dirty and labour-soiled, in ragged and scanty clothes, with heavy eyes and worn faces. In the clothing districts, their faces, necks, and hands are deeply stained with the blue of the dye used for the cloth. From the spinning mills they come covered with the 'flock', or as it is termed the 'fluff' of the yarn – their hair thickly powdered with it – tangled, especially that of the girls, as if no comb could ever penetrate it. . . . I fancied, perhaps wrongly that there was little notice taken of them in the business of the school. . . . The master professed himself unable to include them in the various classes, without materially injuring the progress of the other children.

From the Minutes of the Committee of the Council on Education, 1844; quoted in The Life and Work of Sir James Kay-Shuttleworth *by Frank Smith, 1923.*

234   CHICKABOBBOO   Autumn 1844

At the brewery, where they had been invited by the proprietors, servants in abundance were in readiness to turn upon their giant hinges the great gates, and pass the carriage into the court; and at the entrance to the grand fountain of *chickabobboo* there were servants to receive them and announce their arrival, when they were met, and with the greatest politeness and kindness led by one of the proprietors, and an escort of ladies, through the vast labyrinths and mazes, through the immense halls and courts, and under and over the dry-land of the world, as they were sure to call it when they got home. The vastness and completeness of this huge manufactory, or, in fact, village of manufactures, illustrated and explained in all its parts and all its mysterious modes of operation, formed a subject of amazement in our own as well as the Indians' minds – difficult to be described, and never to be forgotten.

When the poor untutored Indians, from the soft and simple prairies of the Missouri, seated themselves upon a beam, and were looking into and contemplating the immensity of a smoking steeping-vat, containing more than 3000 barrels, and were told that there were 130 others of various dimensions in the establishment – that the whole edifice covered twelve acres of ground, and that there were necessarily constantly on hand in their cellars 232,000 barrels of ale, and also that this was only one of a great number of breweries in London, and that similar manufactories were in every town in the kingdom, though in a less scale, they began, almost for the first time since their arrival, to evince profound astonishment; and the fermentation in their minds, as to the consistency of white man's teachings of temperance and manufacturing and selling ale, seemed not less than that which was going on in the vast abyss below them. The pipe was lit and passed around while they were in this contemplative mood, and as their ears were open, they got, in the meantime, further information of the wonderful modes and operations of this vast machine; and also, in round numbers, read from a report by one of the proprietors, the quantity of ale consumed in the kingdom annually. Upon hearing this, which seemed to cap the climax of all their astonishment, they threw down the pipe, and leaping into an empty vat, suddenly dissipated the pain of their mental calculations by joining in the Medicine (or *Mystery*) Dance. Their yells and screaming echoing through the vast and vapouring halls, soon brought some hundreds of maltsmen, grinders, firers, mashers, ostlers, painters, coopers &c., peeping through and amongst the blackened timbers and casks, and curling and hissing fumes, completing the scene as the richest model for the infernal regions.

From Adventures of the Ojibbeway and Ioway Indians in England, Belgium and France *by George Catlin, 1852.*

235 THE PHILISTINE October 19, 1844

Have called on many master-spinners. Hear they are gratified. Did so before I met the operatives. Addressed a body last night. Admirable meeting; urged the most conciliatory sentiments towards employers; urged too the indispensible necessity of private and public prayer if they desire to attain their end. Told what I felt, that unless religion had commanded my service I would not have undertaken the task. It was to *religion*, therefore, and not to me, that they were indebted for benefits reccived! What a place is Manchester – silent and solemn; the rumble of carriages and groaning of mills, but few voices and no merriment. Sad in its very activity; grave and silent in its very agitation. Intensely occupied in the production of material wealth, it regards that alone as the grand end of human existence. The operatives, poor fellows, to a man, distrust this present prosperity. Have visited print-works, Mr Thomson's, Clitheroe; Mr Dugdale's near Gawthorpe; Mr Field's, Manchester. Thirty-five thousand children, under 13 years of age, many not exceeding 5 or 6, are working, at times, for 14 or 15 hours a day, and also, but not in these works, during the night! Oh, the abomination! Now, therefore, God helping me, I will arise and overthrow the Philistine. Oh blessed Lord and Saviour of mankind, look down on the lambs of Thy fold, and strengthen me to the work in faith and fear, in knowledge, opportunity, wisdom, and grace!

From the Journal of Lord Shaftesbury, quoted in The Life and Work of the Seventh Earl of Shaftesbury *by Edwin Hodder, 1888.*

| 236 | WORDSWORTH | February 16, 1845 |

How can the man who has been constantly publishing poetry for the past forty years, and has at last made the poetry part of the food of the public mind, call himself a man of 'retirement', if he means to include himself. And, if not, how can he complain that he has at last, by his Lake-and-Mountain poetry, created a desire for realizing some of these beautiful descriptions of scenery and elements in the inhabitants of Liverpool and Manchester, which may possibly bring them in crowds by railway to Windermere? My objection to the reasoning of the 'Letters' is that, – 1. There is no danger. 2. It would be a benefit to the humbler classes, greater than the inconvenience to the residents, if there was no danger. Lastly, I have a personal argument against Mr Wordsworth, that he and Rydal can no more pretend to 'retirement' than the Queen. They have both bartered it away for fame. As for Mr Wordsworth, he has himself been crying *Roast Meat* all his life. Has he not even published, besides his poems which have made the district classic ground, an actual prose 'Guide?' And now he complains that the decent clerks and manufacturers of Liverpool and Manchester should presume to flock of a holiday to see the scene of 'The Excursion,' and to buy his own 'Guide-book!' For I utterly deny that the holders of Kendal and Bowness excursion railway tickets would require 'wrestling-matches, horse and boat races, hothouses or beer-shops.' If they come in crowds (which I am afraid they would not), it would be as literally to see the lakes and mountains as the Brighton holiday-ticketers go to see the sea.

From a letter of Barron Field to Henry Crabb Robinson, printed in The Diary, Reminiscences and Correspondence of H. Crabb Robinson, *edited by Thomas Sadler, 1869.*

| 237 | AT FURNESS ABBEY | June 21, 1845 |

Well have yon Railway Labourers to THIS ground
Withdrawn for noontide rest. They sit, they walk
Among the Ruins, but no idle talk
Is heard; to grave demeanour all are bound;
And from one voice a Hymn with tuneful sound
Hallows once more the long-deserted Quire
And thrills the old sepulchral earth, around.

Others look up, and with fixed eyes admire
That wide-spanned arch, wondering how it was raised,
To keep, so high in air, its strength and grace:
All seem to feel the spirit of the place,
And by the general reverence God is praised:
Profane Despoilers, stand ye not reproved,
While thus these simple-hearted men are moved?

From Miscellaneous Sonnets *by William Wordsworth, 1845.*

238   WORDSWORTH   July 1, 1845

The Laureate keeps wonderfully well in the midst of all these troubles even in spite of having a new Edition of his Poems in hand – he has written several short ones of late, one of the last I have asked Kate Southey who is now here to copy for you by way of giving some value to my packet in addition to that which it has as a bearer of good news – of course the Author knows I am sending it to you – & he desires me to say that if he has made you angry by his violence on the Maynooth & Irish Education question he is sure you will be pleased with his kind notice of these Railway Labourers – the Sonnet arose out of a circumstance I told him on my return from a visit to Furness Abbey not many days ago where I had taken three young Arnolds a little Davy & dear Kate Southey – the Sonnet is the literal fact of what we saw – the Railway is carried *profanely* near this holy pile – these poor Labourers seemed to feel that 'once it was holy & is holy still' – not so the Directors – who would have driven streight thro' the *consecrated* enclosure but for Ld Burlington who *ought* to have insisted on a still *greater distance* –

> *From a letter of Isabella Fenwick to Henry Crabb Robinson, published (in part) in* The Correspondence of H. Crabb Robinson with the Wordsworth Circle, *edited by Edith Morley, 1927.*

239   LETTER TO THOMAS COOPER   September 1, 1845

Chelsea

Dear Sir,

I have received your Poem; and will thank you for that kind gift, and for all the friendly sentiments you entertain towards me, – which, as from an evidently sincere man, whatever we may think of them otherwise, are surely valuable to a man.

I have looked into your Poem, and find indisputable traces of genius in it, – a dark Titanic energy struggling there, for which we hope there will be clearer daylight by-and-by! If I might presume to advise, I think I would recommend you to try your next work in *Prose*, and as a thing turning altogether on *Facts*, not Fictions. Certainly the *music* that is very traceable here might serve to irradiate into harmony far profitabler things than what are commonly called 'Poems', – for which, at any rate, the taste in these days seems to be irrevocably in abeyance. We have too horrible a Practical Chaos round us; out of which every man is called by the birth of him to make a bit of *Cosmos*: that seems to me the real Poem for a man – especially at present. I always grudge to see any portions of a man's *musical talent* (which is the real intellect, the real vitality, or life of him) expended on making mere *words* rhyme. These things I say to all my Poetic friends, – for I am in real earnest about them: but get almost nobody to believe me hitherto. From you I shall get an excuse at any rate; the purpose of my so speaking being a friendly one towards you.

I will request you farther to accept this book of mine, and to appropriate what you can of it. 'Life is a serious thing,' as Schiller says, and as you yourself practically know! These are the words of a man serious about it; they will not altogether be without meaning for you.

Unfortunately, I am just in these hours getting out of town; and, not without real regret, must deny myself the satisfaction of seeing you at present.

Believe me to be,
With many good wishes,
Yours very truly,
T. CARLYLE.

A letter of Thomas Carlyle to Thomas Cooper, printed in The Life of Thomas Cooper written by Himself, *1872.*

240   **MANCHESTER**   Autumn 1845

Manchester I found as true a representative of the great manufacturing town of modern England, as York of the old English ecclesiastical city. One receives one's first intimation of its existence from the lurid gloom of the atmosphere that overhangs it. There is a murky blot in one section of the sky, however clear the weather, which broadens and heightens as we approach, until at length it seems spread over half the firmament. And now the innumerable chimneys come in view, tall and dim in the dun haze, each bearing atop its own troubled pennon of darkness. And now we enter the suburbs, and pass through mediocre streets of brick, that seem as if they had been built wholesale by contract within the last half-dozen years. These humble houses are the homes of the operative manufacturers. The old walls of York built in the reign of Edward the First, still enclose the city; – the antique suit of armour made for it six hundred years ago, though the fit be somewhat of the tightest, buckles round it still. Manchester, on the other hand, has been doubling its population every half-century for the last hundred and fifty years; and the cord of cotton twist that would have girdled it at the beginning of the great revolutionary war, would do little more than half-girdle it now. The field of Peterloo, on which the yeomanry slashed down the cotton-workers assembled to hear Henry Hunt, – poor lank-jawed men, who would doubtless have manifested less interest in the nonsense of the orator, had they been less hungry at the time, – has been covered with brick for the last ten years. As we advance, the town presents a new feature. We see whole streets of warehouses, – dead, dingy, gigantic buildings, barred out from the light; and, save where here and there a huge waggon stands, lading or unlading, under the mid-air crane, the thoroughfares, and especially the numerous *cul de sacs*, have a solitary, half-deserted air. But the city clocks have just struck one, – the dinner hour of the labouring English; and in one brief minute two-thirds of the population of the place have turned out into the streets. The rush of the human tide is tremendous, – headlong and arrowy as that of a Highland river in flood, or as that of a water-spout just broken amid the hills, and at once hurrying adown a hundred different ravines. But the outburst is as short as fierce: we have stepped aside into some door-way, or out towards the centre of some public square, to be beyond the wind of such commotion; and in a few minutes all is over, and the streets even more quiet and solitary than before. There is an air of much magnificence about the public buildings devoted to trade; and the larger shops wear the solid aspect of long-established, well-founded business. But nothing seems more characteristic of the great manufacturing city, though disagreeably so, than the river Irwell, which runs through the place, dividing it into a lesser and a larger town, that, though they bear different names, are essentially one. The hapless river, – a pretty enough stream a few miles higher up, with trees overhanging its banks, and fringes of green sedge set thick along its edges – loses caste as it gets among the mills and print-works. There are myriads of dirty things given it to wash, and whole waggon-loads of poisons from dye houses and bleach-yards thrown into it to carry away; steam-boilers discharge into it their seething contents, and drains and sewers their fetid impurities; till at length it rolls on, – here between tall dingy walls, there under precipices of red sandstone, – considerably less a river than a flood of liquid manure, in which all life dies, whether animal or vegetable, and which resembles nothing in nature, except perhaps the stream thrown out in eruption by some mud-volcano. In passing along where the river sweeps by the old Collegiate Church, I met a party of town-police dragging a female culprit – delirious, dirty, and in drink, – to the Police Office; and I bethought me of the well-known comparison of Cowper, beginning,

> 'Sweet stream, that winds through yonder glade,
> Apt emblem of a virtuous maid, –'

of the maudlin woman not virtuous, – and of the Irwell.

From First Impressions of England and its People *by Hugh Miller, written 1846, published 1847.*

241 BIRMINGHAM 1846

Almost all the larger towns of England manifest some one leading taste or other. Some are peculiarly literary, some decidedly scientific; and the taste paramount in Birmingham seems to be a taste for music. In no town in the world are the mechanic arts more noisy: hammer rings incessantly on anvil; there is an unending clang of metal, an unceasing clank of engines; flame rustles, water hisses, steam roars, and from time to time, hoarse and hollow over all, rises the thunder of the proofing-house. The people live in an atmosphere continually vibrating with clamour; and it would seem as if their amusements had caught the general tone, and become noisy like their avocations. The man who for years has slept soundly night after night in the neighbourhood of a foundry, awakens disturbed, if by some accident the hammering ceases: the imprisoned linnet or thrush is excited to emulation by even the screeching of a knife-grinder's wheel, or the din of a coppersmith's shop, and pours out his soul in music. It seems not very improbable that the two principles on which these phenomena hinge, – principles as diverse as the phenomena themselves, – may have been influential in inducing the peculiar characteristic of Birmingham; that the noises of the place, grown a part of customary existence to its people, – inwrought, as it were, into the very staple of their lives, – exerts over them some such unmarked influence as that exerted on the sleeper by the foundry; and that, when they relax from their labours, they seek to fill up the void by modulated noises, first caught up, like the song of the bird beside the cutler's wheel or coppersmith's shop, in unconscious rivalry of the clang of their hammers and engines. Be the truth of the theory what it may, there can be little doubt regarding the fact on which it hinges. No town of its size in the empire spends more time and money in concerts and musical festivals than Birmingham; no small proportion of its people are amateur performers; almost all are musical critics; and the organ in its great Hall, the property of the town, is, with the exception of that of York, the largest in the empire, and the finest, it is said, without any exception.

From First Impressions of England and its People *by Hugh Miller, written 1846, published 1847.*

On August 26, 1846 Mendelssohn conducted the first performance of his Elijah *in Birmingham Town Hall.*

He found no pleasure or relief in the journey. Tortured by these thoughts he carried monotony with him, through the rushing landscape, and hurried headlong, not through a rich and varied country, but a wilderness of blighted plans and gnawing jealousies. The very speed at which the train was whirled along mocked the swift course of the young life that had been borne away so steadily and so inexorably to its fore-doomed end. The power that forced itself upon its iron way – its own – defiant of all paths and walls, piercing through the heart of every obstacle, and dragging living creatures of all classes, ages, and degrees behind it, was a type of the triumphant monster, Death.

Away, with a shriek, and a roar, and a rattle, from the town, burrowing among the dwellings of men and making the streets hum, flashing out into the meadows for a moment, mining in through the damp earth, booming on in darkness and heavy air, bursting out again into the sunny day so bright and wide; away, with a shriek, and a roar, and a rattle, through the fields, through the woods, through the corn, through the hay, through the chalk, through the mould, through the clay, through the rock, among objects close at hand and almost within grasp, ever flying from the traveller, and a deceitful distance ever moving slowly within him: like as in the track of the remorseless monster, Death!

Through the hollow, on the height, by the heath, by the orchard, by the park, by the garden, over the canal, across the river, where the sheep are feeding, where the mill is going, where the barge is floating, where the dead are lying, where the factory is smoking, where the stream is running, where the village clusters, where the great Cathedral rises, where the bleak moor lies, and the wild breeze smooths or ruffles it at its inconstant will; away, with a shriek, and a roar, and a rattle, and no trace to leave behind but dust and vapour: like as in the track of the remorseless monster, Death!

Breasting the wind and light, the shadow and sunshine, away, and still away, it rolls and roars, fierce and rapid, smooth and certain, and great works and massive bridges crossing up above, fall like a beam of shadow an inch broad, upon the eye, and then are lost. Away, and still away, onward and onward ever: glimpses of cottage-homes, of houses, mansions, rich estates, of husbandry and handicraft, of people on old roads and paths that look deserted, small, and insignificant as they are left behind: and so they do, and what else is there but such glimpses, in the track of the indomitable monster, Death!

Away, with a shriek, and a roar, and a rattle, plunging down into the earth again, and working on in such a storm of energy and perseverance, that amidst the darkness and whirlwind the motion seems reversed, and to tend furiously backward, until a ray of light upon the wet wall shows its surface flying past like a fierce stream. Away once more into the day, and

PREMIUM, PAR, DISCOUNT

through the day, with a shrill yell of exultation, roaring, rattling, tearing on, spurning everything with its dark breath, sometimes pausing for a minute where a crowd of faces are, that in a minute more are not: sometimes lapping water greedily, and before the spout at which it drinks has ceased to drip upon the ground, shrieking, roaring, rattling through the purple distance.

Louder and louder yet, it shrieks and cries as it comes tearing on resistless to the goal: and now its way, still like the way of Death, is strown with ashes thickly. Everything around is blackened. There are dark pools of water, muddy lanes and miserable habitations far below. There are jagged walls and falling houses close at hand, and through the battered roofs and broken windows, wretched rooms are seen, where want and fever hide themselves in many wretched shapes, while smoke and crowded gables, and distorted chimneys, and deformity of brick and mortar penning up deformity of mind and body, choke up the murky distance. As Mr Dombey looks out of his carriage window, it is never in his thoughts that the monster who has brought him there has let the light of day in on these things; not made or caused them. It was the journey's end, and might have been the end of everything; it was so ruinous and dreary.

From Dombey and Son *by Charles Dickens, written and published 1846–7.*

The journey was from Leamington to Birmingham, the corn and hay suggest the summer, though the bleak moor and the wild breeze seem to be from another countryside, akin to that of Bamford's Wind of Heaven *(158) and Mrs Gaskell's* Road to Haworth *(286). The apparent contradiction at the end – that the railway had not caused the misery and dilapidation of the Birmingham slums but had 'let the light of day in on these things' is akin to the dialectical situation of Engels on Manchester (230). Compare, in its own way, Charles Kingsley's 'demon bridegrooms' (251). The image is of the Industrial Revolution as a picture of Hell – the dust and ashes of death equated with the dust and ashes of the train, of the slums....*

243   BEYOND ANY DREAMS   January 1847

The time when I first saw the railway uniting Liverpool and Manchester – spanning the bog where human foot could not tread – stands, as I have said, in memory, like an epoch of my life. I looked upon that most poetical and most practical of the grand achievements of human intellect, until people thought I stood and slept; and, when they heard the dream, they said it was very dreamy, indeed. I should fear to tell the dreams which I have now beside the electric telegraph, and on the railways, and within the regions of the god-like inventors and makers of machinery. There is a time coming when realities shall go beyond any dreams that have yet been told of these things. Nation exchanging with nation their products freely; thoughts exchanging themselves for thoughts, and never taking note of the geographical space they have to pass over, except to give the battery a little more of the electric spirit, if the distance which the thought has to go be many hundreds of miles; man holding free fellowship with man; without taking note of the social distance which used to separate them, except, perhaps, the lord, (landed lord or cotton lord,) shall use a little more of the moral electricity, when conveying a thought to a working man, at the opposite end of the social pole, who used to be very distant; that lord may put on a little more of the moral electricity, which shall then be discovered, to carry the instantaneous message of one feeling, one interest, one object, one hope of success from the lordly end, to the working man's end of the social world. Universal enfranchisement, railways, electric telegraphs, public schools (the greatest of the moral levers for elevating mankind named last – because last to be advocated, which should have been first); these are some of the elements of a moral faith, believing in the universal brotherhood of mankind, which I daily hold, and never doubt upon; which I believe will as certainly be realised, as I believe that *good*, and not *evil*, was the object of all creation, and is the end of all existence.

From The Autobiography of a Working Man *by Alexander Somerville (under the pseudonym of 'One Who Has Whistled at the Plough'), written in 1847, and published as a book in 1848.*

244 A GREATER EPIC 1847

I am only got half way in the third book of Thucydides: but I go on with pleasure; with as much pleasure as I used to read a novel. I have also again taken up my Homer. That is a noble and affecting passage where Diomed and Glaucus, being about to fight, recognize each other as old family friends, exchange arms, and vow to avoid each other henceforth in the fray. (N.B. and this in the tenth year of the war!) After this comes, you know, the meeting of Hector and Andromache, which we read together; altogether a truly Epic canto indeed.

Yet, as I often think, it is not the poetical imagination, but bare Science that every day more and more unrolls a greater Epic than the Iliad; the history of the World, the infinitudes of Space and Time! I never take up a book of Geology or Astronomy but this strikes me. And when we think that Man must go on to discover in the same plodding way, one fancies that the Poet of to-day may as well fold his hands, or turn them to dig and delve, considering how soon the march of discovery will distance all his imaginations [and] dissolve the language in which they are uttered. Martial, as you say, lives now, after two thousand years; a space that seems long to us whose lives are so brief; but a moment, the twinkling of an eye, if compared (not to Eternity alone) but to the ages which it is now known the world must have existed, and (unless for some external violence) must continue to exist. Lyell in his book about America, says that the falls of Niagara, if (as seems certain) they have worked their way back southwards for seven miles, must have taken over 35,000 years to do so, at the rate of something over a foot a year! Sometimes they fall back on a stratum that crumbles away from behind them more easily; but then again they had to roll over rock that yields to them scarcely more perceptibly than the anvil to the serpent. And those very soft strata which the Cataract now erodes contain evidences of a race of animals, and of the action of seas washing over them, long before Niagara came to have a distinct current; and the rocks were compounded ages and ages before those strata! So that, as Lyell says, the Geologist looking at Niagara forgets even the roar of its waters in the contemplation of the awful processes of time that it suggests. It is not only that this vision of Time must wither the Poet's hope of immortality; but it is in itself more wonderful than all the conceptions of Dante and Milton.

From a letter of Edward Fitzgerald to E.B. Cowell, printed in Letters of Edward Fitzgerald, *edited by W. Aldis Wright, 1910.*

245   OUR PHILOSOPHY   Spring 1847

In conclusion, I may remark that, whilst considering the state and condition of the powers with which matter is endowed, we cannot shut out from our thoughts the consequences as far as they are manifested to us, for we find them always for our good; neither ought we to do so, for that would be to make philosophy barren as to its true fruits. And when we think of the way in which heat and cohesive force are related to each other, and learn also that the sun is continually giving to the surface of this globe of ours warmth equal to the combustion of sixty sacks of coal in twelve hours on each acre of surface in this climate in the average of the year; and find that of the bodies thus heated, those which ought to remain solid are so circumstanced that they do remain solid; and those which, like *oxygen* and *nitrogen*, in our atmosphere ought to remain gaseous *do* remain gaseous; when we find, moreover, that wonderful substance, water, assuming under the same influence the solid, the fluid, and the gaseous states at natural temperatures, and so circulating through the heavens and the earth ever in its best form; and perceive that all this is done by virtue of powers in the molecules which are indestructible, and by laws of action the most simple and unchangeable, we may well, if I may say it without irreverence, join *awe and trembling* with *joy and gladness*.

Our philosophy, feeble as it is, gives us to see in every particle of matter, a *centre* of force reaching to an infinite distance, binding worlds and suns together, and unchangeable in its permanency. Around this same particle we see grouped the powers of all the various phenomena of nature: the heat, the cold, the wind, the storm, the awful conflagration, the vivid lightning flash, the stability of the rock and the mountain, the grand mobility of the ocean, with its mighty tidal wave sweeping round the globe in its diurnal journey, the dancing of the stream and the torrent: the glorious cloud, the soft dew, the rain dropping fatness, the harmonious working of all those forces in nature, until at last the molecule rises up in accordance with the mighty purpose ordained for it, and plays its part in the gift of *life itself*. And therefore our philosophy, whilst it shows us these things, should lead us to think of Him who hath wrought them; for it is said by an authority far above even that which these works present, that 'the invisible things of Him from the creation of the world are clearly seen, being understood by the things that are made, even His eternal power and Godhead.'

From a Friday Lecture at the Royal Institution by Michael Faraday, from The Life and Letters of Faraday *by Bence Jones, 1870.*

246 ROCHDALE September 13, 1847

The mills! oh the fetid, fuzzy, ill-ventilated mills! And in Sharp's cyclopean smithy do you remember the poor 'grinders' sitting underground in a damp dark place, some dozen of them, over their screeching stone cylinders, from every cylinder a sheet of yellow *fire* issuing, the principal light of the place? And the men, I was told, and they themselves know it, and 'did not mind it,' were all or mostly *killed* before their time, their lungs being ruined by the metal and stone dust! Those poor fellows, in their paper caps with their roaring grindstones, and their yellow *oriflammes* of fire, all grinding themselves so quietly to death, will never go out of my memory. In signing my name, as I was made to do, on quitting that Sharp establishment, whose name think you stood next to be succeeded by mine? In a fine flowing character, Jenny Lind's! Dickens and the other Player Squadron (wanting Forster, I think) stood on the same page.

From a letter of Thomas Carlyle to Jane Welsh Carlyle, quoted in Thomas Carlyle, a History of His Life in London, *by J.A. Froude, 1884.*

247 THE METROPOLITAN POOR November 6, 1847

On Wednesday night last, I left the Society's Office at half-past ten o'clock, accompanied by Mr Jones, and proceeded to the St. Martin's Workhouse; there I found nineteen persons *lying on the pavement*, in the street, unable to obtain shelter within the establishment. They consisted of one man, fifteen women and three children. The porter readily admitted me to examine the casual wards, was very civil, and readily answered all my enquiries. He informed me he had forty-eight persons, male and female, and that the wards were quite full. I examined the male ward, and discovered that the accommodation consisted of beds and rugs, and that the inmates were *in a state of nudity*; or in other words, had no other covering except the rugs, a practice, he informed me, which was introduced and maintained by the paupers themselves, as they were less liable to catch the

THE POOR MAN'S GUARDIAN.

BLESSED IS HE THAT CONSIDERETH THE POOR Ps.XLI

No. 1.   SATURDAY, NOVEMBER 6, 1847.   PRICE ONE PENNY.

ST. MARTIN'S WORKHOUSE.   WEST LONDON UNION.

THE METROPOLITAN POOR.

Martin's Workhouse; there I found nineteen persons *lying on the pavement*, in the street, unable to obtain shelter within the establish— ing that day been sent back from the Fever Hospital. The officers on duty also suffered from fever. He expressed his deep regret at

THE POOR MAN'S GUARDIAN

itch or any other disease from each other. Bread and gruel are supplied to them in the morning before they leave the house. I enquired whether the poor did not suffer from fever, and was informed that they did to a great extent; that they had sent several cases to the Fever Hospital; and by reference to a file which he showed me, proved that deaths were very frequent in consequence, a dead body having that day been sent back from the Fever Hospital. The officers on duty also suffered from fever. He expressed his deep regret at not being able to afford shelter to the poor creatures sleeping on the stones outside, particularly to the children who were crying, although he said he was quite sure the mothers or women in charge of them, were pinching or otherwise inflicting pain on them, in order to excite commiseration and secure a shelter. The door and office windows, I was informed, were constantly being broken by unsuccessful applicants for admission, and the parish authorities were engaged in enlarging the building. His duty commenced at from six or seven a.m. until twelve at night, and he was obliged to attend to all after applications. On leaving the workhouse, I also left behind me the nineteen forlorn miserable creatures, arranging themselves on the bare stones the best way they could, to contend against the inclemency of the night; still scarcely believing it possible, that in this wealthy and charitable metropolis human beings were compelled to sleep in the open streets, from a want of that accommodation which even dogs and pigs have carefully provided for them.

From a letter to the Editor of The Poor Man's Guardian, *No.1, 1847, by Charles Cochrane, Chairman, Poor Man's Guardian Society.*

248   GOD'S HANDWRITING   1848

Those who live in towns should carefully remember this, for their own sakes, for their wives' sakes, for their children's sakes. *Never lose an opportunity of seeing something beautiful.* Beauty is God's handwriting – a wayside sacrament; welcome it in every fair face, every fair sky, every fair flower, and thank for it *Him*, the fountain of all loveliness, and drink it in, simply and earnestly, with all your eyes; it is a charmed draught, a cup of blessing. Therefore I said that picture-galleries should be the townsman's paradise of refreshment. Of course, if he can get the real air, the real trees, even for an hour, let him take it in God's name; but how many a man who cannot spare time for a daily country walk, may well slip into the National Gallery, or any other collection of pictures, for ten minutes. *That* garden, at least, flowers as gaily in winter as in summer. Those noble faces on the wall are never disfigured by grief or passion. There, in the space of a single room, the townsman may take his country walk – a walk beneath mountain peaks, blushing sunsets, with broad woodlands spreading out below it; a walk through green meadows, under cool mellow shades, and overhanging rocks, by rushing brooks, where he watches and watches till he seems to *hear* the foam whisper, and to *see* the fishes leap; and his hard-worn heart wanders out free, beyond the grim city-world of stone and iron, smoky chimneys, and roaring wheels, into the world of beautiful things – *the world which shall be hereafter* – ay, which shall be! Believe it, toil-worn worker, in spite of thy foul alley, thy crowded lodging, thy grimed clothing, thy ill-fed children, thy thin, pale wife – believe it, thou too, and thine, will some day have *your* share of beauty.

From True Words for Brave Men *by Charles Kingsley, 1848.*

249   THINKING BY DREAMING   July 5/6, 1848

With regard to electro-magnetism you may tell Bob that I have not begun the machine he speaks of, being occupied with better plans, one of which is rather down cast, however, because the machine when tried went a bit and stuck; and I did not find out the impediment till I had dreamt over it properly, which I consider the best mode of resolving difficulties of a particular kind, which may be found out by thought, or especially by the laws of association. Thus, you are going along the road with a key in your pocket. You hear a clink behind you, but do not look round, thinking it is nothing particular; when you get home the key is gone; so you dream it all over, and though you have forgotten everything else, you remember the look of the place, but do not remember the locality (that is, as thus, 'Near a large thistle on the left side of the road' – nowhere in particular, but so that it can be found). Next day comes a woman from the peats who has found the key in a corresponding place. This is not 'believing in dreams,' for the dream did not point out the place by the general locality, but by the lie of the ground.

From a letter of James Clerk-Maxwell to Lewis Campbell, printed in The Life of James Clerk-Maxwell *by L. Campbell and W. Garnett, 1882.*

250   A QUIET TALK   July 24, 1848

My father then called me in to make tea for Mr Tennyson in the dining-room, and we had a quiet talk; a powerful, thoughtful face, kind smile, hearty laugh, extremely near-sighted. He spoke of travelling; Dresden, unsatisfactoriness of picture-gallery seeing; the first time he was in Paris he 'went every day for a fortnight to the Louvre, saw only one picture, "La Maîtresse de Titien", the second time looked only at "Narcissus lying by a stream, Echo in the distance and ferocious little Love." Mr Ruskin set his own thought against the united admiration of centuries, but he spoke of a 'splendid chapter on Clouds' in *Modern Painters*.

Then he turned to Geology, Weald of Kent, Delta of a great river flowing from as far as Newfoundland. 'Conceive,' he said, 'what an era of the world that must have been, great lizards, marshes, gigantic ferns!' Fancied, standing by a railway at night, the engine must be like some great Ichthyosaurus. I replied how beautiful Hugh Miller's descriptions of that time are: he thought so too: then spoke of Peach, the Cornish geologist on the Preventive Service, maintaining a wife and seven children on £100 a year, whilst we in one annual dinner, champagne, turtle, etc. spend £25.

From the diary of Mrs Rundle Charles, quoted in Tennyson, a Memoir *by Hallam, Lord Tennyson, 1897.*

251   LINE IRON   Autumn 1848

... Many, many thanks for charming letters; especially the one about the river at night. That I have seen. As a companion, just see the Hungerford Suspension Bridge in a fog; standing on the steamboat pier, the further shore invisible, with two vast lines, the catenary and its tangent line, stretching away as if self-supported, into infinite space; a sort of Jacob's Ladder, one end on earth and one in heaven. It makes one feel very small: so for that matter, do the lines of rail in looking along a vast sweep of railway. There is an awful waiting look about them: a silent forbidden desert to all the world, except the one moment when their demon bridegroom shall rush roaring over them on the path which none but they must go. Does this seem real? It is because the thought is so unspeakable. I wonder whether, in the future ages, men will ever fall down and worship steam-engines, as the Caribs did Columbus's ships. Why not? Men have worshipped stone men and women; why not line iron? Fancy it!

From a letter of Charles Kingsley to Mr Ludlow, quoted in Charles Kingsley, His Letters and Memories of Life, *edited by his widow, 1877.*

THE RAILWAY JUGGERNAUT OF 1845.

It was on September 29, 1848 that Edward Lear was sitting on the sofa of the Ali Bey imitating for his pleasure the sound of the railway and steamboat: Tik tok tik tik etc and Squish Squash Squish Squash.

252   THE EUSTON STATION   November 1848

In a clear winter's night the arrival of an up-train at the platform before us forms a very interesting picture.

No sound is heard in the cold air but the hissing of a pilot engine, which, like a restless spirit advancing and retrograding, is stealing along the intermediate rails, waiting to carry off the next down-train; its course being marked by white steam meandering above it and by red-hot coals of different sizes which are continually falling from beneath it. In this obscure scene the Company's interminable lines of gaslights (there are 232 at the Euston Station) economically screwed down to the minimum of existence, are feebly illuminating the damp varnished panels of the line of carriages in waiting, the brass doorhandles of the cabs, the shining haims, brass browbands and other ornaments on the drooping heads and motionless backs of the cab-horses; and while the blood-red signal lamp is glaring near the tunnel to deter unauthorised intrusion, the stars of heaven cast a faint silvery light through the long strips of plateglass in the roof above the platform. On a sudden is heard – the stranger hardly knows whence – the mysterious moan of compressed air, followed by the ringing of a bell. That instant every gaslight on and above a curve of 900 feet burst into full power. The carriages, cabs, &c. appear, comparatively speaking, in broad daylight, and the beautiful iron reticulation which sustains the glazed roof appears like fairy work.

From an article in the Quarterly Review, *December 1848, by Sir Francis Head, reprinted as* Stokers and Pokers, *1849.*

253 ROOMS NOT CHURCHES May–June 1849

Has your Lordship heard that the Oratorians have opened the Lowther Rooms as a chapel!! – a place for the vilest debauchery, masquerades, &c. – one night a MASQUED BALL, next BENEDICTUS. This appears to me perfectly monstrous, and I give the whole order up for ever. What a degradation for religion! Why, it is worse than the Socialists. What a place to celebrate the mysteries of religion in! I cannot conceive how it is allowed. It cannot ever be licensed or protected by law, since they only have it for a time. It is the greatest blow we have had for a long time; no men have been so disappointing as these. Conceive the poet Faber come down to the Lowther Rooms! The man who wrote 'Thoughts and Sights in Foreign Churches'!!! hiring the Lowther Rooms! Well may they cry out against screens or anything else. I always said they wanted rooms, not churches, and now they have got them. Sad times! I cannot imagine what the world will come to, if it goes on much longer.

From a letter of A.W. Pugin to Lord Shrewsbury, quoted in B. Ferrey, Recollections of A.W. Pugin and His Father, *1861.*

254 THE SHADOW October 7, 1849

Now to bind all this together, and to get a character established as it were which any of the writers may maintain without difficulty, I want to suppose a certain SHADOW, which may go into any place, by sunlight, moonlight, starlight, firelight, candlelight, and be in all homes, and all nooks and corners, and be supposed to be cognisant of everything, and go everywhere, without the least difficulty. Which may be in the Theatre, the Palace, the House of Commons, the Prisons, the Unions, the Churches, on the Railroad, on the Sea, abroad and at home: a kind of semi-omniscient, omnipresent, intangible creature. I don't think it would do to call the paper THE SHADOW: but I want something tacked to that title, to express the notion of its being a cheerful, useful, and always welcome Shadow. I want to open the first number with this Shadow's account of himself and his family. I want to have all the correspondence addressed to him. I want him to issue warnings from time to time, that he is going to fall in such and such a subject; or to expose such and such a piece of humbug; or that he may be expected shortly in such and such a place. I want the compiled part of the paper to express the idea of this Shadow's having been in libraries, and among the books referred to. I want him to loom as a fanciful thing all over London; and to get up a general notion of 'What will the Shadow say about this, I wonder? What will the Shadow say about that? Is the Shadow here?' and so forth. Do you understand?

From a letter of Charles Dickens to John Forster, printed in Forster's
Life of Charles Dickens, *1873.*

255 A POET'S OLD AGE October 8, 1849

I want to ask for your kind offices. You know Tennyson, and you know who Samuel Bamford is, a great, gaunt, stalwart Lancashire man, formerly hand-loom weaver, author of *Life of a Radical*, age nearly 70, and living in that state which is exactly decent poverty with his neat little apple-faced wife. They have lost their only child. Bamford is the most hearty (and it's saying a good deal) admirer of Tennyson I know. I dislike recitations exceedingly, but he repeats some of Tennyson's poems in so rapt and yet so simple a manner, utterly forgetting that anyone is by in the delight of the music and the exquisite thoughts, that one can't help liking to hear him. *He* does not care one jot whether people like him or not in his own intense enjoyment. He says when he lies awake at night, as in his old age he often does, and gets thinking sadly of the days that are gone when his child was alive, he soothes himself by repeating T.'s poems. I asked him the other day if he had got them of his own. 'No,' he said rather mournfully: he had been long looking out for a second-hand copy; but somehow they had not got into the old bookshops, and 14s. or 18s. (which are they?) was too much for a poor man, and then he brightened up and said, Thank God he had a good memory, and whenever he got into a house where there were Tennyson's poems he learnt as many as he could by heart. He thought he knew better than twelve, and began 'Œnone,' and then the 'Sleeping Beauty'. Now I wonder if you catch a glimpse of what I want. I thought at first of giving him the poems this Xmas, but then I thought you would perhaps ask Tennyson if he would give Bamford a copy *from himself*, which would be glorious for the old man. Dear, how he would triumph.

From a letter of Mrs Gaskell to John Forster, quoted in Tennyson, a Memoir *by Hallam, Lord Tennyson, 1897.*

Mrs Gaskell's letter was written five years after Samuel Bamford's Passages in the Life of a Radical, *when he was 61 – he was to live to 84. At the time of 'The Wind of Heaven' (158) he was 33: as he and his wife leave Sheffield, they look forward to seeing their little girl, of whom, the letter says, he thinks sadly when he lies awake at night, twenty-eight years later.*

Mrs Gaskell lived in Manchester from 1832 onwards, after marrying William Gaskell, minister of the Unitarian chapel in Cross Street. She began writing Mary Barton, a Tale of Manchester Life *in 1844, and it was published in 1848. In it she quotes a song of Bamford's.*

Tennyson's poetry was popular with working-class radicals, and he is often quoted in the Christian Socialist, *especially poems expressing idealism and the love of beauty. One may compare Charles Kingsley in 'God's Handwriting' (248), written in 1848. Bamford finding the price of Tennyson's poems prohibitive shows the importance of the later cheap editions, and shows the value, and necessity, of quotations in anthologies, papers and so on.*

256   THE IMPRISONMENT OF ERNEST JONES   1849

Ernest Jones, in the second year of his imprisonment, was so broken in health, that he could no longer stand upright – he was found lying on the floor of his cell, and, then only taken to the prison hospital. He was then told that if he would petition for his release and promise to abjure politics for the future, the remainder of his sentence would be remitted – but he refused his liberty on those conditions, said the work he had once begun he would never turn from, and was accordingly reconsigned to his cell.

As a further illustration of the gratuitous cruelty and petty torture practised towards him, he asked during the period when the cholera was at its height, permission to hear whether his wife (who was in most delicate health) and his little children were still alive – and the permission was refused.

Our readers will perhaps smile at another illustration of prison discipline as applied to him: after 19 months, as we have stated, he was allowed to receive books to read, subject to the supervision of the prison chaplain – and among the books, the admission of which was refused, were D'Israeli's *Coningsby*, Shakespeare's Tragedies, and Macaulay's Essays.

However, he had mental resources of his own. During his imprisonment, and before pen, ink and paper were allowed, he wrote some of the finest poems in the English language. The devices by which he obtained writing materials were amusing. Pens he got by finding occasionally a feather from a rook's wing that had dropped in the prison yard. This quill he cut secretly with a razor, when brought to him twice a week to shave; an ink bottle he contrived to make from a piece of soap he got from the washingshed, and this he filled with ink from the ink bottle when he was allowed to write his quarterly letter; paper was supplied by those quarterly letters, the fly-leaves of a Bible, prayer-book, and of any books he was, as before stated allowed to read. But one poem – The New World – was composed before he had succeeded in securing ink, and this was written almost entirely with his own blood.

From Ernest Jones. Who is he? What has he done?, *a penny pamphlet by either Eli Sowerbutts or James Crossley published in Manchester, 1868.*

257   A CITY OF DIS   November 1849

... a city of Dis (Dante's) – clouds of smoke – the damned etc – coal barges – coaly waters, cast-iron Duke, etc – its marks are left on you ...

From Journal of a Visit to London and the Continent *by Herman Melville, edited by Eleanor Melville Metcalf, 1949.*

258   OLD GILHAM   c.1850

For 60 years, almost without intermission, Old Gilham caught birds. I am assured that to state that his 'catch' during this long period averaged 100 a week, hens included, is within the mark, for he was a most indefatigable man; even at that computation however, he would have been the captor, in his lifetime, of three hundred and twelve thousand birds! A bird-catcher who used sometimes to start in the morning with Old Gilham, and walk with him until their roads diverged, told me that of late years the old man's talk was a good deal of where he had captured his birds in the old times: ' "Why, Ned," he would say to me,' proceeded his companion, ' "I've caught gold-finches in lots at Chalk Farm, and all where there's that railway smoke and noise just by the hill (Primrose Hill). I can't think where they'll drive all the birds to bye and bye. I dare say the first time the birds saw a railway with its smoke, and noise to frighten them, and all the fire too, they just thought it was the devil was come." He wasn't a fool, wasn't old Gilham, sir. "Why," he'd go on for to say, "I've laid many a day at Ball's Pond there, where it's nothing but a lot of houses now, and catched hundreds of birds. And I've catched them where there's all them grand

THE CRIPPLED STREET BIRD-SELLER

squares Pimlico way, and in Britannia Fields, and at White Condic. What with all these buildings, and them barbers, I don't know what the bird-trade'll come to. It's hard for a poor man to have to go to Finchley for birds that he could have catched at Holloway once, but people never thinks of that. When I were young I could make three times as much as I do now. I've got a pound for a good sound chaffinch as I brought up myself." Ah, poor old Gilham, sir; I wish you could have seen him, he'd have told you of some queer changes in his time.'

From London Labour and the London Poor, *by Henry Mayhew, 1851.*

After passenger-life at sea, a man's legs need to be brought into active service somewhat gradually. As we had spent more time than we had meant to at Birkenhead, we determined to rest ourselves for a few minutes, and get start of a few miles into the country by the railroad. A seat, however, on the hard board benches of an English second-class car, crowded, and your feet cramped under you, does not remove fatigue very rapidly.

A heavy cloud darkened the landscape, and as we emerged in a few moments from a dark tunnel, whirling out of the town, big drops of rain came slanting in upon us. A lady coughed, and we closed the window. The road ran through a deep cutting, with only occasionally such depressions of its green-sodded bank, that we could, through the dusty glass, get glimpses of the country. In successive gleams:-

A market-garden, with rows of early cabbages, and lettuce, and peas; –

Over a hedge, a nice, new stone villa, with the gardener shoving up the sashes of the conservatory, and the maids tearing clothes from the drying-lines; –

A bridge, with children shouting and waving hats; –

A field of wheat, in drills as precisely straight, and in earth as clean and finely-tilled, as if it were a garden-plant; –

A bit of broad pasture, with colts and cows turning tail to the squall; long hills in the back, with some trees and a steeple rising beyond them; –

Another few minutes of green bank; –

A jerk – a stop. A gruff shout, 'BROMBRO!' A great fuss to get the window on the other side from us open; calling to the conductor; having the door unlocked; squeezing through the ladies' knees, and dragging our packs over their laps – all borne with a composure that shows them to be used to it, and that they take it as a necessary evil of railroad travelling. The preparations for rain are just completed as we emerge upon a platform, and now down it comes in a torrent. We rush, with a quantity of flying muslin, white ankles, and thin shoes, under an arch. With a sharp whistle and hoarse puffing the train rumbles onward; grooms pick up the lap-dog and baskets; flaunting white skirts are moved again across the track; another rush, in which a diminutive French sun-shade is assisted by a New York umbrella to protect a new English bonnet; a graceful bow in return, with lifting eyebrows, as if in enquiry; and we are altogether crowded in the station-house.

In a few minutes they go off in carriages, and room is left us in the little waiting-room to strap on our knapsacks. The rain slackens – ceases, and we mount, by stone steps up a bank of roses and closely-shaven turf, to the top of the bridge over the cutting.

There we were right in the midst of it! The country – and such a country! – green, dripping, glistening, gorgeous! We stood dumb-stricken by its loveliness, as, from the bleak April and bare boughs we had left at home, broke upon us that English May – sunny, leafy, blooming May – in an English lane; with hedges, English hedges, hawthorn hedges, all in blossom; homely old farm-houses, quaint stables, and haystacks; the old church spire over the distant trees; the mild sun beaming through the watery atmosphere, and all so quiet – the only sounds the hum of bees and the crisp grass-tearing of a silken-skinned, real (unimported) Hereford cow over the hedge. No longer excited by daring to think we should see it, as we discussed the scheme round the old home-fire; no longer cheering ourselves with it in the stupid, tedious ship; no more forgetful of it in the bewilderment of the busy town – but there we were, right in the midst of it; long time silent, and then speaking softly, as if it were enchantment indeed, we gazed upon it and breathed it – never to be forgotten.

From Walks and Talks of an American Farmer in England *by Frederick Law Olmsted, published in England, 1852.*

260   A STREAM OF GOLDEN CLOUD   June 1850

A balloon went up on Saturday Evng. (22 instant) from Vauxhall. The evening was very clear and the Sun bright: the balloon was very high, so that I could not see the car from Queen Square, Bloomsbury, and looked like a golden ball. Ballast was thrown out two or three times and was probably sand; but the dust of it had this effect, that a stream of golden cloud seemed to descend from the balloon, shooting downwards, for a moment, and then remained apparently stationary, the balloon and it separating very slowly. It shews the wonderful manner in which [each] particle of this dusty cloud must have made its impression on the eye by the light reflected from it, and is a fine illustration of the combination of many effects, each utterly insensible alone, into one sum of fine effect. If a cloud of dusty matter, as powdered chalk or road dust, were purposely poured forth under these circumstances, it would give a fine effect both to those on earth and those in the balloon.

From the Diary *of Michael Faraday, edited by Thomas Martin, 1934.*

261   THE SCENERY OF HEAVEN   August 24, 1850

I must tell you how we are situated. We have taken a little house here on the hill-top, where I have a small room to myself, and have, ever since we came here, been deeply immersed in magnetic cogitations. I write and write and write, until three papers for the Royal Society are nearly completed, and I hope that two of them will be good if they justify my hopes, for I have to criticise them again and again before I let them loose. You shall hear of them at some of the Friday evenings; at present I must not say more. After writing, I walk out in the evening, hand-in-hand with my dear wife, to enjoy the sunset; for to me who love scenery, of all that I have seen or can see there is none surpasses that of Heaven. A glorious sunset brings with it a thousand thoughts that delight me.

From a letter of Michael Faraday 'to a friend', printed in The Life and Letters of Faraday *by Bence Jones, 1870.*

Compare 157, Faraday's letter to his fiancée in 1820. The house was in Upper Norwood. On the sunset image, compare Turner who was a friend of Faraday. Turner died in 1851.

Part Four

1851–1886
Confusion

262 THE GREAT EGGS AND BACON 1851

Within the last eighteen years, or more, there has hardly been any public occurrence without a comparatively well-executed medal being sold in the streets in commemoration of it. That sold at the opening of London-bridge was, I am told, considered 'a superior thing', and the improvement in this art of manufacture has progressed to the present time. Within the last three years the most saleable medals, an experienced man told me, were of Hungerford Suspension (bridge), the New Houses of Parliament, the Chinese Junk, and Sir Robert Peel. The Thames Tunnel medals were at one time 'very tidy', as were those of the New Royal Exchange. The great sale is at present of the Crystal Palace; and one man had heard that there were a great many persons coming to London to sell them at the opening of the Great Exhibition. 'The great eggs and bacon, I call it', he said; 'for I hope it will bring us that sort of grub. But I don't know; I'm afraid there'll be too many of us. Besides, they say we shan't be let sell in the park.'

From London Labour and the London Poor *by Henry Mayhew, 1851.*

The years 1849–51 should be the glorious climax of the story of Pandæmonium – the years of King Hudson and the Great Exhibition. But in fact there is a strong feeling of disillusionment and compromise: a recognition of how short reality falls from the dream and the dream also from the reality. In these images there is the contrast of:

dream	real
ideal	real
past	present
freedom	imprisonment
true	false
poetry	life
eggs and bacon	exhibition

263 MAYHEW ON HIS WORK 1851

It surely may be considered curious as being the first attempt to publish the history of a people, from the lips of the people themselves – giving a literal description of their labour, their earnings, their trials, and their sufferings, in their own 'unvarnished' language; and to painting the condition of their homes and their families by personal observation of the places, and direct communion with the individuals.

It may be considered curious also as being the first commission of inquiry into the state of the people, undertaken by a private individual, and the first 'blue book' ever published in twopenny numbers.

It is curious, moreover, as supplying information concerning a large body of persons, of whom the public had less knowledge than of the most distant tribes of the earth – the government population returns not even numbering them among the inhabitants of the kingdom; and as addressing facts so extraordinary, that the traveller in the undiscovered country must, like Bruce, until his stories are corroborated by after investigators, be content to lie under the imputation of telling such tales, as travellers are generally supposed to delight in. . . .

From the Preface to London Labour and the London Poor *by Henry Mayhew, 1851.*

On the same page Mayhew says 'Within the last two years some thousands of the humbler classes of society must have been seen and visited. . . .' This probably means 1849–51. It corresponds with references to the Great Exhibition as 'coming on'. There is a reference to 'Comic Exhibitions': 'The street sale of "Comic Exhibitions" (properly so called) is, of course, as modern as the last autumn and winter; and it is somewhat curious that the sale of any humorous, or meant to be humorous sheet of engravings, is now becoming very generally known in the street as a "Comic Exhibition".'

264 THE TEMPEST PROGNOSTICATOR February 27, 1851

In my first experiments I was desirous of ascertaining whether a number of leeches kept separately, and placed under similar circumstances, would simultaneously give indications of thunder. I found this not to be the case: some appeared to be more sensitive and more prophetic than others; and some appeared to be absolutely stupid. I was, however, convinced of the truth of what the poet Cowper has said with respect to thunder; and although no thunder may take place near where the leeches are, still I discovered that they take cognizance of it if it occur at great distances. As an instance of this assertion, on Thursday, the 7th of August, 1849, I had occasion to take a journey of about fifteen miles west of Whitby. Although it was a beautiful morning, I had before my departure distinct indications from the actions of my leeches, that a storm of some kind was going to take place. In two hours I arrived at Danby Beacon, (about 1000 feet above the level of the sea,) where the sun was shining, and I then beheld, from that elevation, one of the most sublime sights I ever witnessed: the hills from Glazedale to Kildale were crowned with the blackest nimbi I ever saw; forming an amphitheatre of from twelve to sixteen miles in extent, from which issued forked lightning and roaring thunder; and between Rosedale and Westerdale were two water-spouts discharging from the base of the clouds, one of inky blackness, and like an inverted steeple – the other not so dark, but spiral towards its apex. This grand scene reminded me of one of Martin's paintings. When I returned to Whitby in the evening, I found that the day there had been perfectly fine throughout, and that no lightning had been seen, nor any thunder heard.

I was thus confirmed in my previous observations, that it is not thunder which acts upon the leech, but the electrical state of the atmosphere, which precedes thunder; and for that state of the air, all my experiments tend to prove leeches have (if I may be allowed the expression) the most remarkable sympathy. It was thus I found out, that before a storm could take place, there must be a preparatory process in the atmosphere, of which the leech gives unequivocal evidence: and this I found it to do when the weather was fine and undisturbed. Having obtained this fact, I found myself in the predicament of a self-constituted judge; I therefore took it into my head to surround myself with a jury of philosophical counsellors, which was composed of twelve leeches, each placed in a separate pint bottle of white glass, about three inches in diameter, and seven inches in height. I then placed these bottles in a circle, in order, that the leeches might see one another, and not endure the affliction of solitary confinement. Having already analyzed their movements, which I found to be confused and various, I contrived a method to detach those movements, which more immediately appertained to meteorology. For this purpose I invented a metallic tube of a particular form, to insert into the neck of the bottles; to which it would be somewhat difficult for a leech to enter; but which it would enter, and make every effort to do if a storm were preparing. No air was allowed to enter the bottles, except what was admitted at the superior part of the tubes, by the means of small holes perforated in them: care being always taken that no air could enter at the sides of the tubes. The tubes were painted inside with gum-lac, in order that they might be washed clean occasionally, with a camel hair brush, as also to prevent any metallic particles coming in contact with the leeches.

THE TEMPEST PROGNOSTICATOR

Having thus far advanced to my satisfaction, I found I had difficulty to contend with, and that was to know if the leeches entered the tubes during my absence, or in the night time; for it is obvious such might occur without my knowledge, and render my experiments nugatory. Besides, I should have the mortifying reflection of having neglected my duty, when my little comrades (which I presume the author of *Waverley* would have allowed me to call them,) had done theirs. In this, the old adage may be truly applied, that "necessity is the mother of invention," which soon relieved me from my difficulty. I thought if I could get a leech to ring a bell, it would be curious enough, but if I could manage to register such an operation, it would be most satisfactory. Both these objects I soon accomplished. As it would have been preposterous to have a bell for each leech, I made use of a simple contrivance, by placing a bell upon a pedestal, erected on the centre of a circular platform; which bell was surrounded by twelve hammers. From each of these hammers was suspended a gilt chain; each of which played upon a pulley, which was placed in a disk, that was a little elevated above the circle of bottles. By this method, every leech could have communication with the bell. One half of the metallic tubes was left open, so that the interior was exposed: across the entrance of each was placed a small piece of whalebone, which was held up by a piece of wire attached to its centre: these wires were passed through the aperture at the top of each tube, and then hooked on to each chain. After having arranged this mousetrap contrivance, into each bottle was poured rain water, to the height of an inch and a half; and a leech placed in every bottle, which was to be its future residence; and when influenced by the electro-magnetic state of the atmosphere a number of the leeches ascended into the tubes; in doing which, they dislodged the whalebone, and caused the bell to ring.

The apparatus being now ready for action, I beheld an Atmospheric, Electro-magnetic Telegraph, which would communicate to me, at all times, processes that were taking place in the higher regions of the atmosphere, and for hundreds of miles in extent, and would enable me to foretell, with unerring certainty, any storm that was preparing to take place. The leeches appear to be invited to mount into their respective belfries, to participate in that discharge or descent of free caloric, termed electro-magnetism, which had previously been carried up into the atmosphere by evaporation and radiation. Although I am somewhat prepared to proceed with this part of the investigation, it would not at present be in accordance with the line of demarcation I have prescribed to myself, to embarrass this essay with any abstruse matter. I therefore proceed to say that, instead of naming this apparatus an Atmospheric, Electro-magnetic Telegraph, conducted by Animal Instinct, it would be better to give it a name which would convey at once to the mind of the people of all nations its objects: hence I have designated it the 'Tempest Prognosticator', – two words expressive enough for all foreigners to understand.

I may here observe, that I could cause a little leech, governed by its instinct, to ring Saint Paul's great bell in London as a signal for an approaching storm.

From 'An Essay explanatory of the Tempest Prognosticator in the building of the Great Exhibition for the Works of Industry of All Nations'. *Read before the Whitby Philosophical Society, February 27, 1851, by George Merryweather M.D., published 1851.*

265   I CAN'T GET OUT   April 21, 1851

Crystal Palace – bless the mark! – is fast getting ready, and bearded figures already grow frequent in the streets; 'all nations' crowding to us with their so-called industry or ostentatious frothery. All the loose population of London pours itself every holiday into Hyde Park round this strange edifice. Over in Surrey there is a strange agreeable solitude in the walks one has. My mad humour is urging me to flight from this monstrous place – flight 'over to Denmark to learn Norse', for example. Every season my suffering and resistance drives me on to some such mad project and every season it fails. 'I can't get out' . . .

From the Journal of Thomas Carlyle, quoted in Thomas Carlyle, a History of His Life in London, *by J.A. Froude, 1884.*

266   THE OPENING   May 1, 1851

A fine day for the opening of the Exhibition. A little cloudy in the morning, but generally sunny and pleasant. I was struck by the number of foreigners in the streets. All, however, were respectable and decent people. I saw none of the men of action with whom the Socialists are threatening us. I went to the Park, and along the Serpentine. There were immense crowds on both sides of the water. I should think there must have been near three hundred thousand people in Hyde Park at once. The sight among the green boughs was delightful. The boats, and little frigates, darting across the lake; the flags; the music; the guns; – everything was exhilarating, and the temper of the multitude the best possible. I fell in with Punch Greville, and walked with him for an hour. He, like me, thought the outside spectacle better worth seeing than the pageant under cover. He showed me a letter from Madame de Lieven, foolish, with an affectation of cleverness and profundity, just like herself. She calls this Exhibition a bold, a rash, experiment. She apprehends a horrible explosion. 'You may get through it safe; and, if you do, you will give yourselves more airs than ever.' And this woman is thought a political oracle in some circles! There is just as much chance of a revolution in England as of the falling of the moon.

I made my way into the building; a most gorgeous sight; vast; graceful; beyond the dreams of the Arabian romances. I cannot think that the Cæsars ever exhibited a more splendid spectacle. I was quite dazzled, and I felt as I did on entering St. Peter's. I wandered about, and elbowed my way through the crowd which filled the nave, admiring the general effect but not attending much to details.

Home, and finished *Persuasion*. I have now read over again all Miss Austen's novels. Charming they are; but I found a little more to criticise than formerly. Yet there are in the world no compositions which approach nearer to perfection.

From the diary of Lord Macaulay, quoted in The Life and Letters of Lord Macaulay *by George Otto Trevelyan, 1876.*

267 THE SHILLING PEOPLE   after May 26, 1851

But if the other parts of the Great Exhibition are curious and instructive, the machinery, which has been from the first the grand focus of attraction, is, on the 'shilling days', the most peculiar sight of the whole. Here every other man you rub against is habited in a corduroy jacket, or a blouse, or leathern gaiters; and round every object more wonderful than the rest, the people press, two and three deep, with their heads stretched out, watching intently the operations of the moving mechanism. You see the farmers, their dusty hats telling of the distance they have come, with their mouths wide agape, leaning over the bars to see the self-acting mills at work, and smiling as they behold the frame spontaneously draw itself out, and then spontaneously run back again. Some, with great smockfrocks, were gazing at the girls in their long pinafores engaged at the doubling-machines.

But the chief centres of curiosity are the power-looms, and in front of these are gathered small groups of artisans, and labourers, and young men whose red coarse hands tell you they do something for their living, all eagerly listening to the attendant as he explains the operations, after stopping the loom. Here, too, as you pass along, you meet, now a member of the National Guard, in his peculiar conical hat, with its little ball on top, and horizontal peak, and his red worsted epaulettes and full-plaited trowsers; then you come to a long, thin, and bilious-looking Quaker, with his tidy and clean-looking Quakeress by his side; and the next minute, may be, you encounter a school of charity-girls, in their large white collars and straw bonnets, with the mistress at their head, instructing the children as she goes. Round the electro-plating and the model diving-bell are crowds jostling one another for a foremost place. At the steam brewery, crowds of men and women are continually ascending and descending the stairs; youths are watching the model carriages moving along the new pneumatic railway; young girls are waiting to see the hemi-spherical lampshades made out of a flat sheet of paper; indeed, whether it be the noisy flax-crushing machine, or the splashing centrifugal pump, or the clatter of the Jacquard lace machine, or the bewildering whirling of the cylindrical steampress, –

round each and all these are anxious, intelligent, and simple-minded artisans, and farmers, and servants, and youths, and children clustered, endeavouring to solve the mystery of its complex operations.

For many days before the 'shilling people' were admitted to the building, the great topic of conversation was the probable behaviour of the people. Would they come sober? will they destroy the things? will they want to cut their initials, or scratch their names on the panes of the glass lighthouses? But they have surpassed in decorum the hopes of their well-wishers. The fact is, the Great Exhibition is to them more of a school than a show. The working-man has often little book-learning, but of such knowledge as constitutes the education of life – viz., the understanding of human motives, and the acquisition of power over natural forces, so as to render them subservient to human happiness – of such knowledge as this, we repeat, the working-man has generally a greater share than those who are said to belong to the 'superior classes'. Hence it is, that what was a matter of tedium, and became ultimately a mere lounge for gentlefolks, is used as a place of instruction by the people.

From 1851, or the Adventures of Mr and Mrs Sandboys *by Henry Mayhew and George Cruikshank, 1851.*

The first Shilling-day —— going in.

According to the Official Catalogue entrance on the opening day, Thursday, May 1, was by season ticket only. For the next two days the price of admission was £1. The Exhibition was closed on Sundays. On the first Monday, May 5, the price was reduced to 5s. The fourth Monday, May 26, (the twenty-second day of the Exhibition) was the first 'Shilling-day':

From the twenty-second day the prices of admission will be as follows:-

On Mondays, Tuesdays, Wednesdays and Thursdays in each week 1s 0d
On Fridays 2s 6d
On Saturdays 5s 0d

268   ALL PEOPLE THAT ON EARTH   June 5, 1851
DO DWELL

J'étais en effet à Londres dans les premiers jours de juin, l'an dernier, quand un lambeau de journal, tombé par hazard entre mes mains, m'apprit que l'*Anniversary meeting of the Charity children* allait avoir lieu dans l'église de Saint-Paul. Je me mis aussitôt en quête d'un billet, qu'après bien de lettres et de démarches je finis par obtenir de l'obligeance de M. Gosse, le premier organiste de cette cathédrale. Dès dix heures du matin, la foule encombrait les avenues de l'église; je parvins, non sans peine, à la traverser. Arrivé dans la tribune de l'orgue destinée aux chantres de la chapelle, hommes et enfants, au nombre de soixante-dix, je reçus une partie de basse qu'on me priait de chanter avec eux, et *un surplis* qu'il me fallut endosser, pour ne pas détruire, par mon habit noir, l'harmonie du costume blanc des autres choristes. Ainsi déguisé en homme d'église, j'attendis ce qu'on allait me faire entendre avec une certaine émotion vague, causée par ce que je voyais. Neuf amphithéâtres presque verticaux, de seize gradins chacun, s'élevaient au centre du monument, sous la coupole et sous l'arcade de l'est devant l'orgue pour recevoir les enfants. Les six de la coupole formaient une sorte de cirque hexagone, ouvert seulement à l'est et à l'ouest. De cette dernière ouverture partait un plan incliné, allant aboutir au haut de la porte d'entrée principale, et déjà couvert d'un auditoire immense, qui pouvait ainsi, des bancs même les plus éloignés, tout voir et tout entendre parfaitement. A gauche de la tribune que nous occupions devant l'orgue, une estrade attendait sept ou huit joueurs de trompettes et de timbales. Sur cette estrade, un grand miroir était placé de manière à réfléchir, pour les musiciens, les mouvements du chef des chœurs, marquant la mesure au loin, dans un angle au-dessous de la coupole, et dominant toute la masse chorale. Ce miroir devait servir aussi à guider l'organiste tournant le dos au chœur. Des bannières plantées tout autour du vaste amphithéâtre dont le seizième gradin atteignait presque aux chapiteaux de la colonnade, indiquaient la place que devaient occuper les diverses écoles, et portaient le nom des paroisses ou des quartiers de Londres auxquels elles appartiennent. Au moment de l'entrée des groupes d'enfants, les compartiments des amphithéâtres, se peuplant successivement du haut en bas, formaient un coup d'œil singulier, rappelant le spectacle qu'offre dans le monde microscopique le phénomène de la cristallisation. Les aiguilles de ce cristal aux molécules humaines, se dirigeant toujours de la circonférence au centre, étaient de deux couleurs, le bleu foncé de l'habit des petits garçons sur les gradins d'en haut, et le blanc de la robe et de la coiffe des petites filles occupant les rangs inférieurs. En outre, les garçons portant sur leur veste, les uns une plaque de cuivre poli, les autres une médaille d'argent, leurs mouvements faisaient scintiller la lumière réfléchie par ces ornements métalliques, de manière à produire l'effet de mille étincelles s'éteignant et se rallumant à chaque instant sur le fond sombre du tableau. L'aspect des échafaudages couverts par les filles était plus curieux encore; les rubans verts et roses qui paraient la tête et le cou de ces blanches petites vierges, faisaient ressembler exactement cette partie des amphithéâtres à une montagne couverte de neige, au travers de laquelle se montrent çà et là des brins d'herbe et des fleurs. Ajoutez les nuances variées qui se fondaient au loin dans le clair-obscur du plan incliné, ou siégeait l'auditoire, la chaire tendue de rouge de l'archevêque de Cantorbéry, les bancs richement ornés du lord-maire et de l'aristocratie anglaise sur le parvis au-dessous de la coupole, puis à l'autre bout et tout en haut les tuyaux dorés du grand orgue; figurez-vous cette magnifique église de Saint Paul, la plus grande du monde après Saint-Pierre, encadrant le tout, et vous n'aurez encore qu'une esquisse bien pâle de cet incomparable spectacle. Et partout un ordre, un recueillement, une sérénité qui en doublaient la magie. Il n'y a pas de mises en scène, si admirable qu'on les suppose, qui puissent jamais approcher de cette réalité que je crois avoir vue en songe à l'heure qu'il est. Au fur et à mesure que les enfants, parés de leurs habits neufs, venaient occuper leurs places avec une joie grave exempte de turbulence, mais où l'on pouvait observer un peu de fierté, j'entendais mes voisins anglais dire entre eux: 'Quelle scène! quelle scène!! . . .' et mon émotion était profonde quand *les six mille cinq cents* petits chanteurs étant enfin assis, la cérémonie commença.

Après un accord de l'orgue, s'est alors élevé en un gigantesque unison le premier psaume chanté par ce chœur inouï:

>All people that on earth do dwell
>Sing to the Lord with cheerful voice
>(Le peuple entier que sur la terre habite
>Chante au Seigneur d'une joyeuse voix)

From Les Soirées de l'Orchestre *by Hector Berlioz, 1862.*

There is a long passage in the same chapter on the Crystal Palace at dawn on June 7.

269   ONLY MAGIC   June 7, 1851

Yesterday I went for the second time to the Crystal Palace. We remained in it about three hours, and I must say I was more struck with it on this occasion than at my first visit. It is a wonderful place – vast, strange, new, and impossible to describe. Its grandeur does not consist in *one* thing, but in the unique assemblage of *all* things. Whatever human industry has created you find there, from the great compartments filled with railway engines and boilers, with mill machinery in full work, with splendid carriages of all kinds, with harness of every description, to the glass-covered and velvet spread stands loaded with the most gorgeous work of the goldsmith and silversmith, and the carefully guarded caskets full of real diamonds and pearls worth hundreds of thousands of pounds. It may be called a bazaar or a fair, but it is such a bazaar or fair as Eastern genii might have created. It seems as if only magic could have gathered this mass of wealth from all the ends of the earth – as if none but supernatural hands could have arranged it thus, with such a blaze and contrast of colours and marvellous power of effect. The multitude filling the great aisles seems ruled and subdued by some invisible influence. Amongst the thirty thousand souls that peopled it the day I was there not one loud noise was to be heard, not one irregular movement seen; the living tide rolls on quietly, with a deep hum like the sea heard from the distance.

From a letter of Charlotte Brontë to her father, printed in The Brontës' Life and Letters *by Clement Shorter, 1907.*

270   THE LIVING AND THE MARBLE   October 8, 1851

[OCTOBER] 8. WEDNESDAY. – Went again to the Exhibition; the crowd tremendous; at the time I entered 97,000 persons were in the building: in the course of the day nearly 110,000 – one hundred and ten thousand! Vulgar, ignorant, country people: many dirty women with their infants were sitting on the seats giving suck with their breasts uncovered, beneath the lovely female figures of the sculptor. Oh! how I wished I had the power to petrify the living, and animate the marble: perhaps a time will come when this fantasy will be realised and the human breed be succeeded by finer forms and lovelier features, than the world now dreams of. I managed to squeeze into the back and least crowded compartments of minerals etc., and with some difficulty ascended the gallery overlooking the transept, to look down on the sea of heads beneath. All was in motion, every one was moving on, whether they would or not: yet the Times of to-day writes on the deep interest felt for the permanence of the building by the throng that frequented it yesterday! What a fallacy! a mania to go to the place has been excited all over the country by the press, and hence every man woman and child goes or wishes to go, that they may say they have been; but to pretend that this is any proof that the splendid, marvellous, incredible exhibition of nature and art, is or can be appreciated by the ignorant mobs who frequent it, is truly absurd. I remained three hours, and returned thoroughly done up. The only new object I noticed was a splendid piece of opal, and a fine mass of quartz-rock with rich veins of gold, from California.

From the Journal *of Gideon Mantell, edited by E. Cecil Curwen, 1940.*

Fog

November 1851

London. Michaelmas Term lately over, and the Lord Chancellor sitting in Lincoln's Inn Hall. Implacable November weather. As much mud in the streets as if the waters had but newly retired from the face of the earth, and it would not be wonderful to meet a Megalosaurus, forty feet long or so, waddling like an elephantine lizard up Holborn Hill. Smoke lowering down from chimney-pots, making a soft black drizzle, with flakes of soot in it as big as full-grown snowflakes – gone into mourning, one might imagine, for the death of the sun. Dogs, undistinguishable in mire. Horses, scarcely better – splashed to their very blinkers. Foot passengers, jostling one another's umbrellas, in a general infection of ill-temper, and losing their foothold at street-corners where tens of thousands of other foot passengers have been slipping and sliding since the day broke (if this day ever broke), adding new deposits to the crust upon crust of mud, sticking at those points tenaciously to the pavement, and accumulating at compound interest.

Fog everywhere. Fog up the river, where it flows among green aits and meadows; fog down the river, where it rolls defiled among the tiers of shipping and the waterside pollutions of a great (and dirty) city. Fog on the Essex marshes, fog on the Kentish heights. Fog creeping into the cabooses of collier-brigs; fog lying out on the yards and hovering in the rigging of great ships; fog drooping on the gunwales of barges and small boats. Fog in the eyes and throats of ancient Greenwich pensioners, wheezing by the firesides of their wards; fog in the stem and bowl of the afternoon pipe of the wrathful skipper, down in his close cabin; fog cruelly pinching the toes and fingers of his shivering little 'prentice boy on deck. Chance people on the bridges peeping over the parapets into a nether sky of fog, with fog all round them, as if they were up in a balloon, and hanging in the misty clouds.

Gas looming through the fog in divers places in the streets, much as the sun may, from the spongy fields, be seen to loom by husbandman and ploughboy. Most of the shops lighted two hours before their time – as the gas seems to know, for it has a haggard and unwilling look.

The raw afternoon is rawest, and the dense fog is densest, and the muddy streets are muddiest, near that leaden-headed old obstruction, appropriate ornament for the threshold of a leaden-headed old corporation – Temple Bar. And hard by Temple Bar, in Lincoln's Inn Hall, at the very heart of the fog, sits the Lord High Chancellor in his High Court of Chancery.

Never can there be fog too thick, never can there come mud and mire too deep, to assort with the groping and floundering condition which this High Court of Chancery, most pestilential of hoary sinners, holds, this day, in the sight of heaven and earth.

From Bleak House *by Charles Dickens, 1853.*

272   LANE'S NET   1852

In an article on calico printing, which forms part of a recent history of Lancashire, there are a few of the patterns introduced, backed by the recommendation that they were the most successful ever tried. Of one of these, known as 'Lane's Net', there sold a greater number of pieces than of any other pattern ever brought into the market. It led to many imitations; and one of the most popular of these answers line for line, save that it is more stiff and rectilinear, to the pattern in a recently-discovered Old Red Sandstone coral, the *Smithia Pengellyi*. The beautifully-arranged lines which so smit the dames of England, that each had to provide herself with a gown of the fabric which they adorned, had been stamped amid the rocks *eons* of ages before. And it must not be forgotten, that all these forms and shades of beauty which once filled all nature, but of which only a few fragments, or faded tints, survive, were created, not to gratify man's love of the aesthetic, seeing that man had no existence until long after they had disappeared, but in meet harmony with the tastes and faculties of the Divine Worker, who had in his wisdom produced them all.

CALICO PATTERN   SMITHIA PENGELLYI

From The Testimony of the Rocks, or Geology in its bearings on the Two Theologies, Natural and Revealed, *Lecture VI by Hugh Miller, written 1852, published 1857.*

273   A BALLOON VIEW OF LONDON   September 13, 1852

It was late in the evening (a fine autumn one) when the gun was fired that was the signal for the great gas-bag to be loosened from the ropes that held it down to the soil; and immediately the buoyant machine bounded, like a big ball, into the air. Or, rather let us say, *the earth seemed to sink* suddenly down as if the spot of ground to which it had been previously fastened had been constructed upon the same principle as the Adelphi stage, and admitted of being lowered at a moment's notice. Indeed, no sooner did the report of the gun clatter in the air, than the people, who had before been grouped about the car, appeared to fall from a level with the eye; and, instantaneously, there was seen a multitude of flat, upturned faces in the gardens below, with a dense chevaux de frise of arms extended above them, and some hundreds of outstretched hands fluttering farewell to us.

The moment after this, the balloon vaulted over the trees, and we saw the roadway outside the gardens stuck all over with mobs of little black Lilliputian people, while the hubbub of the voices below, and the cries of 'Ah *bal*-loon!' from the boys, rose to the ear like the sound of a distant school let loose to play.

Now began that peculiar panoramic effect which is the distinguishing feature of the first portion of a view from a balloon, and which arises from the utter absence of all sense of motion in the machine itself, and the consequent transference of the movement to the ground beneath. The earth, as the aeronautic vessel glided over it, seemed positively to consist of a continuous series of scenes which were being drawn along underneath us, as if it were some diorama laid flat upon the ground, and almost gave one the notion that the world was an endless landscape stretched up on rollers, which some invisible sprites below were busy revolving for our especial amusement.

Then, as we floated along above the fields, in a line with the Thames towards Richmond, and looked over the edge of the car in which we were standing (and which, by the bye, was like a big 'buck basket', reaching to one's breast), the sight was the most exquisite visual delight ever experienced. The houses directly underneath us looked like the tiny wooden things out of a child's box of toys, and the streets as if they were ruts in the ground; and we could hear the hum of the voices from every spot we passed over, faint as the buzzing of so many bees.

Far beneath, in the direction we were sailing, lay the suburban fields; and here the earth, with its tiny hills and plains and streams, assumed the appearance of the little coloured plaster models of countries. The roadways striping the land were like narrow brown ribbons, and the river, which we could see winding far away, resembled a long, gray, metallic-looking snake, creeping through the fields. The bridges over the Thames were positively like planks; and the tiny black barges, as they floated along the stream, seemed no bigger than summer insects on the water. The largest meadows were about the size of green-baize table covers; and across these we could just trace the line of the South-Western Railway, with the little whiff of white steam issuing from some passing engine, and no greater in volume than the jet of vapour from an ordinary tea-kettle.

Then, as the dusk of evening descended, and the gas-lights along the different lines of road started into light, one after another, the ground seemed to be covered with little illumination lamps, such as are hung on Christmas-trees, and reminding one of those that are occasionally placed, at intervals, along the grass at the edge of the gravel-walks in suburban tea-gardens; whilst the clusters of little lights at the spots where the hamlets were scattered over the scene, appeared like knots of fire-flies in the air; and in the midst of these the eye could, here and there, distinguish the tiny crimson speck of some railway signal.

In the opposite direction to that in which the wind was insensibly wafting the balloon, lay the leviathan Metropolis, with a dense canopy of smoke hanging over it, and reminding one of the fog of vapour that is often seen steaming up from the fields at early morning. It was impossible to tell where the monster city began or ended, for the buildings stretched not only to the horizon on either side, but far away into the distance, where, owing to the coming shades of evening and the dense fumes from the million chimneys, the town seemed to blend into the sky, so that there was no distinguishing earth from heaven. The multitude of roofs that extended back from the foreground was positively like a dingy red sea, heaving in bricken billows, and the seeming waves rising up one after the other till the eye grew wearied with following them. Here and there we could distinguish little bare green patches of parks, and occasionally make out the tiny circular enclosures of the principal squares, though, from the height, these appeared scarcely bigger than wafers. Further, the fog of smoke that over-shadowed the giant town was pierced with a thousand steeples and pin-like factory-chimneys.

That little building, no bigger than one of the small china houses that are used for burning pastilles in, is Buckingham Palace – with St James's Park, dwindled to the size of a card-table, stretched out before it. Yonder is Bethlehem Hospital, with its dome, now about the same dimensions as a bell.

Then the little mites of men, crossing the bridges, seemed to have no more motion in them than the animalcules in cheese; while the streets appeared more like cracks in the soil than highways, and the tiny steamers on the river were only to be distinguished by the thin black thread of smoke trailing after them.

Indeed, it was a most wonderful sight to behold that vast bricken mass of churches and hospitals, banks and prisons, palaces and workhouses, docks and refuges for the destitute, parks and squares, and courts and alleys, which make up London – all blent into one immense black spot – to look down upon the whole as the birds of the air look down upon it, and see it dwindled into a mere rubbish heap – to contemplate from afar that strange conglomeration of vice, avarice, and low cunning, of noble aspirations and humble heroism, and to grasp it in the eye, in all its incongruous integrity, at one single glance – to take, as it were, an angel's view of that huge town where, perhaps, there is more virtue and more iniquity, more wealth and more want, brought together into one dense focus than in any other part of the earth – to hear the hubbub of the restless sea of life and emotion below, and hear it, like the ocean in a shell, whispering of the incessant strugglings and chafings of the distant tide – to swing in the air high above all the petty jealousies and heart-burnings, small ambitions and vain parade of 'polite' society, and feel, for once, tranquil as a babe in a cot, and that you are hardly of the earth, earthy, as, Jacob-like, you mount the aerial ladder, and half lose sight of the 'great commercial world' beneath, where men are regarded as mere counters to play with, and where to do your neighbour as your neighbour would do you constitutes the first principle in the religion of trade – to feel yourself floating through the endless realms of space, and drinking in the pure thin air of the skies, as you go sailing along almost among the stars, free as 'the lark at heaven's gate', and enjoying, for a brief half hour, at least, a foretaste of that Elysian destiny which is the ultimate hope of all.

Such is the scene we behold, and such the thoughts that stir the brain on contemplating London from the car of a balloon.

From The Criminal Prisons of London *by Henry Mayhew and John Binny, 1862; originally published in* Illustrated London News, *September 18, 1852.*

274   HERZEN IN LONDON   Autumn 1852

There is no town in the world which is more adapted for training one away from people and training one into solitude than London. The manner of life, the distances, the climate, the very multitude of the population in which the individual is lost, all this together with the absence of Continental diversions conduces to the same effect. One who knows how to live alone has nothing to fear from the dullness of London. The life here, like the atmosphere here, is bad for the weak, for the frail, for one who seeks a prop outside himself, for one who seeks cordiality, sympathy, attention; the moral lungs here must be as strong as the physical lungs, whose task is to get rid of the sulphuric acid in the smoky fog. The masses are saved by the struggle for daily bread, the commercial classes by their absorption in heaping up wealth, and all by the fuss and hurry of business; but nervous and romantic temperaments, fond of living among their fellows, of intellectual sloth and emotional idleness, are bored to death and fall into despair.

Wandering lonely about London, through its stony lanes and through its stifling passages, sometimes not seeing a step before me for the thick, opaline fog, and running against flying shadows – I lived through a great deal.

In the evening when my son had gone to bed, I usually went out for a walk; I scarcely ever went to see any one; I read the newspapers and stared in taverns at the alien race, and stood on the bridges across the Thames.

On the one hand, the stalactites of the Houses of Parliament would loom through the darkness ready to vanish again, on the other, the inverted bowl of St. Paul's . . . and street-lamps . . . street-lamps without end in both directions. One city, full-fed, lay sleeping, while the other, hungry, was not yet awake – the streets were empty, nothing could be heard but the even tread of the policeman with his lantern. I used to sit and look, and my soul would grow quieter and more peaceful. And so through all this I came to love this dreadful ant-heap, where every night a hundred thousand men know not where they will lay their heads, and the police often find women and children dead of hunger beside hotels where one cannot dine for less than two pounds.

From the Memoirs *of Alexander Herzen, translated by Constance Garnett, 1924–27.*

275   **REFLEX MUSINGS:**   April 15, 1853
         REFLECTIONS FROM VARIOUS SURFACES

>In the dense entangled street,
> Where the web of Trade is weaving,
>Forms unknown in crowds I meet
> Much of each and all believing;
> Each his small designs achieving
>Hurries on with restless feet,
> While, through Fancy's power deceiving,
>*Self* in every form I greet.
>
>Oft in yonder rocky dell
> Neath the birches' shadow seated,
>I have watched the darksome well,
> Where my stooping form, repeated,
> Now advanced and now retreated
>With the spring's alternate swell,
> Till destroyed before completed
>As the big drops grew and fell.
>
>By the hollow mountain-side
> Questions strange I shout for ever,
>While the echoes far and wide
> Seem to mock my vain endeavour;
> Still I shout, for though they never
>Cast my borrowed voice aside,
> Words from empty words they sever –
>Words of Truth from words of Pride.

Yes, the faces in the crowd,
　And the wakened echoes, glancing
From the mountain, rocky browed,
　And the lights in water dancing –
　Each my wandering sense entrancing,
Tells me back my thoughts aloud,
　All the joys of Truth enhancing
Crushing all that makes me proud.

A poem by James Clerk-Maxwell, aged 22, in The Life of James Clerk-Maxwell *by L. Campbell and W. Garnett, 1882.*

276   THE CONCEALED YEARNING   May 4, 1853

The great talk now is Mrs. Stowe and spirit-rapping, both of which have arrived in England. The universality of the phenomena renders it a curious study. A feeling seems pervading all classes, all sects, that the world stands upon the eve of some great spiritual revelation. It meets one in books, in newspapers, on the lips of members of the Church of England, Unitarians, even Free-thinkers.

Poor old Robert Owen, the philanthropist, has been converted, and made a confession of faith in the public papers. One cannot but respect a man, who in his old age, has the boldness to declare himself as having been blinded and mistaken through life; and who, upon the verge of human life, sends forth the concealed yearning of his soul after a spiritual world and an immortality. Yes, indeed, is not the greatest proof, after all, of an immortality the innate longing after it, and the belief in it existing within each human being, whether encased in external intellectual pride, worldly joy, or hardness of heart, and that, too, throughout all ages and shining forth from all mythologies?

Especially are the aristocracy interested in these rappings, which become contagious; a medium of spiritual communication may, in some cases, be developed by the laying on of hands. There is a singular resemblance between it and mesmeric power. The old hobgoblins and brownies seem to be let loose again, for all the spirits appear to be of a singularly low order, frequently lying. Mr Beecher, the brother of Mrs Stowe, has delivered in America a series of lectures to a vast assembly, demonstrating that these phenomena are the work of the devil. Well, perhaps, they may be.

From a letter of Mary Howitt to William Howitt, printed in her Autobiography, *1889.*

277 THE MIND OF MAN July 25, 1853

I have not been at work except in turning the tables upon the table-turners, nor should I have done that, but that I thought it better to stop the inpouring flood by letting all know at once what my views and thoughts were. What a weak, credulous, incredulous, unbelieving, superstitious, bold, frightened, what a ridiculous world ours is, as far as concerns the mind of man. How full of inconsistencies, contradictions, and absurdities it is. I declare that, taking the average of many minds that have recently come before me (and apart from that spirit which God has placed in each), and accepting for a moment that average as a standard, I should far prefer the obedience, affections, and instinct of a dog before it. Do not whisper this, however, to others. There is One above who worketh in all things, and who governs even in the midst of that misrule to which the tendencies and powers of man are so easily perverted.

From a letter of Michael Faraday to Professor Schonbein, printed in The Life and Letters of Faraday *by Bence Jones, 1870.*

278 LIVERPOOL August 20, 1853

This being Saturday, there early commenced a throng of visitants to Rock Ferry. The boat in which I came over brought from the city a multitude of factory-people. They had bands of music, and banners inscribed with the names of the mills they belong to, and other devices; pale-looking people, but not looking exactly as if they were underfed. They are brought on reduced terms by the railways and steamers, and come from great distances in the interior. These, I believe, were from Preston. I have not yet had an opportunity of observing how they amuse themselves during these excursions.

At the dock, the other day, the steamer arrived from Rock Ferry with a countless multitude of little girls, in coarse blue gowns, who, as they landed, formed in procession, and walked up the dock. These girls had been taken from the work-houses and educated at a charity school, and would by-and-by be apprenticed as servants. I should not have conceived it possible that so many children would have been collected together, without a single trace of beauty or scarcely of intelligence in so much as one individual; such mean, coarse, vulgar features and figures betraying unmistakeably a low origin, and ignorant and brutal parents. They did not appear wicked, but only stupid, animal, and soulless. It must require many generations of better life to wake the soul in them. All America could not show the like.

From Passages from the English Notebooks of Nathaniel Hawthorne, *edited by Mrs Hawthorne, 1870.*

A TERRIFIC BANQUET IN AN IGUANODON

December 31, 1853

At the lower end of the park, in a rude and temporary wooden building, almost inaccessible for deep ruts and acres of swamp and mud – a miniature Serbonian bog – Mr Waterhouse Hawkins was steadily engaged in the creation or restoration of a series of now extinct animals, which it would appear were destined to roam, as in their native state, through the deep Penge morasses, or bury themselves in the deep excavations of the park. By the close of the last year, Mr Hawkins had so far succeeded with the formation of some of the members of his monster family, as to be in a position to give effect to a design which he had for some time previously contemplated, of giving a dinner to the Directors and some of his friends within the carcass of one of his antediluvian monsters. The last day of the old year (1853) was selected. Accordingly Professors Owen and Forbes, Mr Gould, Mr Francis Fuller, Mr Belshaw, Mr Ingram, and a number of other gentlemen, assembled to do honour to the unique and novel entertainment. Twenty-one of the guests were accommodated with seats on each side of the table, within the sides of the iguanodon. Professor Owen, one of the most eminent geologists of the day, occupied a seat at the head of the table, and within the skull of the monster. Mr Francis Fuller, the Managing Director, and Professor Forbes, were seated on commodious benches placed in the rear of the beast. An awning of pink and white drapery was raised above the novel banqueting-hall, and small banners bearing the names of Conybeare, Buckland, Forbes, Owen, Mantell, and other well-known geologists, gave character and interest to the scene. When the more substantial viands were disposed of, Professor Owen proposed that the company should drink in silence 'The memory of Mantell, the discoverer of the iguanodon,' the monster in whose bowels they had just dined.

The Professor paid an eloquent tribute to the value of the labours in the wide field of geology and palaeontology of such men as Cuvier, Hunter, and Conybeare. He told the company how the researches of Cuvier in comparative anatomy had provided the means of reconstructing an extinct animal almost from a single fossil-bone, for so perfect was the individuality of each species of animals, and so peculiarly adapted was the construction of their parts, to the purposes for which they were destined, that a skilful observer could tell, with the most perfect accuracy, to what species of animal any particular bone belonged. The researches of Hunter had confirmed the theories of Cuvier, and from a single bone, or a single tooth, Conybeare, Buckland, and others, had succeeded in building up an entire animal. The beast in which he was then speaking, whose original had once roamed through the vast forests of Sussex, had perished there by some great convulsion of nature; a single bone was discovered a few years since by Mantell, and from that fossil-limb the iguanodon had been constructed.

Many other toasts, and many pleasing remarks, beguiled the hours, till approaching midnight suggested the appropriateness of the guests departing to their more congenial homes. Professor Forbes contributed some verses suitable to the occasion. As the thoughts of the learned professor have never yet appeared in print, no apology will be needed for presenting them to the visitor. The poet-geologist having told how the company were indebted to the hospitality of Mr Waterhouse Hawkins, for the opportunity of the spending of the last day of the old year in 'an antediluvian dragon', proceeded thus to the iguanodon, the 'roaring' chorus being taken up by the company in a manner so fierce and enthusiastic, as almost to lead to the belief that a herd of iguanodons were bellowing from some of the numerous pit-falls in Penge Park, in which they had been entrapped: –

> A thousand ages underground
>   His skeleton had lain;
> But now his body's big and round,
>   And he's himself again!
> His bones, like Adam's, wrapped in clay,
>   His ribs of iron stout,
> Where is the brute alive to-day
>   That dares with him turn out?
>   Beneath his hide he's got inside
>   The souls of living men,
>   Who dare our Saurian now deride
>   With life in him again?
>
> (*Chorus*) The jolly old beast
>   Is not deceased,
>   There's life in him again. (*A roar*)
>
> In fairy land are fountains gay,
>   With dragons for their guard:
> To keep the people from the sight,
>   The brutes hold watch and ward!
> But far more gay our founts shall play,
>   Our dragons, far more true,
> Will bid the nations enter in
>   And see what skill can do!
>   For monsters wise our Saurians are,
>   And wisely shall they reign,
>   To spread sound knowledge near and far
>   They've come to life again!

> Though savage war her teeth may gnash,
>   And human blood may flow,
> And foul ambition, fierce and rash,
>   Would plunge the world in woe,
> Each column of this palace fair
>   That heavenward soars on high,
> A flag of hope shall on it bear,
>   Proclaiming strife must die!
>   And art and science far shall spread
>   Around this far domain,
>   The People's Palace rears its head
>   With life in it again.

From Routledge's Guide to the Crystal Palace and Park at Sydenham *by E. MacDermot, 1854.*

280   COKETOWN   January 1854

Coketown, to which Messrs. Bounderby and Gradgrind now walked, was a triumph of fact, it had no greater taint of fancy in it than Mrs. Gradgrind herself. Let us strike the key-note, Coketown, before pursuing our tune.

It was a town of red brick, or of brick that would have been red if the smoke and ashes had allowed it; but as matters stood it was a town of unnatural red and black like the painted face of a savage. It was a town of machinery and tall chimneys, out of which interminable serpents of smoke trailed themselves for ever and ever, and never got uncoiled. It had a black canal in it, and a river that ran purple with ill-smelling dye, and vast piles of building full of windows where there was a rattling and a trembling all day long, and where the piston of the steam-engine worked monotonously up and down, like the head of an elephant in a state of melancholy madness.

From Hard Times *by Charles Dickens, 1854.*

281   BOTTLED COMPASSES   November 16, 1855

Papa has been busy making bottled compasses for Brunel's great ship, who begged him to get at some magnetic results for him, but Papa must experiment in the neighbourhood of much larger masses of iron than he can scrape together here. One thing, however, he had made out, that a needle suspended in water becomes quiet in its true position wonderfully sooner than when, as usual, hung in air – hence bottled compasses. But if thou and Dr Cumming say that the world is at its last gasp, what is the use of inventing any worldly thing, when either destruction or intuition is so nigh at hand? The dear old world! one certainly fancied it in its very infancy blundering over BA *ba*, AB *ab*; but it may be dotage, for truly one sees people nowadays quite *blasés* at twenty. Which was its period of manhood? I suppose Kingsley would not hesitate in giving it to the reign of our Elizabeth. But Kingsley is no prophet of mine, however much he may sometimes rejoice and at others strike me with awe. Ah! and that would only apply to England; and, if I remember rightly, nothing short of the destruction of a world would satisfy Dr Cumming. Oh! the comfort and blessing of knowing that our Future is in other hands than Dr Cumming's; how restful it makes one, and so willing to have the veil still closely drawn which separates Now from Then. It often strikes me that one must look forward to some catastrophe for London, similar in spirit, however diverse in form, to what befell Babylon, Jerusalem, and Palmyra, but the How and When....

From a letter of Caroline Fox to E.T. Carne, published in Memories of Old Friends, *1882.*

Note the use of the word 'quiet' for the compass and the symbolism of the whole letter. Note incidentally it was this very day, as Caroline Fox was writing to Carne, that David Livingstone had his first sight of the Victoria Falls.

282   PHILANTHROPY   December 12, 1855

St. Giles. Winter has set in early and vigorously. Sufferings of the poor very great. The scenes, as recorded in the Police Reports, at the doors of the workhouses, and all night long, are horrifying. Boards of Guardians, Vestrymen, Relieving Officers, and the President of the P.L. Commission, are alike, either brutal, ignorant, or foolish. These things morbidly affect me. They are ever in my mind, and during the inclement season destroy all my comfort, and abate the enjoyment of what, by God's mercy, I possess. All is remediable, but not by one man. And now 'philanthropy' is at a discount; people are nauseated with humanity and 'humanity-mongers', and especially with myself.

From the Journal of Lord Shaftesbury, quoted in The Life and Work of the Seventh Earl of Shaftesbury *by Edwin Hodder, 1888.*

283   THE SILENT SYSTEM   June 1856

There are three distinct rooms where the prisoners pick oakum, one in the misdemeanour prison, and the two others in the felons' prison. We shall choose for our illustration and description the larger one in the felons' prison. It has lately been built on so vast a plan that it has seats for nearly 500 men. This immense room is situated to the west of the main or old prison, close to the schoolroom. It is almost as long as one of the sheds seen at a

THE WORKSHOP UNDER THE SILENT SYSTEM AT MILLBANK PRISON

railway terminus where spare carriages are kept, and seems to have been built after the same style of architecture, for it has a corrugated iron roof, stayed with thin rods, spanning the entire erection. We were told that the extreme length is 90 feet, but that does not convey so good a notion of distance to the mind as the fact of the wall being pierced with eight large chapel windows, and the roof with six skylights. Again, an attendant informed us that there were eleven rows of forms; but all that we could see was a closely-packed mass of heads and pink faces, moving to and fro in every variety of motion, as though the wind was blowing them about, and they were set on stalks instead of necks.

On the side fitted with windows the dark forms of the warders are seen, each perched up on a raised stool. The bright light shines on the faces of the criminals, and the officer keeps his eye rapidly moving in all directions, almost as if it went by clockwork, so as to see that no talking takes place. If a man rest over his work for a moment and raise his head, he sees, hung up on the white walls before him, placards on which texts are printed. One is to the effect that 'IT IS GOOD FOR A MAN THAT HE BEAR THE YOKE IN HIS YOUTH'; another tells the prisoners that 'GODLINESS WITH CONTENTMENT IS A GREAT GAIN'; whilst a third counsels each of them to 'GO TO THE ANT, THOU SLUGGARD, CONSIDER HER WAYS, AND BE WISE'.

We went to the wall where the warders were, and looked up the sloping floor at the dirty gray mass of life; the faces of the men seemed like the flesh showing through a tattered garment.

The building was full of men, and as silent as if it merely contained so many automata, for the only sound heard was like that of the rustling of a thicket, or, better, the ticking of clock-work – something resembling that heard in a Dutch clockmaker's shop, where hundreds of time-pieces are going together.

The utter absence of noise struck us as being absolutely terrible. The silence seemed, after a time, almost intense enough to hear a flake of snow fall. Perfect stillness is at all times more or less awful, and hence arises a great part of the solemnity of night as well as of death. To behold those whom we have seen full of life and emotion – some wondrous piece of breathing and speaking organism, reduced to the inanimateness of the statue, is assuredly the most appalling and depressing sight we can look upon. The stillness of the silent system, however, has, to our minds, even a more tragic cast about it; for not only is the silence as intense and impressive as that of death itself, but the movements of the workers seem as noiseless, and therefore unearthly, as spectres. Nor does the sense of our being surrounded by some five hundred criminals – men of the wildest passions, and almost brute instincts, all toiling in dumb show and without a single syllable escaping from their lips – in any way detract from the goblin character of the sight.

From The Criminal Prisons of London *by Henry Mayhew and John Binny, 1862.*

284 TERRESTRIAL ALL IN CHAOS October 14, 1856
Glenlair

Now I am writing a solemn address or manifesto to the Natural Philosophers of the North, which I am afraid I must reinforce with coffee and anchovies, and a roaring hot fire and spread coat-tails to make it all natural. By the way, I have proved that if there be nine coefficients of magnetic induction, perpetual motion will set in, and a small crystalline sphere will inevitably destroy the universe by increasing all velocities till the friction brings all nature into a state of incandescence, or as H— would say, Terrestrial all in Chaos shall exhibit efflorescence.

From a letter of James Clerk-Maxwell to C.J. Munro, printed in The Life of James Clerk-Maxwell *by L. Campbell and W. Garnett, 1882.*

285 THE RAILWAY TO HEAVEN Summer 1857

I lingered, contemplating the view, till it was time to look for an inn; I chose the *Talbot*, and had no reason to repent my choice. On the way thither, I bought two religious ballads at a little shop, the mistress of which told me she sold 'hundreds of 'em', and they were printed at Otley. As specimens of a class of compositions which are relished and sung, as hymns by a numerous section of the community, they are eminently suggestive. Do they supply a real want? Are they harmless? Are they edifying? Can they who find satisfaction therein be led up to something better? To close this chapter, here follows a quotation from *The Railway to Heaven*:

O! what a deal we hear and read
About Railways and railway speed,
Of lines which are, or may be made;
And selling shares is quite a trade.

Allow me, as an old Divine,
To point to you another line,
Which does from earth to heaven extend,
Where real pleasures never end.

Of truth divine the rails are made,
And on the Rock of Ages laid;
The rails are fix'd in chairs of love,
Firm as the throne of God above.

One grand first-class is used for all,
For Jew or Gentile, great and small,
There's room for all the world inside,
And kings with beggars here do ride.

About a hundred years or so
Wesley and others said they'd go:
A carriage mercy did provide,
That Wesley and his friends might ride.

'Tis nine-and-thirty years, they say,
Whoever lives to see next May,
Another coach was added then
Unto this all-important train.

Jesus is the first engineer,
He does the gospel engine steer;
We've guards who ride, while others stand
Close by the way with flag in hand.

CHORUS
'My Son,' says God, 'give me thy heart;
Make haste, or else the train will start.'

From A Month in Yorkshire *by Walter White, 1858.*

THE ROAD TO HAWORTH

The Leeds and Skipton railway runs along a deep valley of the Aire; a slow and sluggish stream, compared with the neighbouring river of Wharfe. Keighley station is on this line of railway, about a quarter of a mile from the town of the same name. The number of inhabitants and the importance of Keighley have been very greatly increased during the last twenty years, owing to the rapidly extended market for worsted manufactures, a branch of industry that mainly employs the factory population of this part of Yorkshire, which has Bradford for its centre and metropolis.

Keighley is in process of transformation from a populous old-fashioned village into a still more populous and flourishing town. It is evident to the stranger that, as the gable-ended houses, which obtrude themselves cornerwise on the widening street, fall vacant, they are pulled down to allow of greater space for traffic and a more modern style of architecture. The quaint and narrow shop-windows of fifty years ago are giving way to large panes and plate-glass. Nearly every dwelling seems devoted to some branch of commerce. In passing hastily through the town, one hardly perceives where the necessary lawyer and doctor can live, so little appearance is there of any dwelling of the professional middle-class, such as abound in our old cathedral towns. In fact, nothing can be more opposed than the state of society, the modes of thinking, the standards of reference on all points of morality, manners, and even politics and religion, in such a new manufacturing place as Keighley in the north, and any stately, sleepy, picturesque cathedral town in the south. Yet the aspect of Keighley promises well for future stateliness, if not picturesqueness. Grey stone abounds, and the rows of houses built of it have a kind of solid grandeur connected with their uniform and enduring lines. The framework of the doors and the lintels of the windows, even in the smallest dwellings, are made of blocks of stone. There is no painted wood to require continual beautifying, or else present a shabby aspect; and the stone is kept scrupulously clean by the notable Yorkshire housewives. Such glimpses into the interior as a passer-by obtains reveal a rough abundance of the means of living, and diligent and active habits in the women. But the voices of the people are hard, and their tongues discordant, promising little of the musical taste that distinguishes the district, and which has already furnished a Carrodus to the musical world. The names over the shops (of which the one just given is a sample) seem strange even to an inhabitant of the neighbouring county, and have a peculiar smack and flavour of the place.

The town of Keighley never quite melts into country on the road to Haworth, although the houses become more sparse as the traveller journeys upwards to the grey round hills that seem to bound his journey in a westerly direction. First come some villas, just sufficiently retired from the road to show that they can scarcely belong to any one liable to be summoned in a hurry, at the call of suffering or danger, from his comfortable fireside; the lawyer, the doctor, and the clergyman live at hand, and hardly in the suburbs, with a screen of shrubs for concealment.

In a town one does not look for vivid colouring; what there may be of this is furnished by the wares in the shops, not by foliage or atmospheric effects; but in the country some brilliancy and vividness seems to be instinctively expected, and there is consequently a slight feeling of disappointment at the grey natural tint of every object, near or far off, on the way from Keighley to Haworth. The distance is about four miles; and, as I have said, what with villas, great worsted factories, rows of workmen's houses, with here and there an old-fashioned farmhouse and outbuildings, it can hardly be called 'country' any part of the way. For two miles the road passes over tolerably level ground; distant hills on the left, a 'beck' flowing through meadows on the right, and furnishing water power, at certain points, to the factories built on its banks. The air is dim and lightless with the smoke from all these habitations and places of business. The soil in the valley (or 'bottom', to use the local term) is rich; but as the road begins to ascend the vegetation becomes poorer; it does not flourish, it merely exists; and instead of trees there are only bushes and shrubs about the dwellings. Stone dykes are everywhere used in place of hedges; and what crops there are, on the patches of arable land, consist of pale, hungry-looking, grey-green oats. Right before the traveller on this road rises Haworth village; he can see it for two miles before he arrives, for it is situated on the side of a pretty steep hill, with a back-ground of dun and purple moors, rising and sweeping away yet higher than the church, which is built at the very summit of the long narrow street. All round the horizon there is this same line of sinuous wave-like hills, the scoops into which they fall only revealing other hills beyond, of similar colour and shape, crowned with wild bleak moors – grand from the ideas of solitude and loneliness which they suggest, or oppressive from the feeling which they give of being pent up by some monotonous and illimitable barrier, according to the mood of mind in which the spectator may be.

From The Life of Charlotte Brontë *by Mrs E.C. Gaskell, 1857.*

Note on 285 and 286. *Mrs Gaskell visited Haworth for the first time in September 1853 and wrote the letter which formed the basis of the famous opening of Chapter One of the* Life *published in 1857 – in some cases word for word – generally the later account is longer, more philosophical. Charlotte Brontë died in 1855.*

Walter White appears to have visited Haworth in the summer of 1857 and from his account it is clear that there was already quite a 'vast', i.e. a crowd of visitors on account of the Brontës' writings. In many ways the two accounts of the same journey are extraordinarily similar – obviously they could not have known each other.

From Keighley to Haworth is 4 miles. From Keighley the other way it is about six miles to Saltaire to which White went immediately after his Haworth visit. It was built in 1852-3 to designs by Fairbairn. Clearly this was a rising part of the country in the '40s and '50s. It was opening up. And the passing of its romance was celebrated in Wuthering Heights *as the passing of the romance of the lakes at the time of the Lowthers and Curwens by Wordsworth . . . such at least is one's feeling – how far true in fact . . .?*

287   SALTAIRE   c.1857

Saltaire is about a mile from Shipley. It is a new settlement in an old country; a most noteworthy example of what enterprise can and will accomplish where trade confides in political and social security. Here, in an agreeable district of the valley of the Aire – wooded hills on both sides – a magnificent factory and dependent town have been built, and with so much judgment as to mitigate or overcome the evils to which towns and factories have been so long obnoxious. The factory is built in stone in pure Italian style, and has a truly palatial appearance. What would the Plantagenets say, could they come back to life, and see trade inhabiting palaces far more stately than those of kings? The main building, of six stories, is seventy-two feet in height, and five hundred and fifty feet in length. In front, at some distance, standing quite apart, rises the great chimney, to an elevation of two hundred and fifty feet; a fine ornamental object, built to resemble a campanile.

From A Month in Yorkshire *by Walter White, 1858.*

288   SATURN   August 28, 1857

I have been battering away at Saturn, returning to the charge every now and then. I have effected several breaches in the solid ring, and now I am splash into the fluid one, amid a clash of symbols truly astounding. When I reappear it will be in the dusky ring, which is something like the state of the air supposing the siege of Sebastopol conducted from a forest of guns 100 miles one way, and 30,000 miles the other, and the shot never to stop, but go spinning away round a circle, radius 170,000 miles.

From a letter of James Clerk-Maxwell to Lewis Campbell, printed in The Life of James Clerk-Maxwell *by L. Campbell and W. Garnett, 1882.*

On March 23, 1855, the Examiners for the newly founded Adams Prize announced the subject to be 'The Motions of Saturn's Rings', to be adjudged in 1857. Among other things this announcement says: 'It may be supposed (1) that they are rigid; (2) that they are fluid, or in part aeriform; (3) that they consist of masses of matter not mutually coherent. . . .' There is also a reference to 'the newly discovered dark ring'. See The Life.

The 1855 date would explain this relatively late reference to Sebastopol, although of course there were Panoramas and accounts for years afterwards. Note how nearly it is slipping into poetry – and how like Lear is the 'clash of symbols . . .'. This was written from Scotland.

289   THE GREAT MYSTERY   November 9, 1857

We have had streams of hooks and eyes flying around magnets, and even pictures of them so beset, but nothing is clearer than your descriptions of all sources of force keeping up a state of energy in all that surrounds them, which state by its own increase or diminution measures the work done by any change in the system. You seem to see the lines of force curving round obstacles and driving plump at conductors, and swerving towards certain directions in crystals, and carrying with them everywhere the same amount of attractive power spread wider or denser as the lines widen or contract. You have also seen that the great mystery is not how like bodies repel and unlike attract, but how like bodies attract (by gravitation). But if you can get over that difficulty, either by making gravity the residual of the two electricities or by simply admitting it, then your lines of force can 'weave a web across the sky' and lead the stars in their courses without any necessarily immediate connection with the objects of their attraction.

From a letter of James Clerk-Maxwell to Michael Faraday, printed in A Tribute to Michael Faraday *by R. Appleyard, 1931.*

290   THE MATERIAL WORLD   December 6, 1857

I have walked the streets a great deal in the dull November days, and always take a certain pleasure in being in the midst of human life, – as closely encompassed by it as it is possible to be anywhere in this world; and in that way of viewing it there is a dull and sombre enjoyment always to be had in Holborn, Fleet Street, Cheapside, and the other busiest parts of London. It is human life; it is this material world; it is a grim and heavy reality. I have never had the same sense of being surrounded by materialisms and hemmed in with the grossness of this earthly existence anywhere else; these broad, crowded streets are so evidently the veins and arteries of an enormous city. London is evidenced in every one of them, just as a megatherium is in each of its separate bones, even if they be small ones. Thus I never fail of a sort of self-congratulation in finding myself, for instance, passing along Ludgate Hill; but, in spite of this, it is really an ungladdened life to wander through these huge, thronged ways, over a pavement foul with mud, ground into it by a million of footsteps; jostling against people who do not seem to be individuals, but all one mass, so homogeneous is the street-walking aspect of them; the roar of vehicles pervading me, – wearisome cabs and omnibuses; everywhere the dingy brick edifices heaving themselves up, and shutting out all but a strip of sullen cloud, that serves London for a sky, – in short, a general impression of grime and sordidness; and at this season always a fog scattered along the vista of streets, sometimes so densely as almost to spiritualize the materialism and make the scene resemble the other world of worldly people, gross even in ghostliness.

From Passages from the English Notebooks of Nathaniel Hawthorne, edited by Mrs Hawthorne, 1870.

291   LAW AND LIBERTY   March 5, 1858

I have observed that the practical cultivators of science (*e.g.*, Sir J. Herschel, Faraday, Ampère, Oersted, Newton, Young), although differing excessively in turn of mind, have all a distinctness and a freedom from the tyranny of words in dealing with questions of Order, Law, etc., which pure speculators and literary men never attain.

Now, I am going to put down something on my own authority, which you must not take for more than it is worth. There are certain men who write books, who assume that whatever things are orderly, certain, and capable of being accurately predicted by men of experience, belong to one category; and whatever things are the result of conscious action, whatever are capricious, contingent, and cannot be foreseen, belong to another category.

All the time I have lived and thought, I have seen more and more reason to disagree with this opinion, and to hold that all want of order, caprice, and unaccountableness results from interference with liberty, which would, if unimpeded, result in order, certainty, and trustworthiness (certainty of success of predicting). Remember I do not say that caprice and disorder are not the result of free will (so called), only I say that there is a liberty which is not disorder, and that this is by no means less free than the other, but more.

In the next place, there are various states of mind, and schools of philosophy corresponding to various stages in the evolution of the idea of liberty.

In one phase, human actions are the resultant (by par$^{m.}$ of forces) of the various attractions of surrounding things, modified in some degree by internal states, regarding which all that is to be said is that they are subjectively capricious, objectively the 'RESULT OF LAW', – that is, the wilfulness of our wills feels to us like liberty, being in reality necessity.

In another phase, the wilfulness is seen to be anything but free will, since it is merely a submission to the strongest attraction, after the fashion of material things. So some say that a man's will is the root of all evil in him, and that he should mortify it out till nothing of himself remains, and the man and his selfishness disappear altogether. So said Gotama Buddha (see Max Müller), and many Christians have said and thought the same thing.

Nevertheless there is another phase still, in which there appears a possibility of the exact contrary of the first state, namely, an abandonment of wilfulness without extinction of will, but rather by means of a great development of will, whereby, instead of being consciously free and really in subjection to unknown laws, it becomes consciously acting by law, and really free from the interference of unrecognised laws.

There is a screed of metaphysics. I don't suppose that is what you wanted. I have no nostrum that is exactly what you want. Every man must brew his own, or at least fill his own glass for himself, but I greatly desire to hear some more from you, just to get into *rapport*.

As to the Roman Catholic question, it is another piece of the doctrine of Liberty. People get tired of being able to do as they like, and having to choose their own steps, and so they put themselves under holy men, who, no doubt, are really wiser than themselves. But it is not only wrong, but impossible, to transfer either will or responsibility to another; and after the formulae have been gone through, the patient has just as much responsibility as before, and feels it too. But it is a sad thing for any one to lose sight of their work, and to have to seek some conventional, arbitrary treadmill-occupation prescribed by sanitary jailors.

From a letter of James Clerk-Maxwell to R.B. Litchfield, printed in The Life of James Clerk-Maxwell *by L. Campbell and W. Garnett, 1882.*

292 CHANCE 1859

In the case of every species, many different checks, acting at different periods of life, and during different seasons or years, probably come into play; some one check or some few being generally the most potent; but all will concur in determining the average number or even the existence of the species. In some cases it can be shown that widely-different checks act on the same species in different districts. When we look at the plants and bushes clothing an entangled bank, we are tempted to attribute their proportional numbers and kinds to what we call chance. But how false a view is this! Every one has heard that when an American forest is cut down, a very different vegetation springs up; but it has been observed that ancient Indian ruins in the Southern United States, which must formerly have been cleared of trees, now display the same beautiful diversity and proportion of kinds as in the surrounding virgin forest. What a struggle must have gone on during long centuries between the several kinds of trees, each annually scattering its seeds by the thousand; what war between insect and insect – between insects, snails, and other animals with birds and beasts of prey – all striving to increase, all feeding on each other, or on the trees, their seeds and seedlings, or on the other plants which first clothed the ground and thus checked the growth of the trees! Throw up a handful of feathers, and all fall to the ground according to definite laws; but how simple is the problem where each shall fall compared to that of the action and reaction of the innumerable plants and animals which have determined, in the course of centuries, the proportional numbers and kinds of trees now growing on the old Indian ruins.

From The Origin of Species *by Charles Darwin, 1859.*

VISIBLE SYMBOL c.1859

Near the Hall-in-the-Wood rises one of those octagonal columns so common in the manufacturing districts, which serve as visible symbols of the industry that surrounds them. The chimneys in and about Bolton are very numerous, and many of them are of great hight, but all dwindle into pigmy dimensions compared with that near Crompton's former residence, which shoots up into the skies to the height of three hundred and sixty-six feet (by far the loftiest structure in the district), and attracts to it every wandering eye in the surrounding country. Unintentionally it has become a conspicuous landmark, indicating with power and precision the site of his invention. Built for an entirely different purpose, the principal use of this tall and really graceful structure is in connection with numerous steam-engines and furnaces in a huge factory, where some thousands of men and boys are employed in making mule-spinning machinery, not merely for the supply of Europe, and even the outskirts of civilization in Africa; for wherever the humanizing effects of their industry have become known, Crompton's mules and their accessory engines are welcomed and cherished. Thus another unintentional tribute to the

OCTAGONAL CHIMNEY SHAFT AT BOLTON

honour of their inventor is perpetuated by the weekly production of thousand of mule-spindles almost on the very spot of their invention, propelling with regularity, as from a mighty heart, the life-blood which circulates through and sustains this stupendous system of manufacture. from a mighty heart, the life-blood which circulates through and sustains this stupendous system of manufacture.

From The Life and Times of Samuel Crompton *by Gilbert J. French, 1860.*

294   LETTER FROM EDWARD LEAR   July 9, 1859

Washing my rosecoloured flesh and brushing my beard with a hairbrush, –
– Breakfast of tea, bread, and butter, at nine o'clock in the morning,
Sending my carpet-bag onward I reached the Twickenham station,
(Thanks to the civil domestics of good Lady Wald'grave's establishment),
Just as the big buzzing brown booming bottlegreen bumblebizz boiler
Stood on the point of departing for Richmond and England's
                                                metropolis . . . .

From a letter in hexameters from Edward Lear to Lord Carlingford, printed in Letters of Edward Lear, *edited by Lady Strachey, 1907.*

295   DARWIN ON PIGEONS   November 27, 1859

I have found it very important associating with fanciers and breeders. For instance, I sat one evening in a gin palace in the Borough amongst a set of pigeon fanciers, when it was hinted that Mr Bull had crossed his Pouters with Runts to gain size; and if you could have seen the solemn, the mysterious, and awful shakes of the head which all the fanciers gave at this scandalous proceeding, you would have recognised how little crossing has had to do with improving breeds, and how dangerous for endless generations the process was. All this was brought home far more vividly than by pages of mere statements, &c.

April 1860

I must say one more word about our quasi-theological controversy about natural selection, and let me have your opinion when we meet in London. Do you consider that the successive variations in the size of the crop of the Pouter Pigeon, which man has accumulated to please his caprice, have been due to 'the creative and sustaining powers of Brahma?' In the sense that an omnipotent and omniscient Deity must order and know everything, this must be admitted; yet, in honest truth I can hardly admit it. It seems preposterous that a maker of a universe should care about the crop of a pigeon solely to please man's silly fancies.

From letters of Charles Darwin to T.H. Huxley and Sir Charles Lyell, printed in Life and Letters of Charles Darwin, *edited by Francis Darwin, 1887.*

296   DARWIN ON THEOLOGY   May 22, 1860

With respect to the theological view of the question. This is always painful to me. I am bewildered. I had no intention to write atheistically. But I own that I cannot see as plainly as others do, and as I should wish to do, evidence of design and beneficence on all sides of us. There seems to me too much misery in the world. I cannot persuade myself that a beneficent and omnipotent God would have designedly created the Ichneumonidae with the express intention of their feeding within the living bodies of Caterpillars, or that a cat should play with mice. Not believing this, I see no necessity in the belief that the eye was expressly designed. On the other hand, I cannot anyhow be contented to view this wonderful universe, and especially the nature of man, and to conclude that everything is the result of brute force. I am inclined to look at everything as resulting from designed laws, with the details, whether good or bad, left to the working out of what we may call chance. Not that this notion *at all* satisfies me. I feel most deeply that the whole subject is too profound for the human intellect. A dog might as well speculate on the mind of Newton. Let each man hope and believe what he can. Certainly I agree with you that my views are not at all necessarily atheistical. The lightning kills a man, whether a good one or a bad one, owing to the excessively complex action of natural laws. A child (who may turn out to be an idiot) is born by the action of even more complex laws, and I can see no reason why a man, or other animal, may not have been aboriginally produced by other laws, and that all these laws may have been expressly designed by an omniscient Creator, who foresaw every future event and consequence. But the more I think the more bewildered I become; as indeed I have probably shown by this letter.

From a letter of Charles Darwin to Asa Gray, printed in Life and Letters of Charles Darwin, *edited by Francis Darwin, 1887.*

Compare the very important letter of Huxley to Kingsley, on September 23, 1870, on the 'absolute justice of the system of things', 'the Ledger of the Almighty' and 'the gravitation of sin to sorrow' – a statement of causality in the moral and material worlds in many ways Buddhist. Note particularly the reference to Brahmanism, that the young scientists 'all regard orthodoxy as you' – Kingsley that is – 'do Brahmanism'. And remember Shaftesbury on the influence of Brahmanism in the Indian Mutiny. (See Hodder's Life.) *Also see* Life and Letters of T.H. Huxley *for an actual reference to Buddhism by Huxley.*

Huxley had just lost a child – but it is remarkable that this profession of faith, or statement of position as between orthodox religion and science, should come at this very moment. . . .

297 THE SPREAD OF EDUCATION c.1861

I met a woman in Fleet Street, who told me that she came into the streets now and then to get money not to subsist upon, but to supply her with funds to meet the debts her extravagance caused her to contract. But I will put her narrative into a consecutive form.

'Ever since I was twelve,' she said, 'I have worked in a printing office where a celebrated London morning journal is put in type and goes to press. I get enough money to live upon comfortably; but then I am extravagant, and spend a great deal more of money in eating and drinking more than you would imagine. My appetite is very delicate, and my constitution not at all strong. I long for certain things like a woman in the family way, and I must have them by hook or by crook. The fact is the close confinement and the night air upset me and disorder my digestion. I have the most expensive things sometimes, and when I can, I live in a sumptuous manner, comparatively speaking. I am attached to a man in our office, to whom I shall be married some day. He does not suspect me, but on the contrary believes me to be true to him, and you do not suppose that I ever take the trouble to undeceive him. I am nineteen now, and have carried on with my "typo" for nearly three years now. I sometimes go to the Haymarket, either early in the evening, or early in the morning, when I can get away from the printing; and sometimes I do a little in the day-time. This is not a frequent practice of mine; I only do it when I want money to pay anything. I am out now with the avowed intention of picking up a man, or making an appointment with some one for to-morrow or some time during the week. I always dress well, at least you mayn't think so, but I am always neat, and respectable, and clean, if the things I have on ain't worth the sight of money that some women's things cost them. I have good feet too, and as I find they attract attention, I always parade them. And I've hooked many a man by showing my ankle on a wet day. I shan't think anything of all this when I'm married. I believe my young man would marry me just as soon if he found out I went with others as he would now. I carry on with him now, and he likes me very much. I ain't of any particular family; to tell the truth, I was put in the work-house when I was young, and they apprenticed me. I never knew my father or my mother, although my father was, as I've heard say, a well-known swell of capers gay, who cut his last fling with great applause, or, if you must know, I heard that he was hung for killing a man who opposed him when committing a burglary. In other words, he was "a macing-cove what robs," and I'm his daughter, worse luck. I used to think at first, but what was the good of being wretched about it? I couldn't get over for some time, because I was envious, like a little fool, of other people, but I reasoned, and at last I did recover myself, and rather glad that my position freed me from certain restrictions. I had no mother whose heart I should break by my conduct, or no father who could threaten me with bringing his grey hairs with sorrow to the grave. I had a pretty good example to follow set before me, and I didn't scruple to argue that I was not to be blamed for what I did. Birth is the result of accident. It is the merest chance in the world whether you're born a countess or a washerwoman – I'm neither one nor t'other; I'm only a mot who does a little typographing by way of variety. Those who have had good nursing, and all that, and the advantages of a sound education, who have a position to lose, prospects to blight, and relations to dishonour, may be blamed for going on the loose, but I'll be hanged if I think that priest or moralist is to come down on me with the sledge-hammer of their denunciation. You look rather surprised at my talking so well. I know I talk well, but you must remember what a lot has passed through my hands for the last seven years, and what a lot of copy I've set up. There is very little I don't know, I can tell you. It's what old Robert Owen would call the spread of education.'

From the 'extra volume', published in 1862, of Mayhew's London Labour and the London Poor, *this section being written by Bracebridge Hemyng.*

'I'm only a mot who does a little typography by way of variety.' According to the OED, 'mot' is a variant of 'mort', meaning a loose woman or harlot.

298   ODE SUNG AT THE OPENING   January 1862
OF THE INTERNATIONAL EXHIBITION

I

Uplift a thousand voices full and sweet,
  In this wide hall with earth's invention stored,
  And praise the invisible universal Lord,
Who lets once more in peace the nations meet,
  Where Science, Art, and Labour have outpour'd
Their myriad horns of plenty at our feet.

II

O silent father of our Kings to be,
Mourn'd in this golden hour of jubilee,
For this, for all, we weep our thanks to thee!

III

The world-compelling plan was thine, –
And, lo! the long laborious miles
Of Palace; lo! the giant aisles,
Rich in model and design;
Harvest-tool and husbandry,
Loom and wheel and enginery,
Secrets of the sullen mine,
Steel and gold, and corn and wine,
Fabric rough, or fairy-fine,
Sunny tokens of the Line,
Polar marvels, and a feast
Of wonder out of West and East,
And shapes and hues of Art divine!

All of beauty, all of use,
That one fair planet can produce,
   Brought from under every star,
Blown from over every main,
And mixt, as life is mixt with pain,
   The works of peace with works of war.

IV

Is the goal so far away?
Far, how far no tongue can say,
Let us dream our dream to-day.

V

O ye, the wise who think, the wise who reign,
From growing commerce loose her latest chain,
And let the fair white-wing'd peacemaker fly
To happy havens under all the sky,
And mix the seasons and the golden hours;
Till each man find his own in all men's good,
And all men work in noble brotherhood,
Breaking their mailed fleets and armed towers,
And ruling by obeying Nature's powers,
And gathering all the fruits of earth and crown'd
   with all her flowers.

By Alfred, Lord Tennyson, Poet Laureate, published in daily papers and accurate text in Fraser's Magazine, *June 1862.*

From the 'Memoranda' of W.M. Rossetti (published in Ruskin: Rossetti and Pre-Raphaelitism *by W.M. Rossetti, 1899) it is clear that Tennyson's Ode was written before January 29 as on that date Rossetti notes: 'Tennyson's Great Exhibition poem and Albert Dedication in MS. Former not up to the mark. . . .'*

I do not propose to comment on the literary qualities of this poem – only to remind the reader that at the very time when it was written there was a Civil War raging in America, widespread famine in India and consequently frightful unemployment and starvation in Lancashire. The last feudal relations of man and man have been severed and so the poet laureate can 'dream' of peace and brotherhood.

299   THE LOWER PTHAH   1862

I

Lecturer   But listen a moment yet, for that was not quite all my dream. The twilight drew swiftly to the dark, and I could hardly see the great pyramid;

when there came a heavy murmuring sound in the air; and a horned beetle, with terrible claws, fell on the ground at my feet, with a blow like the beat of a hammer. Then it stood up on its hind claws, and waved its pincers at me; and its four claws became strong arms, and hands; one grasping real iron pincers, and the other a huge hammer; and it had a helmet on its head, without any eyelet holes, that I could see. And its two hind claws became strong crooked legs, with feet bent inwards. And so there stood by me a dwarf, in glossy black armour, ribbed and embossed like a beetle's back, leaning on his hammer. And I could not speak for wonder; but he spoke with a murmur like the dying away of a beat upon a bell. He said, 'I will make Neith's great pyramid small. I am the lower Pthah; and have power over fire. I can wither the strong things, and strengthen the weak; and everything that is great I can make small, and everything that is little I can make great'. Then he turned to the angle of the pyramid and limped towards it. And the pyramid grew deep purple; and then red like fire. And I saw that it glowed with fire from within. And the lower Pthah touched it with the hand that held the pincers; and it sank down like the sand in an hour-glass, – then drew itself together, and sank, still, and became nothing it seemed to me; but the armed dwarf stooped down, and took it into his hand, and brought it to me, saying, 'Everything that is great I can make like this pyramid: and give into men's hands to destroy.' And I saw that he had a little pyramid in his hand, with as many courses in it as the large one; and built like that, – only so small. And because it glowed still, I was afraid to touch it; but Pthah said, 'Touch it – for I have bound the fire within it, so that it cannot burn.' So I touched it and took it into my own hand; and it was cold; only red, like a ruby. And Pthah laughed, and became like a beetle again, and buried himself in the sand, fiercely, throwing it back over his shoulders. And it seemed to me as if he would draw me with him into the sand; and I started back, and woke, holding the little pyramid so fast in my hand that it hurt me.

Egypt   Holding WHAT in your hand?
Lecturer   The little pyramid.
Egypt   Neith's pyramid?
Lecturer   Neith's, I believe; though not built for Asychis. I know only that it is a little rosy transparent pyramid, built of more courses of bricks than I can count, it being made so small. You don't believe me, of course, Egyptian infidel; but there it is. (*Giving crystal of* rose Fluor.)

II

Lecturer   But, Egypt, why did you tell me you disliked sewing so?
Egypt   Did I not show you how the thread cuts my fingers? and I always get cramp, somehow, in my neck, if I sew long.
Lecturer   Well, I suppose the Egyptian queens thought everybody got cramp in their neck, if they sewed long; and that thread always cut people's

fingers. At all events, every kind of manual labour was despised both by them, and the Greeks; and, while they owned the real good and fruit of it, they yet held it a degradation to all who practised it. Also, knowing the laws of life thoroughly, they perceived that the special practice necessary to bring any manual art to perfection strengthened the body distortedly; one member gaining at the expense of the rest. They especially dreaded and despised any kind of work that had to be done near fire: yet, feeling what they owed to it in metal-work, as the basis of all other work, they expressed this mixed reverence and scorn in the varied types of the lame Hephaestus, and the lower Pthah.

Sibyl But what did you mean by making him say, 'Everything great I can make small, and everything small great'?

Lecturer I had my own separate meaning in that. We have seen in modern times the power of the lower Pthah developed in a separate way, which no Greek or Egyptian could have conceived. It is the character of pure and eyeless manual labour to conceive everything as subjected to it: and in reality, to disgrace and diminish all that is so subjected; aggrandising itself, and the thought of itself, at the expense of all noble things. I heard an orator, and a good one too, at the Working Men's College, the other day, make a great point in a description of our railroads; saying, with grandly conducted emphasis, 'They have made men greater, and the world less.' His working audience were mightily pleased; they thought it so very fine a thing to be made bigger themselves, and all the rest of the world less. I should have enjoyed asking them (but it would have been a pity – they were so pleased), how much less they would like to have the world made; – and whether, at present, those of them really felt themselves the bigger men, who lived in the least houses.

Sibyl But then, why did you make Pthah say that he could make weak things strong, and small things great?

Lecturer My dear, he is a boaster and self-asserter, by nature; but it is so far true. For instance, we used to have a fair in our neighbourhood – a very fine fair we thought it. You never saw such an one; but if you look at the engraving of Turner's 'St. Catherine's Hill', you will see what it was like. There were curious booths, carried on poles; and peep-shows; and music, with plenty of drums and cymbals; and much barley-sugar and gingerbread, and the like; and in the alleys of this fair the London populace would enjoy themselves, after their fashion, very thoroughly. Well, the little Pthah set to work upon it one day; he made the wooden poles into iron ones, and put them across, like his own crooked legs, so that you always fall over them if you don't look where you are going; and he turned all the canvas into panes of glass, and put it up on his iron cross-poles; and made all the little booths into one great booth; – and people said it was very fine, and a new style of architecture; and Mr Dickens said nothing was ever like it in Fairy-land, which was very true. And then the little Pthah set to work to put fine fairings in it; and he painted the Nineveh bulls afresh, with the blackest eyes he could paint (because he had none himself), and he got the angels down from Lincoln choir, and gilded their wings like his gingerbread of old times; and he sent for everything else he could think of, and put it in his booth. There are the casts of Niobe and her children; and the Chimpanzee; and the wooden Caffres and New-Zealanders; and the Shakespeare House; and Le Grand Blondin, and Le Petit Blondin; and Handel; and Mozart; and no end of shops and buns, and beer; and all the little-Pthah-worshippers say, never was anything so sublime!

From The Ethics of the Dust, *Ten Lectures to Little Housewives on the Elements of Crystallisation, by John Ruskin, 1866.*

I do not know if anyone has noticed the remarkable passage quoted in Galton's Inquiries into Human Faculty *(1883), on a vision of roses obliterated by a cloud of sparks. On the fading of the vision, compare of course Wordsworth's* Immortality Ode. *But the really interesting thing is that both the roses and the sparks correspond to obsessions of Ruskin, as Wilenski pointed out. Roughly speaking, the rose images in Ruskin are connected with Rose de la Touche and the spark images with Whistler and I believe Faraday: at any rate, he is said to have detested Cremorne Lights. On the other hand, compare the famous firefly passage at the end of* Praeterita *(dated June 19, 1889). The real question however is whether all this is pure coincidence or whether the rose-and-sparks visions described in Galton are at all common, that is, derive in any way from a Jungian mass-unconscious (or have some other general origin) and if so whether Ruskin himself might not have had such visions, or known about them, and then connected Rose de la Touche and Cremorne Lights and so on with the visions (rather than the other way round) as he was in the habit of doing in all his thought and writing.*

300 THE QUESTION OF QUESTIONS 1862

The question of questions for mankind – the problem which underlies all others, and is more deeply interesting than any other – is the ascertainment of the place which Man occupies in nature and of his relations to the universe of things. Whence our race has come; what are the limits of our power over nature, and of nature's power over us; to what goal we are tending; are the problems which present themselves anew and with undiminished interest to every man born into the world. Most of us, shrinking from the difficulties and dangers which beset the seeker after original answers to these riddles, are contented to ignore them altogether or to smother the investigating spirit under the feather-bed of respected and respectable tradition. But, in every age, one or two restless spirits, blessed with that constructive genius, which can only build on a secure foundation, or cursed with the spirit of mere scepticism, are unable to follow in the well-worn and comfortable track of their forefathers and contemporaries, and unmindful of thorns and stumbling-blocks, strike out paths of their own. The sceptics end in the infidelity which asserts the problem to be insoluble, or in the atheism which denies the existence of any orderly progress and governance of things: the men of genius propound solutions which grow into systems of Theology or of Philosophy, or veiled in musical language which suggests more than it asserts, take *the shape of the Poetry of an Epoch.*

From 'On the Relations of Man to the Lower Animals', by T.H. Huxley, a lecture of 1860 rewritten in 1862, and published in Man's Place in Nature *in 1863.*

301   BODY AND SOUL   April 21, 1862

We can also form a rough estimate of the efficiency of a man as a mere machine, and find that neither a perfect heat engine nor an electric engine could produce so much work and waste so little in heat. We therefore save our pains in investigating any theories of animal power based on heat and electricity. We also see that the soul is not the direct moving force of the body. If it were, it would only last till it had done a certain amount of work, like the spring of a watch, which works till it is run down. The soul is not the mere mover. Food is the mover, and perishes in the using, which the soul does not. There is action and reaction between body and soul, but it is not of a kind in which energy passes from the one to the other, – as when a man pulls a trigger it is the gunpowder that projects the bullet, or when a pointsman shunts a train it is the rails that bear the thrust. But the constitution of our nature is not explained by finding out what it is not. It is well that it will go, and that we remain in possession, though we do not understand it.

From a letter of James Clerk-Maxwell to Lewis Campbell, printed in The Life of James Clerk-Maxwell *by L. Campbell and W. Garnett, 1882.*

302   TRAVELS IN THE AIR   September 5, 1862

This ascent had been delayed owing to the unfavourable state of the weather. We left the earth at 1h.3m. p.m.; the temperature of the air was 59°, and that of the dew-point 50°. The air at first was misty; at the height of 5,000 feet the temperature was 41°, dew-point 37°.9. At 1h.13m. we entered a dense cloud of about 1,000 feet in thickness, where the temperature fell to 36°.5, the dew-point being the same, thus indicating that the air here was saturated with moisture. At this elevation the report of a gun was heard. Momentarily the clouds became lighter, and on emerging from them at

1h.17m. a flood of strong sunlight burst upon us with a beautiful blue sky without a cloud, and beneath us lay a magnificent sea of clouds, its surface varied with endless hills, hillocks, and mountain chains, and with many snow-white tufts rising from it. I here attempted to take a view with a camera, but we were rising with too great rapidity and revolving too quickly to enable me to succeed. The brightness of the clouds, however, was so great that I should have needed but a momentary exposure, Dr. Hill Norris having kindly furnished me with extremely sensitive dry plates for the purpose. We reached the height of two miles at 1h.22m., where the sky was of a darker blue, and whence the earth was visible in occasional patches beneath the clouds. The temperature had fallen to the freezing-point and the dew-point to 26°.

The height of three miles was attained at 1h.28m, with a temperature of 18°, and the dew-point 13°; from 1h.22m. to 1h.30m. the wet-bulb thermometer read incorrectly, the ice not being properly formed on it. At 1h.34m. Mr. Coxwell was panting for breath; at 1h.38m. the mercury of Daniell's hygrometer fell below the limits of the scale. We reached the elevation of four miles at 1h.40m.; the temperature was 8°, the dew-point minus 15° or 47° below the freezing-point of water. Discharging sand, we attained in ten minutes the altitude of five miles, and the temperature had passed below zero, and then read minus 2°. At this point no dew was observed on Regnault's hygrometer.

Up to this time I had taken observations with comfort, and experienced no difficulty in breathing, while Mr. Coxwell, in consequence of the exertions he had to make, had breathed with difficulty for some time. Having discharged sand, we ascended still higher; the aspirator became troublesome to work, and I also found a difficulty in seeing clearly. At 1h.51m. the barometer read 10.8in. About 1h.52m. or later, I read the dry-bulb thermometer as minus 5°; after this I could not see the column of mercury in the wet-bulb thermometer, nor the hands of the watch, nor the fine divisions on any instrument. I asked Mr. Coxwell to help me to read the instruments. In consequence, however, of the rotatory motion of the balloon, which had continued without ceasing since leaving the earth, the valve-line had become entangled, and he had to leave the car and mount into the ring to readjust it. I then looked at the barometer and found its reading to be 9¾in., still decreasing fast, implying a height exceeding 29,000 feet. Shortly after I laid my hand upon the table, possessed of its full vigour, but on being desirous of using it found it powerless – it must have lost its power momentarily; trying to move the other arm, I found it powerless also. Then I tried to shake myself, and succeeded, but I seemed to have no limbs. In looking at the barometer my head fell over my left shoulder; I struggled and shook myself, my body, again, but could not move my arms. Getting my head upright for an instant only, it fell backwards, my back resting against the side of the car, and my head on its edge. In this position my eyes were directed to Mr. Coxwell in the ring. When I shook my body I seemed to have full power over my muscles of the back, and considerably so over those of the neck, but none over either my arms or my legs. As in the case of the arms, so all muscular power was lost in an instant from my back and neck. I dimly saw Mr. Coxwell, and endeavoured to speak, but could not. In an instant intense darkness overcame me, so that the optic nerve suddenly lost power, but I was still conscious, with as active a brain as at the present moment whilst writing this. I thought I had been seized with asphyxia, and believed I should experience nothing more, as death would come unless we speedily descended. Other thoughts were entering my mind, when I suddenly became unconscious as on going to sleep.

From Travels in the Air *by James Glaisher, 1871.*

Here again is the human being partaking in an experiment (compare later, gas chambers, the Curies, Captain Scott), the human being as a recording instrument. And then the instrument affected by the conditions it is trying to record.

Note that this is exactly what happens, has always happened, to the artist. He makes a subjective ascent to 37,000 feet and endeavours to record his feelings. 'Emotion recollected in tranquillity' – how well it fits Glaisher's account. And compare 'we are laid asleep and become a living soul . . . see into the heart of things'. All this is something like the relation of art to Yoga and similar practices, but taking place now on a material, objective level. 'Realistic' reporting appears to supersede 'artistic' reporting but in fact realism becomes art. This is the identification of subject and object on a new plane.

303   THE UNEMPLOYED   1862

A little past noon, on Friday, I set out to visit the great stone quarries on the southern edge of the town, where upwards of six hundred of the more robust factory operatives are employed in the lighter work of the quarries. This labour consists principally of breaking up the small stone found in the facings of the solid rock, for the purpose of road-mending and the like. Some, also, are employed in agricultural work, on the ground belonging to the fine new workhouse there. These factory operatives, at the workhouse grounds, and in the quarries, are paid one shilling a day – not much, but much better than the bread of idleness; and for the most part, the men like it better, I am told. The first quarry I walked into was the one known by the name of 'Hacking's Shorrock Delph'. There I sauntered about, looking at the scene. It was not difficult to distinguish the trained quarry men from the rest. The latter did not seem to be working very hard at their new employment, and it can hardly be expected that they should, considering the great difference between it and their usual labour. Leaning on their spades and hammers, they watched me with a natural curiosity, as if wondering if I was a new ganger, or a contractor come to buy stone. There were men of all ages among them, from about eighteen years old to white-headed men of past sixty. Most of them looked healthy and a little embrowned by recent exposure to the weather; and here and there was a pinched face which told its own tale. I got into talk with a quiet, hardy-looking man, dressed in soil-stained corduroy. He was a kind of over-looker. He told me that there were from eighty to ninety factory hands employed in that quarry. 'But,' said he, 'it varies a bit, yo known. Some on 'em gets knocked up neaw an' then, an' they han a-whoam a day or two; an' some on 'em connot ston gettin' weet through – it mays 'em ill; an' here an' theer one turns up at doesn't like the job at o' – they'd rather clem. There is at's both willin' an' able; thoose are likely to get a better job, somewheer. There's othersome at's willin' enough, but connot ston th' racket. They dun middlin', tak 'em one wi' another, an' considerin' that they're noan use't to th' wark. Th' hommer fo's leet wi' 'em; but we dunnot like to push 'em so mich, yo known – for what's a shillin' a day? Aw know some odds un i' this delph at never tastes fro mornin' till they'n done at neet, – an' says nought abeawt it, noather. But they'n families. Beside, fro wake lads, sich as yon, at's bin train't to nought but leet wark, an' a warm place to worth in, what con yo expect? We'n had a deeal o' bother wi' 'em abeawt bein' paid for weet days at th' furst; an' they geet it into their yeds at Shorrock were to blame. Shorrock's th' paymaister, under th' Guardians. But, then, he nobbut went accordin' to orders, yo known. At last, th' Board sattle't that they mut be paid for weet and dry, – an' there's bin quietness sin'. They wortchen fro eight till five; an' sometimes, when they'n done, they drill'n o'together i'th road yon – just like sodiurs – an' then they walken away i' procession.'

Written by Edwin Waugh, and published in The Manchester Examiner and Times, *1862, and later in* Home-Life of the Lancashire Factory Folk during the Cotton Famine, *1867.*

This passage – which I quote in direct opposition to the Poet Laureate's Ode (299) – was written by a middle-class journalist simply as a newspaper story. Whether journalism had improved in 150 years the reader may decide by looking back to Defoe (33). Whether the treatment of the unemployed has improved since he may decide by referring to Wal Hannington, The Problem of Unemployment, *where he will find photographs as well as descriptions of stone-breaking in the 1930s, with overseers whose features are themselves evidence of the heightening of the class struggle. To the patronising tones both of reporter and overseer I hope I do not have to draw the reader's attention, but it is worth considering seriously the Fascist drilling of the unemployed referred to at the end, mixing, as Tennyson says,* The works of peace with the works of war.

304   A VERY UNUSUAL THING   November 4, 1862

I went into the city today, to put the £125 I got for the 'Book of Nonsense' into the funds. It is doubtless a very unusual thing for an artist to put by money, for the whole way from Temple Bar to the Bank was *crowded* with carriages and people, – so immense a sensation did this occurrence make. And all the way back it was the same, which was very gratifying.

From a letter of Edward Lear to Lady Waldegrave, printed in Letters of Edward Lear, *edited by Lady Strachey, 1907.*

See also the letters of May 7 where he (from Corfu) has given £5 for the Lancashire poor spinners; and of February 16, where he inquires if The Book of Nonsense *is on all Railway Bookstalls. Compare Shelley's letter to his publisher from Leghorn (note on 154).*

305   GOOD AND EVIL   1863

Notwithstanding the losses and suffering occasioned by strikes, Mr Nasmyth holds the opinion that they have on the whole produced much more good than evil. They have served to stimulate invention in an extraordinary degree. Some of the most important labour-saving processes now in common use are directly traceable to them. In the case of many of our most potent self-acting tools and machines, manufacturers could not be induced to adopt them until compelled to do so by strikes. This was the case with the self-acting mule, the wool-combing machine, the planing machine, the slotting machine, Nasmyth's steam arm, and many others. Thus even in the mechanical world, there may be 'a soul of goodness in things evil'.

   Mr Nasmyth retired from business in December, 1856. He had the moral courage to come out of the groove which he had so laboriously made for himself, and to leave a large and prosperous business, saying, 'I have now enough of this world's goods; let younger men have their chance.' He settled down at his rural retreat in Kent, but not to lead a life of idle ease. Industry had become his habit, and active occupation was necessary to his happiness. He fell back upon the cultivation of those artistic tastes which are the heritage of his family. When a boy at the High School of Edinburgh, he was so skilful in making pen and ink illustrations on the margins of the classics, that he thus often purchased from his monitors exemption from the lessons of the day. Nor had he ceased to cultivate the art during his residence at Patricroft, but was accustomed to fall back upon it for relaxation and enjoyment amid the exploits of trade. That he possesses remarkable fertility of imagination, and great skill in architectural and landscape drawing, as well as in the much more difficult art of delineating the human figure, will be obvious to anyone who has seen his works, – more particularly his 'City of St Ann's', 'The Fairies', and 'Everybody for ever!'

which last was exhibited in Pall Mall, among the recent works of Art by amateurs and others, for the relief of the Lancashire distress.
From Industrial Biography *by Samuel Smiles, 1863.*

Note on 299, 304 and 306. *The Chinese philosopher Chung-Tzu has the saying 'When justice goes out benevolence comes in'. Nasmyth escapes from strike-breaking into the dream-world of 'Everybody for ever' and benevolently exhibits works of art for the relief of the people his system has put out of work. Poetry in Tennyson's Ode (298), journalism in the account of the unemployed (303) and, in this passage, Nasmyth's painting are all seen prostituting themselves to cover the nakedness of oppression.*

306 SCREAMY GANDERS March 15, 1863

A broader creed, – a better form of worship – the cessation of nonsense and curses – and the recognition of a new state of matters brought about by centuries, science, destiny or what not – will assuredly be demanded and come to pass whether Bishops and priests welcome the changes or resist them. Not those who believe that God the Creator is greater than a Book, and that millions unborn are to look up to higher thoughts than those stereotyped by ancient legends, gross ignorance, and hideous bigotry – not those are the Infidels – but these same screamy ganders of the church, who put darkness forward and insist that it is light.

From a letter of Edward Lear to Lady Waldegrave, printed in Letters of Edward Lear, *edited by Lady Strachey, 1907.*

Lear is referring to the battle which developed over the unorthodox views of John William Colenso, bishop of Natal.

307 THE GREAT GULF April 30, 1863

Whether astronomy and geology can or cannot be made to agree with the statements as to the matters of fact laid down in Genesis – whether the Gospels are historically true or not – are matters of comparatively small moment in the face of the impassable gulf between the anthropomorphism (however refined) of theology and the passionless impersonality of the unknown and unknowable which science shows everywhere underlying the thin veil of phenomena.

Here seems to me to be the great gulf fixed between science and theology – beside which all Colenso controversies, reconcilements of Scripture *à la* Pye Smith, etc., cut a very thin figure.

You must have thought over all this long ago; but steeped as I am in scientific thought from morning to night, the contrast has perhaps a greater vividness to me. I go into society, and except among two or three of my scientific colleagues I find myself alone on these subjects, and as hopelessly at variance with the majority of my fellow-men as they would be with their neighbours if they were set down among the Ashantees. I don't like this state of things for myself – least of all do I see how it will work out for my children. But as my mind is constituted, there is no way out of it, and I can only envy you if you can see things differently.

From a letter of T.H. Huxley to Charles Kingsley, printed in Life and Letters of Thomas Henry Huxley, *edited by Leonard Huxley, 1900.*

308   TO HIS NIECE IN HIS OLD AGE   October 1, 1863

So we turn the times over. Here is the first of a new month, and a new season is coming over us, for the rain falls, the winds blow, and the sun shines with a strength and in an order, or rather disorder, that reminds me of an old man, who, purposing to do one thing is drawn off to do another, who, intending to communicate with you, is led away to chat with another girl, and forgets you. However, she is gone. I forget what the thought was like; its end is confusion, and so I come to wakefulness and life again.

From a letter of Michael Faraday to Miss Reid, printed in The Life and Letters of Faraday *by Bence Jones, 1870.*

Compare of course the celebrated 1820 letter to Sarah (157), but also Anima Poetae, *where Coleridge gives a detailed description of the mechanism of this kind of writing, feeling, forgetting and so on....*

309   OVER LONDON   October 9, 1863

Always, however great the height of the balloon, when I have seen the horizon it has roughly appeared to be on the level of the car – though of course the dip of the horizon is a very appreciable quantity – or the same height as the eye. From this one might infer that, could the earth be seen without a cloud or anything to obscure it, and the boundary line of the plane approximately the same height as the eye, the general appearance would be that of a slight concavity; but I have never seen any part of the surface of the earth other than as a plane. Towns and cities, when viewed from the balloon are like models in motion. I shall always remember the ascent of 9th October, 1863, when we passed over London about sunset. At the time when we were 7,000 feet high, and directly over London Bridge, the scene around was one that cannot probably be equalled in the world. We were still so low as not to have lost sight of the details of the spectacle which presented itself to our eyes; and with one glance the homes of 3,000,000 people could be seen, and so distinct was the view, that every large building was easily distinguishable. In fact, the whole of London was

THE SUBURBS OF LONDON IN THE DISTANCE

visible, and some parts most clearly. All round, the suburbs were also very distinct, with their lines of detached villas, imbedded as it were in a mass of shrubs; beyond, the country was like a garden, its fields, well marked, becoming smaller and smaller as the eye wandered farther and farther away. Again looking down, there was the Thames, throughout its whole length, without the slightest mist, dotted over its winding course with innumerable ships and steamboats, like moving toys. Gravesend was visible, also the mouth of the Thames, and the coast around as far as Norfolk. The southern shore of the mouth of the Thames was not so clear, but the sea beyond was seen for many miles; when at a higher elevation, I looked for the coast of France, but was unable to see it. On looking round, the eye was arrested by the garden-like appearance of the county of Kent, till again London claimed yet more careful attention.

Smoke, thin and blue, was curling from it, and slowly moving away in beautiful curves, from all except one part, south of the Thames, where it was less blue and seemed more dense, till the cause became evident; it was mixed with mist rising from the ground, the southern limit of which was bounded by an even line, doubtless indicating the meeting of the subsoils of gravel and clay. The whole scene was surmounted by a canopy of blue, everywhere free from cloud, except near the horizon, where a band of cumulus and stratus extended all round, forming a fitting boundary to such a glorious view.

As seen from the earth, the sunset this evening was described as fine, the air being clear and the shadows well defined; but, as we rose to view it and its effects, the golden hues increased in intensity; their richness decreased as the distance from the sun increased, both right and left; but still as far as 90° from the sun, rose-coloured clouds extended. The remainder of the circle was completed, for the most part, by pure white cumulus of well-rounded and symmetrical forms.

I have seen London by night. I have crossed it during the day at the height of four miles. I have often admired the splendour of sky scenery, but never have I seen anything which surpassed this spectacle. The roar of the town heard at this elevation was a deep, rich, continuous sound – the voice of labour. At four miles above London, all was hushed; no sound reached our ears.

From Travels in the Air *by James Glaisher, 1871.*

310   HERSCHEL AND NASMYTH   Summer 1864

We had a great set-to one day in blowing iridescent bubbles from a mixture of soap and glycerine. Some of the bubbles were of about fifteen inches in diameter. By carefully covering them with a bell glass, we kept them for about thirty-six hours, while they went through their changes of brilliant colour, ending in deep blue. I contrived this method of preserving them by placing a dish of water below, within the bell glass, by means of which the dampness of the air prevented evaporation of the bubble. This dodge of mine vastly delighted Sir John, as it allowed him to watch the exquisite series of iridescent tints at his tranquil leisure.

I had also the pleasure of showing him my experiment of cracking a glass globe filled with water and hermetically sealed. The water was then slightly expanded, on which the glass cracked. This was my method of explaining the nature of the action which, at some previous period of the cosmical history of the Moon, had produced those bright radiating lines that diverge from the lunar volcanic craters. Sir John expressed his delight at witnessing my practical illustration of this hitherto unexplained subject, and he considered it quite conclusive. I also produced my enlarged drawings of the Moon's surface, which I had made at the side of my telescope. These greatly pleased him, and he earnestly urged me to publish them, accompanied with a descriptive account of the conclusions I had arrived at. I then determined to proceed with the preparations which I had already made for my long contemplated work.

Among the many things that I showed Sir John while at Hammerfield, was a piece of white calico on which I had got printed one million spots. This was for the purpose of exhibiting one million in visible form. In astronomical subjects a million is a sort of unit, and it occurred to me to show what a million really is. Sir John was delighted and astonished at the sight. He went carefully over the outstretched piece with his rule, measured its length and breadth, and verified its correctness.

From James Nasmyth, Engineer, an Autobiography, *edited by Samuel Smiles, 1885.*

311 ETERNAL JUSTICE c.1864

I had at this time (about 1864) occasion to go to Birmingham on business, and had left Euston at 9 p.m. I was quietly reading my newspaper in the snug corner of a first-class compartment, containing only two other occupants beside myself. These were two young gentlemen, who appeared much elated at some success, or contemplated success – it might be a race, a Stock Exchange bargain, or any other matter of ordinary interest. Being quite young men they were naturally very enthusiastic, and somewhat loud in their conversation, which rather disturbed my reading. After some remarks by one of them, the other exclaimed, in a very loud tone, 'I wonder what the devil Bessemer will say?' There could be no mistake as to this plain reference to me, since, with the exception of the members of my family, I alone answered to that name. It then occurred to me for the first time that all this excited language and jubilation had some reference to me; I had not the remotest idea as to what had been previously said, or to what it referred. By this time we had reached Watford, and as the train went on I kept my paper before me, but could not prevent my attention being directed to the lively sallies of these young men. Little by little, I became conscious that the exciting cause of this boisterous hilarity was some new joint-stock company that was to be floated in two or three days. It might be a gas company, a brewery, or anything else, for up to this point I had no indication of its nature, and only wondered why they should question as to how Bessemer would receive the news. But one at a time words were dropped that startled me not a little, and riveted my attention to their conversation, which was very much veiled, as though the scheme, whatever it might be, were to be kept a profound secret at present from the outer world. But here and there some casual word or two was dropped, about mines and works, about a journey up from Wales, and what David Chadwick had said about all the shares being taken up in two days for certain. Thus I soon began to grasp the meaning of the fragments I had heard, and to fit these disjointed sentences together; but there was no absolute certainty that I had guessed the true meaning.

We had by this time arrived at Leighton, and my fellow-travellers got out, as I supposed, to take some refreshment, but the train went on without them, and I was left alone to think over this curious incident. Then I remembered that Mr Joseph Robinson, the manager of the Ebbw Vale Company's London offices, lived at Leighton. These young men might probably be his sons; and this formed another startling confirmation of the theory I had arrived at, viz., that the Ebbw Vale Iron Works were going, in a few days, to be formed into a joint-stock company, to take over the works and mines and the other property of the present owners, and that Mr David Chadwick, whose name I distinctly heard, was the financial agent employed to form the company. I was not long in realising all that this meant to me, and I saw that it was necessary to take immediate steps to protect myself. Hence I became very impatient to arrive at the next station, which was Blisworth, and there I got out. It was now about 11 p.m., and the next up train was nearly due. I had by this time worked myself into a considerable state of excitement, and paced the station platform so rapidly as to attract the attention of the station-master, who asked me if anything were wrong, or if he could do anything for me. I said, 'No; I have heard some news on my way down which renders my immediate return to London advisable.' The up train soon arrived, and conveyed me back to Euston. I took a cab to Denmark Hill, where I arrived about 2 a.m., and somewhat alarmed my wife by my return home at such an unseemly hour. Sleep did not come readily that night, my mind was too much disturbed; but in the quiet hours of the early morning I calmly reviewed the whole situation, and rehearsed every detail of the plan of campaign. Then I got a couple of hours' sleep, and by the time breakfast was over I felt sufficiently refreshed, and fully nerved, to carry out the plan which, after renewed consideration, I had determined to follow. I now fully realised the disadvantageous position I should be placed in if this company, with a couple of millions capital, was formed and I was left to fight them single-handed. Even now, after the lapse of so many years, this marvellous revelation, coming as it did at the precise moment necessary to be effective, seems more like an act of eternal justice than one of the ordinary affairs of life.

From the Autobiography of Sir Henry Bessemer, *written about 1896, published 1905.*

Justice having been abolished (see note on 305) the word itself is invoked (in the last sentence of this passage) to sanctify the petty spying of Mr Bessemer. Worth for a moment comparing this episode with the adventures of Sherlock Holmes: the first-class carriage, the overheard fragments, links in the chain of evidence, the mixture of thought and action.

312   THE LITTLE GARRET AT HEATHFIELD   1865

Some months since, we visited the little garret at Heathfield in which Watt pursued the investigations of his later years. The room had been carefully locked up since his death, and had only once been swept out. Everything lay very much as he left it. The piece of iron he was last employed in turning lay on the lathe. The ashes of the last fire were in the grate, the last bit of coal was in the scuttle. The Dutch oven was in its place over the stove, and the frying-pan in which he cooked his meal was hanging by its accustomed nail. Many objects lay about or in the drawers, indicating the pursuits which had been interrupted by death, – busts, medallions, and figures, waiting to be copied by the sculpture-machine, – many medallion moulds, a store of plaster of Paris, and a box of plaster casts from London, the contents of which do not seem to have been disturbed. Here are Watt's ladles for melting lead, his foot-rule, his glue-pot, his hammer. Reflecting mirrors, an extemporised camera with the lenses mounted on pasteboard, and many camera-glasses laid about indicate interrupted experiments in optics. There are quadrant-glasses, compasses, scales, weights, and sundry boxes of mathematical instruments, once doubtless highly prized. In one place a model of the governor, in another of the parallel motion, and in a little box, fitted with wooden cylinders mounted with paper and covered with figures, is what we suppose to be a model of his proposed calculating machine. On the shelves are minerals and chemicals in pots and jars, on which the dust of nearly half a century has settled. The moist substances have long since dried up, the putty has been turned to stone, and the paste to dust. On one shelf we come upon a dish in which lies a withered bunch of grapes. On the floor, in a corner, near to where Watt sat and worked, is a hair-trunk – a touching memorial of a long past love and a long dead sorrow. It contains all poor

WATT'S GARRET AT HEATHFIELD

Gregory's school-books, – his first attempts at writing, his boy's drawings of battles, his first school exercises down to his College themes, his delectuses, his grammars, his dictionaries, and his class books – brought into this retired room, where his father's eye could rest upon them. Near at hand is the sculpture-machine, on which he continued working to the last. Its wooden framing is worm-eaten and dropping into dust, like the hands which made it. But though the great workman has gone to rest, with all his griefs and cares, and his handiwork is fast crumbling to decay, the spirit of his work, the thought which he put into his inventions, still survives, and will probably continue to influence the destinies of his race for all time to come.

From The Lives of Boulton and Watt *by Samuel Smiles, 1865.*

313   **THE TENTH MUSE**   February 1865

Here is one, for instance, lying at the base of all the rest – namely, what may be the real dignity of mechanical Art itself? I cannot express the amazed awe, the crushed humility, with which I sometimes watch a locomotive take its breath at a railway station, and think what work there is in its bars and wheels, and what manner of men they must be who dig brown iron-stone out of the ground, and forge it into THAT! What assemblage of accurate and mighty faculties in them; more than fleshly power over melting crag and coiling fire, fettered, and finessed at last into the precision of watchmaking; Titanian hammer-strokes beating, out of lava, these glittering cylinders and timely-respondent valves, and fine ribbed rods, which touch each other as a serpent writhes, in noiseless gliding, and omnipotence of grasp; infinitely complex anatomy of active steel, compared with which the skeleton of a living creature would seem, to a careless observer, clumsy and vile – a mere morbid secretion and phosphatous prop of flesh! What would the men who thought out this – who beat it out, who touched it into its polished calm of power, who set it to its appointed task, and triumphantly saw it fulfil this task to the utmost of their will – feel or think about this weak hand of mine, timidly leading a little stain of water-colour, which I cannot manage, into an imperfect shadow of something else – mere failure in every motion, and endless disappointment; what, I repeat, would these Iron-dominant Genii think of me? and what ought I to think of them?

From The Cestus of Aglaia, *Chapter 1, by John Ruskin, first printed in the* Art Journal, *February 1865, reprinted in* On the Old Road, Vol.1: Art, *1885.*

314   **THE HUMAN ELEMENT**   June 1865

It was a lovely Autumn evening, and the glorious effects of chromatic aberration were beginning to show themselves in the atmosphere as the earth revolved away from the great western luminary, when two lines might have been observed wending their weary way across a plane superficies. The elder of the two had by long practice acquired the art, so painful to young and impulsive loci, of lying evenly between his extreme points; but the younger, in her girlish impetuosity, was ever longing to diverge and become a hyperbola or some such romantic and boundless curve. They had lived and loved: fate and the intervening superficies had hitherto kept them asunder, but this was no longer to be: a line had intersected them, making the two interior angles together less than two right angles. It was a moment never to be forgotten, and, as they journeyed on, a whisper thrilled along the superficies in isochronous waves of sound, 'Yes! We shall at length meet if continually produced!' (Jacobi's Course of Mathematics, Chap. I.)

We have commenced with the above quotation as a striking illustration of the advantage of introducing the human element into the hitherto barren region of Mathematics. Who shall say what germs of romance, hitherto unobserved, may not underlie the subject? Who can tell whether the parallelogram, which in our ignorance we have defined and drawn, and the whole of whose properties we profess to know, may not be all the while panting for exterior angles, sympathetic with the interior, or sullenly repining at the fact that it cannot be inscribed in a circle? What mathematician has ever pondered over a hyperbola, mangling the unfortunate curve with lines of intersection here and there, in his efforts to prove some property that perhaps after all is a mere calumny, who has not fancied at last that the ill-used locus was spreading out its asymptotes as a silent rebuke, or winking one focus at him in contemptuous pity?

From The Dynamics of a Parti-cle *by Lewis Carroll, first printed in 1865 as an Oxford pamphlet.*

Note on 312, 313, 314. *Matthew Arnold in his essay* The Function of Criticism at the Present Time *contrasts the propaganda addresses (pep-talks) of the capitalists with the 'bleak and inhuman' facts of real life. Life now so bleak, so inhuman, that another Oxford Don – pen-name Lewis Carroll – is seen looking for 'the human element' in supposedly abstract landscapes of Geometry (314). Samuel Smiles (312), the biographer of the engineers and celebrator of Britain's industrial conquests, pauses to moralise on the dust of one of his heroes. In this passage the economic origins of the Victorian sentimentality are clear. Banish human comradeship from life and the naked psyche looks longingly round for an image with which to identify itself. An image of death and tears and despair: withered grapes, funeral palls or again modern machine images which it can make symbolic of a vanished warmth. It is left to John Ruskin (313) to give a correct analysis of modern evil, through the wide vision of one for whom there are still sacred places on earth whose desecration is part of the exploitation of man by man.*

It is true, the *Saturday Review* maintains that our epoch of transformation is finished; that we have found our philosophy; that the British nation has searched all anchorages for the spirit, and has finally anchored itself, in the fulness of perfected knowledge, on Benthamism. This idea at first made a great impression on me; not only because it is so consoling in itself, but also because it explained a phenomenon which in the summer of last year had, I confess, a good deal troubled me. At that time my avocations led me to travel almost daily on one of the Great Eastern Lines, – the Woodford Branch. Every one knows that the murderer, Müller, perpetrated his detestable act on the North London Railway, close by. The English middle-class, of which I am myself a feeble unit, travel on the Woodford Branch in large numbers. Well, the demoralisation of our class, – the class which (the newspapers are constantly saying it, so I may repeat it without vanity) has done all the great things which have ever been done in England, – the demoralisation, I say, of our class, caused by the Bow tragedy, was something bewildering. Myself a transcendentalist (as the *Saturday Review* knows), I escaped the infection; and, day after day, I used to ply my agitated fellow-travellers with all the consolations which my transcendentalism would naturally suggest to me. I reminded them how Caesar refused to take precautions against assassination, because life was not worth having at the price of an ignoble solicitude for it. I reminded them what insignificant atoms we all are in the life of the world. 'Suppose the worst to happen,' I said, addressing a portly jeweller from Cheapside; 'suppose even yourself to be the victim; *il n'y a pas d'homme nécessaire*. We should miss you for a day or two upon the Woodford Branch; but the great mundane movement would still go on, the gravel walks of your villa would still be rolled, dividends would still be paid at the Bank, omnibuses would still run, there would still be the old crush at the corner of Fenchurch Street.' All was of no avail. Nothing could moderate, in the bosom of the great English middle-class, their passionate, absorbing, almost blood-thirsty clinging to life. At the moment I thought this over-concern a little unworthy; but the *Saturday Review* suggests a touching explanation of it. What I took for the ignoble clinging to life of a comfortable worldling, was, perhaps, only the ardent longing of a faithful Benthamite, traversing an age still dimmed by the last mists of transcendentalism, to be spared long enough to see his religion in the full and final blaze of its triumph. This respectable man, whom I imagined to be going up to London to serve his shop, or to buy shares, or to attend an Exeter Hall meeting, or to assist at the deliberations of the Marylebone Vestry, was even, perhaps, in real truth, on a pious pilgrimage to obtain from Mr Bentham's executors a secret bone of his great, dissected master.

From the Preface to Essays in Criticism *(First Series) by Matthew Arnold, 1865.*

316 THE 'FACTORY KING' December 9, 1865

The friends of the late Richard Oastler, and especially those who subscribed to the Oastler Monument Fund, were glad to hear that Mr J. Bernie Philip, the artist entrusted with the execution of the monument, had succeeded, after much labour, in producing a most excellent model of the 'Factory King'. The group consists of three figures: Mr Oastler is represented in a standing attitude, in the strength and vigour of his manhood, such as he was five and twenty years ago, and a more commanding and life-like figure we have seldom seen. The prominent eyes of Mr Oastler, and all the upper part of the head are almost perfect; while the face manifests that kindly gravity for which the living man was so remarkable. The factory boy and girl, the other figures of the group, are very naturally portrayed. It is expected that in about six months from this time, the statue will be cast in bronze metal, and ready for erection. At the suggestion of the artist, the committee resolved that the figures should stand on a massive granite pedestal, and when erected, the monument will present a striking likeness of Mr Oastler, and be admired as a work of art. Bradford has been chosen as the central town of the West-Riding for the erection of the Oastler monument, and it is hoped that the authorities will find an eligible site. It will be an ornament to that borough, and now that the benefits of factory regulations are universally acknowledged, to perpetuate the memory of its most energetic promoter is both a duty and an honour.

Quoted in The Annals of Yorkshire.

317 THE SUICIDE OF BETTY HIGDEN 1865

In those pleasant little towns of Thames, you may hear the fall of the water over the weirs, or even, in still weather, the rustle of the rushes; and from the bridge you may see the young river, dimpled like a young child, playfully gliding away among the trees, unpolluted by the defilements that lie in wait for it on its course, and as yet out of hearing of the deep summons of the sea. It were too much to pretend that Betty Higden made out such thoughts; no; but she heard the tender river whispering to many like herself, 'Come to me, come to me! When the cruel shame and terror you have so long fled from, most beset you, come to me! I am the Relieving Officer appointed by eternal ordinance to do my work; I am not held in estimation according as I shirk it. My breast is softer than the pauper-nurse's; death in my arms is peacefuller than among the pauper-wards. Come to me!'

From Our Mutual Friend *by Charles Dickens, first published in monthly parts 1864–65.*

Twenty years ago, there was no lovelier piece of lowland scenery in South England, nor any more pathetic, in the world, by its expression of sweet human character and life, than that immediately bordering on the sources of the Wandel, and including the low moors of Addington, and the villages of Beddington and Carshalton, with all their pools and streams. No clearer or diviner waters ever sang with constant lips of the hand which 'giveth rain from heaven;' no pastures ever lightened in springtime with more passionate blooming; no sweeter homes ever hallowed the heart of the passer-by with their pride of peaceful gladness, – fain-hidden – yet full-confessed. The place remains, or, until a few months ago, remained, nearly unchanged in its larger features; but with deliberate mind I say, that I have never seen anything so ghastly in its inner tragic meaning, – not by the sand-isles of the Torcellan shore, – as the slow stealing of aspects of reckless, indolent, animal neglect, over the delicate sweetness of that English scene: nor is any blasphemy or impiety, any frantic saying, or godless thought, more appalling to me, using the best power of judgment I have to discern its sense and scope, than the insolent defiling of those springs by the human herds that drink of them. Just where the welling of the stainless water, trembling and pure, like a body of light, enters the pool of Carshalton, cutting itself a radiant channel down to the gravel, through warp of feathery weeds, all waving, which it traverses with its deep threads of clearness, like the chalcedony in moss-agate, starred here and there with the white grenouillette; just in the very rush and murmur of the first spreading currents, the human wretches of the place cast their street and house foulness; heaps of dust and slime, and broken shreds of old metal, and rags of putrid clothes; which, having neither energy to cart away, nor decency enough to dig into the ground, they thus shed into the stream, to diffuse what venom of it will float and melt, far away, in all places where God meant those waters to bring joy and health. And, in a little pool behind some houses farther in the village, where another spring rises, the shattered stones of the well, and of the little fretted channel which was long ago built and traced for it by gentler hands, lie scattered, each from each, under a ragged bank of mortar, and scoria, and bricklayer's refuse, on one side, which the clean water nevertheless chastises to purity; but it cannot conquer the dead earth beyond: and there, circled and coiled under festering scum, the stagnant edge of the pool effaces itself into a slope of black slime, the accumulation of indolent years. Half-a-dozen men, with one day's work could cleanse those pools, and trim the flowers about their banks, and make every breath of summer air above them rich with cool balm; and every glittering wave medicinal, as if it ran, troubled only of angels, from the porch of Bethesda. But that day's work is never given, nor, I suppose, will be; nor will any joy be possible to heart of man, for evermore, about those wells of English waters.

When I last left them, I walked up slowly through the back streets of Croydon, from the old church to the hospital; and, just on the left, before coming up to the crossing of the High Street, there was a new public-house built. And the front of it was built in so wise a manner, that a recess of two feet was left below its front windows, between them and the street-pavement; a recess too narrow for any possible use, (for even if it had been occupied by a seat, as in old times it might have been, everybody walking along the street would have fallen over the legs of the reposing wayfarer).

But, by way of making this two feet depth of freehold land more expressive of the dignity of an establishment for the sale of spirituous liquors, it was fenced from the pavement by an imposing iron railing, having four or five spearheads to the yard of it, and six feet high; containing as much iron and iron-work, indeed, as could well be put into the space; and by this stately arrangement, the little piece of dead ground within, between wall and street, became a protective receptacle of refuse; cigar ends, and oyster shells, and the like, such as an open-handed English street-populace habitually scatters; and was thus left, unsweepable by any ordinary methods. Now the iron bars which uselessly (or in a great degree worse than uselessly) enclosed this bit of ground, and made it pestilent, represented a quantity of work which would have cleansed the Carshalton pools three times over: of work, partly cramped and perilous, in the mine; partly grievous and horrible, at the furnace: partly foolish and sedentary, of ill-taught students making bad designs: work from the beginning to the last fruits of it, and in all the branches of it, venomous, deathful*, and miserable.

Now, how did it come to pass that this work was done instead of the other; that the strength and life of the English operative were spent in defiling ground, instead of redeeming it, and in producing an entirely (in that place) valueless, piece of metal, which can neither be eaten nor breathed, instead of medicinal fresh air and pure water?

There is but one reason for it, and at the present a conclusive one, – that the capitalist can charge percentage on the work in one case, and cannot in the other.

From the Preface to The Crown of Wild Olive *by John Ruskin, 1866.*

---

* A fearful occurrence took place a few days since, near Wolverhampton. Thomas Snape, aged nineteen, was on duty as the 'keeper' of a blast furnace at Deepfield, assisted by John Gardner, aged eighteen, and Joseph Swift, aged thirty-seven. The furnace contained four tons of molten iron, and an equal amount of cinders, and ought to have been run out at 7.30 p.m. But Snape and his mates, engaged in talking and drinking, neglected their duty, and, in the meantime the iron rose in the furnace until it reached a pipe wherein water was contained. Just as the men had stripped, and were proceeding to tap the furnace, the water in the pipe, converted into steam, burst down its front and let loose on them the molten metal, which instantaneously consumed Gardner: Snape, terribly burnt, and mad with pain, leaped into the canal and then ran home and fell dead on the threshold; Swift survived to reach the hospital, where he died too.

319   ENGLAND   December 11, 1866
        Marseille

I have never been so utterly weary of 6 months as of these last: never seeing anything but the dreadful brick houses – and latterly suffering from cold, smoke – darkness – ach! horror! – verily England may be a blessed place for the wealthy, but it is an accursed place for those who have known liberty and seen God's daylight daily in other countries. By degrees, however, (if I don't leave it by the sudden collapse of mortality) I hope to quit it altogether, even if I turn Mussulman and settle in Timbuctoo.

From a letter of Edward Lear to Lady Waldegrave, printed in Later Letters of Edward Lear, *edited by Lady Strachey, 1911.*

320   THE SWINDON RAILWAY WORKS   Spring 1867

This factory is perhaps the largest in the West of England. Here are employed as many as seventeen hundred hands – an army of workmen – drawn from the villages round about. Here are made the engines used upon the Great Western Railway. It is open to visitors upon every Wednesday afternoon, and is a sight well worth seeing. A person is in attendance to show it. The place seems to be built somewhat in the form of a parallelogram. Seven tall chimneys belch forth volumes of smoke. The first thing shown to visitors is an engine room near the entrance. Here are two beams of fifty horse-power working with a smooth, oily motion, almost without noise. The yard beneath is, to a stranger, a vast incongruous museum of iron; iron in every possible shape and form, round and square, crooked and straight. Proteus himself never changed into the likeness of such things. The northern shops are devoted to noise, and the voice of the guide is inaudible. Here is a vast wilderness – an endless vista of forges glaring with blue flames, the men all standing by leaning on their hammers, waiting until you pass, while far ahead sparks fly in showers from the tortured anvils high in the air, looking like minute meteors. This place is a temple of Vulcan. If the old motto '*Laborare est orare*', 'labour is prayer', is correct, here be sturdy worshippers of the fire-god. The first glimpse of the factory affords a view of sparks, sweat, and smoke. Smoke, sweat, and sparks is the last thing that is seen.

Passing between a row of fiery furnaces seven times heated, the visitors enter the rail-mill, where the rails are manufactured. This place is a perfect pandemonium. Vast boilers built up in brick close in every side, with the steam hissing like serpents in its efforts to escape. Enormous fly-wheels spin round and round at a velocity which renders the spokes invisible. Steam hammers shake the ground, where once perhaps crouched the timid hare, and stun the ear. These hammers are a miracle of human manufacture. Though it is possible to strike a blow which shall crush iron like earthenware, to bring down a weight of tons, yet a skilful workman can crack a hazel-nut without injuring the kernel. Gazing upon these wonderful hammers the visitor is suddenly scorched upon one side, and turning, finds that a wheelbarrow load of red-hot iron had been thrown down beside him, upon which a jet of water plays, fizzing off into steam. Springing aside he scarcely escapes collision with a mass of red hot metal wheeled along and placed beneath the steam hammer, where it is thumped and bumped flat. His feet now begin to feel the heat of the iron flooring, which the thickest leather cannot keep out. The workmen wear shoes shod with broad headed iron nails from heel to toe. Their legs are defended by greaves – like an iron cricketing pad; their faces by a gauze metal mask. The clang, the rattle, the roar are indescribable; the confusion seems to increase the longer it is looked upon. Yonder, a glare almost too strong for the eyes shows an open furnace door. Out comes a mass of white-hot metal, it is placed on a truck, and wheeled forward to the revolving rollers, and placed between them. Sparks spurt out like a fountain of fire – slowly it passes through, much thinned and lengthened by the process: which is repeated until at length it emerges in the form of a rail. Here come chips of iron – if such an expression might be used – all red hot, sliding along the iron floor to their destination. Look out for your toes! In the dark winter nights the glare from this place can be seen for miles around; lighting up the clouds with a lurid glow like that from some vast conflagration.

From Jefferies' Land: A History of Swindon *by Richard Jefferies, published 1896.*

321   **IN A RAILWAY CARRIAGE**   Summer 1867

I was on my way from London to Guildford, in a railway carriage, containing, besides myself, one passenger, an elderly gentleman: – presently, however, two ladies entered, accompanied by two little boys. These, who had just had a copy of the 'Book of Nonsense' given them, were loud in their delight, and by degrees infected the whole party with their mirth.

'How grateful,' said the old gentleman to the two ladies, 'all children and parents too ought to be to the statesman who has given his time to composing that charming book!'

(The ladies looked puzzled, as indeed was I, the Author.)

'Do you not know who is the writer of it?' asked the gentleman.

'The name is "Edward Lear",' said one of the ladies.

'Ah!' said the first speaker; 'so it is printed, but that is only a whim of the real author, the Earl of Derby. "Edward" is his christian name, and, as you may see, LEAR is only EARL transposed.'

'But,' said the lady, doubtingly, 'here is a dedication to the great-grand-children, grand-nephews, and grand-nieces of Edward, thirteenth Earl of Derby, by the author, Edward Lear.'

IN A RAILWAY CARRIAGE

'That,' replied the other, 'is simply a piece of mystification; I am in a position to know that the whole book was composed and illustrated by Lord Derby himself. In fact, there is no such person at all as Edward Lear.'

'Yet,' said the other lady, 'some friends of mine tell me they know Mr Lear.'

'Quite a mistake! completely a mistake!' said the old gentleman, becoming rather angry at the contradiction, 'I am well aware of what I am saying: I can inform you, no such person as "Edward Lear" exists!'

Hitherto I had kept silence, but as my hat was, as well as my handkerchief and stick, largely marked inside with my name, and, as I happened to have in my pocket several letters addressed to me, the temptation was too great to resist, so flashing all these articles at once on my would-be extinguisher's attention, I speedily reduced him to silence.

From the Introduction to More Nonsense *by Edward Lear, written 1871 and published 1872.*

322 THE VOWEL FLAME c.1857

I have now to introduce to your notice an astonishingly sensitive flame. It issues from the single orifice of a steatite burner, and reaches a height of 24 inches. The slightest tap on a distant anvil reduces its height to 7 inches. When a bunch of keys is shaken the flame is violently agitated, and emits a loud roar. The dropping of a sixpence into a hand already containing coin at a distance of 20 yards, knocks the flame down. It is not possible to walk across the room without agitating the flame. The creaking of boots sets it in violent commotion. The crumpling or tearing of paper, or the rustle of a silk dress, does the same. It is startled by the patter of a raindrop. I hold a watch near the flame: nobody hears its ticks; but you all see their effect upon the flame. At every tick it falls and roars. The winding up of the watch also produces tumult. The twitter of a distant sparrow shakes the flame down; the note of a cricket would do the same. A chirrup from a distance of 30 yards causes it to fall and roar. I repeat a passage from Spenser: –

> Her ivory forehead full of bounty brave,
>   Like a broad table did itself dispread;
> For love his lofty triumphs to engrave,
>   And write the battles of his great godhead,
>   All truth and goodness might therein be read,
>   For there their dwelling was, and when she spake,
> Sweet words, like dropping honey she did shed;
>   And through the pearls and rubies softly brake
>   A silver sound, which heavenly music seemed to make.

The flame selects from the sounds to which it can respond. It notices some by the slightest nod, to others it bows more distinctly, to some its obeisance is very profound, while to many sounds it turns an entirely deaf ear. In fig. 129 this wonderful flame is represented. On chirruping to it, or on shaking a bunch of keys within a few yards of it, it falls to the size shown in fig. 130, the whole length, a, b, of the flame being suddenly abolished. The light at the same time is practically destroyed, a pale and almost non-luminous residue of it alone remaining. These figures are taken from photographs of the flame.

To distinguish it from the others I have called this the 'vowel flame', because the different vowel sounds affect it differently. A loud and sonorous U does not move the flame; on changing the sound to O, the flame quivers; when E is sounded, the flame is strongly affected. I utter the words, boot, boat, and beat in succession. To the first there is no response; to the second, the flame starts; by the third is thrown into greater commotion. The sound Ah! is still more powerfull. Did we not know the constituion of vowel sounds this deportment would be an insoluble enigma. As it is, however, the flame illustrates the theory of vowel sounds. It is most sensitive to sounds of high pitch; hence we should infer that the sound Ah! contains higher notes than the sound E; that E contains higher notes than O; and O higher notes than U. I need not say that this agrees perfectly with the analysis of Helmholtz.

This flame is peculiarly sensitive to the utterance of the letter S. A hiss contains the elements that most forcibly affect the flame. The gas issues from its burner with a hiss, and an external sound of this character is therefore exceedingly effective. From a metal box containing compressed air I allow a puff to escape; the flame instantly ducks down, not by any transfer of air from the box to the flame, for the distance between both utterly excludes this idea – it is the sound that affects the flame. From the most distant part of the gallery my assistant permits the compressed air to issue in puffs from the box; at every puff the flame suddenly falls. The pulses produced by the issuing air at the one orifice precipitate the tumult of the flame at the other.

When a musical-box is placed on the table, and permitted to play, the flame behaves like a sentient and motor creature – bowing slightly to some tones, and curtseying deeply to others.

From Lecture VI in On Sound *by John Tyndall, published 1867.*

323   THE DAMAGE   October 1867

From noon of October 26th, 1867, to noon of the 28th the weather was very stormy, the wind varying from S.W. to W. and N.W. To the east of St Helen's and Widnes common turnips were *very much* damaged in the leaves; mangel *much* damaged. The bulbs of the turnips, &c., would not be much, if any, less in weight, as the season was too far advanced. I therefore put no damage on those crops. Young clovers in the stubbles were much damaged, but I only put a money value on this in one instance, when the young clover was much advanced in growth. In all other cases I considered there would be no injury of any importance.

The manufacturers considered the damage was by the salt water from the sea. As it was possible this might be the case, I made up in my mind to prove it. I therefore proceeded by rail to Rufford, and then walked across the country, passing between Prescot and St Helen's to Cronton, and then from there by Widnes to Warrington. At Rufford there is a clear sweep from the sea, without any town or works intervening. Here there was not the least damage to be seen, and this was the case until I got in the line of Liverpool and Prescot; then damage was distinguishable to fences and root crops (there was no corn out), but nothing like to the extent as to the east of St Helen's and Widnes. All right about Cronton. From Widnes to near Warrington very bad. This showed that the smoke of Liverpool and Prescot had a bad effect, but not equal to that of St Helen's and Widnes. The sea in that storm did no harm so far inland.

From a report by W. Rothwell, printed in Air and Rain *by R. Angus Smith, 1872.*

324   THE FIRE OF LABOUR   1867

A machine which does not serve the purposes of labour, is useless. In addition, it falls a prey to the destructive influence of natural forces. Iron rusts and wood rots. Yarn with which we neither weave nor knit, is cotton wasted. Living labour must seize upon these things and rouse them from their death-sleep, change them from mere possible use-values into real and effective ones. Bathed in the fire of labour, appropriated as part and parcel of labour's organism, and, as it were, made alive for the performances of their functions in the process, they are in truth consumed, but consumed with a purpose, as elementary constituents of new use-values, of new products, ever ready as means of subsistence for individual consumption, or as means of production for some new labour-process.

From the English translation of Das Kapital *by Karl Marx, written 1867, translation published 1886.*

325   **THE QUEEN OF RED CLAY**   1867

Whether the wives and daughters of Israel under the Pharaohs were also consigned to this unwomanly work in the brick-yards of Egypt, is a question which the Scriptures do not enable us to decide. If they were not sentenced to the same toil as their husbands and brothers, then the brickmakers of the Black Country have improved upon the industrial ethics and economy of the Egyptians, and availed themselves of the cheapness and necessities of female labour, in producing the building material of the country. A writer, who visited the different brick making establishments of the district, estimates that seventy-five per cent. of the persons employed are females; and perhaps two-thirds of these are young girls from nine to twelve years of age. We saw one set of these hands at work at the moulding bench and watched with special interest the several parts they performed. A middle-aged woman, as we took her to be from some dress indications of her sex, was standing at the bench, butter-stick in hand. Apparently she had on only a single garment reaching to her feet. But this appearance may have come from her clothes being so bespattered and weighted with wet clay that they adhered so closely to her person that it was as fully developed through them as the female form of some marble statues through the thin drapery in which they are clad by the sculptor. She wore a turban on her head of the same colour; for only one colour or consistency was possible at her work. The only thing feminine in her appearance was a pair of ear-drops she wore as token of her sex and of its tastes under any circumstances. With two or three moulds she formed the clay dough into loaves with wonderful tact and celerity. With a dash, splash, and a blow one was perfectly shaped. One little girl then took it away and shed it out upon the drying-floor with the greatest precision to keep the rows in perfect line. Another girl, a little older, brought the clay to the bench. This was a heavier task, and we watched her appearance and movements very closely. She was a girl apparently about thirteen. Washed and well clad, and with a little sportive life in her, she would have been almost pretty in face and form. But though there was some colour in her cheeks, it was the flitting flush of exhaustion.

She moved in a kind of swaying, sliding way, as if muscle and joint did not fit and act together naturally. She first took up a mass of the cold clay, weighing about twenty-five pounds, upon her head, and while balancing it there, she squatted to the heap without bending her body, and took up a mass of equal weight with both hands against her stomach, and with the two burdens walked about a rod and deposited them on the moulding bench. No wonder, we thought, that the colour in her cheeks was an unhealthy flush. With a mass of cold clay held against her stomach, and bending under another on her head, for ten or twelve hours in a day, it seemed a marvel that there could be any red blood in her veins at all. How such a child could ever grow an inch in any direction after being put to this occupation, was another mystery. Certainly not an inch could be added to her stature in all the working days of her life. She could only grow at night and on Sundays.

Each moulding woman has two, sometimes three, of these girls to serve her, one to bring the clay, the others to carry away the bricks when formed. What may be just, but equally unfortunate, they are generally her own children if she has any of suitable size and strength; but, for lack of such, she employs the children of equally unfortunate mothers. Whether in cruel or good-natured satire, they are called *pages*, as if waiting on a queen. And she perhaps, is the most directly aimed at in this witticism. Some irreverent wag, looking at her standing by her four-legged throne, with her broad wooden sceptre in her hand, and her yellow turban on her head, might call her the Sultana of Edom, or the queen of red clay, and not travel far from the line of resemblance. Still, there is something painful and cruel in this mock crowning of innocent misfortune. It savours a little of the taunting irony of those ignorant Roman soldiers who platted a crown of thorns for the sublimest brow that ever bore the stamp of humanity or beamed on its weaknesses.

From Walks in the Black Country and its Green Border-Land *by Elihu Burritt, 1868.*

326 NORTHERN FARMER – NEW STYLE c.1868

I

Dosn't thou 'ear my 'erse's legs, as they canters awaäy?
Proputty, proputty, proputty – that's what I 'ears 'em saäy.
Proputty, proputty, proputty – Sam, thou's an ass for they paäins:
Theer's moor sense i' one o' 'is legs nor in all they braäins.

II

Woä – theer's a craw to pluck wi' tha, Sam: yon's parson's 'ouse –
Dosn't thou knaw that a man mun be eäther a man or a mouse?
Time to think on it then; for thou'll be twenty to weeäk.
Proputty, proputty – woä then woä – let me 'ear mysen speäk.

III

Me an' thy muther, Sammy, 'as beän a-talkin' o' thee;
Thou's beän talkin' to muther, an' she beän a tellin' it me.
Thou'll not marry for munny – thou's sweet up' parson's lass –
Noä – thou'll marry for luvv – an' we boäth on us thinks tha an ass.

IV

Seeä'd her todaäy goä by – Saaïnt's s-daäy – they was ringing the bells.
She's a beauty thou thinks – an' soä is scoors o' gells.
Them as 'as munny an' all – wot's a beauty? the flower as blaws.
But proputty, proputty sticks, an' proputty, proputty graws.

V

Do'ant be stunt: taäke time: I knaws what maäkes the sa mad.
Warn't I craäzed fur the lasses mysén when I wur a lad?
But I knaw'd a Quaäker feller as often 'as towd me this:
'Doant thou marry for munny, but goä wheer munny is!'

VI

An' I went wheer munny war: an' thy muther coon to 'and,
Wi' lots o' munny laaïd by, an' a nicetish bit o' land.
Maäybe she warn't a beauty: – I nivver giv it a thowt –
But warn't she as good to cuddle an' kiss as a lass as 'ant nowt?

VII

Parson's lass 'ant nowt, an' she weänt 'a nowt when 'e's deäd,
Mun be a guvness, lad, or summat, and addle her breäd:
Why? fur 'e's nobbut a curate, an' weänt niver git hissen clear,
An' 'e maäde the bed as 'e ligs on affor 'e coom'd to the shere.

Poem by Alfred Tennyson written c.1868 and published in The Holy Grail, *1869.*

327 THE FIRST TASK 1869

Hand-labour on the earth, the work of the husbandman and of the shepherd; – to dress the earth and keep the flocks of it – the first task of men, and the final one – the education always of noblest lawgivers, kings and teachers; the education of Hesiod, of Moses, of David, of all the true strength of Rome; and all its tenderness: the pride of Cincinnatus, and the inspiration of Virgil. Hand-labour on the earth, and the harvest of it brought forth with singing; – not steam-piston labour on the earth, and the harvest brought forth with steam-whistling. You will have no prophet's voice accompanied by that shepherd's pipe, and pastoral symphony. Do you know that lately, in Cumberland, in the chief pastoral district of England, – in Wordsworth's own home, – a procession of villagers on their feast day provided for themselves, by way of music, a steam-plough whistling at the head of them?

From The Future of England *by John Ruskin.*

| 328 | THE GREATNESS OF ENGLAND | 1869 |

Everyone must have observed the strange language current during the late discussions as to the possible failure of our supplies of coal. Our coal, thousands of people were saying, is the real basis of our national greatness; if our coal runs short, there is an end of the greatness of England. But what *is* greatness? – culture makes us ask. Greatness is a spiritual condition worthy to excite love, interest, and admiration; and the outward proof of possessing greatness is that we excite love, interest, and admiration. If England were swallowed up by the sea tomorrow, which of the two, a hundred years hence, would most excite the love, interest, and admiration of mankind, – would most, therefore, show the evidences of having possessed greatness, – the England of the last twenty years, or the England of Elizabeth, of a time of splendid spiritual effort, but when our coal, and our industrial operations depending on coal, were very little developed? Well, then, what an unsound habit of mind it must be which makes us talk of things like coal or iron as constituting the greatness of England, and how salutary a friend is culture, bent on seeing things as they are, and thus dissipating delusions of this kind and fixing standards of perfection that are real!

From Culture and Anarchy *by Matthew Arnold, 1869.*

| 329 | ROUGH-SPUN NATURE | January 1870 |

I bought your vol. (the 'Holy Grail') at Lowestoft; and, when I returned home here for Xmas, found a copy from your new publisher. As he sent it I suppose at your orders, I write about it what I might say to you were we together over a pipe, instead of so far asunder.

The whole myth of Arthur's Round Table Dynasty in Britain presents itself before me with a sort of cloudy, Stonehenge grandeur. I am not sure if the old knights' adventures do not tell upon me better, touched in some lyrical way (like your own 'Lady of Shalott') than when elaborated into epic form. I never could care for Spenser, Tasso, or even Ariosto, whose epic has a ballad ring about it. But then I never could care much for the old prose romances much either, except *Don Quixote*. So, as this was always the case with me, I suppose my brain is wanting in this bit of its dissected map.

Anyhow, Alfred, while I feel how pure, noble and holy your work is, and whole phrases, lines and sentences of it will abide with me, and I am sure, with men after me, I read on till the 'Lincolnshire Farmer' drew tears to my eyes. I was got back to the substantial rough-spun Nature I knew; and the old brute, invested by you with the solemn humour of Humanity, like Shakespeare's *Shallow*, became a more pathetic phenomenon than the knights who revisit the world in your other verse. There! I can't help it, and have made a clean breast; and you need only laugh at one more of 'old Fitz's crochets', which I daresay you anticipated.

From a letter of Edward Fitzgerald to Alfred Tennyson, quoted in Tennyson, a Memoir, *by Hallam, Lord Tennyson, 1897.*

330 LANCASHIRE Spring 1870

With 1870 I returned to my inquiry, and devoted January, February, March, and April again to Lancashire – renewing my work chiefly in the towns I had visited a year before, and entering a few new places. My sorrowful impressions were confirmed. In our old Chartist time, it is true, Lancashire working men were in rags by thousands, and many of them often lacked food. But their intelligence was demonstrated wherever you went. You would see them in groups discussing the great doctrine of political justice – that every grown up, sane man ought to have a vote in the election who were to make the laws by which he was to be governed; or they were in earnest dispute respecting the teaching of Socialism. *Now*, you will see no such groups in Lancashire. But you will hear well-dressed working men talking, as they walk with their hands in their pockets, of 'Co-ops' (Co-operative Stores), and their shares in them, or in building societies. And you will see others, like idiots, leading small greyhound dogs, covered with cloth, in a string! They are about to race, and they are betting money as they go! And yonder comes another clamorous dozen of men, cursing and swearing and betting upon a few pigeons they are about to let fly! As for their betting on horses – like their masters! – it is perfect madness.

From The Life of Thomas Cooper written by Himself, *1872.*

331 FREEDOM March 24, 1870

I protest that if some great Power would agree to make me always think what is true and do what is right, on condition of being turned into a sort of clock and wound up every morning before I got out of bed, I should instantly close with the offer. The only freedom I care about is the freedom to do right; the freedom to do wrong I am ready to part with on the cheapest terms to any one who will take it of me.

From a lecture by T.H. Huxley on Descartes' Discourse on Method, *published in* Lay Sermons, Addresses and Reviews, *1870.*

O 'tis a lovely country! The grey solemn-looking Carboniferous Limestone is the prevailing feature, soft-toned and exquisitely varied by sweetest natural woodland fringing the shores of the famous Bay. Though I had hammered my way through all corners of the neighbourhood in by-gone years (especially 1822 and 1824), and had many times taken peeps at it during my short northern visits of love and duty; yet it was now to me a new country, threaded by railways and covered by towns and villages, where in your old uncle's early days all was in silence and solitude. But this was not all, for in multitudinous nooks and corners, instead of sweet scenery and a bright atmosphere, we saw gigantic furnaces sending into the sky a vapour so dark, that it seemed to have come from the nostrils of Satan. In many places the ground was blood-red; and all around us smelt of fire and brimstone. In fact, our sweet village, the Grange – a name telling one of corn and rural comfort – borders on Low Furness – a country long famous for its iron ore; and truly now, on actual proof, many parts of its surface-deposits are almost a mass of red iron ore (haematite). This ore they are digging away at a rate which would pass belief without the evidence of living sense. Some of the red ore goes, of course, to feed the throats of the gigantic furnaces in the neighbourhood. Other portions are transported by the railway which skirts Morecambe Bay and Duddon Sands. Day by day, forty-four gigantic trains (each composed of carriages varying in number from 50 to 70) were seen dragging their almost endless length and gigantic loads majestically along the undulating line close to the beautiful shore. But we had, each day also, four regular passenger trains, and charming it was to be playing in such trains a game of bo-peep with old father Ocean – a minute or two sweeping along his gently rippling shore – then a grand headland in view against which he wages eternal war of foam and fury. But we took a shorter and quieter line, and shot our way right through the headland. A few minutes of darkness, and then again the bright air and the sparkling sea. We could go to Furness Abbey in about half an hour, passing the fine scenery of the coast of Ulverston – then on through multitudinous iron-works and ore-pits – then by the ancient town of Dalton, in my early years a neat village, now a wonderful congeries of houses. Again on to the westward – for a while once more in pitchy darkness, and then daylight breaking out in the very heart of the sweet grounds that skirt the magnificent ruins of the old Abbey. We several times visited this ground of enchantment, and twice we went on to Barrow – in my working-days a very small fishing village – now a town of about 18,000 inhabitants, and hourly increasing. And instead of the sweet clear sky of olden times it has an atmosphere like that which overhangs the steam furnaces of Leeds or Manchester.

From a letter of Adam Sedgwick to his niece Miss Herschel written from Norwich, August 26, 1870, printed in The Life and Letters of Adam Sedgwick *by J.W. Clark and T.M. Hughes, 1890.*

Compare Wordsworth on Furness Abbey (237). The developments in Morecambe Bay were in part an effect of Sedgwick's own geology.

333   A VAST NUMBER   1871

All the lines carried in one year (1870) somewhere about 307 millions of passengers – in other words, that number of passenger journeys were performed on them. The mail and stage coaches in their best days only conveyed, as we have said, two millions!*

From The Iron Horse or Life on the Line *by R.M. Ballantyne, 1871.*

Compare of course Nasmyth's piece of calico printed with a million spots (310).

334   EVAPORATION   Spring 1871

I have been watching clouds this spring and evaporation, for instance over our Lenten chocolate. It seems as if the heat by *aestus*, throes one after another threw films of vapour off as boiling water throws off steam under films of water, that is bubbles. One query then is whether these films contain gas or no. The film seems to be set with tiny bubbles which gives it a grey and grained look. By throes perhaps which represent the moments at which the evener stress of the heat has overcome the resistance of the surface or of the whole liquid. It would be reasonable then to consider the film as the shell of gas-bubbles and the grain on them as a network of bubbles condensed by the air as the gas rises. – Candle smoke goes by just the same laws, the visible film being here of unconsumed substance, not hollow bubbles. The throes can be perceived like the thrills of a candle in the socket: this is precisely to *reech*, whence *reek*. They may by a breath of air be laid again and then shew like grey wisps on the surface – which shews their part-solidity. They seem to be drawn off the chocolate as you might take up a napkin between your fingers that covered something, not so much from here or there as from the whole surface at one reech, so that the film is perceived at the edges and makes in fact a collar or ring just within the walls all round the cup; it then draws together in a cowl like a candleflame but not regularly or without a break: the question is why. Perhaps in perfect

---

* Many readers may find it difficult to form an adequate conception of such a vast number as 307 millions. It may help one to some idea of it to know that, if a man were to devote himself to count it, one by one, – sitting down after breakfast, counting at the rate of one every moment, and working without intermission for eight hours every day, excepting Sundays, – he would not conclude his task until the thirty-fifth year.

stillness it would not but the air breathing it aside entangles it with itself. The film seems to rise not quite simultaneously but to peel off as if you were tearing cloth; then giving an end forward like the corner of a handkerchief and beginning to coil it makes a long wavy hose you may sometimes look down, as a ribbon or a carpenter's shaving may be made to do. Higher running into frets and silvering in the sun with the endless coiling, the soft bound of the general motion and yet the side lurches sliding into some particular pitch it makes a baffling and charming sight. – Clouds however solid they may look far off are I think wholly made of film in the sheet or in the tuft. The bright woolpacks that pelt before a gale in a clear sky are in the tuft and you can see the wind unravelling and rending them finer than any sponge till within one easy reach overhead they are morselled to nothing and consumed – it depends of course on their size. Possibly each tuft in forepitch or in origin is quained and a crystal. Rarer and wilder packs have sometimes film in the sheet, which may be caught as it turns on the edge of the cloud like an outlying eyebrow. The one in which I saw this was in a north-east wind, solid but not crisp, white like the white of egg, and bloated-looking.

From the Journal of Gerard Manley Hopkins, March 1871, printed in The Notebooks and Papers of Gerard Manley Hopkins, *edited by Humphry House, 1937.*

335   CLOUDS   1871

Whence comes the rain which forms the mountain streams? Observation enables you to answer the question. Rain does not come from a clear sky. It comes from clouds. But what are clouds? Is there nothing that you are acquainted with which they resemble? You discover at once a likeness between them and the condensed steam of a locomotive. At every puff of the engine a cloud is projected into the air. Watch the cloud sharply; you notice that it first forms at a little distance from the top of the funnel. Give close attention and you will sometimes see a perfectly clear space between the funnel and the cloud. Through that clear space the thing which makes the cloud must pass. What then is this thing which at one moment is transparent and invisible, and at the next moment visible as a dense opaque cloud?

It is the *steam* or *vapour of water* from the boiler. Within the boiler the steam is transparent and invisible; but to keep it in this invisible state a heat would be required as great as that within the boiler. When the vapour mingles with the cold air above the hot funnel it ceases to be a vapour. Every bit of steam shrinks, when chilled, to a much more minute particle of water. The liquid particles thus produced form a kind of *water dust* of exceeding fineness which floats in the air, and is called a *cloud*.

Watch the cloud-banner from the funnel of a running locomotive; you see it growing gradually less dense. It finally melts away altogether, and if you continue your observations you will not fail to notice that the speed of its disappearance depends upon the character of the day. In humid weather the cloud hangs long and lazily in the air; in dry weather it is rapidly licked up. What has become of it? It has been converted into true invisible vapour.

From a lecture on The Forms of Water *by John Tyndall given at the Royal Institution, printed 1872.*

Note on 334, 335, 337, 338, 339. *In the years 1870–71, there are two very clear sets of images: clouds (connected with trains) (334, 335); and the gods and animism (337, 338, 339).*

R. Angus Smith among other people was at this time doing elaborate experiments on industrial atmosphere problems, embodied in Air and Rain *(1872) (323).*

In 1871, the year of the Franco-Prussian war, Pissarro, Monet and Sisley were in England. Note the importance to Impressionism of 'the end of animism' in removing the symbolic animistic attributes of objects. Compare Cézanne: 'Le contour m'échappe.'

Through all images – the open air – plein-airisme.

336 THE SUN-FORCE 1871

Lord Lytton told us long ago, in a beautiful song, how

The Wind and the Beam loved the Rose.

But Nature's poetry is more beautiful than man's. The wind and the beam loved the rose so well that they made the rose – or rather, the rose took the wind and the beam, and built up out of them, by her own inner life, her exquisite texture, hue, and fragrance.

What next? The rose dies; the timber tree dies; decays down into vegetable fibre, is buried, and turned to coal: but the plant cannot altogether undo its own work. Even in death and decay it cannot set free the sunbeams imprisoned in its tissue. The sun-force must stay, shut up age after age, invisible, but strong; working at its own prison-cells; transmuting them, or making them capable of being transmuted by man, into the manifold products of coal – coke, petroleum, mineral pitch, gases, coal-tar, benzole, delicate aniline dyes, and what not, till its day of deliverance comes.

Man digs it, throws it on the fire, a black, dead-seeming lump. A corner, an atom of it, warms till it reaches the igniting point; the temperature at which it is able to combine with oxygen.

And then, like a dormant live thing, awaking after ages to the sense of its own powers, its own needs, the whole lump is seized, atom after atom, with an infectious hunger for that oxygen which it lost centuries since in the bottom of the earth. It drinks the oxygen at every pore; and burns.

And so the spell of ages is broken. The sun-force bursts its prison-cells, and blazes into the free atmosphere, as light and heat once more; returning in a moment into the same forms in which it entered the growing leaf a thousand centuries since.

From a lecture by Charles Kingsley given at Chester in 1871, published in Scientific Lectures, *1879.*

| 337 | THE GODS | May 1871 |

You think it a great triumph to make the sun draw brown landscapes for you. That was also a discovery, and some day may be useful. But the sun had drawn landscapes before for you, not in brown, but in green, and blue, and all imaginable colours, here in England. Not one of you ever looked at them then; not one of you cares for the loss of them now, when you have shut the sun out with smoke, so that he can draw nothing more, except brown blots through a hole in a box. There was a rocky valley between Buxton and Bakewell, once upon a time, divine as the vale of Tempe; you might have seen the Gods there morning and evening – Apollo and all the sweet Muses of the light – walking in fair procession on the lawns of it, and to and fro among the pinnacles of its crags. You cared neither for Gods nor grass, but for cash (which you did not know the way to get); you thought you could get it by what the *Times* calls 'Railroad Enterprise'. You Enterprised a Railroad through the valley – you blasted its rocks away, heaped thousands of tons of shale into its lovely stream. The valley is gone, and the Gods with it; and now every fool in Buxton can be at Bakewell in half-an-hour, and every fool in Bakewell at Buxton; which you think a lucrative process of exchange – you Fools Everywhere.

From Fors Clavigera, *Letter the 5th, by John Ruskin, dated May 1, 1871.*

| 338 | ANIMISM | 1871 |

Animism, indeed, seems to be drawing in its outposts, and concentrating itself on the first and main position, the doctrine of the human soul. This doctrine has undergone extreme modification in the course of culture. It has outlived the almost total loss of one great argument attached to it, – the objective reality of apparitional souls or ghosts seen in dreams and visions. The soul has given up its ethereal substance, and become an immaterial entity, 'the shadow of a shade'. Its theory is becoming separated from the investigations of biology and mental science, which now discuss the phenomena of life and thought, the senses and the intellect, the emotions and the will, on a groundwork of pure experience. There has arisen an intellectual product whose very existence is of the deepest significance, a 'psychology' which has no longer anything to do with 'soul'. The soul's place in modern thought is in the metaphysics of religion, and its especial office there is that of furnishing an intellectual side to the religious doctrine of the future life. Such are the alterations which have differenced the fundamental animistic belief in its course through successive periods of the world's culture. Yet it is evident that, notwithstanding all this profound change, the conception of the human soul is, as to its most essential nature, continuous from the philosophy of the savage thinker to the modern professor of theology. Its definition has remained from the first that of an animating, separable, surviving entity, the vehicle of individual personal existence. The theory of the soul is one principal part of a system of religious philosophy, which unites, in an unbroken line of mental connection, the savage fetish-worshipper and the civilized Christian. The divisions which have separated the great religions of the world into intolerant and hostile sects are for the most part superficial in comparison with the deepest of all religious schisms, that which divides Animism from Materialism.

From Primitive Culture *by Edward Burnett Tylor F.R.S., 1871.*

339   THE PLAGUE-WIND   July 1, 1871

It is the first of July, and I sit down to write by the dismallest light that ever yet I wrote by; namely, the light of this midsummer morning, in mid-England, (Matlock, Derbyshire), in the year 1871.

For the sky is covered with grey cloud; – not raincloud, but a dry black veil, which no ray of sunshine can pierce; partly diffused in mist, feeble mist, enough to make distant objects unintelligible, yet without any substance, or wreathing, or colour of its own. And everywhere the leaves of the trees are shaking fitfully, as they do before a thunderstorm; only not violently, but enough to show the passing to and fro of a strange, bitter, blighting wind. Dismal enough, had it been the first morning of its kind that summer had sent. But during all this spring, in London, and at Oxford, through meagre March, through changelessly sullen April, through despondent May, and darkened June, morning after morning has come grey-shrouded thus.

And it is a new thing to me, and a very dreadful one. I am fifty years old, and more; and since I was five, have gleaned the best hours of my life in the sun of spring and summer mornings; and I never saw such as these, till now.

And the scientific men are busy as ants, examining the sun, and the moon, and the seven stars, and can tell me all about them, I believe, by this time; and how they move, and what they are made of.

And I do not care, for my part, two copper spangles, how they move, nor what they are made of. I can't move them any other way than they go, nor make them of anything else, better than they are made. But I would care much and give much, if I could be told where this bitter wind comes from, and what it is made of.

For, perhaps, with forethought, and fine laboratory science, one might make it of something else.

It looks partly as it were made of poisonous smoke; very possibly it may: there are at least two hundred furnace chimnies in a square of two miles on every side of me. But mere smoke would not blow to and fro in that wild way. It looks to me as if it were made of dead men's souls – such of them as are not gone yet where they have to go, and may be flitting hither and thither, doubting, themselves, of the fittest place for them.

You know, if there are such things as souls, and if ever any of them haunt places where they have been hurt, there must be many about, just now, displeased enough!

From Fors Clavigera, *Letter the 8th, by John Ruskin, published 1877.*

340   A LIVING OPTICAL INSTRUMENT Autumn 1871

It is scarcely possible to avoid comparing the eye with a telescope. We know that this instrument has been perfected by the long-continued efforts of the highest human intellects; and we naturally infer that the eye has been formed by a somewhat analogous process. But may not this inference be presumptuous? Have we any right to assume that the Creator works by intellectual powers like those of man? If we must compare the eye to an optical instrument, we ought in imagination to take a thick layer of transparent tissue, with spaces filled with fluid, and with a nerve sensitive to light beneath, and then suppose every party of this layer to be continually changing slowly in density, so as to separate into layers of different densities and thicknesses, placed at different distances from each other, and with the surfaces of each layer slowly changing in form. Further we must suppose that there is a power, represented by natural selection or the survival of the fittest, always intently watching each slight alteration in the transparent layers; and carefully preserving each which, under varied circumstances, in any way or in any degree, tends to procure a distincter image. We must suppose each new state of the instrument to be multiplied by the million; each to be preserved until a better one is produced, and then the old ones to be all destroyed. In living bodies, variation will cause the slight alterations, generation will multiply them almost infinitely, and natural selection will pick out with unerring skill each improvement. Let this process go on for millions of years; and during each year on millions of individuals of many kinds; and may we not believe that a living optical instrument might thus be formed as superior to one of glass, as the works of the Creator are to those of man?

From the sixth edition of The Origin of Species *by Charles Darwin, published January 1872.*

341 AN AFFECTIONATE MACHINE-TICKLING APHID before 1872

But other questions come upon us. What is a man's eye but a machine for the little creature that sits behind in his brain to look through? A dead eye is nearly as good as a living one for some time after the man is dead. It is not the eye that cannot see, but the restless one that cannot see through it. Is it man's eyes, or is it the big seeing-engine which has revealed to us the existence of worlds beyond worlds into infinity? What has made man familiar with scenery of the moon, the spots on the sun, or the geography of the planets? He is at the mercy of the seeing-engine for these things, and is powerless unless he tack it on to his own identity, and make it part & parcel of himself. Or, again, is it the eye, or the little seeing-engine, which has shewn us the existence of infinitely minute organisms which swarm unsuspected around us?

And take man's vaunted power of calculation – Have we not engines which can do all manner of sums more quickly and correctly than we can? What prizeman in Hypothetics at any of our Colleges of Unreason can compare with some of these machines in their own line? In fact, wherever precision is required man flies to the machine at once, as far preferable to himself. Our sum-engines never drop a figure, nor our looms a stitch; the machine is brisk and active, when the man is weary; it is clear-headed & collected, when the man is stupid and dull; it needs no slumber, when man must sleep or drop; ever at its post, ever ready for work, its alacrity never flags, its patience never gives in; its might is stronger than combined hundreds, and swifter than the flight of birds; it can burrow beneath the earth, and walk upon the largest rivers and sink not. This is the green tree; what then shall be done in the dry?

Who shall say that man does see or hear? He is such a hive and swarm of parasites that it is doubtful whether his body is not more theirs than his, and whether he is anything but another kind of ant-heap after all. May not man himself become a sort of parasite upon the machines? An affectionate machine-tickling aphid?

From Erewhon *by Samuel Butler, 1872.*

342 EXTRAORDINARY THINGS March 28, 1872

I can't write at length to describe more particularly the extraordinary things of my last séance on Monday. I had hold in one of my hands of *both* hands of Miss F.'s companion who also rested *both* her feet on my instep and Crookes had equally firm possession of Miss F. The other people present were his wife and her mother and all hands were joined. Yet paper went skimming in the dark about the room and after the word 'Listen' was rapped out the pencil was heard (in the complete darkness) to be writing at a furious rate under the table, between Crookes and his wife and when that was over and we were told (rapped) to light up, the paper was written over – all the side of a bit of *marked* note paper (marked for the occasion and therefore known to be blank when we began) with very respectable platitudes – rather above the level of Martin Tupper's compositions and signed 'Benjamin Franklin'! The absurdity on the one hand and the extraordinary character of the thing on the other, quite staggers me; wondering what I shall yet see and learn I remain at present quite passive with my eyes and ears open.

From a letter of Francis Galton to Charles Darwin, printed in The Life, Letters and Labours of Francis Galton *by Karl Pearson, 1924.*

343 MANUFACTURED ARTICLES September 1873

In the heavens we discover by their light, and by their light alone, stars so distant from each other that no material thing can ever have passed from one to another; and yet this light, which is to us the sole evidence of the existence of these distant worlds, tells us also that each of them is built up of molecules of the same kinds as those which we find on earth. A molecule of hydrogen, for example, whether in Sirius or in Arcturus, executes its vibrations in precisely the same time.

Each molecule therefore throughout the universe bears impressed upon it the stamp of a metric system as distinctly as does the metre in the Archives at Paris, or the double royal cubit of the temple of Karnac.

No theory of evolution can be formed to account for the similarity of molecules, for evolution necessarily implies continuous change, and the molecule is incapable of growth or decay, of generation or destruction.

None of the processes of Nature, since the time when Nature began, have produced the slightest difference in the properties of any molecule. We are therefore unable to ascribe either the existence of the molecules or the identity of their properties to any of the causes which we call natural.

On the other hand, the exact equality of each molecule to all others of the same kind gives it, as Sir John Herschel has well said, the essential character of a manufactured article, and precludes the idea of its being eternal and self-existent.

From the 'Discourse on Molecules' to the British Association by James Clerk-Maxwell, September 1873. Printed in The Life of James Clerk-Maxwell *by L. Campbell and W. Garnett, 1882.*

344 THE DISTURBER 1873–74

On Saturday Boldwood was in the market-house as usual, when the disturber of his dreams entered, and became visible to him. Adam had awakened from his deep sleep, and behold! there was Eve. The farmer took courage, and for the first time really looked at her.

Emotional causes and effects are not to be arranged in regular equation. The result from capital employed in the production of any movement of a mental nature is sometimes as tremendous as the cause itself is absurdly minute. When women are in a freakish mood, their usual intuition, either from carelessness or inherent defect, seemingly fails to teach them this, and hence it was that Bathsheba was fated to be astonished to-day.

Boldwood looked at her – not slily, critically, or understandingly, but blankly at gaze, in the way a reaper looks up at a passing train – as something foreign to his element, and but dimly understood. To Boldwood women had been remote phenomena rather than necessary complements – comets of such uncertain aspect, movement, and permanence, that whether their orbits were as geometrical, unchangeable, and as subject to laws as his own, or as absolutely erratic as they superficially appeared, he had not deemed it his duty to consider.

From Far from the Madding Crowd *by Thomas Hardy, 1874.*

345 **A MEMORABLE FOG** December 9–10, 1873

On December 9 a memorable fog settled down on London. I addressed a telegram to the Trinity House suggesting some gun-observations. With characteristic promptness came the reply that they would be made in the afternoon at Blackwall. I went to Greenwich in the hope of hearing the guns across the river; but the delay of the train by the fog rendered my arrival too late. Over the river the fog was very dense, and through it came various sounds with great distinctness. The signal-bell of an unseen barge rang clearly out at intervals, and I could plainly hear the hammering at Cubitt's Town, half a mile away, on the opposite side of the river. No deadening of the sound by the fog was apparent.

Through this fog and various local noises, Captain Atkins and Mr Edwards heard the report of a 12-pounder carronade with a 1-lb. charge far better than the 18-pounder with a 3-lb. charge, an optically clear atmosphere, and all noise absent, was heard on July 3.

Anxious to turn to the best account a phenomenon for which we had waited so long, I tried to grapple with the problem by experiments on a small scale. On the 10th I stationed my assistant with a whistle and organ-pipe on the walk at the south-west end of the bridge dividing Hyde Park from Kensington Gardens. From the eastern end of the Serpentine I heard distinctly both the whistle and the pipe, which produced 380 waves a second. On changing places with my assistant, I heard for a time the distinct blast of the whistle only. The deeper note of the organ-pipe at length reached me, rising sometimes to great distinctness, and sometimes falling to inaudibility. The whistle showed the same intermittence as to period, but in an opposite sense; for when the whistle was faint the pipe was strong, and vice versa. To obtain the fundamental note it had to be blown gently, and on the whole the whistle proved the most efficient in piercing the fog.

An extraordinary amount of sound filled the air during these experiments. The resonant roar of the Bayswater and Knightsbridge roads; the clangour of the great bell of Westminster; the railway-whistles, which were frequently blown, and the fog-signals exploded at the various metropolitan stations, were all heard with extraordinary intensity. This could by no means be reconciled with the statements so categorically made regarding the acoustic impenetrability of a London fog.

From Lecture VII in On Sound *by John Tyndall, published 1875.*

346 THE LUNAR LANDSCAPE 1874

Let us, in imagination, take our stand high upon the eastern side of the rampart of one of the great craters. Height, it must be remarked, is more essential on the moon to command extent of view than upon the earth, for on account of the comparative smallness of the lunar sphere the dip of the horizon is very rapid. Such height, however, would be attained without great exercise of muscular power, since equal amounts of climbing energy would, from the smallness of lunar gravity, take a man six times as high on the moon as on the earth. Let us choose, for instance, the hill-side of Copernicus. The day begins by a sudden transition. The faint looming of objects under the united illumination of the half-full earth and zodiacal light is the lunar precursor of day-break. Suddenly the highest mountain peaks receive the direct rays of a portion of the sun's disc as it emerges from below the horizon. The brilliant lighting of these summits serves but to increase, by contrast, the prevailing darkness, for they seem to float like islands of light in a sea of gloom. At a rate of motion twenty-eight times slower than we are accustomed to, the light tardily creeps down the mountain-sides, and in the course of about twelve hours the whole of the circular rampart of the great crater below us, and towards the east, shines out in brilliant light, unsoftened by a trace of mountain-mist. But on the opposite side, looking into the crater, nothing but blackness is to be seen. As hour succeeds hour, the sunbeams reach peak after peak of the circular rampart in slow succession, till at length the circle is complete and the vast crater-rim, 50 miles in diameter, glistens like a silver-margined abyss of darkness. By-and-by, in the centre appears a group of bright peaks or bosses. These are the now illuminated summits of the central cones, and the development of the great mountain cluster they form henceforth becomes an imposing feature of the scene. From our high standpoint, and looking backwards to the sunny side of our cosmorama, we glance over a vast region of the wildest volcanic desolation. Craters from five miles diameter downwards crowd together in countless numbers, so that the surface, as far as the eye can reach, looks veritably frothed over with them. Nearer the base of the rampart on which we stand, extensive mountain chains run to north and to south, casting long shadows towards us; and away to the southward run several great chasms a mile wide and of appalling blackness and depth. Nearer still, almost beneath us, crag rises on crag and precipice upon precipice, mingled with craters and yawning pits, towering pinnacles of rock, piles of scoria and volcanic *débris*. But we behold no sign of existing or vestige of past organic life. No heaths or mosses soften the sharp edges and hard surfaces: no tints of cryptogamous or lichenous vegetation give a complexion of life to the hard fire-worn countenance of the scene. The whole landscape, as far as the eye can reach, is a realization of a fearful dream of desolation and lifelessness – not a dream of death, for that implies evidence of pre-existing life, but a vision of a world upon which the light of life has never dawned.

From The Moon considered as a Planet, a World, and a Satellite *by James Nasmyth and James Carpenter, 1874.*

347   **THE POWER TO COME**   before 1875

The people are the power to come. Oppressed, unprotected, abandoned; left to the ebb and flow of the tides of the market, now taken on to work, now cast off to starve, committed to the shifting laws of demand and supply, slaves of Capital – the whited name for old accursed Mammon; and of all the ranked and black-uniformed host no pastor to come out of the association of shepherds, and proclaim before heaven and man the primary claim of their cause; – they are, I say, the power, worth the seduction by another Power not mighty in England now; and likely in time to come to set up yet another Power not existing in England now.

From Beauchamp's Career *by George Meredith, published in the* Fortnightly Review, *1874–75.*

Compare Meredith's famous sonnet, 'Lucifer in Starlight':
>   . . . rank on rank
>   The army of unalterable law.

Both the sonnet and this passage are reminiscent of the early books of Paradise Lost:
>   Mammon, the least erected spirit that fell
>   From heavn . . .

and Meredith's lines about Lucifer:
>   He reach'd a middle height, and at the stars,
>   Which are the brain of heaven, he looked, and sank.

recall Milton, writing of himself:
>	in my flight
> Through utter and through middle darkness borne

in Book III, as well as in Book I:
>	my adventrous Song
> That with no middle flight intends to soar.

Meredith's 'stars, which are the brain of heaven' recall Newton on Space as the brain of God.

348   DELUSIONS OF CRIMINAL PRISONERS   c.1875

Another group of delusions are those of great genius and great inventive power. One man says he is wiser than Solomon, that he has more knowledge in his finger nail than all the Solons in Europe. He has invented a machine by which thieves may be detected when they are breaking into a house, but he will only show it to the governor, for fear some one else should get out the patent first. Another, D.B., has invented a flying-machine, and he can make a pig fly – and 'that is a very unlikely bird'. Now he only wants feathers to make its wings. This he intended to have done with his hair and whiskers, only they have been cut off. However, he completed the machine and tried it, returning to inform his friends that he had put his head through the first heaven, but he could not breathe and had to pull it back again. He only met a raven in his flight, which seemed very much surprised to see him. 'It is a glorious treat to sail around the world in a balloon.' Next time he tries his wings he means to take up a box of cigars to hand to those officers he likes as he passes the prison; but for those whom he hates he shall take up a bottle of vitriol, and drop it on their heads. To prove the value of his machine, he is to walk feet uppermost, along a rope stretched from the 'doom' of St Paul's to the top of the Monument. Unfortunately at the last, he declared he was no longer able to fly, as he had been steeped in salt and water, and was now too weak.

From Memorials of Millbank *by Captain Arthur Griffiths, 1875.*

These 'delusions' have affinities with the imagery of 347 and 'Lucifer in Starlight', as well as with Nasmyth (341) on the lunar landscape, Jules Verne's De la terre à la lune *(1865), and other flight fantasies or 'flights of fancy'.*

349   THE TWO CLAVIGERAE   July 16, 1877

Does then the Physician – the Artist – the Soldier – the good Priest – labour only for escape from his profession? Is not this manufacturing toil, as compared with all these, a despised one, and a miserable, – by the confession of all your efforts, and the proclamation of all your pride; and will you yet go on, if it may be, to fill England, from sea to sea, with this unhappy race, out of which you have risen?

'But we cannot all be physicians, artists, or soldiers. How are we to live?'

Assuredly not in multitudinous misery. Do you think that the Maker of the world intended all but one in a thousand of His creatures to live in these dark streets; and the one, triumphant over the rest, to go forth alone into the green fields?

This was what I was thinking, and more than ever thinking, all the while my good host was driving me by Shenstone's home, The Leasowes, into the vale of Severn; and telling me how happily far away St. George's ground was, from all that is our present England's life, and – pretended – glory. As we drove down the hill a little further towards Bewdley . . . my host asked me if I would like to see 'nailing'. 'Yes, truly.' So he took me into a little cottage where were two women at work, – one about seventeen or eighteen, the other perhaps four or five and thirty; this last intelligent of feature as well could be; and both gentle and kind, – each with hammer in right hand, pincers in left (heavier hammer poised over her anvil, and let fall at need by the touch of her foot on a treadle like that of a common grindstone). Between them a small forge, fed to constant brightness by the draught through the cottage, above whose roof its chimney rose: – in front of it, on a little ledge, the glowing lengths of cut iron rod, to be dealt with at speed. Within easy reach of this, looking up at us in quietly silent questioning, – stood, each in my sight an ominous Fors, the two Clavigerae.

At a word, they laboured, with ancient Vulcanian skill. Foot and hand in perfect time; no dance of the Muses on Parnassian mead in truer measure; – no sea fairies upon yellow sands more featly footed. Four strokes with the hammer in the hand: one ponderous and momentary blow ordered of the balanced mass by the touch of the foot; and the forged nail fell aside, finished, on its proper heap; – level-headed, wedge-pointed,* a thousand lives soon to depend daily on its driven grip of the iron way.

So wrought they, – the English Matron and Maid; – so was it their darg to labour from morning to evening, – seven to seven, – by the furnace side, – the winds of summer fanning the blast of it. The wages of the Matron Fors, I found were eight shillings a week;† – her husband, otherwise and variously employed, could make sixteen. Three shillings a week for rent and taxes, left, as I count, for the guerdon of their united labour, if constant, and its product providently saved, fifty-five pounds a year, on which they had to

---

* Flattened on two sides, I mean: they were nails for fastening the railroad metals to the sleepers, and made out of three-inch (or thereabouts) lengths of iron rod, which I was surprised and pleased to find, in spite of all our fine machines, the women still preferred to cut by hand.

† Sixteen-pence a day, or, for four days work, the price of a lawyer's letter.

feed and clothe themselves and their six children; eight souls in their little Worcestershire ark.

Nevertheless, I hear of all my friends pitying the distress I propose to reduce myself to, in living, all alone, upon three hundred and sixty, and doing nothing for it but contemplate the beauties of nature; while these two poor women, with other such, pay what portion of their three shillings a week goes to provide me with my annual dividend.

From Fors Clavigera, *Letter the 8th, by John Ruskin, 1877.*

350   **ARREOI**   November 15, 1878

If it were universally known that the birth of children could be prevented, and this were not thought immoral by married persons, would there not be great danger of extreme profligacy amongst unmarried women, and might we not become like the 'arreoi' societies in the Pacific? In the course of a century France will tell us the result in many ways, and we can already see that the French nation does not spread or increase much.

From a letter of Charles Darwin to G.A. Gaskell, printed in More Letters of Charles Darwin, *edited by Francis Darwin and A.C. Seward, 1903.*

1877 was the year of the Besant–Bradlaugh trial for publication of Birth-Control pamphlets. Note also that Darwin was in correspondence with Gaskell, Galton and others who were studying heredity. Darwin was in fact subpoenaed as a witness for Bradlaugh in June 1877.

351   A PARADOXICAL ODE   1878
To HERMANN STOFFKRAFT, Ph.D.,
the Hero of a recent work called 'Paradoxical Philosophy'

(After Shelley)

I

My soul is an entangled knot,
Upon a liquid vortex wrought
By Intellect, in the Unseen residing,
And thine doth like a convict sit,
With marlinspike untwisting it,
Only to find its knottiness abiding;
Since all the tools for its untying
In four-dimensional space are lying,
Wherein thy fancy intersperses
Whole avenues of universes,

While Klein and Clifford fill the void
With one finite, unbounded homaloid,
And think the Infinite is now at last destroyed.

II

But when thy Science lifts her pinions
In Speculation's wild dominions,
We treasure every dictum thou emittest,
While down the stream of Evolution
We drift, expecting no solution
But that of the survival of the fittest.
Till, in the twilight of the gods,
When earth and sun are frozen clods,
When, all its energy degraded,
Matter to æther shall have faded;
We, that is, all the work we've done,
As waves in æther, shall for ever run
In ever-widening spheres through heavens beyond the sun.

III

Great Principle of all we see,
Unending Continuity!
By thee are all our angles sweetly rounded,
By thee are our misfits adjusted,
And as I still in thee have trusted,
So trusting, let me never be confounded!
Oh never may direct Creation
Break in upon my contemplation;
Still may thy causal chain, ascending,
Appear unbroken and unending,
While residents in the Unseen –
Æons and Emanations – intervene,
And from my shrinking soul the Unconditioned screen.

Ode by James Clerk-Maxwell, printed in The Life of James Clerk-Maxwell *by L. Campbell and W. Garnett, 1882.*

The Ode is described as 'After Shelley', but note the use of sources other than Shelley, e.g. Gray, Milton on Time and on Christ's Nativity, showing Clerk-Maxwell's astonishing understanding of the idea of an Ode.

352   **THE ELECTRIC LIGHT**   March 14, 1879

I went the other night to see the British Museum lit with the electric light, the superintendent of the Reading Room having offered me a ticket; it looked very well; and I also went last night to the Albert Hall to hear the *Dettingen Te Deum* (which is magnificent), and there I found more electric light, but not so good as at the British Museum. The chorus 'To Thee Cherubim and Seraphim continually do cry' was wonderful. I have counted the 'continually's' and find the word repeated exactly 51 times. If you will say the word 'continually' ten times on each of your five fingers you will find it gives you an idea of the fine effect produced. I heard it years ago, and for some reason or other liked it less than most of Handel's works; but last night quite changed me.

From a letter of Samuel Butler to Miss Butler, quoted in H. Festing Jones, Samuel Butler, A Memoir, *1919.*

353 THE EDISON TELEPHONE 1879

In 1879 the performance of the Edison telephone was illustrated in the theatre of the Royal Institution. Through the kindness of Lord John Manners and the Post Office authorities, a wire, passing through the air from Albemarle Street to Piccadilly Circus, was placed at my service. The two ends of this wire being connected with the public water-pipes at the respective stations, a circuit was established through which a voltaic current could flow. In the circuit, at each end of the air wire, was placed an ordinary carbon telephone (to be referred to immediately), into which the messages were spoken. But while the receiver, at the Circus, of the messages sent from the Royal Institution, was a Bell's magnetic telephone held to the ear, the receiver at the Royal Institution was Edison's loudspeaking telephone. The nephew of Mr Edison, who bore his name, was stationed at the Circus, while Mr Adams operated with the new instrument in Albemarle Street. Passages from Shakespeare, Scott, Tennyson, Macaulay, and Burns, spoken by me through the carbon telephone, were received at the Circus, there repeated by Mr Edison, and returned with an accuracy and loudness which enabled them to be heard throughout the theatre. Not only were selected phrases thus heard, but a poem of Emerson's was read out here from beginning to end, and sent back line by line with extraordinary fidelity and distinctness. Various expressions, moreover, following the quotations, such as 'Excellent!' 'Perfectly satisfactory!' 'Exceedingly good!' were promptly returned and heard with amusing intensity by the audience. Perhaps the most striking illustration of the pliant power of the instrument was its capability to reproduce a whistled tune. Mr Edison's whistling at the Circus was heard in Albemarle Street almost as distinctly as if it had been produced upon the spot. After the lecture I quitted the theatre for a time, during which some members of the audience took my place. On my return I resumed the carbon telephone, and spoke into it. Mr Edison immediately detected this difference of tone, and, on being asked who it was that now spoke, answered correctly. By this new instrument, therefore, the varying qualities of the human voice are in a remarkable degree reproduced.

From On Sound *by John Tyndall, 4th edition, 1883.*

354   NOTHING LIKE THE EARTH   1879

31st July. Some rain early morning. Hot fine evening. Sedge in pond.

1st August. Rain in night: some early morning; fine hot day. Burdock in flower (thistle-like). Thistles in flower in barley so thick as to give it a purple tint over two or three acres.

2nd August. Fine morning. Afternoon cloudy, N.E. wind strong and cool. Night at eleven lightning, continuous came up from N.W. Moonlight brilliant – violet lightning – hailstones, a little larger than a shilling – see roses in the garden and the water glancing in the flashes – thunder louder after storm passed as if blown back by N.E. Wind. Lightning long flashes quivering several seconds.

3rd August. Morning dull, hot. Thrushes and blackbirds do not sing: but did up to within day or two. Willow wren singing zit-zit – yellow hammer very much – greenfinch too.

4th August. Rain early morning: hot fine day.

5th August. Cloudy: evening heavy rain. A little while since plantain flowered in wet ditch.

6th August. Fine morning; showers later. Lightning, heavy thunder. At 4 exceedingly heavy rain. Fog came on in early afternoon – rooks stopped in copse instead of going home to wood – not done it for fifty years – could not find way.

7th. Cloudy morning: afternoon light showers. Branch of sod apple in bloom . . . Rooks fond of maize, Rooks nest in tall Scotch firs: also spruce very high. Bramble still in flower very much: plane trees leaves already brown leathery in spots – wood pigeons calling? Spring and autumn not summer: sparrows in oats, scores, on stalk below grain still green, out for grain.

8th August. Small rain morning: afterwards dry. Barley – thistles rise from roots, not seed: a spindle root. Yesterday saw a small dragonfly: either first or else rare. Swifts still here and screaming.

11th August. Cloudy misty morning: Farmer market morning waiting at stile till another came along with trap, for ride. A large green dragonfly: it is their season then. Last full moon was very high in the sky: near zenith. There is nowhere where you can put £100 and be certain of getting it back again – no deposit (consols pay 90 and receive 94) – nothing like the Earth after all.

12th August. Fine hot N.E. wind. Grasshoppers singing in grass.

15th August. Hot cloudy morning – fine white clouds. Drovers come in, asking for hard biscuits, and toast at the fire: then take tallow candle from table and drop grease from it on biscuit till it would not suck up any more – and eat it as very good: as special relish after 2 days' drinking.

From the Note-books of Richard Jefferies, printed in Concerning Richard Jefferies, *by various writers, published 1944.*

| 355 | MANCHESTER DEVIL'S DARKNESS | August 13, 1879 |

Brantwood

The most terrific and horrible thunderstorm, this morning, I ever remember. It waked me at six, or a little before – then rolling incessantly, like railway luggage trains, quite ghastly in its mockery of them – the air one loathsome mass of sultry and foul fog, like smoke; scarcely raining at all, but increasing to heavier rollings, with flashes quivering vaguely through all the air, and at last terrific double streams of reddish-violet fire, not forked or zigzag, but rippled rivulets – two at the same instant some twenty to thirty degrees apart, and lasting on the eye at least half a second, with grand artillery-peals following; not rattling crashes, or irregular cracklings, but delivered volleys. It lasted an hour, then passed off, clearing a little, without rain to speak of, – not a glimpse of blue, – and now, half-past seven, seems settling down again into Manchester devil's darkness.

Quarter to eight, morning. – Thunder returned, all the air collapsed into one black fog, the hills invisible, and scarcely visible the opposite shore; heavy rain in short fits, and frequent, though less formidable, flashes and shorter thunder. While I have written this sentence the cloud has again dissolved itself, like a nasty solution in a bottle, with miraculous and unnatural rapidity, and the hills are in sight again; a double-forked flash – rippled, I mean, like the others – starts into its frightful ladder of light between me and Wetherlam, as I raise my eyes. All black above, a rugged spray cloud on the Eaglet. (The 'Eaglet' is my own name for the bold and elevated crag to the west of the little lake above Coniston mines. It had no name among the country people, and is one of the most conspicuous features of the mountain chain, as seen from Brantwood.)

Half-past eight. – Three times light and three times dark since last I wrote, and the darkness seeming each time as it settles more loathsome, at last stopping my reading in mere blindness. One lurid gleam of white cumulus in upper lead-blue sky, seen for half a minute through the sulphurous chimney-pot vomit of blackguardly cloud beneath, where its rags were thinnest.

From The Storm-Cloud of the Nineteenth Century *by John Ruskin, published 1884.*

356 THE ROMANCE HAS DEPARTED 1879

A rattling, thumping, booming noise, like the beating of their war drums by savages, comes over the hedge where the bees are busy at the bramble flowers. The bees take no heed, they pass from flower to flower, seeking the sweet honey to store at home in the hive, as their bee ancestors did before the Roman legions marched to Cowey Stakes. Their habits have not changed; their 'social' relations are the same; they have not called in the aid of machinery to enlarge their liquid wealth, or to increase the facility of collecting it. There is a low murmur rather than a buzz along the hedgerow; but over it the hot summer breeze brings the thumping, rattling, booming sound of hollow metal striking against the ground or in contact with other metal. These ringing noises, which so little accord with the sweet-scented hay and green hedgerows, are caused by the careless handling of milk tins dragged hither and thither by the men who are getting the afternoon milk ready for transit to the railway station miles away. Each tin bears a brazen badge engraved with the name of the milkman who will retail the contents in distant London. It may be delivered to the countess in Belgravia, and reach her dainty lip in the morning chocolate, or it may be eagerly swallowed up by the half-starved children of some back court in the purlieus of the Seven Dials.

Sturdy milkmaids may still be seen in London, sweeping the crowded pavement clear before them as they walk with swinging tread, a yoke on their shoulders, from door to door. Some remnants of the traditional dairy thus survives in the stony streets that are separated so widely from the country. But here, beside the hay, the hedgerows, the bees, the flowers that precede the blackberries – here in the heart of the meadows the romance has departed. From the refrigerator that cools the milk, the thermometer that tests its temperature, the lactometer that proves its quality, all is mechanised precision. The tins themselves are metal – wood, the old country material for almost every purpose, is eschewed – and they are swung up into a wagon specially built for the purpose. It is the very antithesis of the jolting and cumbrous wagon used for generations in the hayfields and among the corn. It is light, elegantly proportioned, painted, varnished – the work rather of a coachbuilder than a cartwright. The horse harnessed in it is equally unlike the cart-horse. A quick, wiry horse, that may be driven in a trap or gig, is the style – one that will rattle along and catch the train.

The driver takes his seat and handles the reins with the air of a man driving a tradesman's van, instead of walking, like the true old carter, or sitting on the shaft. The vehicle rattles off to the station, where ten, fifteen, or perhaps twenty such converge at the same hour, and then ensues a scene of bustle, chaff, and rough language. The tins are placed in the van specially reserved for them, the whistle sounds, the passengers – who have been wondering why on earth there was all this noise and delay at a little roadside station without so much as a visible steeple – withdraw their heads from the windows; the wheels revolve, and, gathering speed, the train disappears round a curve, hastening to the metropolis. Then the empty tins returned from town have to be conveyed home with more rattling, thumping and booming of hollow tin – there to be carefully cleansed, for which purpose vast quantities of hot water must be ready, and coal, of course, must be consumed in proportion.

From Hodge and his Masters *by Richard Jefferies, 1880.*

357 THE PRINCIPLE OR FOUNDATION c.1880

Homo creatus est – CREATION THE MAKING OUT OF NOTHING, bringing from nothing into being: once there was nothing, then lo, this huge world was there. How great a work of power!

The loaf is made with flour; the house with bricks; the plough, the cannon, the locomotive, the warship of iron – all of things that were before, of matter; but the world, with the flour, the grain, the wheatear, the seed, the ground, the sun, the rain; with the bricks, the clay, the earth; with the iron and the mine, the fuel and the furnace, was made from nothing. And they are MADE IN TIME AND WITH LABOUR, the world in no time with a word. MAN CANNOT CREATE a single speck, God creates all that is besides himself.

But MEN OF GENIUS ARE SAID TO CREATE, a painting, a poem, a tale, a tune, a policy; not indeed the colours and the canvas, not the words or notes, but the design, the character, the air, the plan. How then? – from themselves, from their own minds. And they themselves, their minds and all, are creatures of God: if the tree created much more the flower and the fruit.

To know what creation is LOOK AT THE SIZE OF THE WORLD. Speed of light: it would fly six or seven times round the earth while the clock ticks once. Yet it takes *thousands of years* to reach us from the Milky Way, which is made up of stars swimming together (though as far from one another as we are from some of them), running into one, and looking like a soft mist, and each of them a million times as big as the earth perhaps (the sun is about that). And there is not the least reason to think that is anything like the size of the whole world. And all arose at a word! So that the greatest of all works in the world, nay the world itself, was easier made than the least little thing that man or any other creature makes in the world.

LUDGATE HILL

From The Principle or Foundation *(An Address based on the Opening of the Spiritual Exercises of St Ignatius Loyola) by Gerard Manley Hopkins, written c.1880, published in* The Notebooks & Papers of Gerard Manley Hopkins, *edited by Humphry House, 1937.*

358 **THE VIEW DOWN FLEET STREET** 1880–81

I know of nothing in any foreign city equal to the view down Fleet Street, walking along the north side from the corner of Fetter Lane. It is often said that this has been spoiled by the London, Chatham, and Dover Railway bridge over Ludgate Hill; I think, however, the effect is more imposing now than it was before the bridge was built. Time has already softened it; it does not obtrude itself; it adds greatly to the sense of size, and makes us doubly aware of the movement of life, the colossal circulation to which London owes so much of its impressiveness. We gain more by this than we lose by the infraction of some pedant's canon about the artistically correct intersection of right lines. Vast as is the world below the bridge, there is a vaster still on high, and when trains are passing, the steam from the engine will throw the dome of St. Paul's into clouds, and make it seem as though there was a commingling of earth and some far-off mysterious palace in dreamland.

From Alps and Sanctuaries of Piedmont and the Canton Ticino *by Samuel Butler, published 1882.*

This passage is quoted in Gloag's Industrial Art Explained *and placed quite correctly opposite Doré's view of Ludgate Hill in 1870 – not 'in the middle of the nineteenth century'. Compare Charles Kingsley on the Hungerford Suspension Bridge (251). Of course Gloag is talking rubbish (compare 'pedant's canon' above). Compare also Monet's 'Gare St Lazare', 1872. And there is a picture of the same view by J.E. Blanche in the Tate Gallery. Compare T.H. Huxley, 371.*

359 **SCIENCE AND POETRY** 1881

I have said that in one respect my mind has changed during the last twenty or thirty years. Up to the age of thirty, or beyond it, poetry of many kinds, such as the works of Milton, Gray, Byron, Wordsworth, Coleridge and Shelley, gave me great pleasure, and even as a schoolboy I took intense delight in Shakespeare, especially in the historical plays. I have also said that formerly pictures gave me considerable, and music very great delight. But now for many years I cannot endure to read a line of poetry: I have tried lately to read Shakespeare, and found it so intolerably dull that it nauseated me. I have also almost lost my taste for pictures or music. Music generally sets me thinking too energetically on what I have been at work on, instead of giving me pleasure. I retain some taste for fine scenery, but it does not cause me the exquisite delight which it formerly did. On the other hand, novels which are works of the imagination, though not of a very high order, have been for years a wonderful relief and pleasure to me, and I often bless all novelists. A surprising number have been read aloud to me, and I like all if moderately good, and if they do not end unhappily – against which a law ought to be passed. A novel according to my taste, does not come into the first class unless it contains some person whom one can thoroughly love, and if a pretty woman all the better.

This curious and lamentable loss of the higher aesthetic tastes is all the odder, as books on history, biographies, and travel (independent of any scientific facts which they may contain), and essays on all sorts of subjects interest me as much as ever they did. My mind seems to have become a kind of machine for grinding general laws out of large collections of facts, but why this should have caused the atrophy of that part of the brain alone, on which the higher tastes depend, I cannot conceive. A man with a mind more highly organised or better constituted than mine, would not, I suppose, have thus suffered; and if I had to live my life again, I would have made it a rule to read some poetry and listen to some music at least once every week; for perhaps the parts of my brain now atrophied would thus have been kept active through use. The loss of these tastes is a loss of happiness, and may possibly be injurious to the intellect, and more probably to the moral character, by enfeebling the emotional part of our nature.

From Recollections of the Development of my Mind and Character *by Charles Darwin, written in 1881 and printed in* The Life and Letters of Charles Darwin, *edited by Francis Darwin, 1887.*

360   IN A MANUFACTURING TOWN   c.1881

As I walked restless and despondent through the gloomy city,
And saw the eager unresting to and fro – as of ghosts in some sulphurous Hades –
And saw the crowds of tall chimneys going up, and the pall of smoke covering the sun, covering the earth, lying heavy against the very ground –
And saw the huge refuse-heaps writhing with children picking them over,
And the ghastly half-roofless smoke-blackened houses, and the black river flowing below, –
As I saw these, and as I saw again far away the Capitalist quarter,
With its villa residences and its high-walled gardens and its well-appointed carriages, and its face turned away from the wriggling poverty which made it rich, –
As I saw and remembered its drawing-room airs and affectations and its

wheezy pursy Church-going and its gas-reeking heavy-furnished rooms and its scent-bottles and its other abominations –

I shuddered:

For I felt stifled, like one who lies half-conscious – knowing not clearly the shape of the evil – in the grasp of some heavy nightmare.

Then out of the crowd descending towards me came a ragged little boy;

Came – from the background of dirt disengaging itself – an innocent wistful child-face, begrimed like the rest but strangely pale, and pensive before its time.

And, in an instant (it was as if a trumpet had been blown in that place) I saw it all clearly, the lie I saw and the truth, the false dream and the awakening.

For the smoke-blackened walls and the tall chimneys, and the dreary habitations of the poor, and the drearier habitations of the rich, crumbled and conveyed themselves away as if by magic;

And instead, in the backward vista of that face, I saw the joy of free open life under the sun:

The green sun-delighting earth and rolling sea I saw –

The free sufficing life – sweet comradeship, few needs and common pleasures – the needless endless burdens all cast aside,

Not as a sentimental vision, but as a fact and a necessity existing, I saw In the backward vista of that face.

Stronger than all combinations of Capital, wiser than all the Committees representative of Labor, the simple need and hunger of the human heart.

Nothing more is needed.

All the books of political economy ever written, all the proved impossibilities, are of no account.

The smoke-blackened walls and tall chimneys duly crumble and convey themselves away;

The falsehood of a gorged and satiated society curls and shrivels together like a withered leaf,

Before the forces which lie dormant in the pale and wistful face of a little child.

From Towards Democracy *by Edward Carpenter, 1883.*

361 THE FIRST WHISPER June 1882

I then sketched the misery of the peasants in the grip of absentee landlords, the turning out on the roadside to die of the mother with new-born babe at her breast, the loss of 'all thought of the sanctity of human life when the lives of the dearest are reckoned as less worth than the shillings of overdue rack-rental'. I analysed the new Act: 'When this Act passes, trial by jury, right of public meeting, liberty of press, sanctity of house, will one and all be held at the will of the Lord-Lieutenant, the irresponsible autocrat of Ireland, while the liberty of person will lie at the mercy of every constable. Such is England's way of governing Ireland in the year 1882. And this is supposed to be a Bill for the "repression of crime".' Bluntly, I put the bald truth: 'The plain fact is that the murderers have succeeded. They saw in the new policy the reconciliation of England and Ireland; they knew that friendship would follow justice, and that the two countries, for the first time in history, would clasp hands. To prevent this they dug a new gulf, which they hoped the English nation would not span; they sent a river of blood across the road of friendship, and they flung two corpses to bar the newly-opened gate of reconciliation and peace. They have succeeded.'

Into this whirl of political and social strife came the first whisper to me of the Theosophical Society, in the shape of a statement of its principles, which conveyed, I remarked, 'no very definite idea of the requirements for membership, beyond a dreamy, emotional, scholarly interest in the religio-philosophic fancies of the past.' Also a report of an address by Colonel Olcott, which led me to suppose that the society held to 'some strange theory of "apparitions" of the dead, and to some existence outside the physical and apart from it.' These came to me from some Hindu Freethinkers, who asked my opinion as to Secularists joining the Theosophical Society, and Theosophists being admitted to the National Secular Society. I replied, judging from these reports, that 'while Secularists would have no right to refuse to enrol Theosophists, if they desired it, among their members, there is a radical difference between the mysticism of Theosophy and the scientific materialism of Secularism. The exclusive devotion to this world implied in the profession of Secularism leaves no room for other-worldism; and consistent members of our body cannot join a society which professes belief therein.'*

From An Autobiography *by Annie Besant, 1893.*

Note first of all the parallel between Ireland and India (and Burma) and 'the first whisper' coming from Hindu students. Note how parallel is the reference to the murders by agents provocateurs *to the murder of Gandhi (January 20, 1948), Aung San (July 19, 1947) and Tin Tut (September 18, 1948). Compare Jung on the theosophical background of the imperialist nations, Holland and Britain.*

Compare also Tylor (338) and compare the volte face of Robert Owen and his conversion to spiritualism in the '50s (278). Remember also of course that after a year or two of socialism, Annie Besant met Helena Blavatsky and went to India and became a member of the Indian National Congress and finally its president.

* National Reformer, June 18, 1882.

We must, however, refresh ourselves by occasional contact with the solid ground of experiment, and an interesting problem now lies before us awaiting experimental solution. Suppose 200 men to be scattered equally throughout the length of Pall Mall. By timely swerving now and then a runner from St James's Palace to the Athenaeum Club might be able to get through such a crowd without much hindrance. But supposing the men to close up so as to form a dense file crossing Pall Mall from north to south: such a barrier might seriously impede, or entirely stop, the runner. Instead of a crowd of men, let us imagine a column of molecules under small pressure, thus resembling the sparsely-distributed crowd. Let us suppose the column to shorten, without change in the quantity of matter, until the molecules are so squeezed together as to resemble the closed file across Pall Mall. During these changes of density, would the action of the molecules upon a beam of heat passing among them resemble the action of the crowd upon the runner?

From 'Atoms, Molecules and Ether Waves' by John Tyndall, first printed in Longman's Magazine, *1882.*

On images of molecules and men, compare H.G. Wells, Anticipations *on the grey 'disordered' mass of people which in the New Republic (Wells is writing c.1901) will re-organise itself into brightly coloured groups – the particles in the grey being of course already coloured – the colour at present being lost in the muddle.*

Compare also Paul Valéry, La Crise de l'Esprit *(1919), in* Variétés *(1924) on diffusion of the inequalities of man similar to diffusion in physics – again the idea of men and molecules. Note the connection also with his poem 'Le Vin' – the diffusion and possible, or rather miraculous, idea of the diffused drop gathering itself together again. Compare p.32 with H.G. Wells on the reintegration of lost colours. Note also Valéry's suggestion of degradation with diffusion.*

Also compare the hæmoglobin test in A Study in Scarlet *by Arthur Conan Doyle (369) with Valéry's poem and passage. Clearly the conflict of diffusion and génie in Valéry is the same as that between the Second Law of Thermodynamics and evolution discussed by Needham who gives the basic quotes from Clerk-Maxwell 1873–75 (343) and Kelvin.*

Compare T.H. Huxley, The Method of Zadig *(1880) and note that impressionism itself represented the extreme diffusion of the central images of painters as established by Giotto, Raphael etc. – through the romanticism of Leonardo, Rubens, Velasquez, Delacroix – and that Cézanne and Seurat's work was to bring together again the diffused molecules into a new shape – génie.*

For the early '80s as the epoch of the New Journalism see The History of the Times, *which begins in 1884. There are many references in these years to 'the papers', 'The Times', 'newspaper proprietors'. But with these references there is also a subtler one connected with them – the crowd, the number of passengers, the phantoms, the molecules, even the bricks and mortar of buildings to replace Holland House (366) – they are all, as Blake said, 'men seen from afar'. . . . These men are sometimes seen as phantoms (365), as 'a million of letters' (363) – remember this is the epoch of Seurat in France. In distinction to them is the individual – runner, newspaper proprietor, Holland House itself, or the ragged little boy of Carpenter (360), or William Morris on the other side of the window (372). . . . Of course the crowd are the New Journalism's readers, the Met's passengers . . . so we see the modern world built up out of atoms and molecules, linked by causality.*

Sherlock Holmes's 'Book of Life', in A Study in Scarlet, *stresses precisely the relation of the drop of water to the Atlantic – compare Valéry on the relation of the wine and the sea – the relation of the individual to the crowd, of the molecule to the gas. It is also worth noting that the science of detection which is here seen arising from natural science was, so to speak, there all the time: Bacon's 'all learning for my province' schemes were precisely connected with the Elizabethan secret service – see Neale,* Queen Elizabeth.

| 363 | THE NUMBER OF PASSENGERS | 1882 |

At a recent meeting of the Metropolitan Railway Company I exhibited one million of letters, in order to show the number of passengers (thirty-seven millions) that had been conveyed during the previous twelve months. This number was so vast that my method only helped the meeting to understand what had been done in the way of conveyance. Mr. Macdonald, of *The Times*, supplied me with one million type impressions, contained in sixty average columns of *The Times* newspaper.

From An Autobiography *by James Nasmyth, edited by Samuel Smiles, published 1883.*

| 364 | MENTAL CHOKING | 1882 |

While sitting on a ledge of rock facing the East, and looking over the wide country stretching away to the horizon beyond the Hudson, it was interesting to think that here we were in a land we had read about all our lives – interesting, and a little difficult, to think of it as some three thousand miles from the island on the other side of the Atlantic whence we had come. Not easy was it either, and indeed impossible in any true sense, to conceive the real position of this island on that vast surface which slowly curves downward beyond the horizon: the impossibility being one which I have vividly felt when gazing sea-ward at the masts of a vessel below the horizon, and trying to conceive the actual surface of the Earth, as slowly bending round till its meridians met eight thousand miles beneath my feet: the attempt producing what may be figuratively called a kind of mental choking, from the endeavour to put into the intellectual structure a conception immensely too large for it.

From An Autobiography *by Herbert Spencer, 1904.*

365 PHANTASMAGORIA 1883

A common form of vision is a phantasmagoria, or the appearance of a crowd of phantoms, sometimes hurrying past like men in a street. It is occasionally seen in broad daylight, much more often in the dark; it may be at the instant of putting out the candle, but it generally comes on when the person is in bed, preparing to sleep, but by no means yet asleep. I know no less than three men, eminent in the scientific world, who have these phantasmagoria in one form or another. It will seem curious, but it is a fact that I know of no less than five editors of very influential newspapers who experience these night visitations in a vivid form. Two of them have described the phenomena very forcibly in print, but anonymously, and two others have written on cognate experiences.

From Inquiries into Human Faculty *by Francis Galton, 1883.*

366 HOLLAND HOUSE Summer 1883

What a grand, memorable, and beautiful place it is! It recalls to my memory the society, political, intellectual, convivial, and genial, of sixty years ago. It recalls the memory of some estimable and some non-estimable persons – all dead and gone; perhaps at the grand garden party of yesterday not one besides myself had ever seen this Palace in its prime, under the famous proprietors, Lord and Lady Holland; and soon, no doubt, the glorious mansion itself, and the noble, ancient park around it, will be consigned to the erection of some thousand edifices; to the domain of brick and mortar. The price it would fetch for building purposes, perhaps half-a-million, will overcome reverence for antiquity, sense of beauty, and all ennobling contemplations. It brought a feeling of sadness over me. But such is progress! And, perhaps, the Prose of the Future may be equal, if not superior, to the Poetry of the Past.

From the Journal of Lord Shaftesbury, quoted in The Life and Work of the Seventh Earl of Shaftesbury *by Edwin Hodder, 1886.*

THE STORM-CLOUD OF THE NINETEENTH CENTURY

February 4, 1884

I

Let me first assure my audience that I have no *arrière pensée* in the title chosen for this lecture. I might, indeed, have meant, and it would have been only too like me to mean, any number of things by such a title; – but, to-night, I mean simply what I have said, and propose to bring to your notice a series of cloud phenomena, which, so far as I can weigh existing evidence, are peculiar to our times; yet which have not hitherto received any special notice or description from meteorologists.

So far as the existing evidence, I say, of former literature can be interpreted, the storm-cloud – or more accurately plague-cloud, for it is not always stormy – which I am about to describe to you, never was seen but by now living, or *lately* living eyes. It is not yet twenty years that this – I may well call it, wonderful, cloud has been, in its essence, recognisable. There is no description of it, so far as I have read, by any ancient observer. Neither Homer nor Virgil, neither Aristophanes nor Horace, acknowledge any such clouds among those compelled by Jove. Chaucer has no word of them, nor Dante; Milton none, nor Thomson. In modern times, Scott, Wordsworth and Byron are alike unconscious of them; and the most observant, and descriptive of scientific men, de Saussure, is utterly silent concerning them. Taking up the traditions of air from the year before Scott's death, I am able, by my own constant and close observation, to certify you that in the forty following years (1831 to 1871 approximately – for the phenomena in question came on gradually) – no such clouds as these are, and are now often for months without intermission, were ever seen in the skies of England, France, or Italy.

In those old days, when weather was fine, it was luxuriously fine; when it was bad – it was often abominably bad, but it had its fit of temper and was done with it – it didn't sulk for three months without letting you see the sun, – nor send you one cyclone inside out, every Saturday afternoon, and another outside in, every Monday morning.

In fine weather the sky was either blue or clear in its light; the clouds, either white or golden, adding to, not abating, the lustre of the sky. In wet weather, there were two different species of clouds, – those of beneficent rain, which for distinction's sake I will call the non-electric rain-cloud, and those of storm, usually charged highly with electricity. The beneficent rain-cloud was indeed often extremely dull and grey for days together, but gracious nevertheless, felt to be doing good, and often to be delightful after drought; capable also of the most exquisite colouring, under certain conditions; and continually traversed by the rainbow: – and, secondly, the storm-cloud, always majestic, often dazzlingly beautiful, and felt also to be beneficent in its own way, affecting the mass of the air with vital agitation, and purging it from the impurity of all morbific elements.

In the entire system of the Firmament, thus seen and understood, there appeared to be, to all the thinkers of those ages, the incontrovertible and unmistakeable evidence of a Divine Power in creation, which had fitted, as the air for human breath, so the clouds for human sight and nourishment; – the Father who was in heaven feeding day by day the souls of his children with marvels, and satisfying them with bread, and so filling their hearts with food and gladness.

From The Storm-Cloud of the Nineteenth Century *by John Ruskin: two lectures delivered at the London Institution on February 4 and 11, 1884.*

368 THE MARCH OF THE WORKERS 1885

(AIR: 'John Brown's Body')

What is this, the sound and rumour? What is this that all men hear?
Like the wind in hollow valleys when the storm is drawing near,
Like the rolling on of ocean in the eventide of fear?
    'Tis the people marching on.

Whither go they, and whence come they? What are these of whom ye tell?
In what country are they dwelling 'twixt the gates of heaven and hell?
Are they mine or thine for money? Will they serve a master well?
    Still the rumour's marching on.

    Hark the rolling of the thunder!
    Lo the sun! and lo thereunder
    Riseth wrath, and hope, and wonder,
      And the host come marching on.

Forth they come from grief and torment; on they went toward health and mirth,
All the wide world is their dwelling, every corner of the earth.
Buy them, sell them for thy service! Try the bargain what 'tis worth,
    For the days are marching on.

These are they who build thy houses, weave thy raiment, win thy wheat,
Smooth the rugged, fill the barren, turn the bitter into sweet,
All for thee this day – and ever. What reward for them is meet?
    Till the host comes marching on.

    Hark the rolling of the thunder!
    Lo the sun! and lo thereunder
    Riseth wrath, and hope, and wonder,
      And the host comes marching on.

Many a hundred years passed over have they laboured deaf and blind;
Never tidings reached their sorrow, never hope their toil might find.
Now at last they've heard and hear it, and the cry comes down the wind,
    And their feet are marching on.

O ye rich men hear and tremble! for with words the sound is rife:
'Once for you and death we laboured; changed henceforward is the strife,
We are men, and we shall battle for the world of men and life;
    And our host is marching on.'

    Hark the rolling of the thunder!
    Lo the sun! and lo thereunder
    Riseth wrath, and hope, and wonder,
      And the host comes marching on.

'Is it war, then? Will ye perish as the dry wood in the fire?
Is it peace? Then be ye of us, let your hope be our desire.
Come and live! for life awaketh, and the world shall never tire;
    And the hope is marching on.'

'On we march then, we the workers, and the rumour that ye hear
Is the blended sound of battle and deliv'rance drawing near;
For the hope of every creature is the banner that we bear,
    And the world is marching on.'

    Hark the rolling of the thunder!
    Lo the sun! and lo thereunder
    Riseth wrath, and hope, and wonder,
      And the host comes marching on.

From Chants for Socialists *by William Morris, 1884–85.*

In 1885 there was sold upon the streets of London a penny pamphlet or rather folder called Chants for Socialists *published by the Socialist League and written by William Morris. This sheet contained among others the tremendous song beginning 'What is this . . .', to be sung by the way to the tune of 'John Brown's Body'. As the first copy of this pamphlet was sold a great English poet had for the first time joined hands truly with the working class and come into it as an equal and as a poet. The Imagination of the Poet and the revolutionary march of the workers in Britain were moving together, consciously resisting the English ruling class, said Lenin/Engels. By nothing is England so glorious said a lesser man, an Oxford Professor, an Inspector of Schools.*

As he spoke, we turned down a narrow lane and passed through a small side-door, which opened into a wing of the great hospital. It was familiar ground to me, and I needed no guiding as we ascended the bleak stone staircase and made our way down the long corridor with its vista of whitewashed wall and dun-coloured doors. Near the farther end a low arched passage branched away from it and led to the chemical laboratory.

This was a lofty chamber, lined and littered with countless bottles. Broad, low tables were scattered about, which bristled with retorts, test-tubes, and little Bunsen lamps, with their blue flickering flames. There was only one student in the room, who was bending over a distant table absorbed in his work. At the sound of our steps he glanced round and sprang to his feet with a cry of pleasure. 'I've found it!', he shouted to my companion, running towards us with a test-tube in his hand, 'I have found a re-agent which is precipitated by hæmoglobin, and by nothing else.' Had he discovered a gold mine, greater delight could not have shone upon his features.

'Dr. Watson, Mr. Sherlock Holmes,' said Stamford, introducing us.

'How are you?' he said cordially, gripping my hand with a strength for which I should hardly have given him credit. 'You have been in Afghanistan, I perceive.'

'How on earth did you know that?' I asked in astonishment.

'Never mind,' said he, chuckling to himself. 'The question now is about hæmoglobin. No doubt you see the significance of this discovery of mine?'

'It is interesting, chemically, no doubt,' I answered, 'but practically –'

'Why, man, it is the most practical medico-legal discovery for years. Don't you see that it gives us an infallible test for blood stains. Come over here now!' He seized me by the coat-sleeve in his eagerness, and drew me over to the table at which he had been working. 'Let us have some fresh blood,' he said, digging a long bodkin into his finger, and drawing off the resulting drop of blood into a chemical pipette. 'Now, I add this small quantity of blood to a litre of water. You perceive that the resulting mixture has the appearance of pure water. The proportion of blood cannot be more than one in a million. I have no doubt, however, that we shall be able to obtain the characteristic reaction.' As he spoke, he threw into the vessel a few white crystals, and then added some drops of a transparent fluid. In an instant the contents assumed a dull mahogany colour, and a brownish dust was precipitated to the bottom of the glass jar.

'Ha! ha!' he cried, clapping his hands, and looking as delighted as a child with a new toy.

From A Study in Scarlet *by Arthur Conan Doyle, 1887.*

After London

I

As, for the most part those who were left behind were ignorant, rude, and unlettered, it consequently happened that many of the marvellous things which the ancients did, and the secrets of their science, are known to us by name only, and, indeed, hardly by name. It has happened to us in our turn as it happened to the ancients. For they were aware that in times before their own the art of making glass malleable had been discovered, so that it could be beaten into shape like copper. But the manner in which it was accomplished was entirely unknown to them; the fact was on record, but the cause lost. So now we know that those who to us are the ancients had a way of making diamonds and precious stones out of black and lustreless charcoal, a fact which approaches the incredible. Still, we do not doubt it, though we cannot imagine by what means it was carried out.

They also sent intelligence to the utmost parts of the earth along wires which were not tubular, but solid, and therefore could not transmit sound, and yet the person who received the message could hear and recognise the voice of the sender a thousand miles away. With certain machines worked by fire, they traversed the lands as swift as the swallow glides through the sky, but of these things not a relic remains to us. What metal-work or wheels or bars of iron were left, and might have given us a clue, were all broken up and melted down for use in other ways when metal became scarce.

Mounds of earth are said to still exist in the woods, which originally formed the roads for these machines, but they are now so low, and so covered with thickets that nothing can be learnt from them; and, indeed, though I have heard of their existence, I have never seen one. Great holes were made through the very hills for the passage of the iron chariot, but they are now blocked by the falling roofs, nor dare any one explore such parts as may yet be open. Where are the wonderful structures with which the men of those days were lifted to the skies, rising above the clouds? These marvellous things are to us little more than the fables of the giants and of the old gods that walked upon the earth, which were fables even to those whom we call the ancients.

From After London *by Richard Jefferies, 1885.*

Apocalyptic Visions

July 6, 1886

I am not much inclined to join the 'Lake District Defence Society'. I value natural beauty so much, and think so highly of its influence that I would make beautiful scenery accessible to all the world, if I could. If any engineering or mining work is projected, which will really destroy the beauty of the Lakes, I will certainly oppose it, but I am not disposed, as Goschen said, to 'give a blank cheque' to a Defence Society, the force of which is pretty certain to be wielded by the most irrational fanatics among its members.

Only the other day I walked the whole length of Bassenthwaite from Keswick and back, and I cannot say that the little line of rails which runs along the lake, now coming into view and now disappearing, interfered with my keen enjoyment of the beauty of the lake any more than the macadamised road did. And if it had not been for that railway I should not have been able to make Keswick my headquarters, and I should have lost my day's delight.

People's sense of beauty should be more robust. I have had apocalyptic visions looking down Oxford Street at a sunset before now.

From a letter of T.H. Huxley to his eldest son, printed in Life and Letters of Thomas Henry Huxley, *edited by Leonard Huxley, 1900.*

372 THE DAY OF THE EARTH 1886

Once more I heard the voice of John Ball: 'Now, brother, I say farewell; for now verily hath the Day of the Earth come, and thou and I are lonely of each other again; thou hast been a dream to me as I to thee, and sorry and glad have we made each other, as tales of old time and the longing of times to come shall ever make men to be. I go to life and to death, and leave thee; and scarce do I know whether to wish thee some dream of the days beyond thine to tell what shall be, as thou hast told me, for I know not if that shall help or hinder thee; but since we have been kind and very friends, I will not leave thee without a wish of goodwill, so at least I wish thee what thou thyself wishest for thyself, and that is hopeful strife, and blameless peace, which is to say in one word, life. Farewell, friend.'

For some little time, although I had known that the daylight was growing and what was around me, I had scarce seen the things I had before noted so keenly; but now in a flash I saw all – the east crimson with sunrise through the white window on my right hand; the richly-carved stalls and gilded screen work, the pictures on the walls, the loveliness of the faultless colour of the mosaic window lights, the altar and the red light over it looking strange in the daylight, and the biers with the hidden dead men upon them that lay before the high altar. A great pain filled my heart at the sight of all that beauty, and withal I heard quick steps coming up the paved church-path to the porch, and the whistle of a sweet old tune therewith; then the footsteps stopped at the door; I heard the latch rattle, and knew that Will Green's hand was upon the ring of it.

Then I strove to rise up, but fell back again; a white light, empty of all sights, broke upon me for a moment, and lo! behold I was lying in my familiar bed, the south-westerly gale rattling the Venetian blinds and making their hold-fasts squeak.

I got up presently, and going to the window looked out on the winter morning; the river was before me broad between outer bank and bank, but it was nearly dead ebb, and there was a wide space of mud on each side of the hurrying stream, driven on the faster as it seemed by the push of the south-west wind. On the other side of the water the few willow-trees left us by the Thames Conservancy looked doubtfully alive against the bleak sky and the row of wretched-looking blue-slated houses, although, by the way, the latter were the backs of a sort of street of 'villas' and not a slum; the road in front of the house was sooty and muddy at once, and in the air was that sense of dirty discomfort which one is never quit of in London. The morning was harsh, too, and though the wind was from the south-west it was as cold as a north wind; and yet amidst it all, I thought of the corner of the next bight of the river which I could not quite see from where I was, but over which one can see clear of houses and into Richmond Park, looking like the open country; and dirty as the river was, and harsh as was the January wind, they seemed to woo me toward the countryside, where away from the miseries of the 'Great Wen' I might of my own will carry on a day-dream of the friends I had made in the dream of the night and against my will.

But as I turned away shivering and downhearted, on a sudden came the frightful noise of the 'hooters', one after the other, that call the workmen to the factories, this one the after-breakfast one, more by token. So I grinned surlily, and dressed and got ready for my day's 'work' as I call it, but which many a man besides John Ruskin (though not many in his position) would call 'play'.

From A Dream of John Ball *by William Morris, 1886–7.*

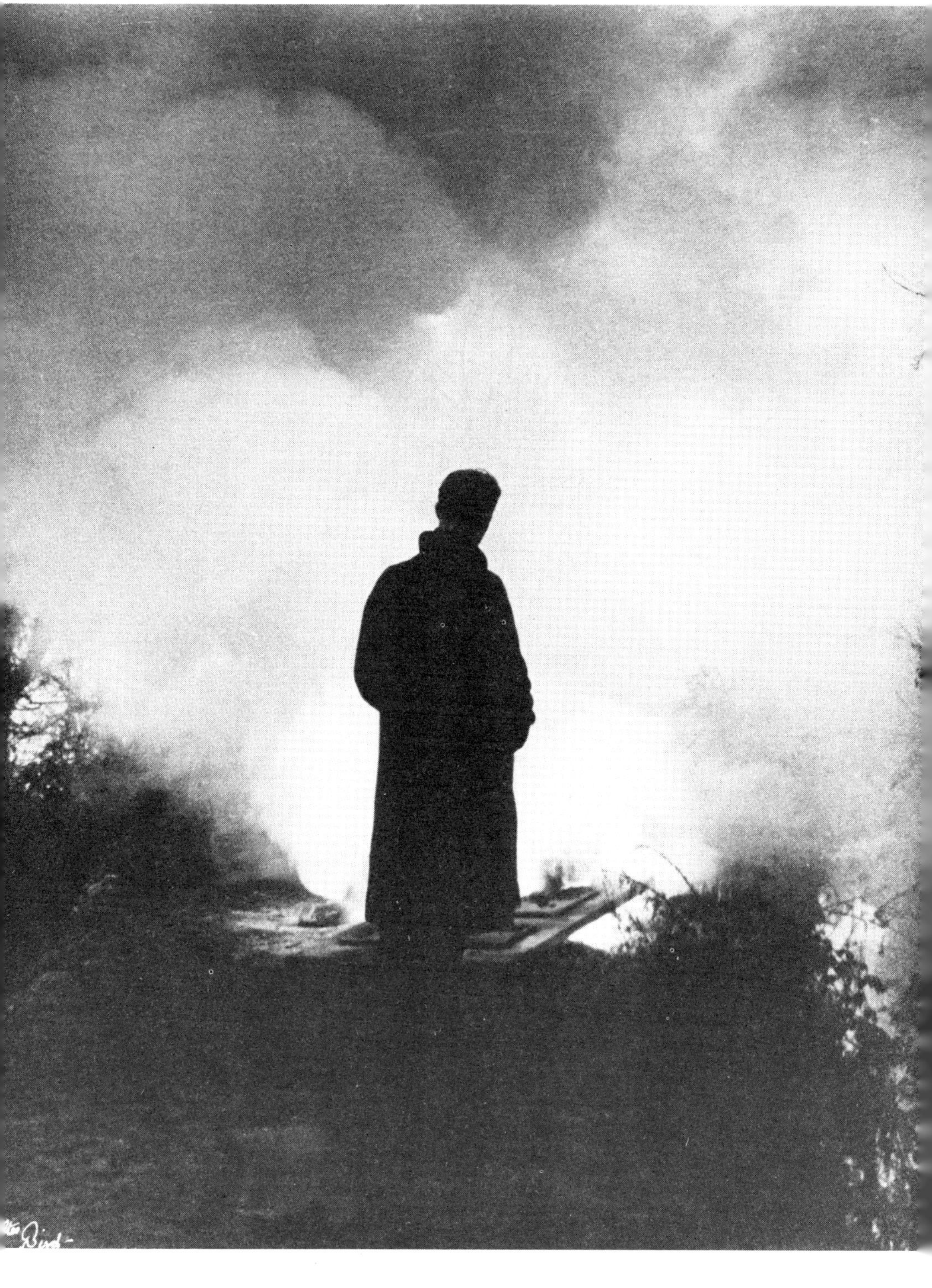

Theme Sequences

THE MAN OF SCIENCE

2   Memorandum
3   God Would Be Much Honored
4   The Boyhood of Genius
5   The Most Stupendious Work in the Whole World
12 Observations
30 Martinus Scriblerus
34 Effects of Lightning in Northamptonshire
35 The York Buildings Dragons
37 Experiment
51 A Perfect Steam-engine
59 Inspiration
71 Blind John Metcalf
72 The Composition of Water
83 The Lunatics
87 The Childhood of Mary Anne SchimmelPenninck
119 The Engine
125 The Extreme Delight
134 Machine for Copying Sculpture
135 Search for Beautiful Forms
138 Davy in Paris
139 A Reform
157 Professional Fancies
159 The Death-bed of Herschel
173 Mr Stephenson
179 Crispations
181 The Salvation of the Triatarsostinus
183 Cholera comes to Manchester
196 The Powers of the Machine
197 Photogenic Drawing
249 Thinking by Dreaming
261 The Scenery of Heaven
284 Terrestrial all in Chaos

310 Herschel and Nasmyth
312 The Little Garret at Heathfield
369 Blood Test

POETRY AND SCIENCE

43 A Love of System
49 Written in Bedlam
101 Facts of Mind
107 The Poet and the Man of Science
112 Newton
113 Newton
116 Chemistry
117 The Cursed Barbauld Crew
126 Rational Toys
132 When the Sun Rises
133 Cottle's Free Version of the Psalms
139 A Reform
141 Demonstration
144 Personification of Fictions
152 The Immortal Dinner
156 The Birth of the Cylinder
160 William Blake
180 Galvanism
181 The Salvation of the Triatarsostinus
190 The Country of the Iguanodon
199 The Ichthyosaurus
215 Mind and Matter
222 Poems
226 In Bedlam
227 Prose
239 Letter to Thomas Cooper
244 A Greater Epic
250 A Quiet Talk
279 A Terrific Banquet in an Iguanodon
314 The Human Element
326 Northern Farmer – New Style
329 Rough-Spun Nature
359 Science and Poetry

THEOLOGY AND SCIENCE

91 Panopticon
105 After Tea

122	Omnipresence
163	Use of the Camera Obscura
169	The Lord's Prayer
201	The Real Sights
208	Indians at the Polytechnic
218	A Too Much Divided Heart
254	The Shadow
272	Lane's Net
276	The Concealed Yearning
277	The Mind of Man
281	Bottled Compasses
295	Darwin on Pigeons
296	Darwin on Theology
300	The Question of Questions
301	Body and Soul
306	Screamy Ganders
307	The Great Gulf
331	Freedom
338	Animism
340	A Living Optical Instrument
342	Extraordinary Things
357	The Principle or Foundation
361	The First Whisper
364	Mental Choking
365	Phantasmagoria

INDUSTRIAL MAN

26	Colledge of Industry
38	The Derby Silk-Mill
46	To the Duke of Bedford, President of The Foundling Hospital
63	Trade
64	An Iron Chieftain
69	Letter to Matthew Boulton
77	Farm Servants
79	Young George Crompton
84	Year 1788
100	Mr Dale's Cotton-Works at New Lanark
115	The Children
136	Spider-Work
143	Mechanic Powers
148	The Produce of the Mind
149	Letter from Venice
150	The Machine-Wreckers of Armata

155	Utopia
175	A Representative Man
184	Man and Machine
193	The Iron Man
194	The Philosophy of Manufactures
205	Imagination
209	Pauper Children Farmed Out
219	A Yorkshire Childhood
223	The Condition of England
228	Christmas Day
230	Classic Soil
231	The Moral Machinery
232	The Due Reward
233	Half-Timers
235	The Philistine
240	Manchester
243	Beyond Any Dreams
256	The Imprisonment of Ernest Jones
278	Liverpool
280	Coketown
286	The Road to Haworth
287	Saltaire
293	Visible Symbol
303	The Unemployed
305	Good and Evil
316	The 'Factory King'
325	The Queen of Red Clay
330	Lancashire
349	The Two Clavigerae
360	In a Manufacturing Town

DÆMONS AT WORK

1	The Building of Pandæmonium
54	Dæmons at Work
55	On the Wye
73	Coalbrook Dale
74	The Evil One
81	Richard Reynolds
120	Portsmouth
124	The Smoke of London
161	Extract from a Play
164	The Black Country
168	The Beautiful Road to Hades

171 This Sheffield
172 The Black Country
186 The Aspect and Character
213 The Devil
214 Faust's Flight
221 Civility to Vulcan
226 In Bedlam
234 Chickabobboo
246 Rochdale
251 Line Iron
320 The Swindon Railway Works
324 The Fire of Labour
355 Manchester Devil's Darkness

MINERS

27 The Mine-Man
33 The Wonders of the Peak
41 The Colliers of Kingswood
42 Easter
47 Wesley in Cumberland
96 The Riot
137 The Felling Colliery Disaster
177 Copy of Union Club Oaths
202 Black Swans
204 Coal-Pipes
207 Sedgwick at Newcastle
220 Shaftesbury's Mines Bill
328 The Greatness of England
336 The Sun-Force

POPULATION AND SUBSISTENCE

24 Of Doubling the People in 25 Years
36 The Children of Ireland
56 The Enclosures
80 Old George Barwell
89 Gleaning
96 The Riot
97 Pantisocracy
98 The Song of the Kings of Asia
99 Food of the Poor of Ingleton
103 Petition Against Enclosure
104 Infant Man

110 The Domestic Affections
114 Somerset
127 The Island of Britain
128 Jerusalem
178 Mr Toogood
192 Letter to Francis Place
223 The Condition of England
225 A Conversation
229 Scrooge and the Second Spirit
247 The Metropolitan Poor
262 The Great Eggs and Bacon
263 Mayhew on his Work
267 The Shilling People
282 Philanthropy
326 Northern Farmer – New Style
329 Rough-Spun Nature
350 Arreoi

THE POWER TO COME

10 A Heathen Place
41 The Colliers of Kingswood
42 Easter
70 The Mob
86 The French Revolution
88 For Church and King
92 Year 1793
93 Tom Paine
95 My Plan
96 The Riot
114 Somerset
154 Peterloo
158 The Wind of Heaven
175 A Representative Man
182 Oastler on the Ten Hours' Bill
185 When the Savage Settles Down
186 The Aspect and Character
212 Kersall Moor
236 Wordsworth (1)
237 At Furness Abbey
263 Mayhew on his Work
266 The Opening
267 The Shilling People
269 Only Magic

270 The Living and the Marble
297 The Spread of Education
298 Ode Sung at the Opening of the International Exhibition
347 The Power to Come
360 In a Manufacturing Town
365 Phantasmagoria
368 The March of the Workers

MAN – ANIMAL – MACHINE

4 The Boyhood of Genius
9 The Water-Insect or Gnat
11 The Nature of Sounds
14 A Mechanical Muscle
16 The Analogy of Nature
18 The Great Gogle-Eyed Beetle
19 Resemblance
25 The Soul of Brutes
28 Compressing Engines
29 Hæmastatics
40 The First Springs
53 The Wooden Horse
118 Simple Naked Scotland
130 The Engine is the Favorite
140 Almost Organic
145 Teredo Navalis
147 Frankenstein
173 Mr Stephenson
174 Opening of the Railway
184 Man and Machine
193 The Iron Man
194 The Philosophy of Manufactures
201 The Real Sights
202 Black Swans
203 Our Origin
242 Dombey in the Train
264 The Tempest Prognosticator
280 Coketown
283 The Silent System
313 The Tenth Muse
322 The Vowel Flame
340 A Living Optical Instrument
341 An Affectionate Machine-Tickling Aphid
344 The Disturber

THE WEATHER IN THE SOUL

- 6 That Hellish and Dismall Cloud
- 7 To Command the Rain
- 8 The Faces of the Sky
- 20 Artificial Spring
- 45 Pure Warm Air
- 48 Providence
- 142 The Road to Putney
- 158 The Wind of Heaven
- 166 Harry and Lucy
- 167 Rays of Darkness
- 217 Carlyle at Leeds
- 264 The Tempest Prognosticator
- 271 Fog
- 308 To his Niece in his Old Age
- 323 The Damage
- 334 Evaporation
- 335 Clouds
- 339 The Plague-Wind
- 345 A Memorable Fog
- 355 Manchester Devil's Darkness
- 367 The Storm-Cloud of the Nineteenth Century

MUSIC AND ARCHITECTURE

- 1 The Building of Pandæmonium
- 11 The Nature of Sounds
- 13 The New Theater
- 15 Sound
- 16 The Analogy of Nature
- 39 The Hoe-Plow
- 50 The Materialist Conception of Music
- 65 Genius
- 66 Memorandum
- 78 The Pantheon
- 129 Encaged
- 162 Saint Paul's
- 198 Quality and Quantity
- 200 Those Beautiful Faces
- 224 The Company's Enterprise and Taste
- 237 At Furness Abbey
- 241 Birmingham
- 253 Rooms not Churches

268   All People that on Earth do Dwell
352   The Electric Light

EARTH AND CREATION

17   The Face of the Earth
43   A Love of System
49   Written in Bedlam
52   The Forming of a Tea-Pot
58   Alloa
61   The Isle of Rum
68   The Invention of Arts
107   The Poet and the Man of Science
108   Blake at Felpham
109   Coleridge at Keswick
118   Simple Naked Scotland
128   Jerusalem
146   The Greatness of Great Britain
153   Keats in the Lakes
206   Brighton
210   Two Hearts
223   The Condition of England
248   God's Handwriting
255   A Poet's Old Age
317   The Suicide of Betty Higden
318   The Pools of Carshalton
327   The First Task
337   The Gods
344   The Disturber
354   Nothing Like the Earth
356   The Romance has Departed
357   The Principle or Foundation
366   Holland House
372   The Day of the Earth

LIGHT

22   The Eduction of Light
31   A Corona, or Image
32   The Solemnity of the Sight
78   The Pantheon
82   Banks
85   In the Cavern
112   Newton

121 Candle-Power of Venus
123 Night Images
167 Rays of Darkness
252 The Euston Station
260 A Stream of Golden Cloud
299 The Lower Pthah
346 The Lunar Landscape
352 The Electric Light

THE RAILWAY

173 Mr Stephenson
174 Opening of the Railway
187 The Steam-Carriages
188 Ville Universelle
189 This New Description of Property
211 From an Old Journal
213 The Devil
214 Faust's Flight
222 Poems
238 Wordsworth
242 Dombey in the Train
251 Line Iron
252 The Euston Station
259 The Country
285 The Railway to Heaven
294 Letter from Edward Lear
311 Eternal Justice
315 The English Middle-Class
320 The Swindon Railway Works
321 In a Railway Carriage
323 The Damage
332 Morecambe Bay
333 A Vast Number
344 The Disturber
363 The Number of Passengers

MEN AND MOLECULES

21 Homogeneous Particles
112 Newton
245 Our Philosophy
260 A Stream of Golden Cloud
273 A Balloon View of London

274 Herzen in London
275 Reflex Musings: Reflection from Various Surfaces
289 The Great Mystery
290 The Material World
310 Herschel and Nasmyth
314 The Human Element
333 A Vast Number
343 Manufactured Articles
362 The Crowd and the Runner
363 The Number of Passengers
365 Phantasmagoria

LONDON

  6 That Hellish and Dismall Cloud
 23 London
 57 An Immense Wilderness
 62 The Song of Birds
 75 The First Aerial Voyage
 94 London
102 The Reverie of Poor Susan
106 Coleridge in London
111 London
124 The Smoke of London
142 The Road to Putney
162 Saint Paul's
165 Carlyle in London
170 London Life
195 Carlyle in London
200 Those Beautiful Faces
216 The Monster
257 A City of Dis
258 Old Gilham
265 I Can't Get Out
271 Fog
273 A Balloon View of London
274 Herzen in London
290 The Material World
309 Over London
345 A Memorable Fog
358 The View down Fleet Street
370 After London
371 Apocalyptic Visions
372 The Day of the Earth

INDEX

Account of the First Aerial Voyage in England, 81, 82, 83
Adventures of the Ojibbeway and Ioway Indians, 227
Aeronautical and Miscellaneous Notebook, 124
After London, 354
Aikin, John, 69, 73
Air and Rain, 315, 324
Alloa, 67–8
Alps and Sanctuaries of Piedmont, 343
Anatomy of Plants, 20
Anima Poetae, 113, 122, 128, 130, 299
animism/materialism,
    author's comments on, xvi, 10, 60, 139, 324
Annals of Agriculture, 79, 97, 107, 112
Annals of the Parish, 88, 101
Annals of Yorkshire, 308
Anticipations, 347
Apology for the Revival of Christian Architecture, 218
Apeal . . . on the Subject of the Riots in Birmingham, 96
Appleyard, R., 281
Arkwright, William, 118
Armata: A Fragment, 144
Arnold, Matthew, 306, 307, 319
Art of Photogenic Drawing, The, 195
atomic theory, 20
'Atoms, Molecules and Ether Waves', 347
Austen, Jane, 258
Autobiography, An (of Annie Besant), 346
Autobiography, An (of James Nasmyth), 348
Autobiography, An (of Herbert Spencer), 349
Autobiography of Sir Henry Bessemer, 303
Autobiography (of Mary Howett), 269
Autobiography and Journals (of B.R.Haydon), 125, 129, 135, 145, 205
Autobiography of a Working Man, 236

Babbage, Charles, 194
Ballantyne, R.M., 322
Bamford, Samuel, 101, 153, 162, 235, 244–5

Barrington, Hon. D., 71
Barwell, George, 85
Beamish, R. 140
Beauchamp's Career, 332
Beddoes, Thomas, 110, 125–7
Bellars, John, 23
Bence Jones, H., 160
Bentham, Jeremy, 99, 112, 135, 139, 307
Berlioz, Hector, 202, 261
Besant, Annie, 346
Besant-Bradlaugh trial, 335
Birch, Thomas, 5, 15
Birmingham, 232
Blake, William, 114, 129–30, 162–3, 169
    author's comments on, 16, 20, 96, 102–4, 110, 348
    'Jerusalem', 127, 136
    other poems, 102, 107, 116, 202
Blanche, J.E., 343
Bleak House, 263
Book of the Great Sea Dragons, 199
Book of Nonsense, The, 297
Book of Ruth, 72
Boswell, James, 71–2, 73 (bis)
Botanic Garden, The, 89
Boulton, Mr of Soho, 73–4, 76, 87
Bowring, J., 139
Brett, Elizabeth, 83
Brewster, Sir David, 17, 18
brick-making in the Black country, 316–17
Brindley, James, 69
British History in the Nineteenth Century, 152
Bronowski, J., xii, 114
Brontë, Charlotte, 262, 279
Brontës' Life and Letters, The, 262
Brunel, I.K., 273
Brunel, M.I., 137–8, 139–40, 168–9
Buckle, William, 80
Bulletin of Stock Prices, 28
Burke, Edmund, 191
Burritt, Elihu, 317
Butler, Samuel, 20, 328, 337, 343
Buxton, C., 145
Byron, Lord, 132, 141, 143

Cambrian, 180
camera obscura, 164, 194–5
Campbell, L. & Garnett, W., 241
Caricature History of the Georges, 41
Carlyle, Thomas, 193, 216–17, 221
  letters, 163–6, 212–14, 230, 238
Carpenter, Edward, 345, 348
Carroll, Lewis, 306
Catlin, G. 227
Cayley, Sir George, 124
Century of Inventions, A, 7
Cestus of Aglaia, 305
Cézanne, Paul, 324, 347
Chalmers, Thomas, 186
Chants for Socialists, 352
Charles Kingsley, His Letters and Memories of Life, 242
Chartists, the, 210–12
children, treatment of, 108, 118, 156–8, 205, 208, 214–15, 219–20, 225, 227–8
Children of Ireland, 41–3
cholera epidemic of 1832, 181–5
Christian Philosopher's Explanation of the General Deluge, 190
Christmas Carol, A, 223
Cicero, 20
Clark, J.W. & Hughes, T.M., 207
Clerk-Maxwell, James, 329
  letters, 241, 276, 280–3, 293
  poems, 103, 269, 336
cloth mills, conditions in, 47–8, 108, 191–3, 205, 213–15, 223, 226, 227
Clough, A.H., 226
Coalbrook Dale, 79, 85–6
coalminers and their families, 23–4, 53–4, 102, 120–1, *121*, 132–4, 179–80, 203–5
Cobbett, William, 142, 170
Coburn, Kathleen, 113
Cochrane, Charles, 240
Colenso, J.W., 298
Coleridge, E.H., 122
Coleridge on Imagination, 114
Coleridge, S.T. 105, 121, 127, 181, 257
  author's comments on, 16, 104, 109–10, 122, 139, 299
  letters, 109, 114, 117, 119, 123
  Notebooks, 112, 121–2, 128, 130
Collected Letters (of S.T. Coleridge), 109, 119, 123
Collections for the History of the Town and Soke of Grantham, 6
'Comic Exhibition(s)', 254
Concerning Richard Jefferies, 339
Conciliation with America, On, 191
Condition of the Working Class . . . in 1844, 223
Corder, Susanna, 112

Correspondence of H.C. Robinson and the Wordsworth Circle, 229
Correspondence of the late James Watt, 79
Criminal Prisons of London, The, 267, 276
Crisis, The, 186
Crompton, Samuel, 284
Crossley, James, 246
Crotchet Castle, 181, 191
Crown of Wild Olive, The, 310
Culture and Anarchy, 319
Curnock, N. 50
Curwen, E.C. 190, 262

Darwin among the Machines, 20
Darwin, Charles, 204, 286, 335, 344
  Origin of Species, 283, 327
Darwin, Erasmus, 69, 86–91 *passim*, 141
Darwin, F., 204
Davy, Sir Humphry 118, 134
  author's comments on, 102–3, 110, 130, 134,
  Memoirs, 102–3, 125
Davy, John, 102
Defoe, Daniel, 28, 36, 38
Derby, 47–8, *48*
Derham, W. 20, 25
Description of the Country from Thirty to Forty Miles round Manchester, 69
Deserted Village, The, 66
diaries, author's observations on, 16–17
Diaries of Edward Pease, 214
Diary (of John Evelyn), 14, 16, 21
Diary (of Michael Faraday) 167, 181, 249
Diary (of Joseph Farington), 118
Diary of Robert Hooke, 16
Diary (of Benjamin Newton), 141
Diary (of Samuel Pepys), 9, 13, 16
Diary, Reminiscences and Correspondence (of H.C. Robinson), 187, 213, 228
Dickens, Charles, 244
  excerpts from, 209, 223, 235, 263, 273, 308
Dickinson, H.W. & Titley, A., 123
Discovery of the Circulation of the Blood, 20
Doctor Darwin, 74
Dombey and Son, 235
Doppler, J.C., 216
Doré, G., *342*, 343
Doyle, Arthur Conan, 347, 353
Dream of John Ball, A, 356
Driver, C., 183
Drummond, Henry, 191
Dugdale, Sir William, 16
Dynamics of a Parti-cle, The, 306

Early Days, 101
Early Letters of Thomas Carlyle, 163–6

Early Letters of William and Dorothy Wordsworth, 115
eclipse, total, 27–8, 29–32
1851, or the Adventures of Mr & Mrs Sandboys, 259
Elements of Geology, 205
Elements of Sir Isaac Newton's Philosophy, 50
Elijah, 232
Elliott, Ebenezer, 221
Emerson, E.W. & Forbes, W.E., 216
Emerson, Ralph Waldo, 216
Enclosure Acts, 37, 65–8, 110–11
Engels, Friedrich, 223–4, 235
Erewhon, 328
Ernest Jones. Who is he? 246
Erskine, Thomas Lord, 144
Essay concerning Human Understanding, 23
Essay explanatory of the Tempest Prognosticator, 257
Essays in Criticism, 307
'Essays towards a Real Character', 16
Ethics of the Dust, The, 292
Evelyn, John, 9, 14, 16, 21
Expedition of Humphry Clinker, The, 67, 68, 72
exploitation, author's comments on, 48–9, 50, 73, 77

factories, conditions in, 47–8, 185, 224–5, 316–17, 334
Faraday, Michael, 238
  Diary, 167, 181, 249
  letters, 160, 250, 270, 299
Far from the Madding Crowd, 330
Farrington, Joseph, 118
farm labourers and their families, 69–70, 85, 110–11, 219–20
Fendall, C.P. & Crutchley, E.A., 141
Fenwick, I. 229
Ferrey, B. 243
Field, Barron, 228
First Impressions of England and Its People, 232
Fitzgerald, Edward, 237, 320
Forman, H.B., 146
Forms of Water, The, 324
Fors Clavigera, 325, 327, 335
Forster, J., 244
Fortnightly Review, 332
Fox, Caroline, 274
Fox, George, 16
Fox Talbot, H. 195
Frankenstein, 141–2
Fraser's Magazine, 289
French, G.J., 53
Froude, J.A., 193

Fry, Elizabeth, 109, 112
Fumifugium, 9
Function of Criticism, The, 306
Funeral Sermon of the Felling Colliery Sufferers, The, 134
Future of England, The, 319

Galt, John, 88, 96, 101
Galton, Francis, 20, 292, 329, 349
Garnett, Constance, 268
Garret Workshop of James Watt, The, 131
Gaskell, Mrs, 235, 245, 279
Gentleman's Magazine, 52
Gilchrist, A., 163
Glaisher, James, 295, 301
Glasgow Mechanics' Magazine, 164
Gloag, 343
Goldsmith, Oliver, 66
Gray, Stephen, 47
Gray, Thomas, 52, 64, 336
Great Exhibition, The, 253–62 *passim*, 259, 288–9
Greig, James, 116
Gresham College meeting and The Royal Society, 5
Grew, Nehemiah, 18–20, *18*
Griffiths, Capt. A., 333
Griggs, E.L., 109
Group of Englishmen, A, 77
Growth of Philosophic Rationalism, The, 139

Hales, Stephen, 26
Halévy, 139
Halley, Dr Edmund, 28
Hammond, J.L. & Barbara, 111, 152
Hankin, Christiana, 86
Hanna, W., 180
Hannington, Wal, 296
Hard Times, 273
Hardy, Thomas, 330
Harvey, William, 20
Hawkins, Thomas, 183, 200
Hawthorne, Mrs, 270
Haydon, B.R., 125, 129, 135, 145, 205
Head, Francis, 243
Head, Sir George, 189, 195
Hemyng, B., 288
Herschel, Mrs. John, 162
Herschel, Sir John, 162, 207, 301–2
Herzen, Alexander, 268
Himes, N.E. 191
History of Derby, 48
History of the Royal Society, The, 5, 10, 14, 15
History of the Times, The, 347–8
Hodder, E., 212
Hodge and his Masters, 341

Hodgson, Rev. J., 134
Holmes, Sherlock, 303, 348
Holy Grail, The, 318, 319
Home Life of the Manchester Factory Folk, 296
Home Tour through the Manufacturing Districts, 189, 195
Hood, Thomas, 223
Hooke, Robert, 9–11, *11*, 12, 16, 20
Hopkins, Gerard Manley, 16, 113, 122, 323, 343
Horse-hoeing Husbandary, 49, *111*
Houghton, John, 28
House of Commons Journal, 111
House, Humphrey, 113
Howitt, Mary, 269
Hungry Forties, The, 215
Hunt, Leigh, 135
Hunt, Robert, 24
Hutton, William, 204
Huxley, L., 299
Huxley, T.H., 286, 293, 320, 343, 347
  letters, 299, 355

Ichthyosaurus, The, 195–9, *199*
Iguanadon, Country of the, 189–90, *189*
Impressionism, 324, 343, 347–8
Industrial Art Explained, 343
Industrial Biography, 298
Ingpen, R. 159
Inquiries into Human Faculty, 292, 349
Iron Horse, The, 322
iron mills, 171, 224–5, 238
Itinerarium Curiosum, 32

James Nasmyth, Engineer, an Autobiography, 172, 216, 302
Jefferies' Land: A History of Swindon, 312
Jefferies, Richard, 312, 339, 341, 354
Jerusalem, 127, 136
John Martin, Painter, 202
Johnson, Samuel, 53, 71–2, 73 (bis)
Jones, Ernest, 246–7
Jones, H.F., 337
Journal (of Gideon Mantell), 190, 262
Journal of a Residence in England of Their Royal Highnesses of Persia, 202
Journal of a Residence for Two Years and a Half, 208
Journal of a Tour to the Hebrides, 72
Journal of a Tour in the Northern Parts, 108
Journal of a Tour in Scotland in 1819, 158
Journal of a Visit to London, 246
Journals (of R.W. Emerson), 216
Journey from Biringham to London, A, 84
Jung, C.G., 346

Kapital, Das, 316
Kay-Shuttleworth, Sir James, 185, 208
Keats, John, 73, 146
Keighley, 278
Kemble, Fanny, 169, 176
King, E.T., 210
Kingsley, Charles, 235, 240–5 *passim*, 286, 325, 343
Knight, William, 76
'Kubla Khan', 110

Lamb, Charles, 116, 119, 145
Lansdowne, Marquis of, 6, 21, 22
Later Letters of Edward Lear, 311
Lay Sermons, Addresses and Reviews, 320
Lear, Edward, 242, 313, *313*
  letters, 285, 297, *298*, 311
Letters and Journals of Lord Byron, 143
Letters of Edward Fitzgerald, 237
Letters of Charles Lamb, 116, 119
Letters of Edward Lear, 285, 297, 298
Letters (of Felix Mendelssohn), 170
Letters of Percy Bysshe Shelley, The, 159
Life and Adventures of Nicholas Nickleby, The, 209
Life and Correspondence of Mrs Hannah More, 105
Life and Letters of Charles Darwin, 204, 285, 286, 344
Life and Letters of Faraday, 160, 238, 250, 270, 299
Life and Letters of T.H. Huxley, 286, 299, 355
Life and Letters of Lord Macaulay, 258
Life and Letters of Adam Sedgwick, 207, 322
Life, Letters and Journals of George Ticknor, 194
Life, Letters and Labours of Francis Galton, 329
Life, Poetry and Letters of Ebenezer Elliott, 221
Life of Beckford, 188
Life of William Blake, 163
Life of Charlotte Brontë, 279
Life of James Clerk-Maxwell, The, 241, 269, 276, 280, 283, 293, 329, 336
Life of Thomas Cooper Written by Himself, 230, 320
Life of Sir Humphry Davy, The, 134
Life of Charles Dickens, 244
Life of Elizabeth Fry, 112
Life of Samuel Johnson, 73
Life of Richard Oastley, The, 183
Life of Mary Anne SchimmelPenninck, 86, 87, 92
Life of James Watt, The, 61, 130
Life of Wedgwood, The, 63

Life and Opinions of General Sir Charles Napier, 212
Life and Times of Samuel Crompton, 53, 85, 284
Life and Work of Sir James Kay-Shuttleworth, 185, 209, 226
Life and Work of the Seventh Earl of Shaftesbury, 212, 215, 221, 228, 274, 286, 349
Linnaean Society, 87
Litchfield, R.B., 114
Liverpool, 270
Lives of Boulton and Watt, 76, 305
Lives of the Engineers, 98
Livingstone, David, 274
Locke, John, 23
'Lockesley Hall', 191
Loftt, Capell, 107
London, *124*, 167, 253, 299–301, *300*, *342*
  Carlyle on, 163–6, 213
  critical descriptions of, 21, 66–7, 101–2, 193, 246, 257, 264–8, 281–2, 355–6
  Holland House, 348, 349
  Hungerford Suspension Bridge, 241–2, 253
  joys of, 70–1, 115–16, 124–5, 170, 343
  St. Paul's, 163–4, 167
  children's service in, 200–1, 202, 260–1
  sea-coale and fog, 8–9, 124, 136–7, 263, 330–1
  Thames Tunnel, 168–9
  and see Great Exhibition
London Labour and the London Poor, 247, 254, 288
Longman's Magazine, 347
Lord Kelvin's Early Home, 210
Lord Monboddo and His Contemporaries, 76
Lowes, Livingstone 109, 122
'Lucifer in Starlight', 332–3
Luddites, 76–7, 131–2, 142–4
Lunardi, Vincent, 80–3
Lunar Society, 87
Lunatics, The, 87
Lyell, Sir Charles, 205, 236
Lyons, Sir Henry, 5
Lyrical Ballads (of William Wordsworth), 113

Macaulay, Lord, 258
MacDermot, E., 273
Manchester, 184–5, 230–2, 339–40
Manchester Examiner & Times, 296
Man's Place in Nature, 293
Mantell, Gideon, 190, 207, 262
Man Without a Mask, 114
Marshall, William, 84

Martin, John & William, 190, 202
Martin, T., 167
Marx, Karl, 316
Mary Barton, 245
Mask of Anarchy, 153–5
Mason, W., 64
Mayhew, Henry, 247, 253–4
  & Binny, J., 267, 276
  & Cruickshank, G., 259
Meerza, N.K., 202
Melville, Herman, 246
Memoir and Correspodence of Caroline Herschel, 162
Memoir of the Life of Sir Mark Isambard Brunel, 140
Memoirs (of A. Herzen), 268
Memoirs of the Life of Thomas Beddoes, MD, 127
Memoirs of Sir T.F. Buxton, Bart., 145
Memoirs of Thomas Chalmers, 186
Memoirs of the Life of Sir Humphry Davy, 102, 125
Memoirs of Richard Lovell Edgeworth Esquire, 64
Memoirs of his (Thomas Gray's) *Life and Writings*, 64
Memoirs of the Ichthyosauri and Plesiosauri, 183, 190
Memoirs of the Literary. . . Society of Manchester, 78
Memoirs of Sir Isaac Newton, 17
Memoirs of Old Friends, 274
Memoirs of Martinus Scriblerus, 27
Memorials of Millbank, 333
Mencius on the Mind, 139
Mendelssohn, Felix, 170, 232
Meredith, George, 332–3
Merryweather, George, 257
Metcalf, E.M., 246
Meteyard, E., 63
Method for Making a History of the Weather, 10, 16
Method of Zadig, The, 347
Micrographia, 11, 20
Miller, H., 232, 264
mills, conditions in, 47–8, 108, 191–3, 205, 213–15, 223–7 *passim*
Milton, 127
Milton, John, 3–5, 15, 336
miners and their families, 23–4, 32–6, 53–4, 102, 120–1, *121*, 132–4, 203–5
Miscellaneous Sonnets (by William Wordsworth), 229
Modest Proposal for Preventing the Children of Ireland. . ., 43
Monet, Claude, 343
Month in Yorkshire, A, 277, 280

Moon considered as a Planet..., 332
Moore, George, 109
Moore, Thomas, 143
Moral and Physical Conditions of the Working Classes, 185
More, Hannah, 97, 104
More Letter of Charles Darwin, 335
More Nonsense, 313
Morely, E., 229
Morning's Walk from London to Kew, 137, 138
Morris, William, 348, 352, 356
Muirhead, J.P., 61
Musaeum Regalis Societatis, 19

Napier, Gen. Sir Charles, 212
Napier, Lt.-Gen. Sir W., 212
Narrative of Mr Watt's Invention, 61, 62
Nasmyth, James, 20, 26, 297–8, 322, 333, 348
  & Carpenter, J., 332
Natura Deorum, de, 20
Natural History of Selborne, The, 75
Newcomen Society, 124
Newton, Sir Isaac, 6, 20, 50, 116–17
  letters, 17, 18
New Translation of the Lord's Prayer, 169
Northern Tour (of William Cobbett), 170
Norton, C.E., 164
Notebooks (of S.T. Coleridge), 112, 113
Notebooks (of G.M. Hopkins), 113, 323, 343
Nowrojee, J. & Merwangee, H., 208

Oastler, Richard, 158, 183, 308
Observations on Modern Gardening, 65
'Ode: Intimations of Immortality', 110
'Ode to a Nightingale', 73
'Ode to the West Wind', 110
Ogden, C.K., 139
Oldfield, George, 215
Oliver, J.W., 188
Olmstead, F.L., 249
Omniana, 127
On the Old Road, 305
Origin and Progress of the Mechanical Inventions of James Watt, 62, 80
Origin of Species, The, 283, 327
Our Mutual Friend, 308
Owen, Robert, 156–8, 346
  and R.D. Owen, 186

Paine, Tom, 101, 108
Pandæmonium, the building of, 3–5, 15, 253
  and Xanadu, 110
Panopticon, 98–9
Panthéon, 84
Paradise Lost, 3–5, 110, 332–3
Paris, J.A., 134

Passages from the English Notebooks of Nathaniel Hawthorne, 270, 282
Past and Present, 217
Paul, Lewis, 53
Peacock, Thomas Love, 181, 191
Pearson, Hesketh, 74
Pearson, Karl, 329
Pease, A.E., 214
Pendered, M. 202
Pennant, T., 70, 72
Penny Magazine, The, 225
Pepys, Samuel, 9, 13, 16
Peterloo Massacre, 146–55
Petition of the Village of Raunds..., 111
Petty Papers, The, 6, 22
Petty-Southwell Correspondence, 21
Petty, Sir William, 6, 22
Phillips, Sir Richard, 137, 138
Philosophical Letters of Ray, 20 (bis)
Philosophical Transactions, 17, 24, 28, 37, 47, 71, 122, 130
Philosophy of Manufactures, 193
Physico-Theology..., 25
Place on Population, 191
Poems of Mr Gray, The, 64
Poems and Prose Remains, 226
Poetical Works and Other Writings (of J. Keats), 146
Political Register, 142
Poole, Tom, 96–7, 103–4, 106, 117
Poor Man's Guardian, The, 239, 240
Pope, Alexander, 27
Popular Romances of the West of England, 24
Praeterita, 167, 292
Priestley, Dr Joseph, 78–9, 90–1, 96
Primitive Culture, 326
prisons, 245–6, 274–6, *275*, 333
Problem of Unemployment, The, 296
Proposals for Raising a Colledge of Industry, 23
Prose Works (of A. Pope), 27
Prothero, R.E., 132
Pugin, A.W., 218, 243
Punch, 223

Quarterly Review, The, 243
Queen Elizabeth, 348

Ramsay, John, of Ochtertye, 54–5
Ray, John, 20, 23
Read's Weekly Journal, 41
Recollections of A.W. Pugin and His Father, 243
Recollections of a Tour made in Scotland, 121
Records of a Girlhood, 169, 176, 179
Rejoice in the Lamb, 60

374

'Researches Chemical and Philosophical', 110
Reveley, Henry, 159
'Reverie of Poor Susan, The', 109
Richard, I.A., 114, 139
Richard Trevithick, 123, 128

Road to Xanadu, The, 109, 122
Roberts, William, 105
Robinson, Henry Crabb, 187, 213
Robinson, H.W. & Adams, W., 16
Robison, Prof. J., 62
Rossetti, D.G., 289
Rossetti, W.M., 289
Rothwell, W., 315
Routledge's Guide to the Crystal Palace and Park, 273
Royal Society, The, 14–15, 86, 249
  author's comments on, 37–8
  Journal of, 5
  Minutes of, 15
  Philosophical Transactions, 17, 24, 28, 37, 47, 71, 122, 130
Royal Society, The, 1660–1940, 5
Rum, Isle of, 69–70
Rundle Charles, Mrs, 241
Rural Economy of the Midland Counties, The, 84, 85
Ruskin, John, 167, 224, 292, 305, 310, 319
  author's comments on, 242, 292, 306
  Fors Clavigera, 325, 327, 335
  Storm Cloud of the Nineteenth Century, 340, 351
Ruskin: Rossetti and Pre-Raphaelitism, 289
Rutland, Duke of, 108

Sadler, T., 213
St. Hildegard, 16
Samuel Butler, A Memoir, 337
Sandford, Mrs H., 103
SchimmelPenninck, Mary Anne, 85–92
Scientific Lectures, 325
Scotland and Scotsmen in the Eighteenth Century, 55
Sedgwick, Adam, 321
Selden-Gott, G., 170
Selincourt, E. de, 115
Shaftesbury, Lord, *Journal* of 212, 215, 221, 228, 274, 286, 349
Sheffield, 170
Sheldon, Dr Gilbert, 14
Shelley, Mary, 142
Shelley, Percy Bysshe, 110, 141, 159, 335–6
  on Peterloo, 152–5
Sherlock Holmes, 303, 348, 352–3
Shorter, C. 262
Sloane, Sir Hans, 20

Smart, Christopher, 16, 60
Smeaton, John, 98
Smiles, Samuel, 76, 98, 298, 305, 306
Smith, Adam, 105
Smith, F., 185
Smith, R.A., 315, 324
Smollett, Tobias, 67, 68, 72
Society for the Betterment of the Condition of the Poor, 107
Soirées de l'Orchestre, Les, 202, 261
Solitary Reaper, The, 72
Somerville, Alexander, 220, 236
Song of Los, The, 107
'Song of the Shirt', 223
Songs of Experience, 102
Songs of Innocence, 202
Sound, On, 315, 331, 338
Southey, Robert, 105, 158
Southwell, Robert, 21
Sowerbutts, Eli, 246
Spencer, Herbert, 349
Sprat, Thomas, 10
Satirical Essays, 26
Stead, W.F., 60
steam engines, 61–2, 79–80, 122–8 *passim*, 128, 158–9, 172–9, 186–9, 195, 203–4, 212, 235–6, 242–3, 242, 248, 273, 284, 311–12, 318–25 *passim*, 355
Stephenson, George, 172–6
Stock, J.E., 127
Stokers and Pokers, 243
Storm, The, 28
Storm Cloud of the Nineteenth Century, 340, 351
Strachey, Lady, 285
Study in Scarlet, A, 347, 348, 353
Stukeley, Dr William, 6, 32
Sturmy, Capt. Samuel, 24
Swift, Jonathan, 27, 43

Table Talk, 181
Talfourd, T.L., 116
Taylor, Tom, 125
Tennant, Smithson, 130
Tennyson, Alfred Lord, 241, 244–5
  author's comments on, 191, 296, 298
  poems, 163, 179, 289, 318
Tennyson, Hallam Lord, 163, 203
Tennyson, A Memoir, 163, 179, 202, 241, 245, 320
Terre à la lune, De la, 333
Testimony of the Rocks, 264
Theory of Fictions, 137
Thomas Carlyle, a History of his Life in London, 193, 214, 221, 238, 257
Thornton, Dr, 169
Ticknor, George, 194

Times, The, 128, 135, 348
Todd, Ruthven, 190
Tom Poole and his Friends, 103, 106, 117
Tom Wedgwood, 114
Tour in Scotland, and Voyage to the Hebrides, A, 70
Tour thro' the Whole Island of Great Britain, 36
Towards Democracy, 345
Town Labourer, The, 152
Tracks in the Snow, 190
Travels in the Air, 295, 301
Trevelyan, G.M., 152
Trevelyan, G.O., 258
Trevithick, Richard, 123, *128*
Tribute to Michael Faraday, A, 281
True Words for Brave Men, 240
Tull, Jethro, 49
Turner, J.M., 250
Turnor, Edmund, 6
Tylor, E.B., 122, 139, 326, 346
Tyndall, John, 324, 347
  On Sound, 315, 331, 338

Ure, Andrew, 193

Valéry, Paul, 347, 348
Verne, Jules, 333
Village Labourer, The, 111
Vision of the Last Judgment, A, 130
Visits to Remarkable Places, 204
Voltaire, Mr, 50

Walks in the Black Country, 317
Walks and Talks of an American Farmer, 249
Wasse, J., 37
Watkins, J., 221

Watt, James, 20, 60–1, 78–9, 303–5, *304*
  and the bust of Sappho, 130
  and the steam engine, 61–2, 76, 87
Waugh, Edwin, 296
Wedgwood, Josiah, 63, 77
Wedgwood, Tom, 110, 114
Wells, H.G., 347
Wesley, John, 50–4 *passim*, 60, 73–4
  author's comments on, 6–7, 23, 50, 158
Whateley, Thomas, 65
Wheatley, H.B., 9
Whistler at the Plough, The, 220, 236
White, Gilbert, 75
White, Walter, 277, 279, 280
Whitelocke, Bulstrode, 16
Wilkins, John, 16
Wilson, Dr P., 131
Wisdom of God, The, 20, 23
Wonders of Geology, 205
Worcester, Marquis of, 7
Wordsworth, Dorothy, 108, 121
Wordsworth, William, 113, 115, 118, 121, 145–6
  author's comments on, 16, 23, 72, 102, 110, 139, 279, 292, 322
  poems, 72, 109, 229
workhouses, 208, 216–17, 238–40, *239*, 274
Works (of J. Bentham), 139
Works of Lord Byron, The, 132
Wren, Sir Christopher, 5, 14–15
Wright, Thomas, 41
Wright, W.A., 237
Wuthering Heights, 279

Young, Arthur, 79
Young, Thomas, 20

Zoonomia, 69, 86